Coming Through

Genevieve Chandler interviewing Ben Horry at his home in Murrells Inlet.
Photograph by Bayard Wootten. North Carolina Collection, University of North Carolina Library at Chapel Hill

Coming Through

Voices of a South Carolina Gullah Community from WPA Oral Histories COLLECTED BY *Genevieve W. Chandler*

EDITED BY
Kincaid Mills, Genevieve C. Peterkin, and Aaron McCollough

FOREWORD BY Charles W. Joyner

THE UNIVERSITY OF SOUTH CAROLINA PRESS

Published by the University of South Carolina Press
Columbia, South Carolina 29208

www.uscpress.com

Manufactured in the United States of America

26 25 24 23 22 7 6 5 4 3

Library of Congress Cataloging-in-Publication Data
can be found at http://catalog.loc.gov/.

ISBN 978-1-57003-721-4 (hardcover)

Contents

Illustrations

Figures

Maps

Acknowledgments

THIS BOOK HAS BEEN MANY YEARS in the making, and the list of those who have contributed insight and effort is quite long. First and foremost, the editors would like to thank the residents of Murrells Inlet, South Carolina. While seeking biographical information on the book's interviewees, we received limitless hospitality in churches along the banks of the Waccamaw as well as in private homes. Special thanks to Rev. George Weathers and the parishioners of New Bethel Baptist Church on Sandy Island; Reverend Hume of Gordon Chapel, African Methodist Episcopal Church, and his parishioners; Henry Small; Peter and Rebecca Carr; Rev. Luther Alston and his wife, Annabel Alston; Mary Brown Smalls (Hagar Brown's daughter); Sarah Deas; Albertina Elliot; Frances and Rosa Pyatt; Elizabeth Robinson; Willamena Pyatt, Wanita Pyatt; Margareet Gore; Essie Tucker; Evelina Knox (daughter of Albert and Ella Carolina, wife of Zackie Knox); Mary Ella Knox and Blondel Knox (Zackie and Evelina's daughters); Sarah Jane Jackson (Welcome Bees's great-granddaughter); Sadie Belamy (Sabe Rutledge's granddaughter); Joanna Brown (Louisa Brown's granddaughter); Vennie Deas Moore; Mrs. Richard Knox (Hagar Brown's granddaughter); Capers Pickett; Kato Singleton (Cato Singleton's grandson); Helen Carr; Drew Knox; Lou Nesbit; and Hattie Smalls.

The project would not have been possible without the academic encouragement and assistance of Anita Goodstein, Tam Carlson, and Don DuPree at the University of the South; Jay Mills; Ian Finseth; J. Edward Chamberlin; and Charles Joyner. Thanks to Suzanne Chapman and to Allison, Olan, and Norma Mills for their support throughout the extended project.

Special thanks are due to the siblings of Genevieve "Sister" Chandler Peterkin: June Hora, Tom Chandler, Bill Chandler, and Joseph "Corky" Chandler. Theirs are the best mullet fries, clam bakes, and oyster shuckings in the lowcountry.

Thanks to the staff of the South Caroliniana Library at the University of South Carolina in Columbia, who hosted and indulged the editors over a number of weeks and diligently retrieved every last box from the inventory of hundreds of boxes of WPA material in the archives. Special thanks to Beth Bilderback of the library for her assistance.

Bayard Wootten's beautiful and stirring photographs, which grace the cover and pages of this book, were for a time lost to the world. Thanks to the Wootten family for not throwing away all those dusty plates, negatives, images, and papers and for generously donating them to the North Carolina Collection of Photography of the Wilson Library at University of North Carolina at Chapel Hill. At UNC, Wootten's materials came into the care and custody of photographic archivist Jerry W. Cotten. Jerry helped us find the long-lost Murrells Inlet photographs. Thanks also to Keith Longiotti who now curates the Wootten collection.

Thanks to librarians, archivist, and document packrats everywhere for caring for all those dusty boxes and shelves full of paper. Thanks to Major McCollough and David Michaels for producing the exceptionally detailed maps. Thanks, finally, to Alexander Moore, Karen Beidel, Pat Callahan, and everyone at the University of South Carolina Press, and to our indexer, Linda Webster.

Foreword

Something More Precious: Genevieve Willcox Chandler and Carolina Folk Culture

Sometimes I wonder if the so-called sophisticate hasn't lost something more precious than he has gained with all his culture and education, all his conveniences, and his complicated way of living.

Genevieve Willcox Chandler

I CAME DOWN TO MURRELLS INLET in the summer of 1969, fresh from research in the Library of Congress. I threaded my way down the narrow main street, lined with boat landings and seafood restaurants, and turned into Genevieve Willcox Chandler's yard. I had read her interviews from the 1930s with former slaves on the rice plantations along the Waccamaw River in South Carolina, which she had conducted as part of the WPA Federal Writers' Project. And I had listened to some of the field recordings John A. Lomax had made in her front yard for the Library of Congress Folksong Archive in 1936, 1937, and 1939. She had gathered some of the finest singers—black and white—from Murrells Inlet, Pawleys Island, and Sandy Island to sing their traditional songs into Lomax's recording machine. Now I drove into her yard, and into her life, full of questions about those years and those people—the ex-slave and dispenser of folk wisdom Hagar Brown, the great singer of spirituals Lillie Knox, and others of her friends who had been dead for a generation.

Summer days on the South Carolina coast are hot and long; but a soft, cooling breeze often wafts in across the salt marsh in the late afternoon, bringing relief to those who live beside the inlet. It is a good time to sit in the shade of the live oaks, sipping iced tea and enjoying the view, sharing stories with friends. How often during the following decade "Miss Genevieve" sat with me in the low afternoon sun at the edge of Murrells Inlet, talking into my tape recorder, dredging up the memories and hopes of time onto the surface of consciousness, sharing in story the history and folklore of her narrow strip of native soil between the Waccamaw and the Atlantic. She told of the masters and the slaves on the rice plantations; of the slave trickster John and his continual sparring for advantage with Ole Maussa; of the animal trickster Buh Rabbit and his continual sparring for advantage with Buh Gator and Buh Bear; of haunts, hags, and plat-eyes; of the folk wisdom of the Gullah proverbs, the haunting beauty of the Gullah spirituals, and the rich expressiveness of Gullah speech.

She had seen more than eighty of such summers, and with a playful twinkle in her mischievous eyes, she proved to be a model of ageless and witty intellect. She spoke expansively, merrily, eloquently. In the last decade of her long life, she became my teacher and my friend. I brought my own students to meet her and to learn from her wisdom. From 1969 until her death in 1980, I cherished the rich memories she shared with me out of a long lifetime of priceless experience.

Genevieve Willcox Chandler's major contribution was her important collection of the oral history, folklore, and speech patterns of the people who lived along the Waccamaw River on the upper coast of South Carolina. As a field-worker for the Federal Writers' Project in the 1930s, she was a pioneer in the study and collection of folklore and oral history and in the fields that are now called creole linguistics and sociolinguistics. While she was not professionally trained in any of these fields and did not analyze her material in an academic fashion, in many ways she anticipated developments in these fields by a generation. Scholars now recognize in her full descriptions of the social context of folklore the work of someone far ahead of her time. Scholars in creole linguistics have praised her careful rendering of the nuances of Gullah, the creole language of the African Americans on the Sea Islands and nearby mainland of coastal South Carolina. Many of those specimens of folklore and oral history, along with fascinating snatches of conversations captured in her "Methodist shorthand," would be acclaimed as "found poetry" and analyzed as sociolinguistics by later generations. Her "field," as a WPA field-worker, was All Saints Parish—that portion of Horry and Georgetown counties that lies between the Waccamaw River and the Atlantic Ocean.

She was born in Marion, South Carolina, on May 21, 1890. Her family moved to Murrrells Inlet in 1910, when her father purchased Wachesaw plantation on the Waccamaw River and the Hermitage at Murrells Inlet. Her achievements were by no means limited to folklore, oral history, and creole linguistics. She was also an artist, a teacher, a museum curator, and a writer of fiction. Her achievements in any *one* of these careers would warrant a claim on our attention. That she was a success in *all* of them is extraordinary. Furthermore there was an underlying unity in the diversity of her accomplishments, for each of her careers was an expression of her love and understanding of the Waccamaw region, its people and their folklife.

As a teacher, she established South Carolina's first night school for illiterate adults near Murrells Inlet in addition to teaching eight grades during the day. This adult-education project was a precursor of the statewide system developed by her friend Dr. Wil Lou Gray. At the time there were no schools for African Americans at Murrells Inlet, and the segregation laws of the state forbade the education of blacks in the schools set aside for whites. So Genevieve Chandler taught adult literacy classes to blacks in her own home, seated around her kitchen table (making it, as the old spiritual calls it, the Welcome Table). She taught similar classes for white adults in the schoolhouse. Her respect for those who were no longer slaves but not fully free either—and for their rich folk culture—was recognized and appreciated in the black community.

As a young teacher, she also was a pioneer in outdoor drama. She and her mother produced *Hiawatha*, based on Henry Wadsworth Longfellow's poem, as an outdoor pageant in Murrells Inlet in 1915. It involved virtually the entire community, with proceeds going to the local school.

During the time she worked with the Federal Writers' Project, she became a successful writer of fiction. Her short stories, based on the folklore of the African Americans who lived along the Waccamaw, were published in *Scribner's Magazine*, *Mademoiselle*, and *Southwestern Review*. An intensely sympathetic approach to her characters and their culture characterized all her work.

When Archer M. and Anna Hyatt Huntington developed four plantations they had purchased along the Waccamaw into a sculptural and botanical garden in the late 1930s, they hired Genevieve Chandler as curator of the Brookgreen Gardens museum, a post she held until 1963. Upon Chandler's retirement, Beatrice Proske of the New York Hispanic Society said of her that "she gave the stranger passing through, unaware of the country or the life around him, a sympathetic insight into its character and history" (*Columbia State*, undated 1963 clipping).

She accomplished all this while teaching Sunday school and playing the organ at Belin Methodist Church and raising a family. Her husband, Thomas Mobley Chandler, died in 1936, leaving her with five children, ranging in age from eighteen months to eleven years.

She was perhaps best known in her last years as an artist. She had studied painting as a young woman at Flora Macdonald College in North Carolina, at the Art Students League in New York, and privately in England; but she set aside her brushes at marriage in 1922 and did not pick them up again until 1962. Soon her watercolors, pastels, charcoals, and pen-and-ink drawings—depicting the scenery and folklife of the Waccamaw region she knew so well—were widely exhibited.

She was not a prophet without honor in her own country. Adger Brown wrote of Chandler's watercolors in the *Columbia State*, South Carolina's capital city newspaper, that they had "a combination of vigorous structure and design and a delicacy of execution which makes them unique." He added that those qualities were each "a reflection of her own personality, one of basic strength and vigor, but mellowed by sensitivity and grace" (November 22, 1964).

Her interviews with former slaves on the rice plantations constitute one of the most important sources extant for the understanding of slavery. Unlike depictions of slavery emanating from the records of the masters and of the masters' guests, these interviews are firsthand evidence of slavery from the perspective of the slaves and their experience. As one of the interviewees, Ben Horry, said to Genevieve Chandler, "I been here! I seen things! I tell you. Thousand of them things happen but I try to forget 'em."

There are, to be sure, a number of objective difficulties in using such sources. They may reveal as much of the time in which they were recorded as of the slavery era. Aged and penniless, struggling to survive during the Great Depression, the former slaves may well have looked back too fondly upon a time when it was the master's responsibility to provide for those too old to work. Moreover the racial etiquette of segregation prevailing in the 1930s did not encourage them to tell whites anything that might disturb them. The climate of fear was evident in Stella Horry's response to Genevieve Chandler's inquiry as to why she did not have electricity in her house, now that the rural electrification program had run power lines past her door. "White folks run me [off] if I do that!" she replied. It is surely a mark of Genevieve Chandler's rapport with African Americans in the Waccamaw region, however, that Stella Horry did not hesitate to confide her fear of white opinion. Nor did the former slaves hesitate to tell Genevieve Chandler of both kindnesses and atrocities they had personally witnessed or experienced in slavery. Both kinds of evidence must therefore be taken into account.

It would be difficult to overestimate Genevieve Chandler's folklore collection, comprising such genres as folk speech, proverbs, folktales, ballads and songs, and folk belief. These are the means by which human beings preserve their memorable experiences and offer comments—sometimes in good-natured humor, sometimes in bitter satire, sometimes in outright protest—on the trivial and the transcendental in their efforts to create a life of meaning and dignity. Her folklore collection is rooted in the real hungers, the real needs, and the real struggles of the people of the Waccamaw, taken verbatim from life itself.

In this collection of Genevieve Willcox Chandler's work, her specimens of folklore, her oral history interviews, and her examples of Gullah conversations have been lovingly and painstakingly assembled by the editors: her daughter Genevieve Chandler Peterkin, Kincaid Mills, and Aaron McCollough. They have searched both extensively and intensively, patiently combing through WPA files in South Carolina and in Washington in order to establish a definitive inventory of her collections. Housed in the Rare Book Room of the Library of Congress, her interviews and folklore collections were long unavailable to the general public. Some of her folklore collections were never sent to Washington at all. A few of her interviews have since been published in facsimile reference volumes for scholars, but most of those in this collection are published here for the first time. In addition Mills and Peterkin searched through the photographs of Bayard Wootten of Chapel Hill, recently donated to the University of North Carolina. This collection is enriched by many photographs taken as she accompanied Genevieve Chandler on some of her interviews. Many of them are published here for the first time.

"At my age," Miss Genevieve said at seventy-five, "you're just beginning to know how to live." A dynamo of energy until her final years, she did not separate her careers, her family, and her great love for the Waccamaw region into watertight compartments. All her careers—as artist, writer, historian, folklorist, linguist, teacher, curator—were directly related to improving the region and depicting its beauties to others. She modestly described her efforts as "a desire to preserve for my children some memories of the area of the Waccamaw Neck."

But her final years were bedridden and painful. Her mind was active to the last, but her body was increasingly feeble. Her death in 1980 at the age of ninety was a release, but many have been enriched by her having lived: not only those of us who had known her, but also those of us who have known her work and those who will learn her work from this collection.

Charles W. Joyner

Introduction

You feel like you got nobody in the world but you—you one.
Things don't look changeable to you till you get over—come through.

Zackie Knox, Murrells Inlet, South Carolina

Zackie Knox's thoughts on "coming through" represent his humble assessment of transformative experiences that helped to shape his own personal life as well as the broader life of the community in which he lived. These thoughts supply a fitting initial glimpse into the range of individual and communal highs and lows chronicled in this book. The interviews collected here document the aspirations, anxieties, joys, and tribulations of the individuals who made up the Gullah community of Murrells Inlet, South Carolina, in the late 1930s. They also present many of the routines and habits of communal life among those people at that moment in history.

Most basically, "to come through" is to undergo a spiritual conversion—to be born again—which (in Knox's account, at least) alleviates one's sense of powerlessness and isolation. "Coming through" (like the similar notion of "catching sense," or becoming aware of one's social obligations) signals the experience of group belonging so fundamental to the Gullah worldview. The following introduction offers an account (part historical, part anecdotal) of the various, connected efforts and circumstances that brought the book about. Undoubtedly the primary effort belongs to Zackie Knox and his fellow informants. If any may be credited with the true authorship of this book, they should be, for the details of their lives make up the book's most clearly demonstrated content. These details were solicited and written down by Genevieve Willcox Chandler, whose presence in the interviews is often (though not always) muted by a detached style.[1] Chandler's efforts were sanctioned and supported by the Federal Writers' Project (FWP), and the collation, annotation, indexing, and computer transcription were done over the course of several years by the editors: Genevieve C. Peterkin, Kincaid Mills, and Aaron McCollough. Insofar as the institutional, cultural, and personal backstories are not made immediately available by the primary texts—the interviews themselves—in this collection, we have addressed them here in the introduction.

We hope that this part of the textual apparatus, along with the biographies and footnotes, will provide readers an informed starting point for working with the materials that make up the book's larger enterprise. Likewise we hope the information here may stimulate further refinement of the complicated historical conversation it presumes to enter. Ultimately we mean in this book for the voices of Zackie Knox and his neighbors to be heard again and as widely as possible and, thus, to "come through" in the most familiar sense: to make safe passage and to be received with clarity.

A Brief History of the Federal Writers' Project

The Federal Writers' Project was a nationwide relief program—one of several branches of the massive Works Progress Administration (WPA) dedicated specifically to employing Americans whose skills and training equipped them for work in the arts and humanities. Upon being established, the FWP almost immediately began styling itself as an instrument for sociocultural curatorship and instruction. National FWP officials imagined a critical part of their job to include the uncovering of an already-present American national identity—one characterized by diversity and continuous self-renewal.[2]

A significant practical feature of the FWP's program—one of particular interest for this book—was an unprecedented narrative-recording effort performed by field-workers like Genevieve Chandler. This effort was only unprecedented, however, in terms of scale. Its true origins may be found in slightly earlier historical and cultural contexts. One such precedent was the antebellum slave narrative, with its inherent critique of social practice, which often capitalized on tense prewar sentiment and the abolitionist politics of its mostly white readership. In the years preceding the Depression, the once-popular genre lost some of its attraction as a salable literary form. This ebb has been attributed to shifting popular tastes following the Civil War, as well as to a concurrent surge of racist attitudes within academic circles, culminating in 1918 with the publication of Ulrich B. Phillips's book *American Negro Slavery*.[3] The slave narrative did persist, however, as a literary genre throughout the late nineteenth century. Booker T. Washington's *Up from Slavery*, published in 1901, stands as an influential and extremely popular turn-of-the-century instance. Furthermore novels like James Weldon Johnson's *The Autobiography of an Ex-Colored Man* (first published anonymously in 1912) drew heavily on tropes and themes common to the slave narrative genre. Thus the FWP initiative may be viewed as a part of continuing social and literary conversations. The autobiographical life histories that began emerging in the late 1920s and early 1930s were brought to light in large part by African Americans themselves, and this in itself represents a significant contribution. Interested in a history that had been obfuscated, distorted, or ignored by men like Phillips, a new wave of scholars sought to produce more-responsible and more-reliable surveys. Advances in anthropology and sociology offered new tools for documenting African American history, while renewed white interest in African American cultural forms such as jazz suggested that the popular climate was becoming more agreeable.[4]

Practically speaking, the true antecedents to the Folklore Project of the Works Progress Administration's Federal Writers' Project date to before 1930 and the privately funded collecting of histories. Committed African American scholars emerged in the late 1920s to fill the gap in the historical record and to rectify the fallacious claims made by the apologists of racism. Working through Fisk University between 1927 and 1929, Andrew P. Watson, a student of the Polish-born anthropologist Paul Radin, began collecting life histories and conversion experiences in and around the Nashville, Tennessee, area. Charles Johnson, also of Fisk University, founded the Social Science Institute there in 1928 and dispatched staff researcher Ophelia Settle to interview ex-slaves in Tennessee and Kentucky.[5] At the same time the historian John B. Cade was heading a similar project under the aegis of Southern University in Scotlandville, Louisiana. A later project that Cade oversaw between 1935 and 1938 at Prairie View State College in Prairie View, Texas, generated four hundred ex-slave interviews ranging over thirteen states.

Initial cooperation from the federal government came in 1934 from the Federal Emergency Relief Administration (FERA) after Lawrence Reddick of Kentucky State Industrial College suggested to FERA director Harry L. Hopkins that relief funds might be routed to unemployed writers—ideally college-educated African Americans. Reddick enlisted the support of Johnson and of Carter Woodson (who is best known for having established, in 1926, Negro History Week, the precursor to Black History Month) for a pilot project employing twelve African American interviewers who collected 250 interviews between September 1934 and July 1935. A larger follow-up project was planned but never materialized. Norman Yetman attributes the project's demise to poor organization at FERA and to shortsighted FERA regulations that obliged the employment of sorely unqualified staff.[6]

In 1935 FERA was dissolved and replaced by the Works Progress Administration. By this time direct relief had fallen into general disfavor among Americans who were eager to get back to work. The WPA, headed by former FERA director Harry L. Hopkins, oversaw the shift from direct relief to work relief and, subsequently, ushered in many of the New Deal's most enormous public works programs. The WPA almost immediately began implementing its arts projects. The writing branch—the Federal Writers' Project—was headed by philanthropist Henry G. Alsberg, who had formerly been a newspaperman and a director of off-Broadway plays. The central ambition of the FWP was to compile and publish the American Guide—five regional volumes as well as a national volume meant to provide a "geographical-social-historical portrait of the states, cities, and localities of the entire United States."[7] This task proved unmanageable and was eventually replaced by the production of guides to individual states. In this somewhat attenuated form though, the American Guide remained the FWP's main focus for the life of the organization. Alsberg is credited with having expanded the FWP's goals, however, to include other peripheral activities. Not the least of these new departments was folklore research. John Lomax was enticed away from his position as honorary curator of the Library of Congress to become the first national advisor on folklore and folkways for the FWP, and "the interview method of collecting folklore and a corollary emphasis upon the collection of life-history materials, both of which [Lomax] introduced, became a hallmark of Writers' Project research."[8] Though ex-slave narratives were being collected independently before 1937, Washington did not back a concerted regional effort until the spring of that year. Lomax's interest in interviews submitted that March by the Florida Writers' Project served as a catalyst for the emphasis on ex-slave narratives that was to come.[9]

Also significant in the transition process from the original plan for an American guide to individual state guidebooks was the establishment of the position of editor for "Negro Affairs" and Sterling A. Brown's appointment to that position. Brown was a respected poet and scholar, and he was also an African American man. He took it upon himself to ensure that FWP treatment of African American materials (including ex-slave narratives but also more general cultural information) was progressive. Brown was a vigilant critic of racial stereotypes, and as Jerrold Hirsch puts it, "Brown did more than correct the work of others. His strictures became rationales for programs he and others advocated."[10] Brown's influence can be felt in the interviews conducted by Genevieve Chandler, especially in the massive number documenting the quotidian tastes, values, and interests of Depression-era African American people like Lillie Knox.

THE FWP, OR "FEDERAL PROJECT NUMBER ONE," officially began on April 1, 1937, with the issuance of specific instructions to individual state directors. Though Yetman claims "Lomax constantly reiterated his insistence upon the importance of recording interview conversations verbatim, with no holds barred,"[11] the official emphases of interviewing practice varied as the project unfolded. A memorandum issued by Alsberg on July 30, 1937, stressed the importance of narrowing the interviewing process down to "one or two of the more interesting and intelligent people, revisiting them, establishing friendly relations, and drawing them out over a period of time."[12] Furthermore the memorandum urged interviewers not to lead their informants or influence their responses. An extensive list of questions was offered in hopes of eliciting a consistent level of pertinent information. Along with these questions, Alsberg's memorandum included "notes by an editor on dialect usage" and an extensive list of words "which should not be used." These directives urged interviewers to privilege "truth to idiom" over "exact phonetic transcription," citing the assumption that "present day readers are less ready for the over-stress of phonetic spelling than in the days of local color."[13] Thus the FWP's method was not utterly self-consistent. Insofar as the project's ultimate goal was a coherent guidebook or set of guidebooks, the government's instructions emphasized accessibility to readers over more-scientific inquiry and reportage. Nonetheless the tendency toward standardization in FWP documents was part of a larger and more complex impulse toward sustainable, communicable diversity: "FWP officials were trying to define a national culture in which individuals and groups could participate as Americans, while retaining their regional, ethnic, and racial identities."[14]

In *Weevils in the Wheat*, Charles Perdue notes that the national interviewing project coalesced as something of an afterthought to the work already being done by regional offices.[15] This can be said to be true more generally of the long progress from the first, privately funded interviewing projects to the federal mandate under which the interviews in the present volume were originally compiled. The quasi-organic, bottom-up organizational development of the enterprise helps to explain many of its methodological inconsistencies, but it also underscores the importance of individual initiative in the project's accomplishments. Finally the most valuable accounts of African American history produced during this era exist thanks to the coordinated labors of real people: African American informants and an eclectic mix of writers committed to presenting lives in all their complexity. Thus the finest interviews of ex-slaves and their children live up to the principle that history is the record, not of heroic deeds performed on a global stage, but rather of men and women acting according to their own needs in a manner shaped by their own cultural norms. In this way the ideological efforts of the FWP and the labors of its field-workers did produce a significant contribution (however problematic) to the historical record.

The Interviewer and the Interviewing Method

> Folk-lore is not as easy to collect as it sounds. The best source is where there are the least outside influences and these people, being usually under-privileged, are the shyest. They are most reluctant at times to reveal that which the soul lives by. And the Negro, in spite of his

> open-faced laughter, his seeming acquiescence, is particularly evasive. You see we are a polite people and we do not say to our questioner, "Get out of here!" We smile and tell him or her something that satisfies the white person because, knowing so little about us, he doesn't know what he is missing. The Indian resists curiosity by a stony silence. The Negro offers a feather-bed resistance.[16]

This observation by Zora Neale Hurston pinpoints an inevitable difficulty in folklore collection and one of the crucial weaknesses of the method by which the Federal Writers' Project obtained ex-slave narratives. Most of the writers employed by the project were from the middle to upper-middle classes and white. The informants were black and either former slaves or their descendants. As several scholars have pointed out, this disparity most likely led many informants to water down their experiences or to tell interviewers "what they wanted to hear," good or bad, with respect to race relations.[17] Genevieve Willcox Chandler was a white woman from a well-established family. To some degree the historical integrity of her work must be contingent upon social pressures beyond her control. In *Them Dark Days*, William Dusinberre rightly identifies a paternalistic attitude in some of Chandler's excursuses, noting for example Chandler's observation in one interview that "most old ex-slaves in the South Carolina lowcountry . . . love and revere the names and memories of their old masters."[18] Chandler managed to do exceptional work within the constraints of the situation however, and Dusinberre's reading of her work depends on numerous flawed assumptions and inattentive readings. The example above, for example, appears somewhat out of context, notably excluding Chandler's puzzlement that "the old couple [Ben and Stella Horry] still live with many old and odd beliefs one being that the white man only is entitled to the good things—the better things."[19] Speaking more generally, it would be a mistake to flatten the complex emotional experiences of these informants to fit current attitudes and beliefs. We must not overlook the distortions of paternalism, but we would also do well to avoid relying too adamantly on assumptions that conflict with what the ex-slaves claimed they felt. Although we may assume that ex-slaves' feelings toward their former owners were complicated, we cannot utterly dismiss the possibility that they included something like love.

Though many writers were conducting interviews and collecting folklore in South Carolina in the mid to late thirties, Chandler managed to set herself apart from her Federal Writers' Project peers who similarly lacked formal linguistic training or degrees in anthropology or folklore. Long after the completion of her work, she has been called a "great folklorist"[20] and "pioneer."[21] Her transcription of Gullah speech has been lauded as astute, offering "tantalizing glimpses of [Gullah] vocabulary and its pronunciation and an opportunity to discover its grammatical rules."[22] William A. Stewart praised Chandler at great length, citing her "impressive background knowledge (including a near-native fluency in the Gullah dialect)"[23] as cogent enough explanation for her success. In fact, Stewart opined, much of Chandler's strength as a scholar came from her lack of academic preconceptions and prejudices.

Whatever training she may have lacked, Genevieve Chandler was a highly educated woman (having begun studies at Flora Macdonald College at age fourteen, she also studied figure drawing at the Art Students' League in New York and, in 1913, studied portraiture in Liverpool). Furthermore, and in no small part due to artistic sensitivity, Chandler *did* possess impressive background knowledge of the Waccamaw Neck region, of the people who inhabited the region, and of the Gullah creole they spoke. Chandler's sympathies and her community involvement were progressive. At age eighteen she began work as a teacher. Chandler taught eight grades in one classroom. Upon detecting that many of the children's parents were illiterate, Chandler decided to return to the schoolhouse in the evenings to teach them.[24] This night work was a forerunner of the statewide adult education system started by Dr. Wil Lou Gray. Chandler did not limit her teaching, though, to white children and white adults in the white school, as the segregation laws of the time required. She taught her adult, illiterate African American neighbors in her own kitchen. By helping the Gullah improve their skills in her private dwelling, Chandler was making a public statement for inclusion, and unwittingly she was also preparing one of many routes to the confidence of those she would later interview.

By the time Chandler began interviewing her neighbors for the Federal Writers' Project, she had lived the better part of her life in Murrells Inlet, South Carolina. In 1908 the Willcox family established itself permanently in the spot where it had formerly vacationed and soon came to be highly regarded in a community where local reputation was still a terribly important commodity. Significantly both the Willcox family and the Chandler family had strong ties to the African American community. Chandler's brother Allston Moore "Dick" Willcox, a doctor, was widely known in the Waccamaw Neck region, and he did much to earn trust and admiration, making house calls to members of the African American community, often at no charge. During the Great Depression, Chandler and her husband, Thomas, were ambassadors of goodwill toward their less fortunate neighbors, employing Lillie Knox long after they could truly afford her services, helping in emergencies,[25] sharing any available surplus with all comers. In 1936 Thomas Chandler suffered a stroke. He died soon thereafter. Against family advice,

Genevieve Chandler insisted on raising her five children alone during the Depression. Her success in this enterprise was due in large part to the income she received while compiling FWP interviews.

In 1936, a year before John Lomax began a nationwide consolidation of ex-slave narratives, Chandler began collecting interviews with African American and white inhabitants of the Waccamaw Neck for the WPA's Federal Writers' Project. Chandler was hired by her lifelong friend Mabel Montgomery, the state director of South Carolina's Writers' Project. From the first extant interviews of May 1936 to the last interviews of October 1938, Chandler's style and method underwent a dramatic transformation. In the earliest dated interviews, Chandler's writing is heavily stylized—delivered from the fixed, quasi-literary perspective of the short stories Chandler published in various national magazines around the same time. As may be seen, for example, in Chandler's interview "Truss Gawd or Ad's Plat Eye" with Addie Knox,[26] the contextualizing, subjective voice tends to reveal more about Chandler herself and the biases and expectations of white culture than it does about Chandler's informants:

> Fourteen. Fourteen human souls she keeps alive with her two hands. Under nourished. Half naked. All in one room. Unmoral. Once a dead baby lay hidden under its sick mother's bed for a week. In a civilized country. And we are Christian.

Most of Chandler's interviews, however, dispense with conventional narrative framing. At their most aesthetically austere, Chandler's texts utterly erase the interviewer's voice and present only the speech of the informants. This can lead to confusion in reading, especially in cases where informants respond to questions that are not present in the written record. Nonetheless, absenting the field-worker does produce a more documentary effect. In the following example, Hagar Brown has clearly been asked a question about alligators—or foodways more generally—but question and questioner have been removed:

> Gator? Eat Gator? My Grandpa have a pond and he shoot one. Eat every part but don't eat the head and feet. Eat body part and tail. Makes chillun fat. Yes. A hawk kin eat! (Meaning that you can eat hawk.) Crow kin eat, too. Fox? I eat 'em. Fox hard to lay hand on. Them thing can out run a ghost. Possum good! Easy to catch possum. Catch in chicken coop. Coon? Coon better than possum; heap cleaner than possum. Coon won't eat everything and possum does. Squirl? Good to flour 'em and put black pepper to 'em and put gravy to 'em. Eel? Dress 'em. Strip 'em down the back. Stuff 'em and bake 'em. And eel skin good for rheumatism.

> Wrap 'em 'round leg. Keep 'em till pain gone. I lick my leg with gasoline and salt.[27]

It should come as little surprise that the stylistic flavor of Chandler's interviews is diverse. Based on surviving memorandums from federal and regional offices, it is clear that methodological instructions were often somewhat contradictory. As noted above, Alsberg discouraged interviewers from focusing heavily on dialect recording. By contrast, undated documentation directed specifically at folklore collecting field-workers states that "field workers will also record unusual dialect, slang, pronunciations, place names, local expressions."[28] In June 1937 Alsberg generally discouraged the sort of literary style Chandler had employed in her earlier interviews:

> I should like to recommend that the stories be told in the language of the ex-slave, without excessive editorializing and "artistic" introductions on the part of the interviewer. The contrast between the directness of the ex-slave speech and the roundabout and at times pompous comments of the interviewer is frequently glaring.[29]

In October 1937, however, Montgomery suggested that informants "be visited several times in order to establish a friendly relation, some material being secured at each visit, and the whole woven into a consecutive story."[30] This "weaving" of various data into a "consecutive story" implies that the artistic and editorial will of the interviewer *should* be engaged in rendering the interviews. Chandler, it seems, considered the various instructions she was given and then proceeded with her own synthesis of practical strategies. Accurate dialect recording was important enough to Chandler that she chose to work against official recommendations.

In "Long Journey Home: Folklife in the South," William A. Stewart is cited praising Chandler's ingenious, intuitive solutions for some of the problems that have led scholars generally to dismiss potential quantitative study of the ex-slave narratives collected by the FWP:

> [Chandler] solved highly technical problems in sophisticated and insightful ways. For example, even knowing Gullah, how was a field-interviewer to get a verbatim or even near-verbatim version of rapid, informal speech without recording equipment?
>
> Her solution was to invent a sort of "short-hand"—actually a form of speed writing—which collapsed individual word spellings (since these have normal Gullah forms which she already knew,) thus allowing her to focus on sentence structure, which was less predictable. And in the case of unusual word pronunciations, she was able to expand the speed writing at that point to include the unusual vowel or consonant.[31]

Rev. Luther Alston recalled the awe inspired by Chandler's recording method: "she would write in shorthand then sing it back. They thought it was so funny weren't nobody could tell what she scratched but her."[32] Whereas most of the ex-slave interviews generated by the FWP were "taken down in pencil or pen, most often after the interview, from memory or from scattered field notes supplemented by memory,"[33] Chandler had found a way to capture and render language patterns with a level of precision otherwise unavailable to other FWP field-workers.

Gullah and Oral Art

> If one pursued the documentary method and looked at facts in their full particularity, as though for the first time, one found no entity to call America. Instead, there were regions, though again if one looked hard enough, the regions gave way and one had communities—which themselves became, on further scrutiny, classes, factions, groups. In short, documenting America turned up such an abundance of what one educator called "localized information" that no generalization with teeth or vigor held. Each town became so unique that the main thing that joined it with the next was the road.[34]

Considering the plenitude of materials generated by the Federal Writers' Project, the work is most exciting as it documents the enclaves of difference and unique cultural identity that have made America the plural entity that it is. The Gullah language is a distinctive dimension of the African American communities that inhabit South Carolina's Waccamaw Neck, and the language is a tangible nexus for multiple cultural idiosyncrasies. In *Down by the Riverside*, Charles Joyner offers the process of linguistic creolization—by which "two or more languages converge to form a new native tongue"—as a model for a larger set of cultural adaptations.[35]

The Gullah language and culture are unique African American inventions engendered by necessity and ingenuity, emerging from the vicissitudes of slave life. Because men and women were seized from various regions of the West African coast and from various tribes, the early generations of slaves on American soil found themselves in linguistic chaos. Speakers of tongues as various as Ewe, Fante, Efik, Ibebio, Igbo, Yoruba, Kimbundu, Tshiluba, Bambara, Vai, Hausa, Wolof, Kikongo, Temme, Twi, Kongo, and Mandinka were hard pressed to find some means of communicating with each other and with the white slave owners. Gullah evolved in response to this problem, mingling English with the lexicons of many African languages. As Patricia Jones-Jackson describes it, "by borrowing words from each other, speakers resolve[d] the communication conflict."[36] The adoption of one common language may also have served to undermine the unique cultural traditions of the various African groups, thus accelerating the process of "detribalization," or broad assimilation.

Gullah retained primarily West African grammatical structures. The most notable deviations from English include abandonment of many prepositions, conjunctions, adjectives, adverbs, and participles; the absence of the grammatical operations that establish continuity between sentences; the uninflected verb; verb serialization; verb reduplication; and an idiosyncratic pronominal system.[37] As subsequent generations were born into slavery and raised with Gullah as their native tongue, the language continued to change. It has changed further in the context of modernization and as the Gullah community has interacted more and more with American mass culture.

According to some analyses, the Gullah of South Carolina, Georgia, and Florida currently belong to a linguistic category termed "post-creole speech communities." That is to say, Gullah creole and its concomitant cultural characteristics have become more difficult to detect and analyze—their distinguishing characteristics have begun to merge with those of the cultures surrounding them. Even so, the transition has been a gradual one—as Jones-Jackson observes:

> Most often we get only a retrospective look at a culture after many of its unique features have been lost. One of the great attractions of the Sea Islands for students of the humanities and social science is that the expected slow pace of change in remote areas will permit a look into the culture as it undergoes transition. As outside forces erode the traditional social structure of the islanders, every attempt should be made to maintain a record of changing language, attitudes, and oral traditions.[38]

Chandler's interviews with Gullah friends and neighbors in Murrells Inlet and its surrounding communities are just such a record, offering a glimpse into Gullah culture at something like a middle point in its long migration across a spectrum of social codes and practices.

Chandler had a remarkable appreciation for Gullah culture and did her best to record faithfully what she saw and heard. The product of her labor and her informants' labors is a curious and rare sort of text: the written transcription of oral art. The effect of such a document is at once revelatory—ethnographically and linguistically—and problematic—because the difference between orality and literacy is more than simply the difference between the spoken word and the written word. Walter J. Ong goes so far as to characterize the rift between the word in oral and literate cultures as initiating a restructuring of the "human life-world":

> In a primary oral culture, where the word has its existence only in sound, with no reference whatsoever to any visually perceptible text, and no awareness of even the possibility of such a text, the phenomenology of sound enters deeply into human beings' feel for existence, as processed by the spoken word. For the way in which the word is experienced is always momentous in psychic life.[39]

By providing a fixed, external tool for recall, Ong argues, literacy has helped lead Western culture to its crowning, analytical achievements. Individual-oriented, authoritative, and permanent text-based sources have been instrumental, for example, in the formulation of the scientific method and the democratic social model. Consonantly, Wallace Chafe argues, "written language . . . is not only preservable through time and space but can be dissected, analyzed, and otherwise manipulated at the leisurely pace essential to scientific investigation as we know it."[40] Other recent scholarship counters these celebratory assessments by recalling the degree to which codified language can be a route to paralyzing orthodoxies.[41] Furthermore the idea that literacy is related to superior cognitive development is hotly debated. Ultimately, the discussion seems to suggest, literacy should not be opposed to illiteracy; rather, different literacies should be recognized. As David Olsen argues, "Literacy is not just a basic set of mental skills isolated from everything else. It is the competence to exploit a particular set of cultural resources."[42] Either way, literacy has been so thoroughly adopted and its effects so thoroughly inscribed upon contemporary life that it and its effects have come to be perceived as a natural and inevitable good. In privileging the written word though, literate mass culture has tended to privilege almost exclusively the visual sense by which the written word transmits its meaning. By contrast, oral culture and its "sound-dominated verbal economy"[43] have relied more heavily on the aural sense for transmission of meaning. As Ong puts it:

> Writing makes "words" appear similar to things because we think of words as the visible marks signaling words to decoders: we can see and touch such inscribed "words" in texts and books. Written words are residue. Oral tradition has no such residue or deposit. When an often-told oral story is not being told, all that exists of it is the potential in certain human beings to tell it.[44]

Cultures with more prominent oral features have charted their own conceptual trajectories, without the "residue" of written words. Insofar as oral tradition has lost pride of place in mass culture, its methods have become increasingly ignored and/or marginalized. Nonetheless orality possesses its own unique tools—alternative ways of confronting, interpreting, and negotiating the world. The oral tradition, differently sustained in different communities, makes way, vis-à-vis these tools, for valuable, different human possibilities. Thus the study and preservation of oral tradition are not atavistic or sentimental exercises. As well as possessing historic and ethnographic value, cultures with prominent oral features also provide us with the opportunity to think and experience "otherwise."

In *When Roots Die*, Jones-Jackson enumerates beliefs, assumptions, and behaviors that differentiate the Gullah lifeworld from the lifeworld of those steeped in literate mass culture, focusing especially on the contextual disjunctions between written storytelling and oral tradition:

> As Western cultures are gifted with a long tradition of written literature, the Gullah performers are likewise gifted with techniques and methods of communicative interactions characteristic of a long tradition of African and African-American oral literature. Unlike the writer, who is often left to create his characters in isolation and solitude, and who is at liberty to take a few days, a week, a month, and in many cases years to fill up a page with words carefully selected to create a certain mood and elicit a certain response, the oral performer must be prepared to create and perform his entire tale within a reasonably short period of time. He does not and cannot perform effectively in isolation. He is influenced immediately by the occasion of the tale, and the atmosphere in which and the audience for whom he is performing.[45]

Temporal concerns and kinesic communicative techniques ("hand movements, a turning of the head, a long pause, a shifting of the eyes, a long knowing stare"[46]) are particularly significant in Jones-Jackson's assessment of the difference between literary and oral storytelling. Chafe offers that "writing sacrifices the benefits of copresence—above all, direct and immediate involvement with another mind,"[47] implying that oral tradition maintains these benefits. Ong notes that aural experience is, in fact, more immediate than any other sense experience, including visual: "A hunter can see a buffalo, smell, taste, and touch a buffalo when the buffalo is completely inert, even dead, but if he hears a buffalo, he had better watch out."[48] The cumulative effect of these techniques, and in fact their cause, is a dialogic relationship between oral culture and its surroundings (the material world as manifested especially in an audience in time). The significance of the work done by an audience cannnot be overstated. The audience must be present, not only for the narrative to take place, but also to propel the narrative forward with cues, questions, and demands.

The elements differentiating literate and oral discourse may be read broadly to inform literate and oral worldviews. Ultimately Ong may overstate the rigidity of the boundaries he finds between literate and oral "noetic" models, but for the purposes of this introduction, his generalizations are helpful. According to Ong, literate tradition has a strong investment in detail-oriented models of specialization, and oral tradition has a commensurate investment in holistic models of perpetuation. Literate tradition tends toward the specific; oral tradition tends toward the general. Even so, oral tradition is arguably more directly informed by immediate experience. While the architecture of oral tales may seem received (and mnemonic devices of repetition may translate poorly when recorded on the page), the vitality of the oral world is in its dependence on the present moment.

The reader must be careful not to judge the voices of the Waccamaw Neck's Gullah citizenry according to habitual literary criteria. Instead, as one approaches Genevieve Chandler's interviews, one should prepare to let oneself be taught a new way of reading. Benjamin Botkin says as much about the entire ex-slave narrative project in his introduction to *Lay My Burden Down* (1945):

> Oral statements of ex-slaves may seem crude and casual. But as folk-say—what the people have to say about themselves—and oral literature on an illiterate or a semiliterate level, they will be found to possess literary qualities of their own. . . . They have the forthrightness, tang, and tone of people talking, the immediacy and concreteness of the participant and the eyewitness, and the salty irony and mother wit which, like the gift of memory, are kept alive by the bookless world.[49]

Though much *is* lost in the translation from spoken word to textual artifact, and thus, as Jones-Jackson observes, transcribed narratives can "appear as short, loosely strung together episodic tales,"[50] much has been retained. As noted earlier, Chandler's interviews are stylistically diverse. Certainly questions remain regarding the degree to which any FWP interviews were actually verbatim transcriptions of Botkin's "folk-say." At their most astute, though, Chandler's texts represent a tremulous bond between oral and literary traditions. As with all attempts to render "different literacies" in print, Chandler's method must represent a distortion of the event it proposes to document. All the same it represents something far superior to other dialect recording approaches of the period.

The interviews in this volume are products of literacy insofar as they are portable, written records, but they differ in their means of production from almost all other literary documents. John Blassingame has critiqued the historical utility of FWP interviews, citing limitations in focus, brevity, internal inconsistencies, unstable relationship between tone and "facts," subtle nuances, and uncertain chronologies.[51] In doing so, Blassingame has adopted narrow models of history and historical reliability. In effect Blassingame's critique attempts to discredit FWP interviews categorically on grounds that they are not easily reducible to Anglo-American historical discourse convention. We believe that much of the value inherent in these documents derives from their very resistance to literate convention. By maintaining many of the trappings of oral discourse, they offer, for a belated audience, the "next-best thing" to verbatim speech and performance. In order to work with these documents, a reading audience is obliged to imagine itself in the same cocreative, copresent position of the countless audiences that have again and again collaborated in the oral composition process.

FWP interviews, in general, may or may not live up to the project's stated ambitions: "to let the ex-slaves, and through them slavery and freedom, speak for themselves."[52] What can be said with certainty is that this collection of interviews represents a community peopled by real human beings with real personalities. Once a reader learns to *listen* to these people on the page, she will be little troubled by questions of their historical worth. These interviews represent something epic, but the Gullah men and women of the Waccamaw Neck are not the stylized heroes of Homeric Greece, they are differently stylized African American men and women who have endured and prevailed in a history of enslavement, emancipation, Jim Crow disenfranchisement, and economic depression.

The Present Project

The idea of compiling Genevieve Chandler's work into book form was certainly not our own nor, for that matter, was it a new one. Even while Chandler was still writing for the FWP, she herself had planned to compile a selection of the interviews that would be accompanied by Bayard Wootten's photographs. The seeds of that book project most likely died with Hurricane Hazel in 1954. During the storm, Chandler lost all of her copies of the FWP interviews and of the Wootten photographs. In the course of his graduate studies, Charles Joyner worked with the material and with Chandler herself. He had contemplated the idea of putting together a book of the interviews and had tried to persuade Genevieve "Sister" Peterkin, Chandler's daughter, to produce a book based on her mother's work. Kincaid Mills's interest in the project began in 1991 when he first encountered Chandler's interviews while doing research on the Gullah culture of South Carolina's Waccamaw Neck as an undergraduate at the University of the South. During the decade and a half since then, he (and the other editors) have been assembling the book you now hold.

Sources of Interview Material

Though somewhat esoteric, some of Chandler's interviews did find their way into print between the late thirties and the early nineties. George P. Rawick's *The American Slave: A Composite Autobiography*, volumes 2 and 3, *South Carolina Narratives*, for example, contained those ex-slave narratives housed at the Library of Congress Rare Books Room. Rawick's supplement series contained more Chandler interviews, which he had retrieved from the Library of Congress Archive of Folk Song and the South Caroliniana Library. The South Carolina WPA publication *South Carolina Folk Tales*, edited by Mabel Montgomery, contained many of the Murrells Inlet stories about Brer Rabbit, hags, and ghosts. That particular volume modified, or "normalized," the language of the interviews.

The present project was driven by two primary concerns. The first was to make the material available to a broad readership. The interviews had been tremendously useful in our study of the Gullah community. For anyone studying the Gullah people along the Waccamaw, the broader Gullah culture of the southeastern seaboard, slavery, emancipation, Reconstruction, the Jim Crow South, or the Depression of the 1930s, these documents could be invaluable. Second, we wanted to make the book more than a disorderly compendium of Chandler's interviews. We felt that the story of the Waccamaw Gullah community should be told to as many people as possible and that its voice and history should be heard.

Consolidating Chandler's work was, in itself, a labor-intensive and time-consuming endeavor. Because FWP materials were originally collected in each state headquarters before portions were sent on to Washington and the Library of Congress, the most extensive collection of Chandler's FWP interviews is housed in the South Caroliniana Library at the University of South Carolina. Documents never sent to Washington ultimately found their way to this repository. Thus much of the initial work was done in Columbia, South Carolina.

Unfortunately Chandler's work lay dispersed through hundreds of boxes of material containing everything from writing instructions for field-workers to the manuscript of "South Carolina: The WPA Guide to the Palmetto State." In this disarrayed condition, Chandler's interviews were then and still remain relatively inaccessible. Navigation of the materials was aided by the collections of two earlier workers in the same hedgerow. Jay Mills, a plantation archeologist working on the Waccamaw Neck region (and Kincaid Mills's brother), and Charles Joyner, the historian and folklorist, had both compiled their own fairly exhaustive sets of interviews by consulting the library's index and methodically culling the result from South Caroliniana's boxes. From these sources, we were able to consolidate some 350 pages of interview material. Often the pages were second- and even third-generation photocopies of typed or carbon pages. The interviews obtained from Mills, Joyner, and the South Caroliniana Library collection were themselves in no discernible order. Furthermore it became apparent that the library indexes upon which previous researchers had depended were incomplete. Ultimately the only way to obtain a complete listing of Chandler's work was to search South Caroliniana's collection box by box and page by page. In his own collection at the time, Kincaid Mills had some 200 separately titled interviews. A solid week of flipping pages yielded roughly 400 additional transcriptions. The amount of material Chandler had collected in her two-year tenure with the Federal Writers' Project was overwhelming. Even excluding the Anglo-American informants, there were still 1,330-odd pages of typescript to contend with.

Editorial Method

Discrepancy between the amount of material and the number of pages that could fit comfortably between two covers preempted the desire to produce one volume containing all of Chandler's African American interviews. Part of the editorial task was thus strictly organizational: to separate the interviews into chapters arranged by speaker. Each chapter, as imagined, would begin with a short biography or character sketch, further supplemented, when possible, by period photographs. Knowing some of the speaker's history and seeing a photographic image of the speaker promised the reader the fullest access to the text and to the lives the text represents.

Chandler's African American material contains several interview types: ex-slave narratives, life stories, folklore, group conversations, sermons, songs, and spirituals. More broadly, these variations can be associated with one of two basic genres: narrative and song. All told, there were just over one thousand pages of typescript narrative and approximately three hundred pages of song. The line between these forms is fairly distinct. For practicality's sake, three volumes will be produced. The current volume is primarily narrative in substance. A subsequent volume containing the songs and spirituals will follow.[53] A third volume containing supplementary narratives and songs from Chandler's informants (both black *and* white) is also planned.

Documentary copies of Chandler's interviews vary greatly in legibility. The top sheet is of course the most legible, while the carbon copies trend toward illegibility the deeper one goes into the onion sheets. From photocopied originals, coeditors Aaron McCollough and Kincaid Mills retyped the interviews keystroke for keystroke and typo for typo. (Initially we even employed Courier, a monospaced typeface, to facilitate comparison of our transcribed text with the original typescripts.) Where words were illegible, we searched for more pristine copies to work from. Where this was impossible or yielded no better results, we noted the fact in the text within brackets. Our decision not to edit or correct the text for misspellings and typos is intended to be in keeping with Chandler's own efforts to record the conversations "verbatim." As previously noted, Chandler was fluent in Gullah. She knew its lexical aberrations and its complex grammatical and syntactical structures. Chandler also understood that Gullah speech—including its rhythms, cadences, and intonations—was significant in its own right. Her task in recording the Gullah people went far beyond the job of a scribe. She endeavored to record oral language onto paper and in so doing created something new. Under these conditions the fine editorial line between misspelling and phonetic spelling, typo and intonation becomes elusive. Our "correction" of the material at this level could jeopardize the integrity of the original collection method.

To improve the text's readability, we have, however, standardized certain formatting in the texts. Indentations, dashes, and the style of headings have been made uniform throughout. Extra spaces within parentheses, following opening quotation marks, and following a sentence's terminal punctuation have been deleted. And in a handful of cases, bracketed information has been added to clarify who is speaking. Within the body of each informant's interviews, we strove to group texts chronologically. Though Chandler did not date many of her interviews, we were able to devise a rough chronology by observing certain typographical clues. In the heading of each of the original interviews, information is provided for identification of project number, interviewer's name, and interviewer location. This data appears in a number of standardized forms, each particular to a period of time. The various standardized headers can be estimated to correspond to date ranges by matching undated interview header styles with dated groupings. In addition, contextual evidence within the interviews helps to further narrow the margin of error.

By including biographical information, footnotes, and photographs, this book has been designed to help mitigate the difficulty the reader will face in working with these transcriptions of oral discourse—transcriptions made more daunting by their origins in a very specific cultural and historical milieu. The biographies draw information from what Chandler tells about her speakers, from what the speakers reveal about themselves in the telling of their life stories, and from what informants reveal about one another. U.S. Census data is often used to confirm or complicate claims made by Chandler and her informants or to find leads on the ages of informants, the names of spouses and children, and occupations.

Genevieve Peterkin, having traveled with her mother on many if not most of her interviewing excursions and having been a Gullah scholar in her own

Genevieve Chandler and Bayard Wootten visiting Emelia Holmes in the Freewoods. *Photograph by Bayard Wootten. North Carolina Collection, University of North Carolina Library at Chapel Hill*

right, has been a tremendous source for biographical information on her mother's informants. She continues to have a relationship with informants and their families, and thus she has provided introductions to many community members. The richest and most rewarding part of this project was seeking out local elders and the families of the informants. Their recollections inform much of the book's editorial documentation.

A Short Note on the Photographer

All of the photographs that appear in this volume are the work of Bayard Wootten, an exceptional American artist in her own right.[54] She, like Chandler, was a professional career woman and a single mother long before either circumstance was a widely acceptable commonplace. Wootten shared with Chandler an interest in the representation of culture and the documentation of life in the lower class. Raised in New Bern, North Carolina, Wootten was a fellow southerner. Though they were very different in many ways, these two women's similarities surely made for a compatible working relationship between them.

How Wootten and Chandler came to know of one another is uncertain, but Wootten was associated with the North Carolina office of the Federal

Writers' Project through her friend William Terry Couch, the former director of the University of North Carolina Press who became the assistant director of the state FWP. Also, though the two photographers may never have met in person, Wootten and Doris Ulmann are linked because they both did much of their work in the southern Appalachian Mountains, because they were both prominent in the "pictorialist" photographic movement,"[55] and because they shared billing in various photography exhibitions. Significantly, Ulmann worked in the South Carolina lowcountry with Chandler's cousin, Pulitzer Prize–winning novelist Julia Peterkin, around 1932. The fruits of their labors came in the 1933 publication of *Roll, Jordan, Roll.* It is possible that Wootten and Chandler were acquainted one way or another through this nexus of relationships. Sculptor Anna Hyatt Huntington was also a mutual acquaintance of Wootten and Chandler. Though they already knew each other at the time, Wootten's trip to Murrells Inlet to photograph Huntington's collection of outdoor sculpture at Brookgreen Gardens (where Chandler was hostess/curator) may have inaugurated the collaboration suggested by the Wootten photographs presented in this volume.

Though Wootten and Chandler never completed the book they had planned to publish together, Wootten had already had and continued to have success in publishing her own work as photographic illustration in a number of prominent places, including Alex Mathews Arnett and Walter Clinton Jackson's *The Story of North Carolina* (1933); Charles Morrow Wilson's *Backwoods America* (1934); Muriel Earley Sheppard's *Cabins in the Laurel* (1935); the Garden Club of North Carolina's *Old Homes and Gardens of North Carolina* (1939); the WPA's *North Carolina: A Guide to the Old North State* (1939); Olive Tilford Dargan's *From My Highest Hill: Carolina Mountain Folks* (1941); and in books exclusively dedicated to her work, *Charleston: Azaleas and Old Bricks* (1937) and *New Castle, Delaware, 1651–1939* (1939).

A Note on the Biographies

In the following pages, we have done our best to gather concrete biographical information about the men, women, and children Genevieve Chandler interviewed. Our primary intent has been to provide historical and social context. In doing so, we have relied heavily on U.S. Census Records. These records have been enormously helpful in clarifying many of the relationships between interviewees as well as in identifying community figures who are only obliquely referenced in the interviews. Caution is necessary, however, when it comes to using these records. They are, after all, only as reliable as the men and women who set them down. Particularly problematic in this case is the default reliance on Western European models of patrilineal descent for identifying relationships within separate households. Traditionally the Gullah family seems to have favored a more matrilineal emphasis.[56] Furthermore familial and communal ties appear to have been far more fluid than European models because of the terrific hardships imposed by slavery. The disruption and dispersal of families obliged creative solutions for insuring that children were cared for and that a sense of belonging could be maintained across plantations, states, and even continents. As a result it may be a mistake to emphasize too much the specific blood relations between the interviewees found here. It seems that the most important social unit was not the nuclear family but a broader, clanlike community clustered among other, similar communities. As Patricia Guthrie has recently argued, it appears that priority was placed on where a person "caught sense" (began to be aware of his or her social obligations) rather than on who one's biological parents were.[57] Although the exact phrase "catch sense" does not appear, similar problems and solutions appear to have prevailed in the African American communities documented in this book.[58] High infant, childhood, and adult mortality rates hardly disappeared with emancipation. Indeed isolation, impoverishment, and otherwise pernicious conditions persisted in the South Carolina lowcountry through the Great Depression. Lack of adequate nutrition, poor medical and dental care, abject poverty, and the surrounding mosquito-infested swamps created unfavorable conditions for longevity. The 1880, 1900, and 1910 U.S. Censuses asked the following questions: "Mother of how many children" and "Number of the children living." In the Waccamaw district of Georgetown County and the Socastee district of Horry County, the answers to these questions suggest mortality rates of 40–50 percent among children. The number of young widows and widowers is equally remarkable. During this period, poverty, racism, and a general lack of opportunity for self-improvement also motived southern black men and women to move from rural to urban areas and often northward. In this tumultuous period of high mortality rates and migration, children were often left with grandparents, aunts and uncles, extended family, or neighbors. Motherhood and fatherhood appear often to have had more to do with the responsibilities and necessities of group survival than with any strict grammar of biological inheritance. In this book, the Knoxville community, Hagar Brown's Corner, and Sandy Island provide crucial points of reference as *places* that took precedence over patrimony.

Notes

1. Official FWP directives mandated the careful excision of reference to the interviewer. Interviewers were also encouraged to restrain impulses to add editorial color to their work. Chandler's interviews typically follow these instructions, but not always.

2. In *Portrait of America: A Cultural History of the Federal Writers' Project* (Chapel Hill: University of North Carolina Press, 2003), Jerrold Hirsch provides a rich portrait of what he describes as an American romantic nationalist and pluralist tradition informing FWP practice. Hirsch stresses the ways in which FWP officials sought to and often succeeded in introducing America to itself, not as a culture of great potential improving through the partial *contributions* of its various subcultures, but rather as a culture of manifest accomplishment produced and maintained by the *participation* of its subcultures in their full complexity.

3. Norman R. Yetman, *Life under the "Peculiar Institution"* (New York: Holt, Rinehart, and Winston, 1970), 341. Furthermore, as Charles Joyner has observed, the antebellum slave narratives were problematic as historical or sociological sources, "marred both by their frankly propagandistic purpose and by the narrowness of their sample of the slave population." At the same time, Joyner stresses the degree to which these narratives "are guilty of no more special pleading than the accounts of the slaveholders, abolitionists, and travelers whose writings constitute standard fare for historians." Joyner, foreword to *A Comprehensive Name Index for the American Slave*, ed. Howard Potts (Westport, Conn.: Greenwood Press, 1997), viii.

4. Yetman, *Life under the "Peculiar Institution,"* 340–42

5. Charles L. Perdue Jr., introduction to *Weevils in the Wheat: Interviews with Virginia Ex-Slaves*, eds. Charles L. Perdue Jr., Thomas E. Barden, and Robert K. Phillips (Charlottesville: University Press of Virginia, 1976), xi–xii. See also Charles Joyner, foreword to *A Comprehensive Name Index*, ix.

6. Yetman, *Life under the "Peculiar Institution,"* 345.

7. Ibid., 346.

8. Ibid., 348.

9. Ibid., 351–52.

10. Hirsch, "Portrait of America: The Federal Writers' Project in an Intellectual and Cultural Context" (Ph.D. diss., University of North Carolina, 1984), 46.

11. Yetman, *Life under the "Peculiar Institution,"* 352.

12. Henry G. Alsberg, memorandum, reprinted in George P. Rawick, ed., *From Sundown to Sunup: The Making of the Black Community* (Westport, Conn.: Greenwood Publishing, 1972). See appendix D in this volume.

13. Ibid., 176.

14. Hirsch, "Portrait of America," 23.

15. "Although ex-slaves had been interviewed under the aegis of FERA, the FWP interviews were not a direct extension of that activity. Instead, the FWP interviewing of ex-slaves seems to have begun initially in separate states and then to have expanded into a national project as the Washington office became aware of the interviews." Perdue, introduction to *Weevils in the Wheat*, xv.

16. Zora Neale Hurston, *Mules and Men* (New York: Harper and Row, 1990), 2.

17. See John W. Blassingame, "Using the Testimony of Ex-Slaves: Approaches and Problems," *Journal of Southern History* 41, no. 4 (1971): 490; Rawick, *From Sundown to Sunup*, xviii–xix; Paul D. Escott, *Slavery Remembered: A Record of Twentieth-Century Slave Narratives* (Chapel Hill: University of North Carolina Press, 1979), 6–17;

Rawick, ed., *The American Slave: A Composite Autobiography, Supplementary Series 1* (Westport: Greenwood Press: 1977), xix–xli, lxxxvi–cvi; Yetman, *Life under the "Peculiar Institution,"* 3–4; C. Vann Woodward, "History from Slave Sources," *American Historical Review* 79 (April 1974), 470–81; Eugene Genovese, "Getting to Know the Slaves," *New York Review of Books*, September 21, 1972, 16–19; Genovese, *Roll, Jordan, Roll: The World the Slaves Made* (New York: Pantheon, 1974), 676; Thomas F. Soapes, "The Federal Writers' Project Slave Interviews: Useful or Misleading Source," *Oral History Review* 2 (1977): 33–38; David Thomas Bailey, "A Divided Prism: Two Sources on Black Testimony on Slavery," *Journal of Southern History* 46, no. 3 (1980): 381–404.

18. William Dusinberre, *Them Dark Days: Slavery in the American Rice Swamps* (New York: Oxford University Press, 1996), 417.

19. Dusinberre dedicates an entire chapter of *Them Dark Days* to evaluating Chandler's work. Perhaps in service of that monograph's broader agenda, Dusinberre's evaluation of Chandler and her work is marred by numerous methodological flaws. As evidenced above, he quotes selectively and somewhat irresponsibly to support his claims. On occasion he misquotes—from an interview with Ben Horry, for example, Dusinberre substitutes the word "master" for "overseer" as part of his claim that "Chandler could not delude herself into imagining that the memory of Dr. Magill was revered by his bondsmen and bondswomen: Magill's 'Oregon' plantation, Chandler admitted, 'from all accounts, had a cruel master'" (423). Most unfortunately, however, Dusinberre takes excessive liberty in his interpretation of aporias and subtexts in Chandler's interviews. One of several glaring examples follows his claim that "another element in the blacks' perception of slavery was their sense of being dishonored" (424). Although few would dispute Dusinberre's claim here, his use of Sabe Rutledge as an example is curious in a number of ways. Dusinberre reports, "In slavery times, Sabe Rutledge said with a stutter (stuttering sometimes being associated with suppressed anger), planters did not have even horses or mules: 'Didn't have nothing but ox. And the colored folks—they came next to the ox.' No doubt Rutledge's remark was born of experiences like the one Kemble reported, of cattle freely grazing among the wooden markers of the slaves' dishonored graves" (424). Oddly the full text of Rutledge's interview seems to bear not at all on Rutledge's sense of honor or dishonor. Instead the comments quoted by Dusinberre belong to Rutledge's meditation on transitions in agricultural cultivation and coastal topography. The stutter, which Dusinberre interprets creatively (to say the least), does not precede Rutledge's comments about plowing methods used in indigo farming. Instead it precedes his observation that the beach was once a field. No mention of graves is made whatsoever. Limitations of space and purpose prevent further explication of many similar weaknesses and distortions in Dusinberre's estimation of the Chandler materials. Readers should draw their own conclusions about what the interviews reveal. By the same token, readers should look to Dusinberre's work as a caveat against using specific, individualized interview material to draw overly emphatic conclusions about historical generalities.

20. "Long Journey Home: Folklife in the South," *Southern Exposure* 5, no. 2–3 (1977): 119.

21. Walter B. Edgar, introduction to *South Carolina: The WPA Guide to the Palmetto State* (Columbia: University of South Carolina Press, 1988), xiii.

22. Charles Joyner, *Down by the Riverside: A South Carolina Slave Community* (Urbana: University of Illinois Press, 1984), 197.

23. "Long Journey Home: Folklife in the South," *Southern Exposure* 5, no. 2–3 (1977): 119.

24. Genevieve C. Peterkin and William P. Baldwin, *Heaven Is a Beautiful Place* (Columbia: University of South Carolina Press, 2000).

25. Ibid. According to Peterkin, Thomas Chandler saved the lives of two Sandy Island men who nearly drowned when a cow they were ferrying across the river upset their raft.

26. See pages 121–24 in this volume.

27. See page 23.

28. Unsigned, undated memorandum to field-workers in folklore, p. 2, box D-3-23 #2, South Caroliniana Library collection. See appendix B in this volume.

29. Alsberg, memorandum, in Rawick, *From Sundown to Sunup*, 178. In this volume, see appendix C, 365–66.

30. Memorandum from Mabel Montgomery to "workers who prepare ex-slave stories," October 1, 1937, p. 1, box F-3-19, South Caroliniana Library collection. See appendix A in this volume.

31. "Long Journey Home: Folklife in the South," *Southern Exposure* 5, no. 2–3 (1977): 119.

32. Rev. Luther Alston, interviewed by Kincaid Mills and Genevieve Peterkin, October 9, 1993.

33. George P. Rawick, ed., *The American Slave: A Composite Autobiography Supplement, Series 1*, Vol. 11, *North Carolina and South Carolina Narratives* (Westport, Conn.: Greenwood Press: 1977), xxx.

34. William Stott, *Documentary Expression in Thirties America* (New York: Oxford University Press, 1973), 110.

35. Joyner, *Down by the Riverside*, xx–xxi.

36. Patricia Jones-Jackson, *When Roots Die: Endangered Traditions on the Sea Islands* (Athens: University of Georgia Press, 1987), 140.

37. Ibid., 132–46.

38. Ibid., xx.

39. Walter J. Ong, *Orality and Literacy: The Technologizing of the Word* (London: Routledge, 1982), 73.

40. Wallace L. Chafe, *Discourse, Consciousness, and Time: The Flow and Displacement of Conscious Experience in Speaking and Writing* (Chicago: University of Chicago Press, 1994), 42.

41. See J. Edward Chamberlin, "Doing Things with Words: Putting Performance on the Page" in *Talking on the Page: Editing Aboriginal Oral Texts,* ed. Laura J. Murray and Keren Rice, 69–90 (Toronto: University of Toronto Press, 1999).

42. David Olsen, *The World on Paper: The Conceptual and Cognitive Implications of Writing and Reading* (Cambridge: Cambridge University Press, 1994), 43.

43. Ibid., 73.
44. Ibid., 11.
45. Jones-Jackson, *When Roots Die*, 32–33.
46. Ibid., 33.
47. Chafe, *Discourse, Consciousness, and Time*, 44.
48. Ong, *Orality and Literacy*, 32.
49. Benjamin Botkin, *Lay My Burden Down: A Folk History of Slavery* (Chicago: University of Chicago Press, 1961), xiii.
50. Jones-Jackson, *When Roots Die*, 36.
51. Blassingame, "Using the Testimony of Ex-slaves," 473–92.
52. Botkin, *Lay My Burden Down*, viii.
53. The exceptions are songs incorporated in a narrative or songs, like "The Ballad of the 1893 Storm," that are narrative in form and especially specific to this community and its history.
54. Jerry W. Cotten's book on Wootten provided much of the data for this section. For more detail on Wootten as a person and an artist, see Cotten, *Light and Air: The Photography of Bayard Wootten* (Chapel Hill: University of North Carolina Press, 1998).
55. Pictorialism was one of many artistic movements at the beginning of the twentieth century to take advantage of new mechanical innovations to distract audiences from the industrial realities that made those very innovations possible. Defining characteristics of pictorialist work include "softness of contrast and tone, a diffused 'atmospheric' look, and even dreamlike appearances." Cotten, *Light and Air*, 14. Typically the pictorialists strove to establish a strong affective quality in their work. They preferred the impressionistic to the realistic, stressing the value of artistic intention and the well-wrought thing. Among the most famous pictorialists are Edward Weston, Edward Steichen, Gertrude Käsebier, Alvin Langdon Coburn, Imogen Cunningham, and Clarence White.
56. William R. Bascom, "Acculturation among the Gullah Negroes," *American Anthropologist*, n.s., 43, no. 1 (1941): 48.
57. Patricia Guthrie, "'Where'd You Catch Sense?' Plantation Membership on St. Helena Island," *Transforming Anthropology* 3, no. 2 (1992): 1–9.
58. Two expressions, however, come very close to the manner and meaning of the phrase Guthrie documents. Louisa Brown recalls, "When I first have sense, I 'member I walk on the frost bare-feet. Cow-belly shoe" (p. 38). In reconstructing her own past, Liza Small reports, "When I know myself, I started to Turkey" (p. 342).

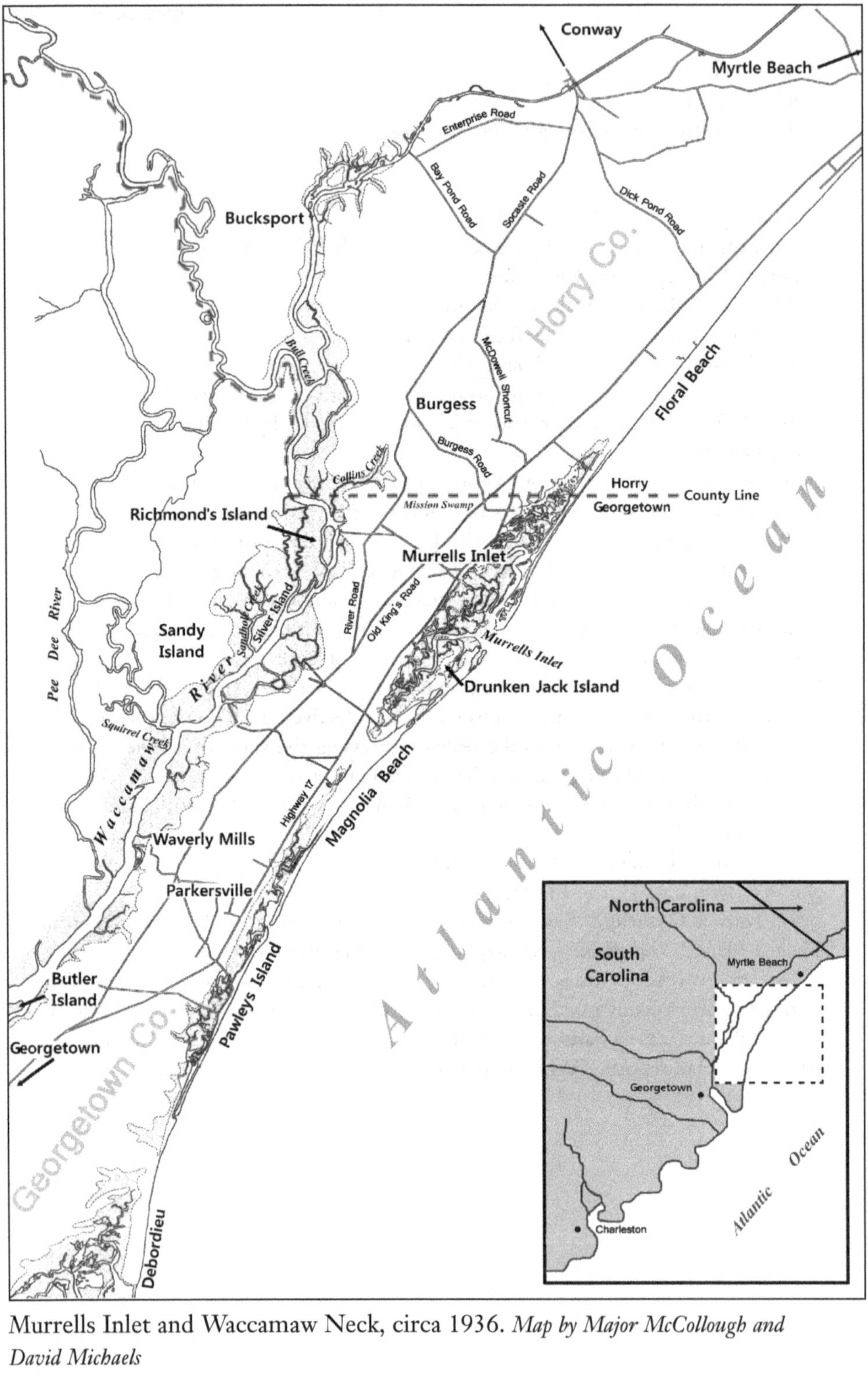

Murrells Inlet and Waccamaw Neck, circa 1936. *Map by Major McCollough and David Michaels*

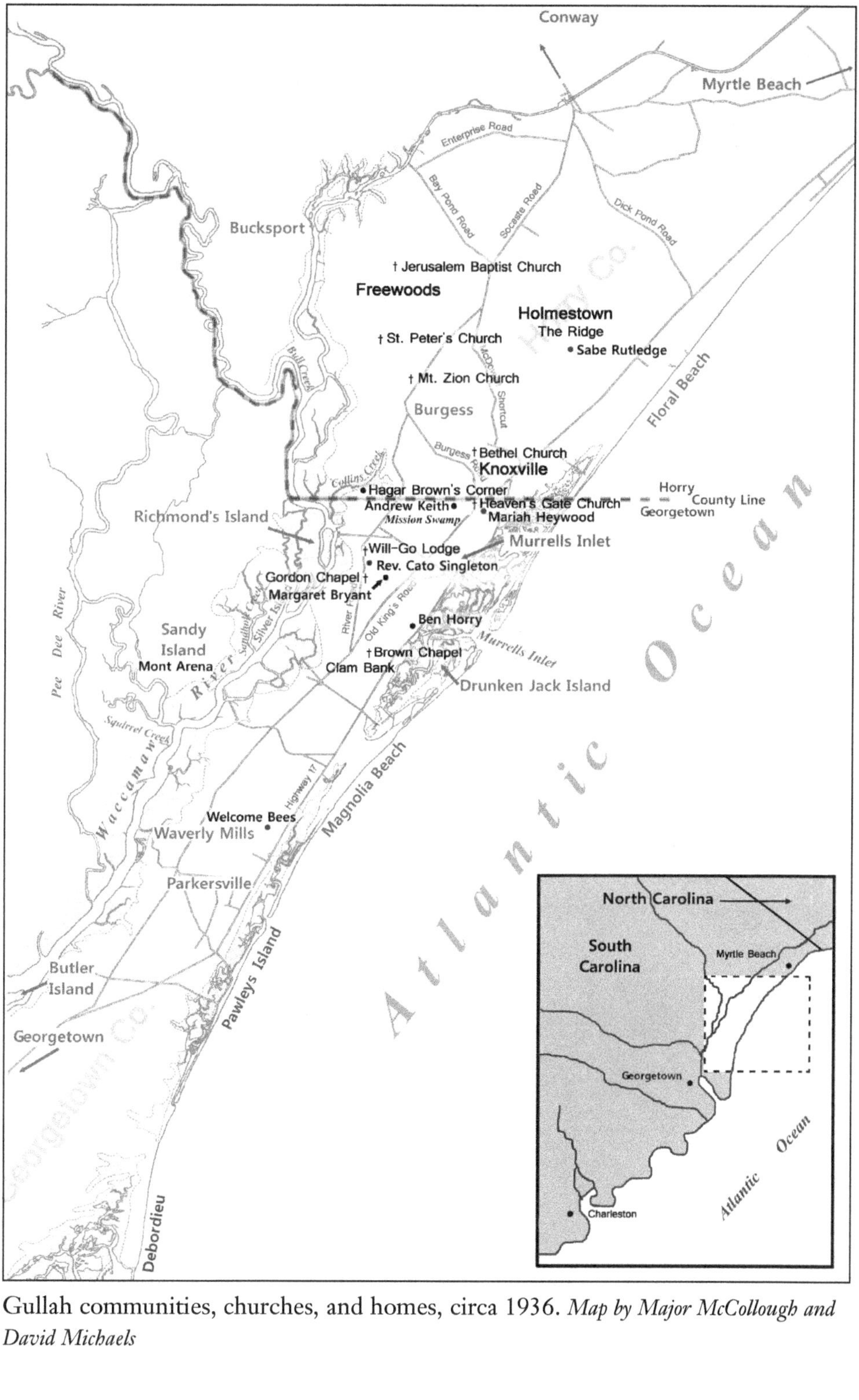

Gullah communities, churches, and homes, circa 1936. *Map by Major McCollough and David Michaels*

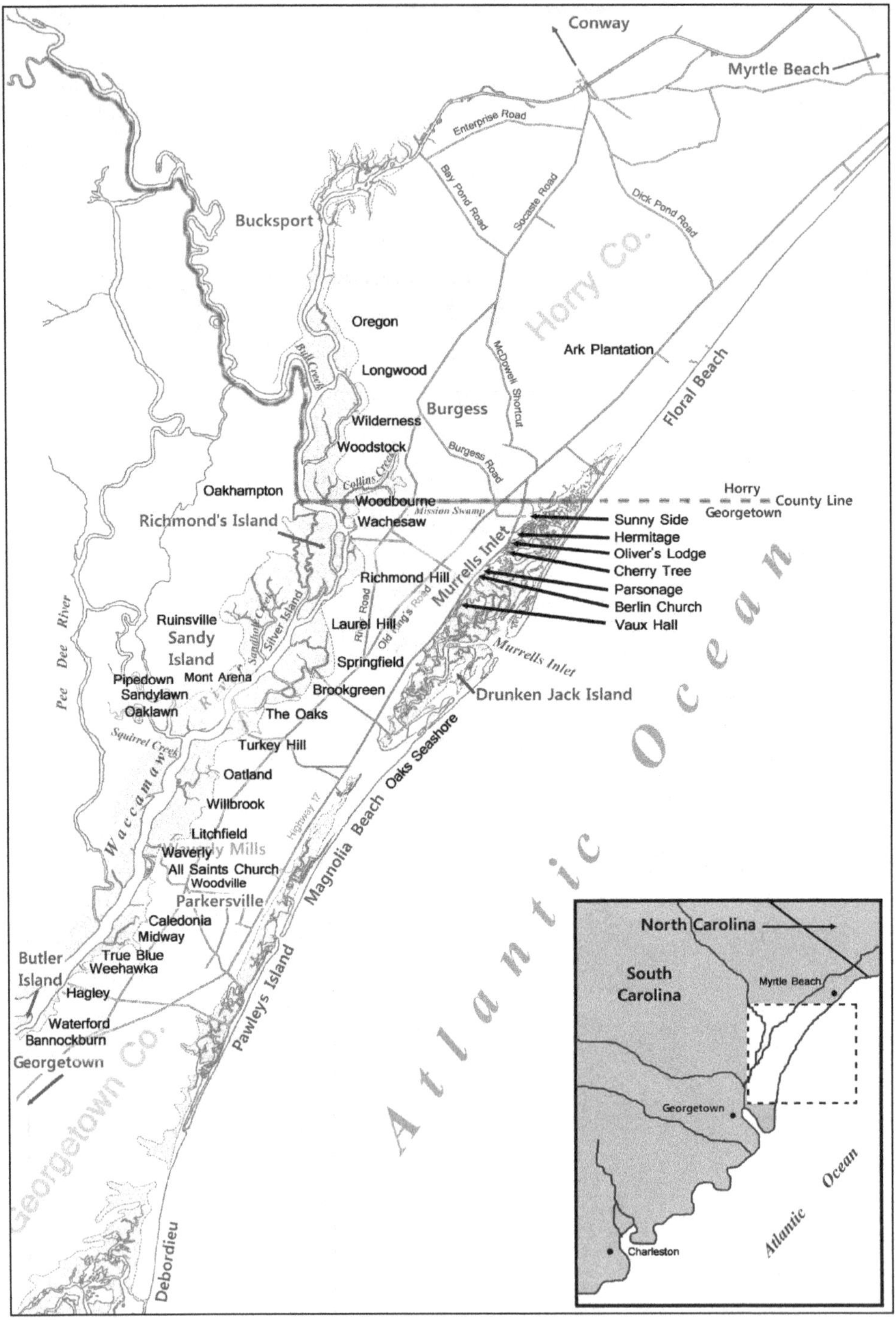

White plantations, homes, and churches, circa 1936. *Map by Major McCollough and David Michaels*

Coming Through

Welcome Bees

Welcome Bees was something of a local legend by the time Genevieve Chandler interviewed him. He was reputed to be the oldest man in the community, and Chandler certainly would have been familiar with him as such. Perhaps because deference to elders is a strong feature of Gullah culture, Bees's true age was of paramount concern for him and for Chandler. These interviews also offer the reader a taste of Chandler's descriptive scene setting as well as Bees's account of how the Civil War was perceived by slaves as it was occurring.

When Chandler interviewed Bees in 1938, he claimed to be 104, placing his birth sometime around the year 1834. Bees was recorded as being 37 at the time of the 1880 United States census, which would have made him 95 in 1938. The census of 1900 reports that he was born on June 1, 1842, which would have made him 96 in 1938. Neither census can be considered completely reliable however. They are helpful guides in establishing and delineating histories, but they are also problematic sources of data. In this case Bees's own testimony may be more credible than the early census information. Various clues in Bees's interviews point toward his true age, however vaguely. His report, for example, that he was 30 when South Carolina seceded from the Union would make him approximately 107 when interviewed. Bees's suggestion, circa 1937, that he had been 35 at the time of his son Isaac's birth puts him at 104. Bees claimed to have been 12 years old when Benjamin Allston Sr. (1765–1847) died. Because Allston was the father of the woman who owned Bees (Martha Allston Pyatt), it is plausible the death would have been a landmark event in the young man's life—one he would likely remember with clarity. If the memory is accurate, Bees was 103 when Chandler interviewed him.

The Methuselah-like legend of Welcome Bees has grown through the years in Murrells Inlet and the surrounding communities. In fact some claim that he lived to be 119 and, even at that advanced age, was not taken by natural causes but by a speeding automobile.

Bees's talents as a master carpenter were highly prized and rewarded during his years as a slave. Based on his talents, he was afforded a degree of freedom

Welcome Bees at home. *Photograph by Bayard Wootten. North Carolina Collection, University of North Carolina Library at Chapel Hill*

that unskilled slaves did not have. By Bees's own account, "Have you own carriage. Go anywhere you want to go." This privileged status most likely also benefited Bees as he started life as a free man. He took part in the construction of batteries at Little River, Charleston, and Florence, presumably during the Civil War or just before. He also worked in the construction of Oatland plantation's church (which he calls Nanny Gully), built before the Civil War by Rev. James Belin as a Methodist church for the blacks and poor whites. The church was moved to Murrells Inlet in 1925 and renamed Belin Church. Later it was moved to its current location off Highway 501 between Myrtle Beach and Conway and again renamed, this time as Bethea Methodist Church. At this ultimate location, it was established with an integrated congregation.

In later life Bees made West African–style sweetgrass baskets of the sort employed in rice cultivation and processing. In fact the 1930 census lists his occupation as "Basket Maker." By the 1920s and 1930s, this was something of a lost art on Waccamaw Neck. Subsequently, many involved in rice production depended on Bees's baskets.

Bees was one of eleven children born to Dolly and Sam who were brought from Virginia to Oatland plantation on the Waccamaw by the Pyatt family. Bees was born at Oatland. He was married twice, first to Mary Bees and then to Emma Bees. He offered the following account of his progeny: "My wife had fifteen head. All dead cept three boy—one gal . . . Grands? Fifteen head . . . Ober twenty-head o' great-grand."[1] According to U.S. Census data, Bees's children included Isaac, Samuel, Susan, Jonas, and John.

Many of the other ex-slaves whom Chandler interviewed were children during the Civil War, and as a result, their memories of slavery are often imperfect. Bees witnessed the war years as a young man. Thus his reflections on growing up, living, and working as a slave on the eve of war and as a free man during Reconstruction are among the most valuable of any included in this book.[2]

1. The 1910 U.S. Census lists Mary, fifty-four years old, as Bees's wife. It indicates that they had been married thirty-five years and that she had had fifteen children, only six of whom had survived.

2. The 1910 U.S. Census indicates that Welcome Bees owned his farm and home free of mortgage. According to the record of Henry Marlow, who administered the 1930 census in Murrells Inlet, Welcome Bees was the only resident of his home and a renter. His was the 125th house visited. The 126th residence visited housed Bees's son John, daughter-in-law Maria, and grandchildren John Jr. and Estell. These same records indicate John was a carpenter and that he could read.

Welcome Bees. *Photograph by Bayard Wootten. North Carolina Collection, University of North Carolina Library at Chapel Hill*

Visit with Uncle Welcome Bees—Age 104 Years

The road is perfectly camouflaged from the King's Highway by wild plums that lap overhead. Only those who have traveled this way before could locate the 'turn in' to Uncle Welcome's house. When you have turned in and come suddenly out from the plum thicket you find your road winding along with cultivated patches on the left—corn and peas—a fenced-in garden, the palings riven out by hand, and thick dark woods on the left. A lonesome, untenanted cabin is seemingly in the way but your car swings to the left instead of climbing the door-step and suddenly you find you are facing a bog. The car may get through; it may not. So you switch off and just sit a minute, seeing how the land lies. A great singing and chopping of wood off to the left have kept the inmates from hearing the approach of a car. When you rap therefore you hear, 'Come in.'

A narrow hall runs through to the back porch and off this hall on your right opens a door from beyond which comes a very musical squeaking—you know a rocking chair is going hard—even before you see it in motion with a fuzzy little head that rests on someone's shoulder sticking over the top. And the fuzzy head which in size is like a small five-cent cocoanut, belongs to Uncle Welcome's great-grand. On seeing a visitor the grand, the mother of the infant, rises and smiles greeting, and, learning your errand, points back to the kitchen to show where Uncle Welcome sits. You step down one step and ask him if you may come in and he pats a chair by his side. The old man isn't so spry as he was when you saw him in the fall; the winter has been hard. But here it is warm again and at most four in the April afternoon, he sits over his plate of hopping John—he and innumerable flies. At his feet, fairly under the front of a small iron stove, sits another great-grand with a plate of peas between her legs. Peas and rice, 'hopping John.' (Someone says peas and hominy cooked together makes "limping Lizzie in the Low-Country. But that is another story.)

[*Visitor:*] "Uncle Welcome, isn't Uncle Jeemes Stuart[3] the oldest liver on Sandy Island?"
Welcome: "Jeemes Stuart? I was married man when he born. Jeemes rice-field. (Worker in rice-field)[4] posed himself. In all kinds of weather. Cut you down, down, down. Jeemes second wife gal been married before but he[5] husband dead.

3. Little is known about this man or the validity of his claim to be the oldest man on Sandy Island. Presumably he was the namesake of the first rector of All Saints Church, James Stuart (a loyalist during the Revolutionary War, who served at the church from 1772 to 1777).

4. The writing in parentheses is Genevieve Chandler's own normalizing gloss on what Welcome Bees is saying. This represents the first of many examples throughout Chandler's work of such glossing. Official WPA protocol discouraged faithfulness to difficult dialects. Chandler nevertheless included Gullah speech as she heard it, often providing these parenthetical summaries as a concession.

5. Patricia Jones-Jackson explains the Gullah pronominal system thus: "Whereas English employs separate pronouns to specify masculine, feminine, and neuter genders,

"I couldn't tell the date or time I born. Your Maussa (Master) take it down. When I been marry, Dr. Ward Fadder (Father)[6] aint been marry yet. My mother had twelve head born oatland.[7] He bought my mother from Virginia. Dolly. Sam he husband name. Sam come from same course. When my mother been bought, he been young woman. Work in rice. Plow right now (Meaning April is time to plow rice fields). I do carpenter work and mind horse for plantation. Come from Georgetown in boat. Have you own carriage. Go anywhere you want to go. Oatland church build for colored people and po-buckra.[8] I helped build that church. The boss man, Mr. Bettman. My son Isaac sixty-nine. If him sixty-nine, I one hundred four. That's my record. Maussa didn't low you to marry till you twenty-two. Ben Allston[9] own Turkey Hill.[10] When him dead, I was twelve years old. Me! (Knocking his chest)"

Welcome Bees—
Parkersville, S. C.
(Near Waverly Mills, S. C.)
Age 104.

Uncle Welcome Bees—Age 105
Waverly Mills, S. C.
(Verbatim)

"The morest licking I ever get been from my Maumer. Licking for misbehavior. Go out Sunday and catch squirrel and shinny on the ball[11] on Sunday. Maumer tie you hog fashion. Throw me down, lick me till one side done. Turn me over, lick me till other side done.

---

some speakers of contemporary Gullah adhere to a system in which gender is unspecified and the same pronoun, *e* [I], may be used to refer to males and females in the nominative and genitive cases. 'E blink e eye,' for example can be translated either 'He blinked his eye' or 'She blinked her eye.' . . . Specifications are indicated largely through context and prefixing." Jones-Jackson, *When Roots Die: Endangered Traditions on the Sea Islands* (Athens: University of Georgia Press, 1987), 145.

6. Arthur Belin Flagg Sr. (1828–1893), killed in the hurricane of 1893, also known as the Flagg storm.

7. Oatland plantation, owned and managed by Martha Allston Pyatt, John F. Pyatt's widow.

8. A derogatory Gullah term used to refer to poor whites. It is a combination of both new- and old-world terms: the *po* is derived from the English "poor" while the *buckra* is a West African term for "Caucasian."

9. Benjamin Allston Sr. (1765–1847), Martha Pyatt's father.

10. Turkey Hill plantation, owned by William Heyward Trapier, who married into the Pyatt family.

11. A reference to dancing, which was considered sacrilegious.

"Mister White[12] carry forty or fifty tousan' (thousand) man from town. Say he goin' to Washington to get old Lincoln head. Come back without old Lincoln head. Say he went out the notion. Stid o' he gettin' Lincoln head 'fore he through Lincoln get his'n.

"What the General 'blong to this country name? General Lee and Grant to Richmond Hill. Last place they had the war! All the fightin' done out yonder.[13]

"Last time I see Mr. White, he come say: (I come to tell wonneh (you all—) good-bye!' When he get there battle begun. Three day and three night fight. Regular man slaughter. Not eat; not drink. Shot Captain White. Shot on horse. End Captain White. Horse run three miles. Retreat today. Bury dead tomorrow. Back again. Do'em just like a hog. Here come one-half bushel o' grape shot. Captain cry: 'Close up! Close up! Close up!' They close up. Gun mow 'em down.

"War? Kill the lil' baby to the breast. Them the one do THAT. Yankee fight for free WE. When the old Rev. war,[14] that the thing bring the thing on. South and Northern state been together so." (Illustrates—fingers interlacing.) "Yankee jine in and help South lick the English Nation back. Then the South gettin' up strong. Raise they own President—they own Governor! Own sumptin'—to eat! Yankee when he come to the Cap'n to Bucksville there on Waccamaw, he say 'We coming back to take this country!' And here say, THEY FIGHT TO FREE NIGGER!

"Thing sho' change. Missus, air-plane good. Car on road good too, but bless God, kill up too much o' people! That how come you find me walk the ditch. I too fear car in the road. I took the first road to the west.

"String on my finger? Why I wear 'em? Missus, I too plagued with the cramp. And twine out the store kinder ease 'em. Cut 'em out—kinder ease 'em. Tie up both thumb with twine for ease the cramp. I ain't wuth!

12. Captain Richard Green White of the Georgetown Rifle Guards.

13. Although General Lee and General Grant did not fight the last pitched battle of the Civil War at Richmond Hill, Welcome Bees's point illustrates how the Gullah people often viewed the world around them. Historical facticity and barriers of time and space could be less significant than the specific relevance an event held within the confines of the Gullah world. Julia Peterkin also makes this point in her short story "Seeing Things": "To the Negroes, this bit of earth has a definite entity. It is the center of the whole universe, with Heaven, the home of the Great-I-Am, in the sky, straight overhead." To Welcome Bees, the Civil War was about one thing, slavery. More specifically it was about the abolishment of slavery. The last battle of the war was fought and won for the slaves by the Union on the day when Welcome Bees and the rest of the slaves were told that they were free.

14. The Revolutionary War.

"Chillun? My wife had fifteen head. All dead cept three boy—one gal."
Visitor: "How many grands, Uncle Welcome?"
Uncle Welcome: "Grands? Fifteen head."
Visitor: "How many great-grands?"
Welcome: "Ober (over) twenty-head o' great-grand."
Visitor: "That all, Uncle Welcome? That all?"
Welcome: "Missus, that all I talk 'bout."

"Heaven, Missus? Heaven is above! They was a mix up all kind of a how. God Almighty command Gabriel to put that wicked angel out the battlement o' Heaven.

"I 'members too good Cap'n White gone on to Washington to fight the Yankee. Three, four thousand man he got to Georgetown. He had a cask o' whiskey. Old Mahogany run.[15] All get tight. Feelin' big. Want to list 'em now. Feelin' big. Go to Washington and fetch old Lincoln own head!

"I gone to make a battery to Little River and to Charleston and to Florence.

"I 'member song sing when we rowin' Cap'n White to town on the Waccamaw!

"'Caesar kill the Mausser fatten' hog!
Hallie—loo! Hallie—loo!

"Get him to town Cap'n White carry forty or fifty thousand man from Georgetown. Here we goin' down the river. Rowin' Cap'n White to Georgetown:

"'Caesar boy—Caesar!
Poor Caesar gone kill the Mausser fattenin' hog!

(A r-r-r-r-Rap!) (A noise made with oar and tongue, sudden, startling)
He condemn to hang!'
Caesar boy—Caesar!
Poor Caesar boy condemn to hang!
Caesar boy—Caesar!
Caesar kill poor Mausser fattenin' hog!'

"Sing! You sing. Uster row Cap'n White to town:

1. "Oh, where Mausser William?
Sing 'Glory in my soul!'
One day gone—Another come!
Sing 'Glory in my soul!'

15. Rum.

2. "WE'll broke bread together!
   Sing 'Glory in my soul!'
   Pender Meddlesome—Meddle everbody!
   Sing 'Glory in my soul!'

3. "Oh, where Danny Blue-jay?
   Sing 'Glory in my soul!'
   Pender Meddlesome—meddle everbody!
   Sing 'Glory in my soul!'"

Source: Uncle Welcome Bees—Age 105
(Can be proved by Mausser Tombstone to Turkey Hill graveyard). February 1938.
Waverly Mills, S. C.
(Sings[16] given exactly as sung by Uncle Welcome. Dramatically sung and acted but little tune.)

[***Visitor:***] "Uncle Welcome, what color are young eagles?"
Welcome (age 105 yrs.): "Noung one white like a geese. I KNOWS. Was to Nanny Gully church. (That YOU church now. White people move them to Murrells Inlet)[17] Was Sunday mornin'. I been a mind my fadder rice and this noung man mind HE Pa rice. Four of we been mind rice. Was a tall pine. Eagle make a nest and we say we gwine cut the tree. And this noung man say: 'I gwine climb up and get'em! I gwine climb the tree!' And here he gone! He gone to the top and he trow one the eagle out the nest. That how come I know. I see'em I tell you! White like a geese.

"And we look up and see the old eagle comin'! Just a speck! Just a speck! Far as we see that eagle comin' she cryin':

"'E! E! E! E! E!'

"'Fore he git there. When we see him we hear him cryin,'

"'E! E!. E! E! E!'

"And we shriek:

"'Come down! Come down! Come down off the tree!'

"And the boy call down: 'Eagle can't hurt me! I gwine get the 'nother one!'

"And here come the old eagle! He LAM[18] him wid he wing! He fly off and here he come back and he LAM him wid he wing. And the three time he come

16. Gullah term for songs.

17. This church, originally located at Oatland plantation, was known to the whites as Oatland Church. It was later moved to Murrells Inlet and renamed Belin Methodist Church after Rev. James L. Belin, who had ministered to the slaves and Native Americans before the Civil War.

18. To hit.

Lam that boy here the boy he come down to the ground out that tree! And he lie there.

"No. He ain't dead. He ain't dead till next day. And we ain't tell! He brudder been there. Sampit Dunmore been there and Primus been there and nudder one again. Solomon! Solomon been there!

"Talk we? No. We ain't tell. We scare for tell. The boy ain't have business climb that big pine on the Lord's day. He ain't tell hisself. Them old people something else. We too fear. NO. We ain't tell'em.

"After Freedom that been my brudder field, but he ain't his own now. The tax take'em way."

Source: Welcome Bees (age 105)
Waverly Mills, S. C.
July 15th., 1938

Will Bees

We have found no definitive information on Will Bees in the extant sources.

Uncle Will Tells a Story (Enoch Arden)

"One time they wuz two neighbor—her live close togedder. This lady husband went to he home and get he old police (valise) and get all he clothes and left home. Leff (left) he little daughter and he wife right dere (there.) And he gone off from home. Get 'em a good job. Find a good fore-man out dere and gone and forgot he wife and little dater (daughter). He wouldn't WRITE nor SEND. Several years he been off from home. Bout ten years or nine. It was coming on Easter. He little girl come home and tell her Mamma,

"My play-mate going get 'em a Easter dress." So she Mamma tell 'em,

"Gal, get out way from me! Your Daddy gone from here so long—and he wouldn't write nor send!

So one day, more than all, him and fuh fore-man fall out. Now so be he mind lick 'em back home to he wife. So he take up he old police and get back home. And when he got back home, sharp twelve o'clock that night, he see the light in duh house and gone there and knock to the door. Ain't get no answer. Knock to the winder; ain't get no answer. The old man back off! Say, Diss (this) my house! I gwine in there to-night."

So he gone to window again. Knock the window loose. He start in—for go through the window! He say, "I gwine in!"

And when he get he whole body in, the udder (other) man who was in knock 'em back through the window and leff (left) he old coat hang up in the window on a nail. He run off, look back, cry out and say,

"I jump through the window
I jump through the door!
The people don't know
The trouble I in!"

"So his partner tell 'em, 'NO! Sho the people don't know. Huccome (how come) you went from home so long and didn't write nor send? Tell (till) you wife done marry wid nother man—nother mans supporting you wife and daughter. And now you want to come her and boss. When you neither write nor send!"

An' him went back tuh find 'nother job an' 'nother fore-man."

Uncle Will Bees—75 or 80
Murrells Inlet, S. C.
August 15th, 1937

Hagar Brown

Hagar Brown was one of Genevieve Chandler's principal informants. Because she was an elder member of the community, she was able to share some remarkable memories, and she retained an investment in traditional folk beliefs that had already begun losing traction in the later 1930s. In this set of interviews, readers find, for example, reference to the punishment of slaves by masters and patrollers. Brown also offers accounts of supernatural phenomena, including "hants" and "hags."

Hagar Brown lived in her eponymous community, Hagar Brown's Corner, within two miles of Genevieve Chandler's Wachesaw plantation home. Brown was a frequent visitor. When Chandler interviewed her, Brown was in her late seventies and no longer capable of much physical labor. Nevertheless, between her own gardening, odd jobs, bartering, and the care of neighbors, Brown did manage to eke out a reasonable existence.

Because Chandler's finances were meager, she drew as much as possible from easily accessible subjects. Driving to find informants consumed gas and time, and both were precious commodities. The less driving she had to do, the more time she had to interview, and the interviews, after all, were what made her money. Clearly, Brown was frequently interviewed because she was frequently available. Beyond mere convenience, however, Brown offered Chandler a wide breadth of experience coupled with an enthusiastic personality. Born into slavery but raised in freedom, Brown offers a unique perspective on the community's history. Her charisma attracted the attention of documentarians Bayard Wootten, John, Ruby, and Alan Lomax. John A. Lomax even made note of Hagar in his account of Ben Small's funeral.[1]

Brown also may have cared for the Chandler children from time to time. Regardless of the tasks she performed, her wit and wisdom made her a popular fixture in the Chandler home for several years. Whereas other community

1. "Suddenly Mom Hagar, the mother of Ben Small's wronged wife, left a group and came back swiftly to the grave. She waved her hands over it and stared up through

members offered labor in the Chandler home for a wage or an occasional meal, the primary commodities Brown had to offer were her stories and songs. Even after Chandler moved to Murrells Inlet, no small distance from Brown's home, Brown still walked to the house once a week to spend some time and get what she called her "'visions" (provisions).

At the end of her visits, Brown would produce a crocus sack to be filled with foodstuffs. Chandler's family had a garden that supplied corn and field peas. They also had a milk cow. When Brown visited, she could count on corn, peas, and milk. Lillie Knox filled the sack with a variety of other foods. Brown segmented the sack with knots, which separated different items. Additional foodstuffs could include grits, cornmeal, fatback, coffee, and sugar. This peculiar toting method prompted Chandler to observe that Brown looked like she was carrying a string of sausages home with her.

Brown was born in Columbia, South Carolina, toward the end of the Civil War. Her family was moved there to avoid Sherman's army during its march to the sea. Brown's mother and father were laborers at the Oaks plantation. She was one of four daughters (Emmeline, Getty, Hagar, and Katrine) born to Sally Doctor. Brown's husband, Caleb, died in a Georgia penitentiary after having been falsely accused of stealing pigs. The Browns had several children; in one interview Brown recites an incomplete list, including Samuel, Elias Arthur, Beck, a first Sally, and a second Sally. After losing one daughter named Sally, Brown was urged by her own mother to name a second daughter Sally also. Brown does not mention her daughters Mary Brown Small or Mattie Brown Collins. Nor does she mention her son Joshua, who was forced to flee the community after shooting a white neighbor, Van Turberville. According to Mary Small, the Brown family had believed Joshua escaped until they were later told he was captured and lynched upriver at Longwood plantation.

In many ways Hagar Brown was the matriarch of her community. She was mother, grandmother, and great grandmother to many. She was also a midwife, and in that role she brought even more members of the community into the world.

---

the trees at the sky. What she was saying I could not understand. Perhaps it was Cherokee, for she was half Indian; perhaps Gullah speech, for she came from Sandy Island. 'What were you saying, Aunt Hagar,' I asked. She looked at me steadily out of her small, hard, black eyes. 'Ben's soul's done wropped up in de care of de Lord, and nothin' mo' in dis world kin harm him.' And she glided off into the woods muttering and mumbling." John A. Lomax, *Adventures of a Ballad Hunter* (New York: Macmillan, 1947), 214.

Hagar Brown: "Lord bless this house and keep the soul." *Photograph by Bayard Wootten. North Carolina Collection, University of North Carolina Library at Chapel Hill*

Mom Hagar (Verbatim Conversation)

Mom Hagar Brown lives in her little weathered cabin on forty odd acres left by her husband, Caleb Brown. Caleb died in Georgia where he had been sent to the penitentiary for stealing a hog that another man stole. Aunt Hagar has grands settled all around her and she and the grands divide up the acreage which is planted in corn, sweet potatoes, cotton, and some highland rice. She ministers to them all when sick, acts as mid-wife when necessary, and divides her all with her kin and friends—white and black. She wages a war on ground-moles, at which she laughs and says she resembles. Ground-mole beans almost a foot long protect and decorate her yard. She has apple and fig trees, and scuppernong grape vines grow rank and try to climb all her trees.

(Monday morning she hobbles up on a stick—limping and looking sick) Comes in kitchen door.

Lillie:[2] "Aunt Hagar, how you?"

Hagar: "Painful. Doctor tell me I got the tonsil. Want to represent me one time and take them out. I say, 'No Doctor! Get in hospital, can't get out! Let me stay here till my change come.'[3] Yeddy?[4] I ain't wuth! Ain't wuth! Ain't got a piece o' sense. Yeddy? Ellen[5] say she want God to take she tommorrow? When you ready it's 'God take me now! All right son!" (greeting Zackie who enters kitchen.)

Zackie:[6] "Aunt Hagar, how you feel?"

Hagar: "I ain't wuth son. How's all?"

Zackie: "Need a little more grits!"

Lillie: "Hear Zackie! Mom Hagar, that ain't hinder him ordering another!" (The fact that food is scarce doesn't limit Zackie's family.)

Hagar: "You here bout this Jeremiah broke in somewhere—got all kinds likker and canned things and different thing?"

Zackie: "Must a broke in that place call 'Stumble Inn!' (Very seriously) That Revenue man been there."

2. Lillie Knox, the Chandler family's housekeeper and friend (see her interviews, beginning on p. 125).

3. "Till my change come" is a euphemism for death.

4. "Yeddy" is a Gullah expression that can mean many things depending on context. In this case, Hagar Brown uses "Yeddy?" as a rhetorical device somewhat like the use of "Listen" at the beginning of a tale.

5. Probably Ellen Godfrey, who ultimately moved to Conway, South Carolina. She would have been ten years old at the time of this interview.

6. Zackie Knox, a brother of Lillie Knox's husband, Richard (see Zackie's interviews, beginning on p. 238).

Hagar: "I yeddy last night! Say he there in news-paper. Mary[7] say, 'see 'em in paper!' Mrs. White gone to child funeral. That been in paper too. Mary see that in paper. Easter[8] say old lady gone dere. Doctor say better go. Child sick. Child seven years old. Fore they det there tell 'em say, 'Child dead!."

"People gone in patch to pick watermillon. Ain't want child to go. You know chillun! Child gone in. Ain't want 'em for go. You know. Child pick watermillon. Ketch up one—I forgotten what pound they say. Roll. Roll duh watermillon. Roll 'em on snake! They say, Snake bite 'em?' Child say, 'No. Must a scratch.' See blood run on boy leg. Child get unconscion that minute. Gone right out. Jess so. Ease out so. I cry. I cry!"

Lillie: "You know 'em, Mom Hagar?"

Hagar: "No! No! Lill, fever got me! Cold got me till my rump dead. Got hospital boy rouse one time say, 'Ma, less go home! Red stripe snake bite me.'"[9]

Hagar: "Klu Klux?" (Chin cupped in hand—elbow on knee—looking way off—)

"Reckon that the way them old timey people call 'em. Have to run way, you go church. Going to come in to ketch you or do any mischievous thing—come carry you place they going beat you—in suit of white. Old white man to Wilderness Plantation. Parish old man name. Treat his wife bad. Come to house, ain't crack. Come right in suit of white. Drag him out—right to Woodstock[10] there where Mr. Dan get shoot. Put a beating on that white man there till he mess up! 'Oman never gone back to him yet!

"A man wuz name (I forgot what the man name wuz)—wuz a white man mess round wid a colored woman and they didn't do a God thing but gone and put a beating on you, darling! Come in. Grab you and go. Put a beating on you till you can't see. Know they got a good grub[11] to lick you wid. They git done you can't sit down. Ain't going carry you just for play with."

[Visitor:] "Mom Hagar, you wanter vote?"

Hagar: "Oh my God!"

7. Mary Brown Small, Hagar Brown's daughter, who married Ben Small.

8. Easter Brown Wright, Hagar Brown's granddaughter, who married Cephus Wright.

9. A coral snake, the most poisonous snake in North America.

10. Woodstock plantation.

11. Gullah term for stick.

[Visitor:] "Aunt Hagar are the colored people happier now than the old timey slavery time people?"
Hagar: "Young people now got the world by force. Don't care. Got more trick than law low. Tricky! Can't beat the old people. Can't equal to 'em. Some the young people you say 'AMEN' in church they make fun o' you. Every tub stand on his own bottom. Can't truss 'em.

"Ma say some dem plan to run way. Say, 'Less run! Less run!' Master ketch dem and fetch dem in. Lay 'em cross barrel. Beat dem till dey wash in blood. Fetch 'em back. Place 'em cross the barrel—hogsket barrel—Christ! They ramp wash in blood! Beat Me sister. He sister sickly. Never could clear task—like he want. My Ma have to work he self to death to help Henritta so sickly. Clear task to keep from beat. Some obersheer[12] mean. Oaks labor. (Meaning her Ma and ma's family were laboring on Oaks Plantation—the plantation where Gov. Joseph Allston and Theodosia his wife lived on Waccamaw) Mother Sally Doctor. Ma got four chillun. One was Emmeline, one Getty, one Katrine one Hagar! I older than Gob (Katrine).[13] Could a call doctor for Gob if I had any sense." (Big nuff to gone for doctor when Gob born.)

"Stay in the field!
Stay in the field!
Stay in the field till the war been end!"
(This is Aunt Hagar's favorite song)

Mom Hagar Brown—age 77
Murrells Inlet, S. C.
July 4th, 1937.

12. Plantation overseers, generally drawn from poor white families in the region, were responsible for managing the drivers (members of the slave class who had direct authority over field hands). Generally an overseer's responsibilities were extensive, and his performance was typically not only "judged by the condition and productivity of the slaves but also by the physical condition of the plantation." Charles Joyner, *Down by the Riverside: A South Carolina Slave Community* (Urbana: University of Illinois Press, 1984), 69.

13. Here Hagar Brown refers to her sister Katrine with a basket name, Gob. Basket names are a vestigial feature of West African tradition that lives on in Gullah culture. They are to be used only by family members and close friends. Under slavery, basket names served as a kind of shibboleth. A slave was, in effect, one person for the master and another among intimates. In this way one maintained a personal identity in spite of a system that was often dehumanizing.

Mom Hagar en Hag[14]

"Dey juss lak-uh-we. But they come in all fashion. Come in any kind of how. Suck yuh en draw yuh blood. Feared uv'um. Feared o' hag. Talk to 'em en cuss'em. Doan stop wid dat! Talk out loud en say,

'White people tell me whut tuh do. White people gib me uh plan!"

En I feel all roun onder th' bed. 'Go way! White people tell me whut tuh do? Dey ride me, all rite! Drowsy! Can't open yuh eye! Jump rite on yuh. Hag ride yuh! Hag ride people! Hag ride yuh, all rite! Slip dem skin off en come een row!"

"Lucien Ant Nellie[15] body chile. Dem other, She dopts."

Mom Hagar Brown
(age 70)
Murrells Inlet, S. C.
(Submitted: Dec.30, 1936)

Introduction

Mom Hagar Brown, age seventy-seven, often assists at 'bornings', especially those of her 'grans' and 'great-grans.' She owns fifty acres. On some of these cleared acres, squatter like, are cabins (one quite primitive, yet with a peculiar charm that is inseparable from all primitive things, built of logs) and in these cabins are grans, one daughter and Aunt Hagar's 'great-grans.' Most of these she has assisted into the world. This may account for her feeling of responsibility. She is really mother of a clan.

The following verbal picture was painted by the old lady who acted the whole scene taking each part in turn. It is hard to understand the conversation unless one sees the moving, gesticulating old Mom Hagar, with all her expressions of joy, pain, relief and disgust.

"Trouble over! Gal, you aint know! Mah back and leg broke! Ay, Lord, my leg broke! I grunt and complain. Leetle gran gal come behind! Morkin (mocking) me! Yuh eye! You sharp face! Wait! Wait!

14. A hag is one of various supernatural creatures that inhabit Gullah lore. As with the belief in supernatural beings in general, belief in hags originally grew out of the African concept of the spirit. In the case of the hag, the disembodied spirit of a living person roams the earth, skinless, perpetrating bad dreams on its victims, and "riding" them in their sleep. Hags share many characteristics with witches and nightmares of western European culture.

15. Cinchy Lance.

"When you get old
Lak uh me
Yuh nose run
En yuh eye can't see!

"Easter chicken hatch! Gawd knows, he get out the nest! Tuh my house. Easter say, 'Grandma I wantuh bathe! Gwine. Keep dem chillun! Cephus,[16] less go! (Let us go.) Gone on.

(Cephus come rap on door.): 'Ma!'

'What you wanter Ma, man?'

"Lord, from uh burning world! Faid tuh lef'em (Afraid to leave them)—dese chillun. Dat leetle one might meddle th' lamp, and dey all burn up here. Kill ez yuh go! Hurry up, less we go frum here! Boy, run fuh cun Becky! (Old Granny woman[17] in th' Free Woods).

"Easter dis here lingering pain.

"Cun Becky come.

(I say): 'Cephus, I make a little thin bread. Reckon you wanter eat! "Cephus stay chillun. Walk round. Cephus feel—feel!

Walk off.—

'Wah! Wah!'

I yell, 'Whoop! Whoop!'

Cephus, 'Coming!'

'Doan run, boy! Hit gal!' (It is a girl). (Not worth running for!)

Whole hill holler!

'Coat! Coat! Coat!' (To catch baby in)

Rachel:[18] 'Tank Gawd! Tank Gawd! Too glad it a gal! Make me feel too cheap Cephus a boy and me but gal!'

'Better get yinnah gun! Gals on the hill! Whole hill done gal! Boys coming.' (Boys will be coming after girls.)

Cephus say, 'Got mah gun in shooting position. Gal too omanish.'

Rachel got four gal; Easter got two gal; Roy[19] one gal—
one boy. Pigeon pair."[20]

16. Cephus Wright, husband of Hagar Brown's granddaughter Easter Brown Wright.

17. Another term for a midwife.

18. One of Hagar Brown's granddaughters.

19. Roy Brown, Hagar's grandson.

20. Boy and girl twins. Also a family consisting of a son and daughter only, so called after a pigeon's brood, which usually consists of a male and a female.

Given by—Mom Hagar Brown
(Age 77, Colored).
Murrells Inlet, S.C.
Feb. 22, 1937
(Acted and re-counted by Aunt Hagar who, fond of dramatizing, acts all parts and gives direct words of absent actors in scene.)

"I tell Mattie[21] 'I gwine carry my coat. I might wet!' Mind! Had a time to Salem[22] yestiddy! I shout[23] my coat out! Put 'em on bench. Coat gone! Man's less house and land and I say, 'Coat gone! Lord will pervide!' Shout till I shout out my coat. Sperrit take me, I shout out my coat.

"Abraham Wright going to preach tonight. I say, 'I'm a leese (least) among the postle.' Ax everybody to come out and see the fun!

"Where Mattie marry? Right to my do (door)! Mattie marry to my do! (door) People dere like the leaf on duh tree. Had a flowers yard. And people dance and beat the flowers down till they wuzn't a flowers been in that yard. Brass band and kittle drum and the bass and them horn!

"Coat gone! I say 'Trust God and go to cross! Dat you battle ax!' Ay, King! Do, Massa!

"Teena got duh rock in he yad (yard) and you want 'em? Aint gie 'em to yinnah? I go dere and tief 'um! Tief 'um out duh yad! Big rock?"

(It was impossible to decide whether my old saint was going to throw all her principle overboard and 'tief' for me or not. Her eyes were full of mischief—her expression and tone militant.)

Mom Hager Brown, age 77
Murrells Inlet, S. C.
June 21, 1937.

21. Mattie Collins.
22. Salem Church.
23. Shouting is one of many West African forms of worship incorporated into Gullah Christianity. Akin to spirit possession, shouting occurs during ecstatic religious gatherings. The urge to shout often comes during the singing of spirituals. The congregation begins singing softly, gradually reaching a crescendo. Clapping of hands and stomping of feet complement the singing. Women tend to do the shouting. When one feels moved by the spirit, she leaves her pew, comes into the aisle, and begins to clap her hands, shuffle her feet, and sing. Men tend to sing bass on the songs and prepare to catch the shouters who frequently faint. In the case Hagar Brown presents in this interview, someone has taken the opportunity of Brown's absence from her pew to steal her coat.

(Verbatim conversation)

[Visitor:] "Mom Hagar, how many children has Aunt Liddy?"
Hagar: "Far as I know got Fessor (Professor), Knox, Willie, Dave, Shedrick.[24] I wash today. Clothes been wash on the line. Line come down 'Yop! Yop!' So sorry dat line fall. Wanter cry. Big washing. Line come down 'Blop! Lord Jesus! Have a time today.

"Slaves? Dey put 'em in the grave live! And you holler under the dirt till you weary and hafter dead. Old timey people talk! My Ma does talk fore she dead. Beat! Beat! Beat the box. Yeddy my Ma talk 'em. I say, "Good thing I aint been here! ' Ma say, 'No, dater, you couldn't do nothing—not a thing.' Yeddy too much o' thing.
Yeddy! Aint want to lie! And I ain't going to crack!

"Ben cut a log there for toe don't wet! Go cross the log!"[25]

Mom Hagar Brown—age 77
Murrells Inlet, S. C.

Mom Hagar
(Verbatim)

Hagar: "Oh, my Savior! If I ever come there and wheel my patched coat on the wharf. I'll destroy the worrel! They tell me! I scared o' Sandy Islant people."[26]

"You see Benjy? How old Gabe[27] when you see him? How old Gabe? He 'round seventy sumptin'. My Lord! Looker old man Todd.[28] He most a hundred."
Lillie: "Mom Hagar?"
Hagar: "Mama?"
Lillie: "Gabe got fifty acres to left his chillun!"

24. Liddy Collins and her children, Fessor, Knox, Willie, Dave, and Shedrick Collins.

25. Here Hagar Brown is referring to making a log bridge.

26. Hagar Brown's fear of Sandy Islanders stems from their insularity and attendant cultural practices that she found mysterious. For example, Sandy Islanders allegedly kept track of any of their number who strayed to other communities so as to ensure their bodies were returned to the island for burial after they died. Sandy Islanders were known to have taken the body out of a home without the family's knowledge.

27. Gabe Lance (see interviews beginning on p. 274).

28. Probably the same "old man Todd" mentioned later by Lillie Knox in the interview titled "Todger Todd."

Hagar: "Land a good thing to look after. I'll work till I loney[29] in the field.

'Stay in the field!
Stay in the field!
Stay in the field till the war been end!"

"I 'member and I 'member well when I wuz on my prayin' ground! 'Member when I get my thing! (Religion)

"Old Laurel Hill Church been by that big old mustard shed (muster shed). I come through! Right there to old Laurel Hill been my prayin' ground. Man come fetch me from that sea, put me in a big white house. White like-a snow! I sing and shout!

"'How happy are the child of God
When he know he sin forgiven!'

"Somebody kept tryin' to tech me. I walkin'! Walkin'! And a big white man with he hands folded jest so say, 'Let her 'lone! Leave her 'lone. I been that-a-way myself.' He layin' down! Layin' down hands cross he breast! No common head o' man! Spirit o' God! Then I feel somebody tech me. My jaw been lock Thursday night twelve o'clock. Saturday I come through! Couldn't eat; couldn't eat! Them old timey people, couldn't fool 'em.

"Gator?[30] Eat Gator? My Grandpa have a pond and he shoot one. Eat every part but don't eat the head and feet. Eat body part and tail. Makes chillun fat. Yes. A hawk kin eat! (Meaning that you can eat hawk.) Crow kin eat, too. Fox? I eat 'em. Fox hard to lay hand on. Them thing can out run a ghost. Possum good! Easy to catch possum. Catch in chicken coop. Coon? Coon better than possum; heap cleaner than possum. Coon won't eat everything and possum does. Squirl? Good to flour 'em and put black pepper to 'em and put gravy to 'em. Eel? Dress 'em. Strip 'em down the back. Stuff 'em and bake 'em. And eel skin good for rheumatism. Wrap 'em 'round leg. Keep 'em till pain gone. I lick my leg with gasoline and salt.

"Teeth? First time I gone doctor take out five! Next time take out all. All out.[31]

29. Looney, or crazy.

30. Here Hagar Brown is most likely responding to a specific question from Genevieve Chandler. Chandler has probably chosen to omit the question itself, perhaps to make herself more transparent and to emphasize the authority and sincerity of her interviewee.

31. This is a reference to Huntington's Brookgreen Clinic, where Dr. Herbert Hucks of Georgetown was the dentist.

"Me, I got no certificie.[32] Can't sit there and let the gal die. Call come day or middle night, I gone! Sometimes strike the young moon, gone right in. I ax Mausser, "When time Julie ready? he say

"'June.'

"But gal ain't big nuff for that. But I know he'll gone in this mont'."

Mom Hagar Brown, Age 77? Murrells Inlet, S. C.

Mom Hagar Arrives on Monday Morning (enters the house, 'stepping in high cotton')

"Mom Hagar, what was the text[33] yesterday?"

"Good! But me aint no hand to fetch no text![34] I ax Andrew.[35] I couldn't get 'um, daughter" (She said Datter with a short 'a') Me ain't have no head to fetch no ting. Beg Andrew to scratch the text and bring you Gracious God! Jesus! We had a sermont yestidday! Mudder Day! Mudder Day all over the world! That man preach! He preach Mudder Day! He ring down on Mudder Day. Mudder teach chillun right. Clare (I declare) that man preach Mudder Day till he preach me out my sense! Know I won't be here nother Mudder's Day. Got to move! (shout) Say, Mudder Day, again, I ain't here! Baby in arms. Rachel own. Got the child. Had to pitch up! Rachel call:

"Git 'um from Grand Ma! Git 'um fore Grand Ma drop!"

"Fire[36] take the church. Heart commence to turn over! I say, 'Take this child! Take 'um!' Rachel take the baby (Aunt Hagar shouted up and down the aisle) Rose on for Mudder and suit of white. Great Lord! The whole thing been jump! Fire take the house! (The Lord's spirit filled the church), I done! Easter got the baby. You know. I want to rush her out all I can. (She said kin!) Anything I want, I hold out my hand and say, 'Jehovah, I pend on you!' (Cross fox-terrier runs into kitchen) Look at puppy! Do, Lord! Ain't going meddle me, enty? I look on Easter. She mudderliss and fadderliss child. Them chillun!'

"Berry? Everything plow up. Plow up! Put in four sacks of fertilize. Allus (always) rake straw and rotten' em in coop and pen and put you ashes in wash water. Make good fertilize. Tater bed aint so tick (thick) with sprout yet.

32. Midwifery certificate. Though Hagar Brown did not possess this license, she was an active midwife.

33. The text in question is the Bible verse from the previous Sunday's church service.

34. Here Hagar Brown is refering to her fading memory.

35. Andrew Keith.

36. Spirit.

"Lil, you say how Gracie? Fine! Fine! Fine! Gracie fine! Walk way to Moody house.[37]

"You take this to Sandy Island? (Looking at photograph of old friend.)

"That's Liddy![38] That's Liddy! That's Liddy! Sho as you born to die.' That's him sho! 'Here you gal!' (Addressing the photograph) That's him! That's him! (Aunt Hagar was very pleased and overcome by the wonder of photography) Man! That's him!. (Aunt Hagar said 'Dat's' very emphatically when she meant 'That's.)

"Aunt Hagar, all those pains in your limbs must be caused by a bad tooth. Any roots in your mouth?"[39]

"Aint tooth in my head! I tell 'em, 'Tooth do this, take'um out! Every one.! 'Toot out! All!'"

"Aunt Hagar, you've been around a lot when new babies come, did you ever have any trouble?"

"Live they help they self down; dead it tough time. Foot foremost? Some come head fust (first.) Foot fore-most they wise! Plenty sense! Glad when they come foot fore-most—they wise. Cod? (Caul)[40] Dat's Cod. (That's a caul!) Thin lak a paper. You call 'em veil? Some calls 'um 'coil.'
Take that off. Make tea outer (out of) um (them.) Feed baby till he all gone. Take the spell off. Can't see 'um. Can't see hant. When 'um born take 'um from he face. Make tea. Feed 'um till he all gone. Drink 'em all. Spell take off. Can't see 'um."

(In the last paragraph Mom Hagar tells how to counteract the evil of being born with a caul. When asked, "Why undo the spell?" she answered, "Scare 'um. See hant keep 'em scare all the time.")

She still does one washing for a family of five and helps her Grand, Easter, with another weekly. She insists she wants to 'die in the field.' That is 'die in harness'—work till the end.)

(When Mom Hagar leaves the house she always says on the doorstep, arms lifted toward Heaven, "God bless the house and keep the soul.)

Mom Hagar Brown
77 Years old (almost 78)
Murrells Inlet, S. C.
Georgetown County.

37. Jim Moody.
38. One of Bayard Wootten's photographs taken on Sandy Island.
39. The questions here are delivered by Genevieve Chandler.
40. A child born with a caul, or placenta, covering its face is reputed to have second sight, or the ability to see spirits.

Scraps of Verbatim Conversation

[Visitor:] "Ant Hagar, you know something I want to know."
Mom Hagar: "Ef et een mah hed, its—blong-tuh-yuh—yuh done got hit!"
[Visitor:] "Is Mr. Burgess out in the savannah, a cunjur man?[41] I heard so."
Mom Hagar: "Yeddy duh so, too!" Willie en Mack Burgess do debbil wuk. When I shum, dey gib me duh time ub duh day."
Mom Hagar: "Duh oldest libber een th' Free Woods?[42] Can't tell. Ben mammy, Annie[43] en me one mont (month) chillun. Semelia[44] seem tuh look older. Ain uh reglar ole people een duh woods now. Semelia got uh long stick to walk, but when yuh look een 'e face, ain so ole. Tink 'e say we bout sebenty-eight. I glad tuh see all diss chillun so livery. When Gawd en Hebben fuh yuh, th' worrel can't do yuh no ham."
Mom Hagar: "No, darlin! No, my darlin! Drop ded en kick! Shum. Ef yuh doan ca me,[45] I wauk frum heah."

Given by Mom Hagar Brown (age 78, colored)
Murrells Inlet, S. C.
(Submitted: Dec. 31, 1936)

(Ex-Slave talks Verbatim)
Binkie Hit by Car

"Dat dark-skinned man have duh teet (had the tooth-ache) and duh boss give him sumptin for duh teet. And Lill give him dinner and duh coffee. And he set right here and the Cap'n ain't make 'em go back to work. Old lady Binkie he cousin. Sech[46] a testimony leave! You know how people'll do. Give her

41. Conjuring, or hoodoo as it is also known, involves the manipulation of both the natural and the supernatural worlds. The conjure man or woman serves the dual role of healer and caster of spells in Gullah culture. He or she uses charms and magic concoctions to produce specific tangible results, from curing the sick to banishing evil spirits to hexing enemies on demand. In Carribean Creole culture this practice goes by the name voodoo.

42. The Freewoods lie in Horry County on the northern part of the Waccamaw Neck. There are two stories explaining the region's name. One tradition holds that this particularly rough land north of the rice growing plantations provided some sanctuary for slaves on the run. A competing tradition suggests that the name naturally emerged as the region was settled by freed slaves directly following the Civil War.

43. Benjamin Small, Hagar Brown's son-in-law, was Annie Small's son.

44. Amelia Holmes.

45. Call me.

46. "Such" is often pronounced *sech* in Gullah and in the southern black vernacular.

testimony jess (just) like you will do. (Come on Pinnacle,[47] fuh eat) Shout and class walk right out to her death!"[48]

Birthing Julie Baby

"Julie baby come! Gie 'um a name so they kin turn 'em in. Just hafter turn in he mudder and fadder, how old he is and how old is he Daddy. Put 'em in. How old he Mammy—put 'em in; if he farmer, put 'em in. Put dat down dere.[49] Dat going! Call duh doctor name—BECK![50] If Cun Becky to a patient and can't come, I put it through. After I get 'em through, I tell 'um 'Go get Cun Becky!' Ain't cut cord. That HIM business! (Cun Becky's—who is a licensed mid-wife). If I ain't got 'em in when she come, then she gwine to it and we fight 'emem. When he come" ('He' means Cun Becky) "I tuh sleep. Tell 'em 'Woman, water on fire. Fuh warm.' I right in chair sleep by stove. Julie in bed. After he git over, gal so glad! So I tell 'em, 'Sleep all you want to sleep' You done fight that big fight. Is a battle fought all right! Wrop 'em up and wrop 'em (baby) up warm. Kinder coolish you know! (August in S. C. Hot little cabin) Did coolish cause after while I get up and put on sweater. Work hard. That a stirring business when you get there. Lay on he Ma bed foot.

("I bet I hide 'em and they never get 'em!" (Referring to her bottle of milk—for which she had walked miles.)[51]

"I jess rub. Put 'em straight. That Julie stand on my back! When I gone in (in too the room where the sick woman lay waiting for help to birth her child) I tell 'em, 'I come to kill or be kill, Gal! You ready?

"How I come? Walk! Wake me up. Chillun so scare! I walk. Water splash! Splash, 'I ain't know when I fell out the bed! I say, 'Whey is I? Feel! Walk the foot log—fall off. Can't take the log. Get to house, kick out my wet shoe. Draw my string tight! Have my string draw. Tell Julie 'Come on! Come on! Do like I tell you. Come on!'

"Here first light, Lucille come hail! I say, 'Lucille, Touble over! What I gie 'em fuh eat? Gie 'em a leetle piece o' slip-jack (slap-jack—pan-cake—

47. Rev. Aaron Pinnacle.

48. Meaning that Binkie was hit and killed by an automobile on her way home from church.

49. Here Hagar Brown is refering to the subject fields of a birth certificate.

50. Dr. Beck, a highly respected African American doctor practicing in Georgetown, South Carolina. Beck's signature was required on birth certificates.

51. The Chandlers had one of the few dairy cows in the area. Hagar Brown and many other people depended on them for milk. Brown would often deliver an interview in exchange for milk and other foodstuffs.

batter-cake) leetle bread soft and tea. Tell that gal, 'Do Julie, do don't kill you sef fuh eat!' (Do don't kill your self eating.")

Rattlesnake

"I been gwine in the woods. Here duh road; here duh rut. I been see rattle-snake in we woods! I look and here the snake head jess so! (She illiustrated, by holding up one long brown, skinny finger, the way the snake held his head up) Got on he cross![52] (His blood up!) I can't kill 'em! Throw stick and limb at 'em. One day agin gone in woods. Get stick and scrange for iron. (Make ironing fire) Cut the scrub oak. See a log. Pick up the log. Pick up the log here the snake onder the log in he (quoil!) quile! Run get LE-roy. Bring he gun. Pull down.—Leroy git a long pull! (A long piece of grape-vine) He pull 'em and pull 'em to the yard! Sich a snake! I been for pitch chunk at 'em. (Chunks of 'lightard'—light-wood knots) Leroy finish 'em wid he gun. I throw at 'em snake go,

"DI! DI! DI!DI! DI!DI! DI!DI!

"I pick up my coat (lifted her petticoat and skirt—she demonstrated by lifting knee high) and through the woods I gwine! Run so I ain't know how hard I gwine!

"Got a sack (pushing her jar of milk down in a flour sack). So nobody ain't know what I got. Truss God!"

Missus: "Come back Monday! Do Mom Hagar, please don't die fore Monday!"

Hagar: "IF I wash to Miss Gillikin I'll come. If I ain't come—I ain't wash. If I does wash, I be here. Truss God till the end!"

Mom Hagar Brown (acting midwife)
(unlicensed)
Age—77-9 (born 'Reb time day")
Murrells Inlet, S. C.

(Some recollections of Mom Hagar Brown)

Visitor: "Mom Hagar, how old did you say you were?"

Hagar: "Don't take care of my age! Had me gang of chillun
when ma die. I had Samuel, I had Elias, I had Arthur, I had Beck. Oh, my God! Man, go way! I had Sally. I had Sally again. I didn't want to give the name 'Sally' again. Say, 'First Sally come carry girl.' Ma say, 'Gin 'em name 'Sally!' I faid (afraid) that other one come back for him. Had to do what Ma say. Had to please 'em. Ma name Sally. Ma chillun Catrine, Hagar, Emmeline,

52. The snake seemed "cross," or angry.

Gettie. I born Columbia. Come Freedom, when we left Columbia, ma finer[53] till we get in Charston.[54] Freedom come, battle till we get 'Oaks.' (Battled till they reached the 'Oaks Plantation—.') Stay there till people gin (begin) move bout. Come Watsaw. Gone 'Collins Creek.' In the 'Reb Time'[55] you know, when they sell you bout—Massa sell you all about. Broke through them briar and branch and thing to go to church. Them patrol[56] get you. Church 'Old Bethel.' You don't know 'em. Been gone!

"I yeddy ma! (heard my mother) Ma say, 'I too glad my chillun aint been here Rebs time! Gin you task you rather drown than not done that task! Ma say Auntie poor we weak creeter, couldn't strain. Ma had to strain to fetch sister up with her task. Dere (there) in rice-field. Ma say they on flat going to islant (island), see cloud, pray God send rain! When rooster crow, say they pray God to stop 'em! Rooster crow, broke up wedder! When rooster crow, scare 'em. Broke up rain! Ma say they drag the pot in the river when the flat going cross. Do this to make it rain.[57] Massa! Don't done you task, driver wave that whip, put you over the barrel, beat you so blood run down! I wouldn't take 'em. Ma say, 'I too glad my chillun aint born then!'

"Any cash money? Where you gwine get 'em? Only cash the gospel! Have to get the gospel. Give you cloth! Give you ration! Jess (just according) many chillun you got. Ma say chillun feed all the corn to fowl. Chillun say,

'Papa love he fowl!
Papa love he fowl!
Three peck a day!
Three peck a day!

53. Feeling well.

54. Chandler uses this spelling of Charleston more than once, and we believe it to be intentional.

55. A reference to the antebellum era and thus to the institution of slavery.

56. Patrollers were hired by plantation owners to police the large tracts of wooded land and swamp between their rice fields. The job was more often than not filled by poor, unlanded whites. Some suggest the wildernesses between plantations afforded slaves a degree of freedom of movement and provided ideal cover for runaways. Patrollers endeavored to limit the benefits the woods gave the slaves. Their powers included both capture and punishment, tasks they performed with infamous cruelty.

57. The ritual of dragging a pot in the river was thought to bring rain. Rain, or the lack of it, determines the success or failure of an agricultural community. By controlling the weather, the community might in part control its own destiny. Also, the slaves didn't have to work during inclement weather: "in case of heavy rains and

"Parent come to door. Not a grain of corn leave! Poor people! Come, drop! Not a grain! Everybody on the hill help. One give this; one give that. Handle 'em light! (Very careful with victuals). Gone you till Saddy (Saturday.) (Will last you until Saturday when you are rationed again.)

"When Ma get down, she say, 'I gone leave! I gone leave here now! But, oh, Hagar! Be a mudder and fadder for Katrine!'

"I say, (I call Katrine 'Gob') I say, 'Better tell Gob to look atter me!'

"Ma say, 'When I gone I ax the Master when he take me, to send drop o' rain to let true believer know I gone to Glory!'

"When they lift the body to take 'em to the church, rain, 'Tit! Tit! Tit! Tit!' on the house! At the gate, moon shine out' Going to the church! Bury to the 'Oaks.'

"Gob say, 'Titty,[58] all you chillun bury at Oaks. Ma to Oaks. How come you wanter bury Watsaw?'[59]

"I say, 'When the trumpet sound, I yeddy!' (When the trumpet sounds, I'll hear it!)

"I marry right to Collins Creek hill. Big dance out the door! I free! I kick up! Ma, old rebs time people!"

Mom Hagar Brown

Age—(She says 'Born first o' Freedom' but got her age from a contemporary and reported 77*)*

Murrells Inlet, S. C.

A Little Seasonin'

"How you, Mom Hagar? Come on in out the cold!"

"Lill, gall, I not worth! Not worth a cent!"

"What that in that sack?"

"Pea. Pea for them chillun. All the 'tater in my hill—two for them chillun; one for me. But my 'tater rotten down! Rotten down!

What you know, Lill?"

And Lill replied:

"Nothin'. Nothin'. What you know, Mom Hagar?"

"You hear 'bout the fight? I meet the news to the church. I laugh in that church! 'Quack! Quack! Quack! Quack!' Not laughin' so much at the fight! I was laughin' at GOB tellin' 'bout the fight. Fightin' over a little slice o' meat—

---

thundershowers the slaves were dismissed from work and allowed to return home." Joyner, *Down by the Riverside,* 44.

58. An informal term for sister.

59. Wachesaw plantation.

a seasonin' o' butts! Now wasn't that something to be fightin' over? You know if Ezzoline buy that meat with money from her own labor, she ain't had a big slice to lend nobody! What Ezzoline got to buy meat with?"

"The way Gob tell me, Big Teena daughter, Sadie, loan a seasonin' o' butts to Ezzoline, Teena step-mama. Ezzoline borry the meat for her collards. Just a little slice o' butts. And she didn't turn it back!

"Now time come Sadie need that meat. She cookin' cow-peas and some home-made rice for them chillun dinner and have not even a bacon rind to season it. When she gone to Ezzoline house—the house right cross a little field—she meet the house empty. So beings she HAD to have that slice o' meat she gone on in and get it—and it take all in the house. Seems like they was just one little piece in the box. So Sadie take it and gone on and put it in her pot o' peas. And it was just-a poppin' and bubblin' when Sadie hear Ezzoline comin'.

"Seems like Ezzoline was countin' on puttin' that slice o' butts in her own pot to season her turnips. (That where she was when Sadie gone there—down in the turnip patch gettin' her dinner.) Seems like she washed the turnips and then went to the meat box and found it empty and then here she follow Sadie steps home! And she must-a been mad by time she cross that field. She call Sadie (now 'scuse me for the word)—and then they gone down to quarrelin'. And Gob say, 'fore Sadie know what she plannin', Ezzoline broke a lamp over Sadie head and then smashed up Sadie flash-light the same way!

"One them chillun must-a got scared and run for her Grand-ma, Big Teena, 'cause next news here come Teena! Off the job! Leave her work and come stick in hand. She come up and join in. She say:

"'I come to settle, and settle with a fight!'

"And Teena haul back with that young oak stick and knock Ezzoline down and all them chillun of Sadie and Big Teena pile up and cover her:

"But Ezzoline couldn't be keep down. Here she rise up out that pile o' chillun and rise with the rake in her hand! And she kiss her step-daughter! She kiss Big Teena with that rake! Rake hit Teena right here under her right eye and tear from her eye clean cross her cheek! Teena so big! Ezzoline so little and skinny! That make it seem funny. Ezzoline gettin' her meat back! Takin' it off Teena face! And here Teena end up in the doctor's office!

"When Ezzoline through with that rake, she wheel! She say:

"'I goin' home and get my gun! I'll kill one and wound the rest!'

"And it look like every one though she the one goin' be kill! Teena and Sadie and all that gang o' chillun sweep clean! All run! The yard CLEAN! Leave Ezzoline house, yard and all!

"Yes. Teena is so big they laugh and say:

"'How come you let Ezzoline run you and Sadie and all them chillun?

"Teena tell 'em:

"'You could see Ezzoline wasn't stoppin' short o' murder and you know the old sayin': 'Coward dog carries whole bones!"

"Teena not able to be on the job this mornin'. She still under the doctor. Ezzoline, she restin' in bed. That lamp or flash light, one, leave a mark on Sadie. She's stayin' in. They say her head so bind up nothin' showin' but one eye.

"Step-mama kissin' her step-daughter with a rake and hittin' her step-grand-daughter with a lamp and flash-light 'bout a little seasonin' o' butts meat! "You know they goin' to law! Case have to put off till they able to travel. None able to get to the Magister[60] house. Nobody able to 'tend that trial yet. That slice o' butts not worth what it goin' cost to pay that doctor and take 'em all to the trial."

Source:

Lillie Knox and Mom Hagar Brown
Murrells Inlet, S. C.

Cunjur Bag[61]

"I know I ain't goin' be the one peep in there. 'Cause I ain't make my peace yet. Know it will make you fall dead. Wouldn't have time to crook."[62]

Mom Hagar Brown Murrells Inlet, S. C.

Superstitions

"A child that never know he Pa can sho cure thrash.[63] Just have to blow in the baby mouth and it'll sho cure'em!"

Mom Hagar Brown
Murrells Inlet, S. C.

"If you let a child drink water out a stranger shoe it'll cure 'thrash.' Meet him in the road say: 'Loan me your shoe a minute! Give the baby water to drink out'em and that'll sho cure up the 'thrash.'"

60. The magistrate.

61. The conjur bag is used by the conjur man or woman as a container for a magic spell. For more on the conjur man or woman, see page 26, note 41.

62. To become stiff with rigor mortis.

63. Yeast infection of the mouth.

Salutations

Zack: "What you say, Mom Hagar?"
Hagar: "I'm tanksful I outer the dirt.[64] As for feeling I ain't got a feeling. How dem chillun?"
Zack: "Cryin' for bread."
Hagar: "And another one comin'? Hush boy! It hot this mornin'. Too hot to count money!"[65]

Mom Hagar

"I tell you we HAD a time to Gordon[66] Sunday! Such a nice time. The Revents took for his text 'The 'Noung People.' He preached the disbehaviour of the 'noung people. Tryin' to follow fashion and smokin' cigret. If they don't MIND ME, I'll cut a light for the State to see, I'll cut they head with the ax! Lay 'em open and tell Uncle Sam to take me."

Mom Hagar

"Mary! Gie this to Cun Becky! Baboon[67] sent 60 cts. Pay as he kin! Pay as he kin! She jew (due)[68] on that last child she take he wife. That make $1.60 he pay on the chile!"

Hager: "Struck a knot now!

Bubba Son[69] the one kill that other man. He kill Ham. He sho did. You know a lot of murdering has done here.

64. Not dead and buried. This is an example of a manner of phatic greeting common in Gullah. For a similar example, refer to Margaret Bryant's interview where she responds to Genevieve Chandler's "how are you?" with "I ain't wuth" (p. 46). Neither greeting can be taken literally since the former is obvious and the latter suggests grave illness.

65. Hagar Brown is not interested in hearing about Zackie Knox's financial woes.

66. Gordon Chapel.

67. Baboon Singleton, son of Sadie Singleton.

68. This reference is to money owed the midwife for the delivery of Baboon Singleton's child.

69. Ben Francis.

He jest wuz lying there drunk. They say half the people were coming by the house and he had two guns (Ben did). Held 'em up! Wouldn't let 'em pass! Say he gwine kill 'em all! Say he Daddy kill his Mother. Say he murder her and he going to get him! Held up he Ma funeral procession! Some run through the woods! I hear 'em on church grounds. They say, 'Ben drunk! Come to tend he Mother funeral drunk!

When we all come by, he jest laying there on the poarch. Some say, 'Call him! Let him come on and see the last o' his mother!' I say, 'No, man! Let sleeping dog lie!'

Mr. Francis (Ben Pa) after the burying done say he going home and let boy know who were boss! He say he boss 'em if he were no bigger than ants! 'I show him today!'

All the mans say,

'That's a man! 'A old pot! I tell you bout pot!' 'That what I call a man!'

Ag him on. Ag him on. And Ben likened to kill his Daddy. A man can't shoot wid two guns in he hand. What he going to pull the trigger wid? What going hinder him? Say they take the two guns and hide 'em. Ain't Ben's wife relation to you?"

Lillie: "Yes. Fuss (first) cousin. But it take financial to take little trips. I ain't gone to Hannah.[70] I ain't got cash to throw way. She get gainst the wall she'll find me.

"Aunt Riah[71] say, 'Gal, you get all you joke from you Pa! Say Papa say, 'Miss Hess, Aunt Riah say look in the right hand corner of her trunk and give me one of those dollar you find!'

Miss Hess tell Aunt Riah and she say, "Hess, you look in dere and if you find a dollar in right hand corner it more dan I know!"

Then Papa 'ud say,

"Miss Hess, fix me up a bag 'o them cold biscuits out you Ma safe!

Say she got a scrub (broom) now Papa make for her. She say I kin BORROW it but I must bring it back."

Mom Hagar Reports

Zack: "Goin'?"

Mom Hagar: "Ain't goin'. I GONE! Preacher gone to bury the dead!"

Zack: "Monday? Today?"

70. Hannah Francis.

71. Mariah Heywood.

Hagar: "I fall down! Could hear my inside cry! Just been to we Lodge.[72] I turn back. Rub! Rub! Rub! I keep wood. Make fire. Had a wedder I tellin' you! Tote my wood. I have the water. Most die on the go! Gone to get the Connune. (Commune) Wanter get'em so bad! Preacher gone to bury the dead. Cato in the pulpit."[73]
Lillie: (enters) "Hello Mom Hagar! How you feelin'?"
Hagar: "Got a chance! Tank God for the chance! How's all?"
Zack: "All well to my house only them chillun needin' some grits."
Hagar: "Stop, Zack, 'bout them chillun always hongry.'
Zack: "Where there no fool, there no fun!"
Hagar: "Like to stay here you feed me!"
Zack: "Ain'ts you come for feed? Say you so full of pain. I hear how you shout to Salem yestiddy! They say you make so much a racket—"
Hagar: "Them chillun say, 'Grandma, you ain't got good sense ain't he? Gone to church and shout and you got the leg! 'I tell dem:' I wants to stay here and pray and shout by myself! Get out o' here! Get out and GONE! 'I full them full o' hominy and send dem on home. Tell 'em, 'Get out my house!'"
Lillie: "Want some coffee?"
Hagar: "Stop! Plenty 'nouf! I tell Jehovah,'O King, send You angel 'round and protect me!'"
Zack: "When old people get like Mama and Aunt Hagar, the only way to run them out is to BURN them out!"
Hagar: "Calvin gone! Night Calvin[74] gone I hear outcry. I say: "Oh Lord! Oh Lord! Come King!' Boy bring outcry. I hear dem holler that-a-way comin' cross the field. I say: 'Who dat?'"

"'Joe!'

"'What Joe?'

"'KIT Joe!'

"'What 'tis?'

"'Come to let you know Calvin drownded.'

72. The meeting place for the Ellen Will-Go Society, a nondenominational prayer group that may predate the Civil War. Some sources suggest the Will-Go is meant to indicate that the prayers made by the society *will* go to heaven. Others contend that the Will-Go is a reference to the society's community service ethic—e.g., members *will go* where their help is needed. The name Ellen in the title is said to refer to Ellen Horry.

73. Cato Singleton, former driver at Richmond Hill plantation. Later in life, Singleton also preached.

74. Calvin Bryant, drowned at the Ark plantation (now known as Surfside Beach).

"'Mattie[75] come down the path wavin' her arms, Holler: 'OH MA!'

"'Mattie , don't kill me! What 'tis?'

"'Calvin DROWNDED!' I bust loose:

"'Poor Fed! Poor Fed! (Fred)—Calvin's mother)[76]

"I hear them chillun behind me. Them chillun duh mock me,
'Poor Fed! Poor Fed! I ask Mattie:
"How Sarah take it? Hess? Anna?'

"Go on gal. Hunt the book for me. Want the book. Mary comin' Wednesday to paper[77] me up for holiday. Don't disfurnish youself.[78] I don't wants to be a robber! You hear I lose all my pig? Somebody give that hog some slop and top and all and the baby come dead!"

SOURCE: *Mom Hagar Brown—77 Lillie Knox—36*
Zack Knox—30 Sept. 1938
Murrells Inlet, S. C.

75. Mattie Brown Collins, one of Hagar Brown's daughters.

76. Margaret Bryant.

77. Before the introduction of drywall or wood paneling—and when plaster was prohibitively expensive for most people—the preferred interior wall covering was pasted newspaper. An example of this can be seen in the photograph on page 4.

78. The *r* is commonly dropped in the possessive pronoun "your."

Louisa Brown

Louisa Brown was born around 1857, presumably at Turkey Hill plantation where she married her husband, Watson Brown. According to U.S. Census data, the couple had eleven children, six of whom were still living in 1900. Among the children were Allen, Joe, Edwin, Washington, and Saraphine. As adults, the children appear to have lived in adjacent homes. In her conversation with Chandler, Brown related many of the Waccamaw Neck's historic and fabled events: the evacuation of slaves upriver ahead of the invading Union army; the 1886 quake; and the 1893 hurricane. She also witnessed the more subtle changes that came with Reconstruction, as her pithy description of generational difference demonstrates: "we 'lamp-oil chillun'; they 'lectric light' chillun now!"

Ex-slave Story (Verbatim)

"My old man[1] can 'member things and tell you things and he word carry. We marry to Turkey Hill Plantation. Hot supper. Cake, wine, and all. Kill cow, hog, chicken and all. That time when you marry, so much to eat! Finance wedding![2] Now—

"We 'lamp-oil chillun'; they 'lectric light' chillun now! We call our wedding 'lamp-oil wedding.' Hall jam full o' people; out-of-door jam full. Stand before the chimbley.

"When that first war[3] come through, we born. I don't know just when I smell for come in the world.

"Big storm? Yinnah talk big storm hang people up on tree?[4] (Noah!) Shake?[5] I here in house. House gone, 'Rack-a-rack-a-racker!'

1. Her husband, Watson Brown.
2. Louisa Brown is indicating regret that African Americans must now finance many things that had previously been the responsibility of the slaveholder.
3. The Civil War.
4. The 1893 hurricane, also known as the Flagg storm because it reduced the prominent Flagg family literally to a man, Dr. Ward Flagg.
5. The earthquake of 1886.

"My husband run out—with me and my baby left in bed! Baby just come in time of the shake.

"When I first have sense, I 'member I walk on the frost bare-feet. Cow-belly shoe.

"My husband mother have baby on the flat[6] going to Marion and he Auntie Cinda have a baby on that flat.

"From yout (youth) I been a Brown and marry a Brown; title never change.

"Old timey sing?

1. "Wish I had a hundred dog
And half wuz hound!
Take it in my fadder field
And we run the rabbit down!
Chorus: Now he hatch
He hatch!
He hatch!
And I run the rabbit down!
2. I wish I had a hundred head o' dog
And half of them wuz hound
I'd take em back in my bacco field
And run the rabbit down.
Chorus: Now he hatch—he hatch!
He hatch—he hatch!
Now he hatch—he hatch!
And I run them rabbit down!

That wuz a sing we used to have on the plantation. Then we make up sing—we have sing for chillun. Make 'em go sleep. Every one have his own sing.

"Bye-o-baby!
Go sleepy!

6. In 1862 the regiments defending the Waccamaw Neck had dwindled enough that Colonel Arthur Middleton Manigault "warned the planters that they should be ready to move their Negroes 15 or 20 miles inland with provisions for one year and to hold their plantation flats in readiness to provide the necessary transportation." George C. Rogers Jr., *The History of Georgetown County, South Carolina* (Columbia: University of South Carolina Press, 1970), 396. Federal troops went up the Waccamaw River to Laurel Hill plantation in July 1862, and it was around this time that the planters actually began moving their slaves inland to prevent defection and unrest.

Bye-o-baby!
Go sleepy!
What a big alligator
Coming to catch
This one boy!"

Diss here the Watson one boy child!
Bye-o-baby go sleepy!
What a big alligator
Coming to catch this one boy!

Emmie Jordan: "Missus, I too plague with bad heart trouble to give you the sing!"

Song and conversation Given by
Mom Louisa Brown (Born time of 'Reb people War')
Waverly Mills, S. C.
Near—Parkersville, S. C.

Sam Brown

There is no record of Sam Brown in the U.S. Census data for Horry or Georgetown counties, and he is not remembered by the contemporary residents of the Murrells Inlet area. The story he tells, however, is the first instance in this volume of a folktale in the trickster tradition. Slaves are both perpetrators and victims of the trickery in this case, but the violence and cruelty of overseer and driver also feature prominently.

Uncle Sam Brown: "You yeddy the story o' the two boy and the Master? The two boys always 'blive they didn't get 'nouf food. Always think they needin' more corn than the Overseer share'em out.[1]

"So these two boy gone and slip a board in the barn. Night time they gone to that loosen board and load they sack. Full'em up wid the Maussa corn.

"And the Overseer get on to it. He send the Driver and tell him: 'When they slip they hand through that loosen board, take a hatchet and chop he hand off!'

"Night time come and boy gone back to the place where they have loosen the board and first boy stick he hand in and Driver been hide in the barn.

1. A reference to slave food rations. According to James L. Michie's research on Richmond Hill plantation, slave diets comprised food items produced by the plantation, crops grown in small slave gardens, as well as flora and fauna from surrounding forests and streams. Therefore slaves were partially responsible for supplementing what their masters gave them to eat. See Michie, *Richmond Hill Plantation, 1810–1868: The Discovery of Antebellum Life on a Waccamaw Rice Plantation* (Spartanburg, S.C.: Reprint Company, 1990). In *Time on the Cross: The Economics of American Negro Slavery* (Boston: Little, Brown, 1974), authors Robert Fogel and Stanley Engerman report that the bulk of the slave diet came from eleven foods: beef, pork, mutton, milk, butter, sweet potatoes, white potatoes, peas, corn, wheat, and minor grains. Other foods that found their way into the slave diet were fish, fowl, game, sugar, fruit, vegetables, corn bread, fat meats, and molasses.

Driver make a chop down and chop off the boy hand! Boy turn to he partner and tell'em:

"'Already got mine! You get yours!' (Draw he hand out. Stick'em under he coat.)

"Now the 'nother boy stick he hand in. Say:

"'Oh, somebody chop off my hand!'

"First boy pull out he hand. Show'em. Say:

"'Mine too! Mine too!'

"Both the boy have but the nubbin' leave. Jest the nubbin'!'

"Why he ain't tell he partner? HE catch and call 'tief, want he partner to catch too!"

SOURCE: *Uncle Sam Brown (Age 50 plus)*
July 17th., 1938
Brook Green, S. C.

(Sounds like Leopold in Africa—on ivory coast)

Margaret Bryant
(Granddaughter)

Margaret Bryant is her grandmother's namesake. Genevieve Chandler interviewed both of them. The younger Margaret's father, Calvin Bryant, was the elder Margaret Bryant's son. As the younger Margaret mentions in her interview, Calvin Bryant drowned in 1937 in an accident at Sabe Rutledge's fishing operation on the Ark plantation.

Uncle Sabe's wife:[1] "Say he done all he KIN. Wife do all she kin. Turn her over to the Lord."
Margaret Bryan: "I dream Sunday night Grandma was sick. I say, 'I goin' home! I SHO goin' home! I goin' home this mornin'. Mr. Lon, can you drive me to the station?' He say, 'All right Margaret. I bring you and I promise you can go when you take notion. You ready?' And here I am. I know just as well I goin' meet bad news! And here, when I step off to the beach, first boy I see Uncle Quinvy's King Agrippa and he ax me, 'You hear 'bout your Grandma burn out last Satdy night ain't you?'

"How you makin' out?"
Uncle Sabe's wife: "I comin' long. Sabe good but he old. He good as he can be. He scrab (scrabble) 'round. Brokin' in corn this week, when he not to the fishery."
Margaret: "Cun Andrew be been[2] mean to patch up Grandma house ever since Pa[3] drownded to the fishery last year but never didn't get to it. Good he didn't. If he'd a put a part on it he'd a lose all."

1. Nancy Rutledge.

2. The "be" of "be been" is an example of preverbial marking to indicate verb tense. For further discussion, see Patricia Jones-Jackson, *When Roots, Die: Endangered Traditions on the Sea Islands* (Athens: University of Georgia Press, 1987), 141.

3. Calvin Bryant.

"I tell Grandma I sho glad Mr. Frank hold her so she not go back in that house! She too worry over lossing her pocket-book. Had in 'em three dollar. I say, 'By the help of the Lord can get more house to stay in but can't get no more Grandma.'"

Uncle Sabe wife: "How the house catch nohow?"

Margaret: "Ain't no tellin'. Two them Mazyck boy was comin home from meeting' way down the road and it happen they see the light through the pine thicket and come running. They was a-whoopin' and a hollerin'. Must been them that wake up Daisy. Daisy say when she wake she hear the fire roarin' and she too scare to do more than throw them seven head o' sleepy chillun in the corn patch and lead Grandma out. Them two boys drag out a few pieces but they leave the trunk and chair too close up to the fire and they all catch and burn up. That house been frame with the pure heart pine. They say it was sho a hot fire for the size.

"Where they sleep to? They gone right in Mr. Frank Wallace house next door. It happened he was up off and on with a sick mule. The mule die. Die this morning. When I leave all hands was digging up the lot. Making a hole right there to the stable door to bury that mule. Didn't have no way to haul him off. The LAW won't let you haul critter off nowhere nohow. Have to bury them. Before time they just drag critter off and leave dem in the woods."

SOURCE: Aunt Sabe Rutledge (70 plus)
The Ridge (Near Floral Beach)
Margaret Bryan (18?)
Murrells Inlet, S. C.
Sept. 15th., 1938

Margaret Bryant
(Grandmother)

Genevieve Chandler most likely sought out Margaret Bryant because she was one of the oldest members of the community and because she was a former slave. In this interview Bryant recounts her Civil War memories, particularly the appearance of Union troops at Wachesaw plantation and the reaction of the plantation's owner and underlings. Bryant also discusses some folk beliefs concerning breach births and cauls.

As a child Margaret Bryant and her twin brother, Michael, belonged to Doctor Allard Flagg and nursed with Flagg's son Allard Jr. Bryant's father, Michael One, was a carpenter. As the "number one carpenter," One's duties included more than simple carpentry. He was often the plantation architect, engineer, timber man, lumber-mill operator, building crew chief, and foreman. One was also in charge of the maintenance and upkeep of all the plantation buildings. In short, Michael One held the most highly skilled labor position among the slaves, a position that carried a good deal of prestige. It comes as little surprise that the planter treated the One family with a degree of flexibility. Since Bryant's parents were skilled laborers, she most likely enjoyed some luxuries that other slaves did not.

Margaret Bryant's mother, Mary One, was a model of productive slave resistance and a perfect example of the freedoms that were possible for certain slaves. After an overseer accused Mary One of failing to complete a task, she threatened to kill herself. Rather than allow One to make good on her threat to destroy herself and rather than physically punishing her, the master transferred her from Sandy Island to the weaving room at Wachesaw plantation, thereby defusing the situation. Thereafter Margaret One Bryant and Mary One wove cloth, some of which they sold to whites in the area, presumably for their own profit.

As an adult, Margaret Bryant lived on the southern boundary of Richmond Hill plantation (present-day Turntable Road). U.S. Census data for 1910 indicates that she was married to Benjamin W. Bryant, a literate carpenter.

Margaret Bryant at her home. *Photograph by Bayard Wootten. North Carolina Collection, University of North Carolina Library at Chapel Hill*

They appear to have had at least four children (Sarah, Ellen, Calvin, and Cora). In subsequent years Bryant lived as a widow. By the time the 1930 census was taken, she lived as a member of her son Calvin's household. This is likely the setting for the interview that follows.

(Some recollections of 'The Reb Time day' given by Aunt Margaret Bryant)

Visitor: "How are you Aunt Margaret?"
Margaret: "Missus, I ain't wuth! I ain't wuth!"[1]
Visitor: "Aunt Margaret you've been here a long time. How old are you?"
Margaret: "I can't tell you my age no way in the world! When freedom come, I been here. Not big nuff (enough) for work for the Reb, but I been here Reb time. Been big nuff (enough) to know when Yankee gun-boat[2] come to Watsaw (Wachesaw). Whole gang o' Yankee come to the house and didn't do a thing but ketch (catch) a gang o' fowl and gone on. And tell the people (meaning the slaves) to take the house and go in and get what they want. The obersheer (overseer) hear the Doctor[3] whistle to the gate and wabe (wave) him back. And then the Doctor know the Yankee been there and he gone on to the creek house and get all he gold and ting (thing) out the house and gone—Marion[4] till Freedom then he come back.

"Yankee come in that night. Moon shine lak a day. Stay in the Doctor house that night. Morning come, take a gang o' fowl and gone on!
Visitor: "Aunt Margaret, what was your name before you were married?"
Margaret: "Margaret One. Brother and sister? I ain't one when I come here. Ain't meet aunty, uncle—none. Me and my brudder Michael[5] wuz twin. I ain't meet none when I come here. All been sell. Me and my Ma One here. Mary One. Husband title, husband nichel (initial) been 'One.' Number one carpenter—give 'em that name Michael One—and he gibe 'em that name. Born Sandy Island. Been to landing to Watsaw when gun-boat come. Just a sneak long! Boat white. Hab (have) a red chimbley (chimney.) Didn't try to carry we off. Tell 'em 'Go and help youself.' Been after the buckra. (The Yankee trying to catch the buckra.)

1. See page 33, note 64, on common phatic greetings in Gullah.

2. On July 29, 1862, Federal troops, led by a liberated slave pilot named John E. Uptegrove, went up the Waccamaw River in one of two vessels—the *Norwich* or the *Pocahontas*. They anchored at John D. Magill's Richmond Hill plantation, just south of Wachesaw.

3. Allard Belin Flagg was the owner of Wachesaw plantation.

4. Marion, South Carolina.

5. Michael One.

"I see my Ma dye with some bush they call 'indigo,'[6] and black walnut bark. Big old pen for the sheep - folds.

"My Pa sister, Ritta One had that job. Nuss (nurse) the chillun. Chillun house. One woman nuss (nurse) all the chillun while they ma in the field—rice field. All size chillun. Git the gipsy (gypsum) weed. Beat 'em up for worm. Give 'em when the moon change. Take a bucket and follow dem. And tell the Doctor how much a worm that one make and that one and count dem (them). When the moon change, do that.

"I have one born with caul. Loss he caul. Rat carry 'em. Ain't here; he see nothin. (The custom seems to be, to preserve the caul.)

"Child born feet fore-most see 'um too." (See spirit) "Talk chillun? Put duh switch. Put you 'Bull pen.'[7] Hab 'um (have them) a place can't see you hand before you. Can't turn round good in there. Left you in there till morning. Give you fifty lash and send you to work. You ain't done that task, man and woman lick!

"Couldn't manage my ma. Obersheer (overseer) want to lick ma, Mary One say, 'Going drownded meself![8] I done my work! Fore I take a lick, rather drownded meself.'" Obersheer gone tell the doctor. Tie her long rope. Right to Sandy Island. Man hold the rope. Gone on. Jump in river. So Doctor say, 'You too good labor for drown. Take dem (them) to Watsaw.' Me and she and man what paddle the boat. Bring her to weave. Two womans fuh card; two spin. Ma wop 'em off. Sail duh sheckel (shuttle) through there.

"Po- buckra come there and buy cloth from Ma. Buy three and four yard. Ma sell that, have to weave day and night to make up that cloth to please obersheer. Come big day time. 'Little chillun, whey (where) Mama?' Tell 'em Ma to the weaving house. Don't have money fuh pay. Bring hog and such like as that to pay.

"You know Marse Allard[9] age? Me and Marse Allard suck together. Me and Marse Allard and my brudder Michael. My ma fadder mix wid (with) the Injun.[10] Son Larry Aikens. Stay Charston (Charlestown). Just as clean!

6. Indigo was a plant brought by slaves from West Africa that produced a valuable blue dye. It became one of South Carolina's first export products.

7. Solitary confinement.

8. "Meself" commonly replaces the standard English "myself" in Gullah usage.

9. Allard Flagg.

10. In the early days of European and African settlement of the South Carolina coast, the new settlers and the indigenous Creek peoples shared the land, interacting but maintaining distinct cultures. As the plantation system prospered with the successful

(Meaning Larry, her Uncle, very bright skin. Mixed with Indian.) See 'em the one time. Come from Charston bring Doctor two horse."

Given by Aunt Margaret Bryant
Age—(Born before Freedom)
Murrells Inlet, S. C.

---

cultivation of rice, it demanded more land and more labor. Those Creek who were not pushed west by European expansion were often absorbed by the slave population on the plantation.

Reverend Albert and Ella Carolina

In these interviews of husband and wife Albert and Ella Carolina, special attention is paid to historical and fabulistic narratives. Albert Carolina focuses on church history, particularly on the history of the Heaven's Gate Methodist congregation, but also on the more general history of clandestine religious practices under slavery. Ella Carolina discusses the infamous Flagg storm of 1893, delivers a trickster tale, and relates a folktale concerned with courtship practices.

Albert and Ella Carolina lived in Horry County near the town of Burgess and the community of Knoxville. Albert's maternal grandfather was Native American, and his maternal grandmother was native African. In his interview he states his own guess regarding his age as "bout seventy-seven since I start," but at the end of the same interview Chandler records his age as eighty-seven. According to the 1910, 1920, and 1930 U.S. Census data for Horry County, his age at the time of his interviews would have been between 78 and 81. The 1910 census finds Albert (age 51) and Ella (age 34) raising their son James (age 2); they have been married fourteen years. Albert's occupation is listed as "lumber wood" and their location as "log camp." By 1920 the number of children living in their home has expanded significantly to include Hazzard M. (age 17), Rosa M. (age 15), James A. (age 12), Eva (age 9) and Flora (age 6 months). Several of the Carolina children may have been adopted. Additionally this census indicates that Ella's mother, Lucrecia Burgess, age 102, lived with them. Albert's occupation is listed here as farmer, and the three older children are listed as working on the home farm. In the 1930 census, James (age 23), a daughter Elizabeth (age 12), and a grandson James (age 3) are reported to be living in the Carolina home. The Carolina's daughter Evelina lived next door with her husband, Zackie Knox, and their daughter Mary (age 2).

Carolina continued working late into life. He was also an itinerant minister, preaching occasionally at Heaven's Gate Church. A significant piece of

Reverend Albert Carolina on the front porch of his home. *Photograph by Bayard Wootten. North Carolina Collection, University of North Carolina Library at Chapel Hill*

local lore suggests Albert Carolina had a somewhat idiosyncratic and witty personality. According to Hagar Brown's daughter Mary Smalls, Carolina once responded to Brown's criticism of his crooked plowing thus: "Dis is de way, dis is de new kin I got. En wen ebrybody see e, dey goin try it."

Ella Carolina was also a farm laborer. Her mother was Sisby Borrice (a name Chandler glosses as Thisbe Burroughs). Ella Carolina had four sisters and two brothers. The 1910 census places her age at 61 by 1937, but she clearly states in her interview that she was born in 1855. She also implies she remembers the dedication of Heaven's Gate Church in 1870, which would place her age at approximately 82.

Together, Albert and Ella Carolina raised Evelina Knox, Arthur, James, Hazzard, Rosa, and Flora Carolina.

Heaven's Gate Church
(Verbatim conversation by Uncle Albert Carolina.):

When asked about the founding of Heaven's Gate colored Methodist church Rev. Albert Carolina answered:

"In the beginning of Freedom they separate us from whites.

'Sixty one the war begun;
Sixty four the war was o'er.'

"Rev. Zacharias Duncan wuz the man. He the one built Heaven Gate church. Brother Henry Smith and Brother David Kidd and old man Jackson Heywood wuz the old ones built it. Some more been there. Can't think of them. Old man Jim Beaty wuz one. Can't remember no more. He wuz Allston man. (That means he was a slave owned by the Allstons) Uncle Dave Kidd, he owned a tract of land in the Savannah.

"Brought us up in Sabbus (Sabbath) school. Sunrise prayer-meeting. Ten o'clock Sunday school. Leven o'clock service again. Three o'clock service again. Eight at night—service again. Raise us taughen (taught) in the church. Steal off Slavery time in they own house and have class meeting. Driver come find'em, whip'em. Th' patrolls come riding down th' road. Four plait whip. Two big black dog. White pat-roller. Ketch without pass, they whip me. Crawling. (I was crawling). But I walk then and walk every[1] since! Bo-cart. Dat's what they call it—'Bo-cart.' (Crude home made baby walker.) Bout seventy seven years since I start. Remember nother thing going on in them time. Mausser gin (give) the women a task. Didn't done it. Next day didn't done it. Saturday come, task time out! Driver! I tell yuh th' truth, you could hear those people, 'Murder! Murder!'

1. "Every" commonly replaces the standard English "ever" in Gullah usage.

"Judge Kershaw was a fine man. His boy William—I and William born the same day.

"We never has met th' bed yet, without family prayer—and never get up without it. Didn't low them with a book in they hand. The Driver learn you at night if he like you. Try to out-wage (educate) you at night. Didn't have any school.

"Mother's father Indian. Brighter than, who? Who round here bright as my Grand-father? Hannah! Hair was long. Wouldn't stay home. Lives in th' swamp. Wouldn't stay out. Grand-mother wuz African. She had a little bowl make out of clay."[2]

Uncle Albert Carolina, age 87 (colored)
Murrells Inlet, S. C.
March, 8th. 1937
(A description followed of how his grand-parents built a kiln of clay pots and baked them.)
(Submitted: March 25, 1937)

Told by Daughter of Mom Sisby Borrice (Thisbe Burroughs?)

"My Ma have seven in all—two boy and musser (must-a) be four girl. Seven in all! (Dat dog name 'Penny.' Can buy sumpin' with him!) Now Crissie, she Flagg labor.[3]

"When the Big Storm come, lemme see if the buttle[4] been stayin' there! Old Buck house[5] have no servant hall for womens.

"He been ragin' all night! Pitchin' and dodgin' all night! Water didn't rise up on land till mornin', then it DID storm! Storm so strong just like somebody pelt you—lick you with a rock. Couldn't cook no breakfast. Couldn't catch up no fire in that stove that mornin'. Had to make up some tea—and eat light-bread.

2. Probably a reference to colono ware, a ceramic style brought by slaves from Africa. Colono ware bowls are made entirely by hand, brown or black in color, and usually coarse, with little or no ornamentation. At the beginning of the eighteenth century, planters had access to cheaper ceramics, which they passed on to their slaves. As a result, colono ware began to disappear around the same time. James L. Michie, *Richmond Hill Plantation, 1810–1868: The Discovery of Antebellum Life on a Waccamaw Rice Plantation* (Spartanburg, S.C.: Reprint Company, 1990).

3. One of the Flagg family's slaves.

4. Butler.

5. A summer home in Murrells Inlet belonging to the shipbuilding Buck family.

"I stay in the kitchen till he got KNEE deep in the yard. I get to the field corner and I look back every thing coming! Big barn o' corn. House and all! All the servants hall—little servant house and all coming! Chicken, cow and all. What didn't ruin didn't 'scape for they life. All drowned in the field.

"Everybody have flat cottage house on the beach, lost!

"Buttle tell me 'I goin' leave!' Time for go! Say he couldn't stay there to the crick edge and just drowned and perish in the storm. Water knee deep in the yard, time to go! Like Sodom and Gomarrah! Lot's wife oughter bear (obey) orders! I lift my skirts and left! Big piano and ALL gone. Salt water kill all growin' thing dead.

"I born in 1855. Heaven Gate Church delegate in 1870. (Dedicated) My brother born the year it delegate; sister she born the year after it delegate. My sister say it peace didn't 'clare she'd a been a half hand in the field. Half-hand? Half-hand does half task. Half acre. Rice field work whole acre been a task.[6]

"Animal? Story 'bout animal? Lemme see! Been so long now. Uster have 'em by heart. Lemme see 'bout the rabbit! Rabbit nuster loves to go to dance. Have a story 'bout Budder Wolfe cut off Budder Rabbit tail. Reason why Budder Rabbit tail so short now. Start to party. Budder Rabbit ax Budder Wolfe to be he riding horse. Budder Rabbit so tricky. Get near where the dancing house Budder Rabbit spur 'em. All the pretty girl is see Budder Rabbit fine riding horse. All laughed at Budder Wolfe. They tell me Budder Wolfe chop off Budder Rabbit tail. Budder Rabbit always been tricky. Wuz story 'bout Budder 'Gator and Rabbit. Budder 'Gator wuz on tussick.[7] On a big log sleepin' in the hot sun. Budder Rabbit say:

"'Some day good!'
Some day bad!'

"All the time tell Budder 'Gator that. Budder Gator say:

"'No, Budder Rabbit. All day good! All day good!'

"One time Budder 'Gator sleep on the bank in the hot sun. Budder Rabbit find 'em. Stick dry mash[8] all 'round 'em. No way to go set fire! Swinge 'em! [9] Swinge 'em! GOOD. 'Fore Budder 'Gator get to the river he SICK. He say:

6. Every job on the plantation was broken into tasks, with a task roughly defined by Plowden C. J. Weston as "as much work as the meanest hand can do in nine hours, working industriously." Slaves themselves were assigned tasks according to their age and abilities. Charles Joyner, *Down by the Riverside: A South Carolina Slave Community* (Urbana: University of Illinois Press, 1984), 44.

7. A clump of grass.

8. Kindling.

9. Singe, or burn, them.

"'Budder Rabbit tell me,
"'"Some day good
Some day bad!"'

"There was a story 'bout the eggs. Wuz a girl (must be a girl. Don't seem like it were boy.) One was disobedient one; one obedient one. Good one and bad one. Come to old lady house. Old lady tell 'em:

"'Feed my cat! Feed my cat!
Cook for 'em
Cold the bittle[10]
And give 'em to 'em!

"Cat wouldn't eat 'em. Didn't cold 'em. (Disobedient one!) Take every egg that jump up and say:

"'Take me! Take me!
Take me! Take me!'

"Break one to every mile post. Going to seek he fortune. (Find fortune at end.)

"Good girl (obedient one) go in house and cook and feed cat. And cat done eat all. Tell girl:

"'Every egg that jump up and tell you take 'em—TAKE 'EM. And every mile post broke one! Broke one!'

"And this been the OBEDIENT, good one. And she done it all and come out to a good end. Both gone seeking fortune and fortune must been a husband and the first one got a husband devil to'em. And other one got a King son or something.

There was once a old woman have one son and now he son want to married. (Show you 'Parents must not always pick love for chillun.') So old lady every girl the boy go to see she break 'em up. Wouldn't let 'em marry NONE the girl in the neighborhood. And after she wouldn't let get marry, one Sunday afternoon up the road come a fine young girl. Steppin' down the lane. And mother didn't know who it was. Mother not knowin' who it was, admire that girl.

"Now THAT the one I want you to marry!
" " " " " " " " " "
" " " "
" " " "

10. Cool the food.

She 'vite 'em in. Boy want to take 'em home. Evenin' part of the day. Mother tell 'em, 'Hitch up carriage and take 'em home!' Have four dog. Have a name for all of 'em. (One must have name o' PLATE)[11] Boy tell Ma:

"When you see this white plate get red, turn my plate loose."

Ever mile post get to gal countenance change. Every mile post gettin' uglier and uglier. Get to last mile post she turn to DEVIL with a long tail on 'em! No gal now! Mother had drop sleep! When she wake and turn dog loose, want to get loose so bad one broke he leg! You can't pick love for chillun. Have to pick for they self!"

Source: Mom Ella Calina, Burgess, S.C. (Horry County) October 1937.

11. Ella Carolina is suggesting that one of the dogs was named "Plate."

Martha Cox

Genevieve Chandler picked Martha Cox up in her automobile as she was walking home to Burgess, South Carolina, from Conway, South Carolina. Otherwise, Cox does not appear in Mrs. Chandler's work, and little biographical information is available. According to the 1930 U.S. Census, however, Martha Cox does show up as the employee (the census uses the term "servant") of Amanda Macklen. According to that record, Cox was a widow. She was about seventy when Chandler interviewed her, and the interview probably took place between May and October of 1937.

Aunt Martha

From her walk, a rhythmical swing, arms swinging in front and head held so erect and from the fact that her skirt was girded up to give her legs freedom of action, I guessed she belonged in the Free Woods or somewhere lower down, so I stopped my car.

"Auntie, where you going?"

"Burgess postoffice,[1] Missus."

"Walking home from Conway?"

"Yes, Missus!"

"Get in. We're going your way. This Doctor sister."[2]

"You the doctor sister? I see duh fabor.[3] Tank God missus. Yonneh stay to Flagg sea-shore?"

Her hair was not plaited, but the strands were tightly bound in white twine. The braids were so tight they bristled off at various angles. It developed that she had been to town to see the doctor. Having been sick ("Had the

1. At this time the Burgess, or Freewoods, community post office was the only official institution that identified the community by name.

2. Dr. Dick Willcox, Genevieve Chandler's older brother, was highly respected in the African American community for his generosity and medical expertise. His status provided Mrs. Chandler a unique entrée to her interviewee's confidence.

3. Favor, or resemblance.

dissipate,[4] Missus") she had ridden up with the rural delivery mail. The mailman left her—for what reason she could not make clear—and so she "Took her foot in her hand[5] and was walking thirty long, tedious miles, though she had been sick with the 'dissipate' for five months. Her only burden or bundle was a bottle of 'doctor's medicine.' (To distinguish it from home remedies and peddlers' medicine—patent remedies that are peddled and 'recommend to cure any disease.')

As we rode along it was readily learned that this was Aunt Martha's first ride in a car. She kept exclaiming at the rate we were covering ground. And it was some miles before she relaxed and began to make conversation. The sun was getting low and that furnished her with a theme.

"If I know you been go take me by Miss Oliver[6] I sho like to look at she fowl. Robinson Nesbit got a fool boy, Bannister,—kinder cracky. (Cracked brain). Him carry duh fowl. Dat a fool boy. Fasten up the fowl every night. Gone in coop. Call up chicken. Tree (three) gone! Aint eat 'em. Aint sell 'em. Myself. Tief my chicken! Going debt 'em! Going debt 'em! (Law 'em)
Can't debt 'em less you see 'em. Got to carry eye witness to law. Can't carry reckon so and guess!

"Missus, I sho like to get home fore duh sun gone. Got to truss[7] duh chicken up.

"Robert Jones he too fool. Nesbit fool boy Bannister go in my fowl house and truss up my chicken and sell to Robert, and Robert fetch 'em to the white people. I know my fowl anywheee. Him going tell me how him come by duh fowl. Him a fool boy. Aint eat 'em myself. Aint sell 'em. If I ketch 'em, I going debt 'em!"

Martha Cox—Age about 70
Murrells Inlet, S. C.
Burgess P.O. (Horry)
(Her age been lost)

4. Unidentified, lingering illness.

5. This Gullah phrase indicates that Martha Cox was carrying her shoes so as to walk more freely and quickly.

6. Emma Oliver, wife of William Oliver, who ran a boardinghouse in Murrells Inlet called Oliver's Lodge.

7. To tie at the feet.

Will Deas

Compared to some of the "old livers" Chandler interviewed, Will Deas (pronounced 'days') was a rather young man, approximately fifty-five. His dispatches on animal behavior, though, seem to come from an older man within him. Deas was a ditcher, or ditchdigger, by profession, but he chose not to address this activity in the interviews. Instead he talked excitedly about eagles, red bugs, sharks, and whales. An innocent curiosity characterizes his voice, but something of the sage appears in his deep appreciation for nature. According to the 1910 census, Deas was married to Peggy Deas with whom he had two children (Maggie and Joseph). At the time of that census, he was twenty-seven. Also at that time the Deases were the neighbors of Matthew Grant, another of Chandler's interviewees. The 1930 census offers a relative wealth of information. Dating him as forty-eight years of age, it also indicates that he owned his home, that he could read, and that he was employed in public works. Furthermore his wife is listed as Anna. She was also literate, and the couple had four children living with them: Morris (age seventeen), Emma (age eleven), William Jr. (age eight), and Luther (age six).

The Eagle
(Verbatim)

Will: "I don't much 'bout it. Tell you the little which I have. Eagles which live up in the mountains, they tell me is the King Bird of the air. Miss, call them a King Bird of the air! (Let me get a chunk here for you to set down on. What you call them wood bug? Red bug.[1] Them thing make you scratch night time till you have for get up out of bed and rub with carry-sene. (kerosene). King Bird,—and a very wise bird. When time for those eagle to hatch out young one, they goes up to the tree. They 'zamine that tree. Zamine trunk. Must be the tallest tree can be find in the woods. They take their bills and wings and try that tree from the trunk up and if it not solid, they will build their nest on that tree. They left that tree and go to another. That one sound they go up to the top and 'zamine the limbs where they goin' build they nest. After they

1. Of the family Trombiculidae; a common chigger.

done pick place for nest, they go out and get thorns. Then they'll go back and get a lot of sticks,—and they line that on top of the thorns. Then they'll go and get a whole lot of soft trashes and things and line up that nest right thick and soft. Then, after that, they lay two eggs in that nest."

Mike:[2] "Lay more egg than that! Then they began to hatch on that egg,—sit on that egg. And she'll stay right there and the man eagles he'll go, you know, and bring food back—just like a man do his family. And when she done hatchin' those bird, she stay there with them considerable while until she feel that they have strength enough. Then she commence to stir the nest She moves away those trashes, and she take away the sticks and she leave those thorn in the bottom. And the young bird stir on those thorn, they stick them. Want to learn the young bird to get out. By and by the small eagle will hopped out on a limb. Hopped out on a limb!

"Now the Mother eagle want to learn them how to fly. She'll pick one up and she'll sail way up in the element. Carry them way up. When she think she got them high 'nouf, she dodges from under them and the little bird way up there try to catch on her own opinion. Then the big bird fly off and watch her. And she watch her trying to fly till she think she getting tired. Then she run to her and catch her on her back. Then she'll take her back to the tree,—and she let her rest there. She let her rest there! Then, when she think she rest enough, she take her out again. She carry her up again into the element. Dart from under her again! And as she dart from under them,—the little eagle, she goes to flying! And she let her fly again till she think she got tired. Then she run to her and catch her (on her back) again. She take 'em back to the tree. When she think both of 'em strong 'nouf to go, She took both out together and she sail way up! And as she turn them loose this time, she seem to said to her little birds,

"Go, now, birds and defend you own self. Through with you."

You find that instruction in the Bible.

SOURCE: *Uncle Will Deas (ditcher)*
September 1937, Parkersville, S. C. (Georgetown County)

(Verbatim)

"Old Aunt Crissia say 'Onpossible to get straight wood from crooked timber.'"

"So! Dat so! You tink[3] you kin and you put dem in the sun and it'll warp and twist. Man the same way! Put'em in the kiln. Give'em test. Find'em same

2. Mike Maybank.
3. "Tink" commonly replaces the standard English "think" in Gullah usage.

way. Now Jonah. He try to run from God. Don't coward! Gulf shark now kin swallow a man. Shovel nose[4]—dey 'bout dese wide! They can take common sailors right in.

"Whale supspose to be the largest fish in duh water. Most qualify fish at that time. Wuz a casket God prepare. They set seine. Big hawse-line reach from dat barn and more. Take up anchor and could not beach'em. Two gulf shark in the bag. Two big mule can scacely pull dem. Whale is a lawful reef fish. Classify by dat name.

"Finally boy foot strike that shark. Send plantation. Get double team. Hitch'em. Pull. Git grit in that net. Fight and fight. Take six and more men to put dem in duh team. Make a manure.[5] Make shark steak. I would 'preciate if I had dem now. They are climatize—tasable."[6]

SOURCE: *Given by: Uncle Will (W. P. A. Ditcher.)*
Parkersville, S. C.
April 1938.

4. Probably a hammerhead shark.
5. The inedible parts of the shark were used as fertilizer.
6. They have a pleasing taste.

Ellen Godfrey

IN AUGUST 1937 ELLEN GODFREY PROCLAIMED, "My birthday the seven of October coming. . . . Come seben of October been a hundred." She remembered being twenty-three when Federal troops demanded the surrender of her master, Mayham Ward, in the latter half of 1865,[1] placing the year of her birth as 1842. The 1900 census lists her birth date as May 8, 1840. Regardless, between 95 and 99 years old, Ellen Godfrey was a vestige from another era.[2] Born on Longwood plantation in Horry County, Godfrey labored as a weaver during slavery. After emancipation she worked for Arthur Belin Flagg as a nurse to his family: "I gib the old Doctor (Dr. Ward Flagg) sweet potato when he two week old." Her third husband, Harry Godfrey, also worked for the Flaggs. Together they witnessed the 1893 hurricane, known in the region as "the Flagg storm" because it killed nearly the entire Flagg family. By simple virtue of her longevity, she was herself a witness to many of the most important events in her community. Often Godfrey played an instrumental role in those events. As a result, perhaps, Godfrey was treated as a cherished matriarch and a prized community possession by her neighbors. Her vivid recollections of the slave evacuation to Marlboro during Sherman's invasion and the ensuing emancipation give some of the best insights into the drama of slavery and liberation to be found in Genevieve Chandler's interviews.

It is possible that Chandler knew Godfrey personally before she interviewed her in Conway, South Carolina. Godfrey may have worked previously along the Murrells Inlet creek near Chandler's home. Raised at Longwood plantation,[3] she had been a part of the community with which Chandler was

1. George C. Rogers Jr., *The History of Georgetown County, South Carolina* (Columbia: University of South Carolina Press, 1970), 426.

2. The 1920 U.S. Census for Horry County placed Godfrey's age at seventy, which would have made her eighty-seven in 1937.

3. Longwood plantation was owned by Joshua John Ward (1800–1853), one-time lieutenant governor of the state. Along with Longwood, Ward owned Brookgreen, Oryzantia, Alderly, Prospect Hill, Springfield, and Rose Hill. After his death, his

most familiar. If Chandler had not known Godfrey personally, she would certainly have known of Godfrey through local lore.

Sadly, Godfrey outlived most, if not all, of her children. Godfrey was married three times, last and most happily to Harry Godfrey, who was ten years her senior according to the 1900 U.S. Census. By her own recollection and according to census records, she raised between eleven and seventeen children, some of whom were either stepchildren or adoptees: Wenus, Jane, Harry, two sets of twins (Isaac and Rebecca, David and Caneezer), 'Lizabeth, Martha, Patient, Harry, Edmund, James, Kate, Janie, Jennie, and Fred. The twins as well as the youngest, Kate (who was born the year before the 1893 hurricane), were Godfrey's own children.

Godfrey was also one of the founding members of Salem Baptist Church.

Aunt Ellen Godfrey
(Ex-Slave)
(Verbatim Conversation)

(Aunt Ellen is a misfit in her present environment. Born at Longwood Plantation on Waccamaw in 1837, all she knows is the easy, quiet life of the country. And the busy, bustling 'RACE PATH' near which her Grandson lives with whom she makes her home doesn't make a fitting frame for the old lady. All day she sits in a porch swing and when hungry, visits a neighbor. The neighbors (colored—all) vie with each other in trying to make her last days happy days. She says they do her washing and provide necessary food. When you start her off she flows on like the brook but usually her story varies little. She tells of the old days and of the experiences that made the greatest impression—the exciting times during the 'Confedrick' war—the 'Reb time day.')

Visitor: "Aunt Ellen home?"

Aunt Ellen's neighbor (from the washtub): "No'um. She right cross there on the 'Race Path'" (So called because in Conway's early days races were run—horse races—on this street.)

Visitor: "Are you one of the neighbors who take such good care of Aunt Ellen?"

Neighbor: "No'um. I'm off all day. I work for Miss Bernice."

Visitor: "Miss Bernice who?"

Neighbor: "Miss Bernice something nother. I can't keep up with that lady title! See Aunt Ellen white cap yonder?"

---

estate and its plantations were managed by his oldest son, Joshua Ward. The Ward estate during this period owned some 1,100 men, women, and children, earning it the dubious distinction of being the largest slaveholding institution in the country.

Aunt Ellen (Sitting on chair at back door leaning on cane.)

"I want everybody come to my birthday! Seventh o' October coming be a hundred. Baby one dead jew (due) time! Five daughter—one sanctify preacher. Seven one—one Portssmith Virgina. All dead! All dead! Marry three times; all the husband dead! My last baby child—when the Flagg storm kill everybody on the beach, (1893) the last child I have out my body been a year old!

"Last time I gone see the old Doctor,[4] rap! rap!

Doctor: "Come in!" Gone in.

Doctor: "Great God! Looker Aunt Ellen! For the good you take care Daddy Harry, God left you live long time!"

Ellen: "Flat 'em all up to Marlboro![5] (All the slaves) Ten days or two weeks going. PeeDee[6] bridge, stop! Go in gentlemen barn! Turn duh bridge! Been dere a week. Had to go and look the louse on we. Three hundred head o' people been dere. Couldn't pull we clothes off. (On flat.) Boat name Riprey. Woman confine on boat. Name the baby 'RIPREY!' Mama name Sibby."

(***Neighbor:*** "Aunt Ellen been looking for you all day! Keep saying she got to go home. A white lady coming and she got to be there!")

Aunt Ellen: "Doctor come on boat. By name Doctor Lane. White lady come tend woman. Get to Marlboro where they gwine. Put in wagon. Carry to the street. Major Drake Plantation. One son Pet Drake. Wife leetle bit of a woman.

"I see Abram Lincoln son Johnny! Talk with him! Gimme tobacco. I been to loom. Weave. Sheckle flying—flying sheckle!

(Singing): "Tech (touch) me all round my waist!
Don't tech my water-fall!
Gay gal setting on the rider fence!
Don't tech my water-fall!"

"Clothes gone to wash this morning. (Can't go today.) Clothes gone.

"I been here so long—I ax Jesus one day carry me next day! Can't make up my bed. Like an old hog sleep on a tustick." (I always heard it 'Toad on a tussock'—and you?)

4. Dr. Ward Flagg at Brookgreen plantation.

5. Marlboro, South Carolina. See page 38, note 6, regarding the movement of slaves inland during the summer of 1862.

6. The Pee Dee River, west of the Waccamaw. According to the WPA's *Palmetto Place Names* (1941; Spartanburg, S.C.: Reprint Company, 1992), 83, the river's name can be attributed either to a Native American tribe, the Pee Dees, or to the letters "P.D." carved into many trees in the region by the explorer Patrick Daly.

(Four lean cats prowled about sniffing around the wood-pile where a boy was scaling some pale, dead fish.)
Visitor: "Aunt Ellen, how could you cook on the flat?
Aunt Ellen: "Dirt bank up. Fire make on dirt. Big pot. Cook. Fry meat. Come PeeDee get off flat. Bake. Bake. Iron oven. Stay PeeDee week. Bake. Pile coals on oven top." (Another slave told of scaffold—four posts buried and logs or planks across top with earth on planks. On this pile of earth, fire was made and on great bed of coals oven could be heated for baking. 'Oven' means the great iron skillet like vessel with three legs and a snug lid. This oven bakes biscuit, pound cake, and some old timers insist on trusting only this oven for their annual fruit cake. It works beautifully on a hearth. Put your buttermilk biscuit in, lid on and pile live-oak coals on top. Of course only the ones who have done this a long time know when to take the lid off.)

"Dirt camp to stay in—to hide from Yankee." (Her gestures showed earth was mounded up.)
Visitor: "Like a potato bank? A potato hill?"
Ellen: "Dat's it! Pile 'em! Gone in dirt camp to hide we from Yankee. Have a Street Row of house. Yankee coming. Gone in dirt camp.

"I been weave. My loom at door. Six loom on dat side! Six loom on dis side! I see 'em coming. Hat crown high as this." (She measured off almost half of her walking stick—which had a great, tarnished plated silver knob.) "And I tell 'em 'Yankee coming!' I talk with Abram Lincoln own son Johnny and, bless your heart I glad for Freedom till I fool!"

(Singing)
'Freedom forever!
Freedom everymore!
Want to see the Debbil run
Let the Yankee fling a ball
The Democrack will take the swamp!'

"Massa been hide. Been in swamp." (This is history. All the old men, too old for the army, hid in Marlboro swamps and were fed by faithful slaves until Yankees passed on. My grandmother and mother gave vivid accounts of this—my mother telling of the sufferings of the women—mental—worrying about her feeble old grandfather down there with the moccassins)[7]

7. Water moccasin, *Agkistrodon piscivorus,* a venomous snake. Also called cottonmouth.

Ellen: "Yankee officer come. 'Where Mahams Ward[8] and John J. Woodward? Come to tell 'em take dese people out the dirt camp! Put we in flat. Carry back!' (In first story Aunt Ellen told the Yankee Captain said, 'Tell 'em be Georgetown to salute the flag!')

"Put food and chillun in flat. We been walk." (Walking back to Waccamaw) We gone. (See 'um! See their feet like the children of Israel in Green Pastures!) In man's house. Man say, 'Come out! You steal my turnip!' Brush arbor. Night come. Make camp. Way down the road somewhere! Make a big bush camp. All squeze under there. Left Marlboro Monday. Come Conway Friday sun down! Hit Bucksville, hit a friend. Say 'People hungry!' Middle night. Snow on ground. Get up. Cook. Cook all night! Rice. Bake tater. Collard. Cook. Give a quilt over you head. I sleep. I sleep in the cotton. I roost up the cotton gone in there." (Burrowed down in the cotton—'rooted' it up)" December. Winter time. Cook all night. Corn-bread, baked tater, collard. Git to Bucksport, people gin to whoop and holler! Three flat gone round wid all the vittles." (And with the very young and very old) Easier coming home. Current helped. Going up against the current, only poles and cant hooks—tedious going) "Git 'Tip Top'[9] (Plantation) all right. Come home den! Git to double trunk (rice-field trunk)[10] at 'Tip Top' Whoop! Come bring flat! Mother Molly dead on flat! Bury she right to Longwood grave-yard. Nuss. (nurse) Sam'l Hemingway bury there. Horse kill 'em in thrashing mill.[11] Child name Egiburt bury there too. Horse gwine round in thrashing. He lick the horse. Horse kick 'em. Whole gang white jury come!

"Sing and pray all the time. Pray your house. Pray all the time. (I wish to God I could get some of you clam!)

"Salem Baptist? I helped build Salem! I a choir in Salem!"

Aunt Ellen Godfrey
Age 99 years 10 months
Conway, S. C.

8. Mayham Ward (1837–1866), son of Joshua John Ward, one-time owner of Brookgreen plantation.

9. Henry Buck renamed Woodbourne plantation Tip Top after he acquired it from Jacob Motte Alston in 1858.

10. Sluice gates used to flood and drain the rice fields with the tides, as dictated by the cultivation schedule.

11. Initially the threshing process was done by hand. The heads of grain were expertly separated from their stalks with flailing sticks. By Ellen Godfrey's era, threshing mills were doing this onerous task. In this case the motive power was provided by a horse.

Conversation of Aunt Ellen Godfrey—Age 99 Years, Conway, S. C. June 25th.

"Would gone wid you Missus, but I waiting on the 'Relief.' He wuz going to bring me the dress and shoe and ting. My birthday the seven of October coming. We Massa have give we good shoe. Right her Longwood Plantation. Massa was kind—you know. Send slam to England gie me good clothes and shoe. I been a weave when the Yankee come. I been on the loom to Marlboro deestrict. A man place they call Doctor Major Drake. Got a son name Cap and Pet. Oh, Jesus, been here too long! In my ninty-nine now. Come seben of October been a hundred. Three flat "(flat boats used for rice field work) "carry two hundred 'o people and all they things. We hide from Yankee but Yankee come and git we. Ask whey " (where)" Massa. (Massa in swamp! I in buckra house. I say, 'Dem gone! Gone to beach.' Say,'Tell'em to be in Georgetown to bow unto flag.' Dat time I been twenty-three year old. Doctor Flagg didn't born, He a pretty child and so fat! Love duh Doctor too much! Born two weeks after freedom. He Ma gone Georgetown. Granny git'em there. Melia Holmes! Aint no more dan chillun to me! "(Aunt Melia is eighty-eight or nine—bony and cripple)" She have two twin sister Laura and Serena. When the Freedom I was twenty-three years old.—over the twenty-five. Great God hab a mercy! Couldn't do dat! Colonel Ward keep a nice place. Doctor McGill[12] people hab to steal for someting[13] to eat. Gie'em rice—peas. Four cook for chillun. One nurse". (Aunt Ellen said 'Nuss') " "Make the boy go get'em clam. That same Dr. Ward GrandPa. Great big sack 'o clam! Give you cow clabber. Shay'm". (Share them—the clabber)" and put on bittle for eat.

"Hagar Brown! She darter (daughter) got a abscess in her stomach. Save Rutledge! I nuse (nurse) Sabe. I nuss'em. Her pappy my cousin. I been big young woman, I nuss Sabe.

"Albert Calina a christian-hearted people. Christian hearted boy.Relief come, I gie'em my age. My birthday over, I wanter go right home to Heaven. Great Dow! 'Looker Aunt Ellen!' (That is what Dr. Wardie say when I gone (see'um) 'In you ninety-five! What make you good, you take care of you husband! ' Harry Godfrey waiting man! Marry twice time. He duh last—

"Andrew Johnson? Dropsy? I have wid every chillun—Oh, I buss (burst) one time. Buss here" (Illustrating by drawing line across stomach) " Till it get to my groin it stop! Every time I get family I swell. Never have a doctor

12. John D. McGill, the owner of Richmond Hill plantation, was reputed to be the cruelest slave owner on the Waccamaw.

13. The *h* is commonly dropped in the pronunciation of of "thing."

'Granny'[14] for me yet. My Mary good old Granny. Catch two set 'o twin for me. Isaac and Rebecca; David and Caneezer.

"Sell all my fowl and ting—five dollars—me and old man two come to town to we chillun.

Been Marlboro four year. Yankee foot where they put on stirrup red. Most stand lak a Mr. Smoak—Big tall—Abraham Lincoln own son Johnny! 'You jess as free as ribbon on my hat!' That what he say. I been weave. Sheckle!" (Aunt Ellen worked foot and hand and mouth in illustrating how the shuttle worked back and forth—and the music it made)".

"Conch? Eat'm many time! Take'em bile! Grind'em up!

"Welcome Beas? She son get kill in Charston, Welcome Beas son courting my gal.

"Tom Duncan? He child to me. He wife Suzannah. I know duh fambly. I gone knock to duh door.

'Come in! Come in! Come in! 'Here duh beard! " (And Aunt Ellen measured on her chest to show how long Dr. Flagg's beard was).

"Old Daddy Rodgers and merry wuz she !
The old man wuz cripple
And Mary wuz blind.
Keep you hat on you head.
Keep you head warm
And set down under that sycamore tree!
My kite! My kite!
My kite! My kite!
Two oxen tripe!
Two open dish 'o cabbage!
My little dog!
My spotted hawg!
My two young pig a starving!
"Cow in the cotton patch. Tell boy call dog drive pig out cotton!
Heah duh song;
"Send Tom Taggum
To drive Bone Baggum
Out the world 'o wiggy waggum!"

14. Midwife.

(This last song chanted out by Aunt Eleanor Godfrey, age 99, is really a gem. She said 'Bone Baggum' boney old white cow. 'Wiggy waggum' is a picture word making one see the soft, wagging tufts of white cotton)

Given by Aunt Eleanor Godfrey
Age 99 (100 come seben of Oct.)
June 25th,1937
Conway, S. C.

Mom Ellen Godfrey

Good God! Wuz a day! The old man Harry Godfrey been the best husband I happen on. He were Dr. Arthur[15] cook. Git married dem time Cap'n boss give you a big weddin'. River-side cook. Marry in day give'em dinner; of a night—supper. Water-millon lay in the field like log.

"Tink he storm, Harry?"

I say: "Great God. Look at the black-bird! Mean business." Fly down. Light on piazza. T'ick as hop. Look like a judgment. Gone on in. the rain in he road cyart. Oh, Lord, I cry more when that Flagg storm come! More dan one time. 'Leven head o' chillum. Wenus, Jane, Harry, Isaac, 'Lisabeth, Martha—every one o' dem and Kate duh baby one. She turn out to be a sanctify preacher. Gone off to preach. Didn't hear from dem yet since she leave.

I can't drink de milk. He bind me.[16]

SOURCE: *Mom Ellen Godfrey*
Age 100 yrs.
Conway, S. C.

Mom Ellen
Ex-slave.

"Now this divorce business! I know a woman try that once and the law give her alimony but I say if she not try that, 'stead of alimony she'd a get ALL."

Mom Ellen—age 101 "Come October seven!"

"I gib the old Doctor[17] sweet potato when he two weeks old. He a good child. He eat'em good as ever. I down here with the jumpin' back ache. I write the old doctor and he send me two pills and one white powder. And I not have the jumpin' backache since.

15. Dr. Arthur Flagg.
16. Apparently Ellen Godfrey was lactose intolerant.
17. Dr. Ward Flagg.

"When the 'Shake' shake, my last child would year old in Jinuary.

"Eagle take a baby outer the basket. Sabie? Sabie? Sabie tell yinnah? Sabie KNOW. I nuss (nurse) Nuss the baby.

"Eagle got a stone in he nest.[18] Everbody want dem. Dem bring too good luck.

"After the doctor storm they find old Miss,[19] she shoe been unbutton to ONE button. They find young Miss roll up, in a roll o'wire. He tie he face up not to see he chillun beat to death. Tie up in a towel. I find little Eben[20] coat in a hole. Fine little coat. Stocking hanging out on bush like rag. Young Artur[21] wife, doctor brudder wife name Miss Ma——.[22] One daughter to town to school. Call dem 'Baby.' Lettle A——[23] lettle girl so! I have the buckra clothes in my house. I gone in the basket and put he Grandma clothes on drownded child.

"I live to see the seven of October come I'll be 101. I is the dog-minder and the cat-minder. I not able to wash a kandkercher. Pray! I can pray! I spect to tie my boat to Jerusalem wharf. I gwine run through Jerusalem street and bathe in the bathin' pool.

"I didn't see dem head and didn't see dem foot. I could tell dem build. I sleep hongry dat night! Oh, my God, my chillun gone! Wash out! Carry out to sea!"

SOURCE: *Mom Ellen Godfrey—age 101*
Conway S. C.—Sept. 1938

18. An eagle is reputed to keep a stone in its nest, which is said to bring good luck to whomever acquires it.

19. Georgianna Flagg.

20. Charles Ebenezer Belin Flagg.

21. Arthur Belin Flagg Jr.

22. Martha A. Flagg.

23. According to the burial records of All Saints' Episcopal Church, the following Flaggs were buried following the 1893 storm: Dr. Arthur Belin Flagg Sr.; his wife, Georgianna Ward Flagg; their adult sons Arthur Belin Flagg Jr. and Charles Ebenezer Belin Flagg; Arthur Jr.'s wife, Martha Ann Labruce Flagg; and their children—Albert, Joshua John Ward, Alice, Martha, and Eben. Arthur Sr.'s son Joshua John Ward "Dr. Ward" Flagg and daughter Georgianna survived. His older brother Allard and Allard's family also survived. Other Flaggs, and community members not related to the Flaggs, may have been lost in the storm as well, but their deaths never recorded.

Matthew Grant

MATTHEW GRANT'S PENCHANT FOR STORYTELLING comes through clearly in Genevieve Chandler's interviews. Like so many of his neighbors, Grant was deeply impressed by supernatural phenomena. He made sense of these phenomena by casting them in a narrative frame.

Born in 1876, Grant would have been in his sixties when he was interviewed at his home in Parkersville near Pawleys Island. According to U.S. Census data, he married Elizabeth Grant, and they had at least eight children (Georgia, Joshuay, Jefferson, George, Lucien, Herman, Mack, and Jessie). He worked as a farm laborer and also as laborer in public works. By 1930, according to the census report for that year, he owned his own home, which had an estimated value of eight hundred dollars. He is also listed as being able to read and write. Grant's neighbor was Will Deas, whose interview is also found in this volume.

Regarding Hags (Verbatim)

"One time, Miss, wuz a boy wuz courtin' a girl. And he didn't know the girl wuz a HAG. And he gone to court the girl and he settin' round by the fire and he watch them and he watch the father and the mother in the room settin' down. And just 'bout 'leven o'clock the girl Pa take a bottle off the mantle and rub 'em on he arm—he TWO arm! And he fly through the chimbley! And she Ma come (whole fambly settin' side the fire) and she gone to the mantle and she take the bottle and rub 'em on he arm and him gone fly through the chimbly. And he sister and him brother follow he Ma and he Pa. Sister, Brudder, Mudder, Pa and after dem gone him done the same thing and HIM gone! And when gal him courtin' she gone and rub on she and HIM gone through the chimbley and left the young man him ONE. Him gone and rub him one and rub him and HIM gone through the chimbley. And he gone the same place the old man come! And a bexation come 'tween him and the old man. Get entangle there. Gone right to place where he was to hag that night!

Day catch dem! Old lady and gal and all know how to shift to dey skin. But the boy he didn't! Come a confusion 'tween them. Boy learn to fly. Dem could get back. Dem know how to come back. 'Cause that dem TRADE. Finally they have to kill out all that family—all that race o' people. The boy finally tell the Maussa how it was. Maussa do way with all o' them. Put' em in a barrel o' tar and BURN DEM UP.

Skin? The man left he skin in the LOFT. He been know how to get in he skin. But the boy didn't know! Boy tell zackly how it is and do way with all o' dem! Come there and fly inside there. You kin hear the house crack! That the hag comin' in. Put your parents to sleep then them JUMP ON YOU. Hag a REAL PERSON. They just learn that trade."

Mathew Grant
Parkersville
(Near Pawley's Island, S.C.)
Born 1867

Budder Deer and Budder Cooter[1]

"The King have a daughter. Budder Deer and Budder Cooter all two both wantin' the King daughter. Budder Deer and Budder Cooter runnin' race for the King daughter. Courtin' the King daughter. Had a ten mile race. Tell 'em anyone can beat the race get the daughter. Budder Cooter tell Budder Deer he can't run on the land. Run in the ditch! Budder Deer tell him:

"Anywhere you run all right! I know I goin' get the gal! You foot too short! YOU can't run!'

"Budder Cooter ax him:

"When us race come off?'

"'Tursday!'

"'Tursday?'

"'Yes! Right here the first mile post!'

""'Well,' Budder Cooter tell Budder Deer, 'I goin' show you something. I goin' show you what a short foot man do with a long foot man!'

"King count and the race start. (Cooter got in ditch and get nine other cooter in ditch—one on every mile post and him make the ten! Him goin' start right here!) So after they ready the gal settin' side she fadder. King say:

"'Now, boy, here the time!'

"Cooter get in ditch. Budder Deer take the road. Hit the first mile post

"'Hey, Budder Cooter!'

"'Here Budder Cooter stick he head out he ditch,

"'Come on man! I gone on! Thought you could run!'

1. A tale similar to Aesop's "The Tortoise and the Hare." In this case the tortoise is referred to by his lowcountry name, Cooter. The deer fills the hare's role.

"Budder Deer jump ten foot! Here he gone high tailin' down the road! Come to next mile post! Budder Cooter been there first! Same way ever time. Hit the ten mile post

"'Hey, Budder Cooter!'

"Here I is, Budder Deer! I turnin' back, boy! Been here till I turnin' back!'

"When Budder Deer get back to the startin' place here he find Budder Cooter done get out the ditch, beat the race and stand side the gal have the gal HUG UP!

"Budder Deer fall dead!

"Been skinin' deer from dat time up till now! Deer run from dog—run right in the gun mouth!"

(Ever time a young man hang a cooter on a limb he get way; old man hang 'em can't get way! Young man tie 'em, go back there to find 'em he gone! Nebber shee'um! He gone!)

SOURCE: *Matthew Grant, Born 1887. Parkersville, S.C.*

Loney "Noonie" Heywood

Loney "Noonie" Heywood grew up as a member of the Heywood family living in Knoxville, within a mile of Sunnyside. Her mother and father were Loney (or Salony) and William Heywood. She was the sister of Walter, Hattie, Rosa, Rebecca, Jannie, Essie, Minnie, Mary, and Obertha Heywood. She was also related—probably as a great-niece—to ex-slave and fellow Chandler informant Mariah Heywood. Always known as Loney Heywood to the African American community, the white community seems to have called her Noonie or Noontoo. In the 1930s Heywood worked as a nurse for Genevieve Chandler's children. They remember her as an affable companion, prone to giggling fits.

Heywood's interviews are some of the most finely delineated portraits, if mainly in their eccentricity, to be found in the volumes of material that Chandler collected in her tenure on Murrells Inlet. Apparently Heywood stuttered heavily, a point that Chandler not only recorded but addressed in an aside in a transcription of Heywood singing lullabies: "Noontoo stutters something AWFUL in conversation."[1] Heywood also had a beautiful singing voice, made up her own versions of popular songs, and possessed a powerful, sometimes wild, imagination. Her animal stories, for example, are almost apocalyptic in their resonance. Along with Heywood's simply styled songs, these stories evoke a Blake-like coupling of innocence and experience.

Noontoo's Story

Once I was sitting away in a wild desert. I heard a terrible noise. WHEN I hold up my head I seen a great big bird with a great big tree limb carryin' it to build his nest. I came to his nest. I climbed and looked in the nest. He had it all seal up in there DARK. Had seal it up with pine top and burr and vine and all.

The mother eagle lay her eggs in there and the father eagle had all kind of wild beast meat restore in the hollow for his young. But one day it was cold and rainy and all the meat was gone and the mother eagle said to father:

1. Forthcoming in a volume of song and spirituals collected by Genevieve Chandler.

Loney "Noonie" Heywood. *Photograph by Bayard Wootten. North Carolina Collection, University of North Carolina Library at Chapel Hill*

"We haven't got anything to eat today!" Father eagle turn 'round and look up and down. He seen a little lamb runnin' cross the field and he said:

"We will be happy. 'Bog Eagle! Bog Eagle! Hawk won't give you chicken but we'll have meat anyhow.'" Then he swoop down on the lamb and took him up with his claws and carried him home. The 'noung one was afraid of it but he said to them: "We will have all kind of meat!" And he start skinnin' the lamb. And when the lamb blood begin to drop on the mother eagle wing she said to the 'noung one:

"'Bog Eagle! Bog Eagle! Hawk won't give us meat but we have meat anyhow!'"

And all start eatin'.

When the food give out again the father eagle go way off to where a mother was workin' in a field. She have put her baby in to a basket at the end of the row. And the woman name Molly, was pickin' peas and singin'. She and the other colored people singin':

"I wants to be ready!
I wants to be ready!
I wants to be ready
To walkin Jerusalem just like John!"

The father Eagle heard them singin'. He say: 'I will show you what I will do with that basket.' And he swoop down and carry that baby far away! Away he went. Then the baby start cryin'.

When the mother come to the end of the row the baby was gone!

She look 'round. She didn't seen any body track. She hear a cry. She look up. She say:

"Oh the angle must -a come from Heaven and took my baby back!"

Planter[2] Cat

"It musser been thirty or twenty nine years ago. Papa remembers all 'bout it. A great big old thing just taken down Mission Swamp. Went like a baby Papa said; Aunt Maria said it went like a ox bellowin'. All the women and children would look up at first dark. Everybody was afraid. "Wow—ough! Wow—ough!" And that kept up till everybody was so scared they put the dogs in the woods and they TREED it. A great big old wild-cat and everbody sayin' panter cat!"

SOURCE: *Noonie Heywood—Age 25(?)*
Sept, 15th., 1938
Murrells Inlet, S. C.

2. Panther.

Mariah Heywood

AT THE TIME MARIAH HEYWOOD WAS INTERVIEWED, her family lived on the road to Burgess close to Knoxville, the home of the extended Knox family. It is through the Knoxes that Chandler would have had the strongest association with Heywood. The Heywoods also used the Willcox property to access the creek.

Heywood lived her early life as a house servant at Sunnyside along the creek at Murrells Inlet, merely a mile north of the Willcoxes' later home, the Hermitage. This was a life of relative privilege. Benjamin Faneuil Dunkin presented Mariah to his daughter Anna Washington Dunkin Alston and her husband, Charles Alston, as a gift. As a result of Heywood's status within the white family, she cultivated a pride rare among slaves. Despite apparent satisfaction with the state of freedom, Mariah also put great stock in Charles Alston's reluctance to concede defeat at the end of the Civil War: "My Massa, Major Charles Allston, was the last one to gone to Georgetown and gone under the Flag!" In short, she respected honor and imagined quality in her white family elevated her by association. She expressed pride in being one of the last slaves freed: "Free everywhere else and we wasn't free Sunnyside till June third or second. Sunday we got our Freedom. Bright day too. Our colored people fare just like the white wearing, eating, drinking. I wuz raise on the cream of earth." This pride in her enslavers was mixed with the sweet elation of freedom: "I know when Lincoln shoot the chain of slavery off my neck. And I hear the gun. I hear SHOOT and the house shake and water shake out the glass. The gun shoot to Georgetown!"

Heywood was born Mariah Brockington in 1855, the same year as Charles and Washington's daughter, Mary R. Alston, so Heywood was eighty-two when Chandler interviewed her. She had two younger brothers, Smart Robert Brockington and Harrison Franklin Brockington, born free ("mancipation children"). According to U.S. Census data, she was the daughter of Peter and Hester Brockington. By 1910 her husband, Jackson Heywood, was not working and was, in fact, physically disabled. As the primary wage earner, Mariah Heywood raised between ten and eleven children (Hester A., Martha E., Peter, Joe, Robert, Ben Henry, Harry, Anna, John, Julia, Ester B., and perhaps

William). Mariah Heywood was also a very active participant in Heaven's Gate Church. At the time of her interviews, at least, she was the "oldest 'communion steward' . . . 'THE MOTHER OF HEAVEN'S GATE.'"

Aunt Mariah Heywood

Aunt Mariah Heywood, born in 1855, was 'Allston labor' on Waccamaw Neck. Given as a bridal present to 'Miss Susan Alston' by her father, Mr. Duncan Alston of Midway Plantation Waccamaw,[1] Aunt Mariah has for the last fifty years lived much in the past when 'I wuz raise on the cream of the earth' and her head is just a little higher and her backbone just a little stiffer than that of the average colored person because of pride—family pride—in her people—her white people. And as one can readily see from her testimony, her chief cause for her pardonable snobbery seems to be that her Massa was the last man to surrender and "swear gainst his swear."

Her sons, one of whom is a preacher in the Methodist Conference and 'one a zorter—a locust' and her youngest son John[2] (who got all the credrick) have built her a comfortable house (painted a bilious yaller) which she keeps clean and sweet with flowers in the front yard—two treasured plants having been sent by her brother (born after mancipations) clean from Pittsburgh.

The fact that she was raised by aristocrats shows plainly in her dealing with both races and she is a leader in church activities and her opinion valued when a vote is taken about school matters.

Being the oldest 'communion steward' she is affectionately spoken of as 'THE MOTHER OF HEAVEN'S GATE'—the Methodist church founded in Murrells Inlet community by colored leaders shortly after Mancipation.

"Aunt Mariah, you home?"
"Missus, what you brought me?"
"- - - - - - - - - - - -
"I too thank you."
(Soon she began to reminesce)

1. Apparently Chandler was confused. Mariah Heywood's owner was Benjamin Faneuil Dunkin, chancellor of the Court of Equity of South Carolina and owner of Midway plantation. He apparently gave Mariah to his daughter Anna Washington Dunkin Alston and her husband, Charles Alston, in 1855. According to family records the Alstons were married in May 1847, so it would seem Mariah was not a wedding present. Rather it may have been that one or both of her parents were part of the dowry or that Mariah's moving to the Alston household was associated with the birth of the Alston's daughter, Mary Rutledge Alston, in 1855.

2. John Heywood.

Mariah Heywood. *Photograph by Bayard Wootten. North Carolina Collection, University of North Carolina Library at Chapel Hill*

"You could hear 'em over there slamming and banging. The Yankee tear up the Dr. Flagg house[3] but they didn't come Sunnyside.[4] Bright day too! Old man Thomas Stuart lead 'em to Hermitage. Had team they take from Mr. Betts[5] and team they take from Dr. Arthur to Woodland.[6] Free everywhere else and we wasn't free Sunnyside till June third or second. Sunday we got our Freedom. Bright day too. Our colored people fare just like the white; wearing, eating, drinking. I wuz raise on the cream of earth.

"They wuz glad. Sign a contract for your boss you would work the same and get pay the end of the year—and tend you when you sick all the same." (The same medical attention to be given that was given before 'Freedom') "Big guns shooting![7] House jar to Sunnyside and one day water shake out the

3. The Hermitage was Dr. Allard Belin Flagg's summer home.

4. Sunnyside was constructed by Jacob Motte Alston, owner of Woodbourne plantation. He sold the home to his brother Charles Alston.

5. Rev. Charles Betts, a Methodist circuit rider.

6. Woodland, the Murrells Inlet home of Edward Thomas Heriot.

7. In 1862 a Union gunboat traveled up Flagg Creek in Murrells Inlet, opening fire on the salt works on the Hermitage beach front. Sunnyside was not fired upon because the creek was too shallow. According to a Georgetown County history, "the salt works were destroyed, but the Federals were driven away by a force of twenty-five

glass! Miss Susan[8] take her spyglass and stand behind one them big posses (posts) and spy them big boats shooting! And boss[9] say, 'Don't get in front of them posses—they might shoot you!'

"Yankee come to Mrs. Belin[10] and Parson Betts. And they tell Mrs. Belin, they want her to know no more slave holding and she thank 'em and she say, HE people wuz always free! Grandma Harriet, (Harriet Mortor wuz her title but that time they always gone by they Master title). Joe Heywood wuz Joe Belin—he was Parson Belin man—he take the Heywood title after mancipation. Poinsette (Uncle Fred) ALWAYS carry that title. That day, all the right hand servant[11] always take they Massa title.) When the big gun shooting, old people in the yard, 'Tank God! Massa, HE COMING!' (Referring to 'Freedom') 'HE COMING!' (Guns gone just like thunders roll now!) Chillun say, "What coming? What coming? What coming, Grandma?'

'You all will know! You all will know!'

"Massa live 'Wee ha kum'[12] for years. We are fifty-five (55) chillun. Mary Rutledge Allston and I one year chillun." (She and Mary R. Allston born same year.) "My Missus have four chillun—Mary Rutledge, Susan Bethune, Marsa Pink and Marse Fanuel. (Benjamine Nathaniel!)[13]

"Four years of the war been hold prayer-meeting." (Praying for 'freedom'). Lock me up in house. Me, I been PRESent to Miss Minna[14]—'Miss Mary![15] We, us lock up! My brother and I listen! (Two brother mancipation chillun. Smart Robert Brockington and Harrison Franklin Brockington in Pittsburgh. I nuss (nurse) him—jess like you hold that book.) Old people used to go to Richmond Hill, Laurel Hill and Wachesaw have these little prayer-meeting.

---

men. In the last week of [July] they broke up 'the salt boilers, stole 2 boiler heads and wantonly scatter'd the Salt into the Sand.'" George C. Rogers Jr., *The History of Georgetown County, South Carolina* (Columbia: University of South Carolina Press, 1970), 402.

8. Susan Bethune Alston, daughter of Charles and Anna Washington Dunkin Alston.

9. Charles Alston.

10. Hesse Belin.

11. One's "right hand servant" was chosen early in life and was usually around the same age as the person he or she served. From childhood playmate to life companion, this servant would ultimately act as a handmaid or footman, always an intimate to the man or women served, but also always a slave.

12. Thomas Pinckney Alston, father of Charles Alston, owned Weehawka plantation until 1858, when he sold it to Plowden Weston.

13. Mary Rutledge Alston, Susan Bethune Alston, Thomas Pinckney Alston, and Benjamin Faneuil Alston.

14. Anna Washington Dunkin Alston.

15. Mary Rutledge Alston and Mariah Heywood were born the same year.

All bout in people house. Hold the four year of the war. Great many time the chicken crow for day. Hear the key. We say 'Yeddy!' Change clothes. Gone on in the house. Get that eight, seven o'clock breakfast.

"Parson Glennie (Rector All Saints, Waverly lived at Rectory there and did wonderful work teaching and preaching to slaves as well as whites—preaching at beautiful St. Mary's chapel, built by Plowden Weston at Hagley[16] for the slaves of materials from England—baptismal font from this chapel now in Camden Episcopal church and stained glass also removed before chapel burned some few years ago.) At this period—prior to mancipation Waccamaw slaves were usually educated in the faith of their masters—the Episcopal.) Parson Glennie come once a month to Sunnyside. Parson Glennie read, sing, pray. Tell us obey Miss Minna. (I wuz little highest.) Two of us 55 chillun![17] We'd fight. She knock me. I knock back! Wouldn't take a knock! She say, 'I tell Parson Glennie! Lord won't bless you! You bad.' I say, 'You knock me, I knock you!'[18]

"Have a play-house. Charlie[19] buy from Mott.[20] Used to summer it at Magnolia.[21] Row from Bull Creek once a month to Chapel. (10 miles or more) Put them All Saints eleven o'clock service. Four best men his rowsmen. Fuss (first) year war we tuh Bull Creek. Nobody go (to All Saints) but Missus and Massa[22] and the four rowsmen.

"Flat going from Midway to Cheraw.[23] Beat rice on flat. (Couldn't grind corn) Kill chicken. Gone to protect from Yankees—to hide! When they come (to Cheraw). Sherman[24] coming from MONDAY till SATDY! Come on RAIL! Said 'twas a shocking sight! When Sherman army enter Cheraw, town full of sojers. Take way from white people and give horses colored people! Didn't kill none the horses. (On Sunnyside on Waccamaw) Cheraw Yankee kill horses!

16. Hagley plantation, where Camden Episcopal Church was built for the African American community.

17. Both Mariah Heywood and Mary Rutledge Alston were born in 1855.

18. As Heywood suggests, she and Mary Rutledge Alston grew up together and, in the process, shared some equal footing. If Mary hit Mariah, Mariah hit back. Obviously, black violence against whites was rarely condoned, but these two children managed, for a time at least, to operate outside that double standard.

19. Charles Alston.

20. Jacob Motte Alston, Charles's half brother, from whom Charles purchased Sunnyside.

21. Magnolia Beach.

22. Anna Washington Dunkin Alston and Charles Alston.

23. From Midway plantation to Cheraw plantation on the Pee Dee River.

24. General William Tecumseh Sherman's troops raided the Waccamaw.

(Indeed—YES! It is history in Marlboro, near Cheraw they were killed and thrown in the wells to pollute the water.)"

"Mr. Charley horse, couldn't nobody ride but him! Father-in-law (Mr. Duncan to Midway) had a pair of grey—BUCK and SMILER. Driver, Tom Carr. Come in carriage every month to Sunnyside. Get the family. Go and spend ten days—Midway! Family wuz MYSELF, MISS MINNA, and the three and the Massa and Miss Susan. Mary Huger one my Missus sister. One marry a Huger to Charleston.[25]

"Major Charles say he'd die in Sunnyside yard fore he'd go there (Georgetown) and take off his hat and 'swear gainst my swear.' He'd die in Sunnyside yard. My Massa, Major Charles Allston, was the last one to gone to Georgetown and gone under that flag! He was Charles Jr., but after Confederick was he was Major Charles! Major Charles the last man off Waccamaw gone under the flag! At Georgetown. Went down in row-boat. My fadder gone and tell old man Tom Nesbitt to have his boat and four of his best mens. Got to go off a piece! Pa gone. Have boat ready. Ma got up. Cook a traveling lunch for 'em. Fore day! Blue uniform. Yellow streak down side—just like this streak in my dress. Yellow bar!" (Most of 'em had to rob dead yankees or go naked) "LAST GENTLEMAN GONE UNDER THE FLAG![26]

"Walking up and down the piazza! Say, can I go to town and swear gainst my slave?" Can I? Up and down!

"I hear bout them slave try to run way. Aunt Tella Kinloch eye shot out. Marsh (baby) cry! Mother say take her apron and stuff the child mouth. Blockade (patrollers) wuz hiding. Shot in range of that sound. Row! Row! Row! Put everything in jail! All in jail! Mr. McCuskey tell us! He wuz one of the men help lynch. I got married 1873. They wuz talking bout the time (war) "Mr. McCuskey told us Nemo Ralston was one. Say he never see a fatter man. Fat in there in shield! Like a fattening hog! (They running way from

25. Again Chandler seems to have confused some of the members of the Alston family. Charles and Anna Alston had four children: Thomas Pinckney, born March 26, 1848; Benjamin Faneuil, born December 27, 1849; Susan Bethune, born March 13, 1853; and Mary Rutledge, born June 13, 1855. A corrected sentence might read: "Family wuz myself, Miss Minna (Mary R. Alston) and the three (Thomas P., Benjamin F., and Susan B. Alston) and Massa (Charles Alston) and Miss Anna (Anna Washington Dunkin Alston)." Joseph Asbury Groves, *The Alstons and Allstons of North and South Carolina* (Atlanta: Franklin Printing and Publishing Company, 1901), 85–86.

26. George Rogers Jr. notes, "General John P. Hatch issued an order on April 25 [1865] commanding the planters of Georgetown and Charleston districts to take an oath of allegiance to the United States, after which they were to assemble their freedmen and inform them that they were free. Equitable contracts in writing were then to be made with the freedmen. The planters must provide subsistence until the crops

Oregon[27]—Dr. McGill place). Say they put four horses to him—one to every limb. Stretch 'em. And cut horses and each horse carry a piece! Mr. McCuskey was one help lynch Nemo.

"Uncle William Heywood didn't birth till after mancipation. Not a thing to do with slavery time! But I know when the big gun shooting to free me! Yankee come and free Waccamaw! No slave hold. Whole neck free but us! Last people free on 'Neck.' MY MAJOR last one to went under flag to Georgetown! Old man Moses Gibson and Peter Brockington build Sunnyside kitchen

"I wuz birth November 5th, 1855. Mr. Buck say, 'Aunt Mariah, know your birth?'

"'Yes, sir!'

'Aunt Mariah, you too old to work! You born 1800 go on home raise your chicken!'

Aunt Mariah Heywood
Age—82
Murrells Inlet, S. C.

Questioner: "Aunt Maria, what did you know 'bout the old Doctor?'[28]
Maria: "All I know, he a nice gentleman from start to finish. Been know him since before the time of the Big Storm.

"In that Big Storm old man Bob Vereen wife, water lick every clothes off her. And they was a gang of naked people hangin' on that tree! And the breaker had lick every clothes off'em. The old Cap'n see his wife turn loose and he loose his grip and make a grab and they lock together and down they gone![29] Bob Vereen and his wife both save. Mom Adele drownded. She was Uncle Tom Ma.

"Dr. Wardie had plant that tree when he was a boy. Water lift dem. Float them up in that 'Beach Cedar' and they ketch.

"Old man Parrish'son was killefirst of 'mancipation. Old Cap'n say:

"'Go to stable Peter and get my horse!'[30]

"When Pa went Pa find two dead man layin' right to the line and other one his cousin from Pee Dee. Cap'n say:

---

were gathered, at which time the freedmen were to receive one-half of the crop." Rogers, *History of Georgetown County*, 424. The accuracy of Heywood's claim is uncertain, though Charles Alston Jr.'s father is recorded as having taken the oath at Darlington Courthouse on August 21, far earlier than most of the surrounding planters.

27. Both Oregon plantation and Richmond Hill plantation were owned by Dr. John D. Magill (1795–1864).

28. Dr. Ward Flagg.

29. Dr. Arthur Belin and Georgianna Flagg.

30. Peter Brockington, Mariah Heywood's father.

"'Take my horse Peter, and ride down to Brook Green and see what yousee and hear what you hear!'

"One of them dead man was Mr. Ward big Driver. Gang of white men come and question Parrish Vereen. My Pa stop and cut bresh and cover they face. (Nobody ride that horse but Pa!)"

"He ride. They run. Couldn't get close to him! These people scare. Pa run dem down.

"Young Cap'n was engaged to one of dem T—— girl. He wanted Pauline but look like he always get in company with Lucy, the oldest.

"Willie Brown come by the morning of the storm. Come riding down the King Road horse-back ten o' clock in the morning. Storm get over by then. Time we see him say: 'Light and come in!' He say:

"'No! Ain't you hear Magnolia islant[31] float off and all the people drownded?'

"That upsot everybody and mens all came to the seashore and find that Miss Kessire (Desire) house all bust open! A big stump wash up and bust up 'gainst the door.

"Katrine been in the house when the water come. Katrine say:

"'My God, here I goin' drown up here in this house way from all my chillun!'

"House lift up by a big water and drop back on block 'BIM'! Hit the block! At Sunnyside salt water full up the well and they have to shovel the dead mash (marsh) out the house. And it gone in the windows! They all there and wouldn't go to the woods when the water rainin.'

"Cap'n Allard[32] land to The Oaks Seashore. Come over on top of the house. (Ask Fred Poinsett! He'll give the whole inscription!) One top float off—off the out house and they watch it and it come by the window and they active boy and they watch it and it come by the window and they active boy and they jump out the window and got on the roof and had a cat on top and the horse come swimming on behind. (Cat kill by Huntington.[33] Doctor ready to war!)"

SOURCE: *Aunt Maria Heywood*
Age 80 olus
Murrells Inlet, S. C.
July 1938
(Born Sunnyside Plantation before the war)

31. The Flagg family was on Magnolia Beach when the great storm of 1893 hit.
32. Allard Belin Flagg.
33. Archer M. Huntington, heir to a railroad fortune. Huntington bought Brookgreen plantation, where Dr. Ward Flagg then continued to live. He also acquired the

Ex-slave Talks

"Money sent here to help the poor, needy, destiny (destitute) people. If my blind girl not need help and I not need help, WHO DO?

"We goin' trust God and suffer together. I know when Lincoln shoot the chain of slavery off my neck. And I hear the gun. I hear SHOOT and the house shake and water shake out the glass. The gun shoot to Georgetown!

"Joe gone. Zack gone. The same God there and I trust God and live on. Both Hess and Matt sick with high blood.[34] Soon as I bury we don't know WHAT comin'. I see the hint of it now. My God tell me to tell (till) the earth! I can't sign 'gainst my land! The lady talk. She tell me I needy. I tell her 'YES'M.' But I can't sign 'gainst my land. If I just can hold on to my land! I a BURN CHILD. I BURN! I'faid! I'faid!

"A 'nother one come. A man come tell me I give $24 they'll rush that pension through. I have two white friend tell me not to sign NOTHIN'."

SOURCE: *Aunt Maria Heywood*
Born before Freedom.
Waccamaw Neck, Georgetown County
Lived Sunnyside Plantation. October, 1938.

---

adjacent plantations Springfield, Laurel Hill, and the Oaks. Before Huntington's death, this land was incorporated as Brookgreen Gardens; ownership was given to a self-perpetuating board of trustees. The gardens feature works by renowned American sculptors including Huntington's wife, Anna Hyatt Huntington, and the estate is dedicated to the study of southeastern flora and fauna.

34. High blood pressure.

Monday Samson Holmes

Chandler interviewed Holmes at the Ark plantation fishery, which served as a community gathering ground for both blacks and whites during the mullet fishing season. Here Chandler interviewed people as they feasted on the fall's fattened mullet or as they waited for the next catch. Holmes was born and raised near the Ark at Wilderness plantation in Horry County. According to informant Essie Tucker, Holmes was a descendant of David Holmes—a manumitted slave originally from Norfolk, Virginia, who purchased land in the Freewoods that became Holmestown. By the time of the 1920 census, Holmes was a widower, having lost his first wife, Emma. Chandler placed Monday Samson Holmes's age at around eighty to eighty-five; the Horry County 1920 census placed him at fifty-five (and thus he would have been seventy-three in 1938). The 1930 census recorded his age as seventy-one. Holmes himself claimed that he was no taller than his walking stick "when freedom clear." Perhaps, then, he was five in 1865 and thus nearly seventy-eight in 1938. Holmes came from a large family with ten brothers. He names six: Joe, Dickie, Willie, Frank, Jacob, and Ellis. Only one sister is on record: Nancy Holmes Rutledge, whose husband, Sabe Rutledge, operated the fishery at the Ark. Holmes had at least three children—a son, Sol, and two daughters, Lenora and Patient. Holmes worked with lumber and as a farmer. At the time of his interview with Chandler, he planned to marry a woman named Liza Johnson, most likely the widow Eliza Johnson listed as his neighbor in the 1930 U.S. Census.

Ex-slave Talks

Mundy Holmes: "I some where close a hundred. Mundy Holmes. When Freedom clear, I a little boy 'bout so high." (Measures on poplar stick. Shiny from use. Coca-cola cap stuck on end.)"

"First thing I 'member is the Lord's pray." (He recites it.) "Our Father pray. My Ma make me learn that.

"I have two chillun. Sol,[1] and that die the other day; Patient—and that marry Tyler Carr. That my one daughter.[2]

"I see thing in my time. I see'um make some haul and fish pile high as that sand hill there.[3] Didn't been so much a seine. Now they not four mile apart. The beach lined with seine. Don't catch them fish like they 'nuster been.

"I don't get deer meat 'cept when the white man kill dem and I eat to he house. When they in the bay and the dog go in, here come the old buck first and doe right behind him.

"A boy drown right here. Have the line 'round he hand. Shark in the net, Take right on out to sea. Find the boy way up yonder to Little River. Piece of rope still tie to he hand.

"'Nother boy drown right here. Done eat a big belly full o' fish. Gone in swimmin'. Brudder see him in trouble. Gone to save him. Suck hole pull him down. Brudder make a dive to miss that suck hole. He one come back. Sea rough like he is now. Just such a day.

"Woods fire? Woods take a-fire have to work I'm tellin' you to save my fence. That the worst time I EVER have. I save'em! Lor, but I work to save that fence!

"I make a little rice out in the Holmes-town. A little corn. A little 'tater. Me one. Ain't a critter to my name. Take these two hand. I plant cotton. Boll weevil take all way from me!

"I some where close a hundred. I bet I go somewhere 'round there. I 85 or 80. You know the Big War what free the colored people not TODAY you know.

"Missis, you hear 'bour hat 'tentious money? I go to Conwayborough.[4] I gone to LEAF OFFICE.[5] I ain't have the straightness of that 'tentious money yet!

"Family collection done that. I is hear 'bout that ox get kill and sell but that nothin' but FAMILY COLLECTION.

1. Sol Holmes.

2. It is not clear what Holmes means by "one" here. He may mean to indicate that Patient Holmes is his only living daughter. The 1910 U.S. Census suggests he already had a fifteen-year-old daughter at that time with his wife, Emma. According to the same record, Emma had borne four children, three of whom were still alive, and the couple had been married for twenty-five years.

3. Ark plantation fishery.

4. Conway, South Carolina. Named for the Revolutionary War general Robert Conway, it was known as Conwayborough until 1881.

5. Relief office.

"Ellen? Ellen Godfrey? I know him when he big 'noung woman have breast in he stummick to Longwood.[6] I born to WILDERNESS PLANTATION. ——— to WOODSTOCK. Ellen? I know him like a book. Elsie. He a Granny. (Midwife)

"Pa chillun? Oh my God! I have ten head o'budder! Oldest budder, one name Joe; one name Dickie; one name Willie; one name Frank; one name Jacob; one name Ellis. Yes. Ten head. I 'blive that all. My RIGHT name been Samson[7] but I never been call dat YET. Name Samson outer the Bible. Calls me MONDAY[8] 'cause I born that day.

"What kinder dog that? That just a house dog.

"Yes'm? I fixin' to married. Name Miss Liza Johnson!"

SOURCE: *Uncle Monday Samson Holmes*
Holmes-town in the Free Woods
Horry County, Burgess, S. C.
Age—"Close on to a hundred. Must been 85 or 80."

6. Longwood plantation.
7. Monday Holmes's given name.
8. Monday Holmes's basket name. See page 18, note 13, for more on basket names.

Ben and Stella Horry

A PROPERTY OWNER ALONG THE CREEK at Murrells Inlet and an erstwhile entrepreneur, Ben Horry led a life in the community marked by agitation and conflict. As Chandler's interviews with him attest, legal troubles were one of Horry's major preoccupations. Allegedly, much of this trouble was self-inflicted—stemming from dishonest and self-serving tendencies. Zackie Knox reports that Horry's legal troubles began when he tried to sell his sister's share of land without her knowledge or permission.

The struggle over ownership of his fourteen and three-quarters acres of land kept him constantly involved with lawyers—having to "step to" Conway (a walking round-trip of some forty miles) often more than once a week trying to sort out his legal problems. In an interview with Chandler, Horry himself recounted an incident in which he was shot for trespassing. Others have suggested that, in fact, Horry habitually cursed his neighbor, Joe Baruchs, from the steps of the man's house. Apparently the aforementioned shotgun blast was the culmination of one such encounter. At one point Horry was ostracized from the church because of his bootlegging operation. He ultimately mended his ways but not before losing out to a white bootlegger and not without staging a dramatic return to the fold.

Horry was born into slavery on December 13, 1852, at Brookgreen plantation.[1] Horry's father, Define (glossed by Chandler as "Divine"), later became Colonel Joshua Ward's "head man" at Brookgreen—a position Ben Horry also came to fill. According to U.S. Census data, Horry's mother's name was Bess, and he had a younger sister, Daphney. Horry was married twice (first to Mary, then to Stella Horry), had a stepson (Miller), and had several children of his own (Charles Henry, Ben, Bill, Dinah, Christine, Mary, and Georgie). Horry was a fisherman, steamboat worker, cook, and, as mentioned above, a bootlegger. In August 1937 he was eighty-seven years old.

1. In 1870 the U.S. Census recorded Ben Horry's age as fourteen, which would date his year of birth to circa 1856.

Stella Horry was Ben Horry's second wife—and some twenty years his junior. Her one short interview indicates that she shared her husband's distrust of the white community. Although electric power was available to the Horrys, Stella explains her reluctance to adopt the new technology with the gnomic claim that "white folks run me if I do that." In one of her interviews with Ben Horry, Genevieve Chandler has interpreted Stella's statement as evidence she clung to old ways of white entitlement: "the old couple still live with many old and odd beliefs one being that the white man only is entitled to the good things." In effect, Chandler assumed that Stella feared she would be punished by whites for presuming to use technology reserved for them. It is possible, of course, that Stella meant something a bit subtler. By accepting the white man's electricity, perhaps she feared she would give up something of her, and the black community's, fledgling autonomy.

Uncle Ben Horry

(Uncle Ben lives in his own cabin with his second wife, Stella. Formerly almost inaccessible, the new Coastal Highway has put Uncle Ben and Aunt Stella in the world. The rural electricity program has current right at their door. Aunt Stella was asked 'Why don't you have lights, Aunt Stella?' and she replied, 'White folks run me if I do that!' So you see the old couple still live with many old and odd beliefs one being that the white man only is entitled to the good things—the better things. Like most old ex-slaves in South Carolina low country, they love and revere the names and memories of their old masters.)

"Right now, I oldest one from Longwood to Prospect—see dere? (Pointing to forest wall—great pines and live-oaks in front of the cabin)—Look! I know when he cleared and plant! Josh Ward[2] have potato there. I have manure and plant tater. I been here, daughter!" (He pronounces it 'Dater' with a short 'a')

(Aside: "Stella, mind now! Don't quarrel me to-night! What you do?"
Aunt Stella: The second wife—some years his junior—probably 65—"I do nuff!")

"Got to go up there and cook supper to the Schoolfield house." (This was Uncle Ben's announcement as he crawled in-to the car with a bucket in which were his shoes. He was walking down the Coastal Highway and not staying where he belonged—on the shoulder!) "Got to cook crab and ister (oyster). Ain't got much to cook. They don't eat much. Got a gal there to fry fish. They

2. Joshua Ward (1830–1869), son of Joshua John Ward (1800–1853) and owner of Springfield and Brookgreen plantations. During the Civil War, Ward captained a battery of light artillery. Around 1864 he resigned from the army and went to England for the duration of the war.

Ben Horry at his home. *Photograph by Bayard Wootten. North Carolina Collection, University of North Carolina Library at Chapel Hill*

give me recommend for cook. Been get the sea foods for 'em for five year. Iron oven the way we raise." (Aside to his wife) "Stella, if that man come there, see that sack there? Tell that man I put fire there. Gie 'em fork and knife. Tell 'em eat all he want!") (Uncle Ben arranges oyster roasts.)

"That man to Schoolfield house want me to stay and sleep wid 'em. All women gone. Tell me keep the man and lock up the house when he gone. I tell 'em too much o' tief!"

Lillie: "Aunt Stella, ain't you fraid when Uncle Ben stay out all night?"

Uncle Ben: "Stella keep pot o' water boil and tief come she trow 'em!"

Visitor: "Uncle Ben tell Lillie bout your father[3] and the whiskey jug."

Uncle Ben: "You see, to Brookgreen we nuster plant rice and my fadder had the barn key. He kinder boss man. He nuster (used to) take me and go out woods night time."

(Aside to mother of child at pump—"Take care dat child!")

"Fadder take me out woods night time (What you say, Primus?) and I hold storch (torch) for him see for trash (thrash) out rice what he take out the barn. Rice been money dem time you know. And he take he rice and gone on down to town for get he liquor. And he come from town wid whiskey. Boss find it out. Five or six chillun and always give us rations. Broke that jug and when they call his name (put rations in pile you know—pile for every one been in fambly) when they call my fadder name but a piece o' broken jug there is discourage him from whiskey—. He come from town and been drop the jug and it break up. And Boss know. Far as I can remember he keep give 'em that broken jug bout a year. You see he sponsible for key. Seem like I member right where we go beat that rice. Pine tree saw off and chip out make as good a mortar as that one I got. Dan'l, Summer, Define! Define the oldest brother my fadder have. Young Missus Bess, Florence, Georgia, Alice. Those boys the musicianer—go round play for the girl."

(***Aunt Stella:*** Interrupting, "You orter be carry money with you. Get the meat. I ain't going no whey (where)."

Lillie: To Primus who has walked up.

"Handful back yet?" (Handful his wife's basket name.)[4]

3. There is some confusion in Ben Horry's account of who his father was. Later in this interview, for example, he says that Define Horry was one of his uncles. In another interview, however, Horry clearly states that Define was his father's name (p. 97). The contradictory reports are probably due to an error on Genevieve Chandler's part, either in her note taking or in her transcription of her notes.

4. See page 18, note 13, for more on basket names.

Primus: "No. This man bacco barn burn up."
Lillie: "What?
Primus: "Mr. Len barn. Must'er been asleep!"
Lillie: "Rich most cure all his'n. Taint mine! Rich tease me. He say, 'MY bacco; YOUR kitchen!'"
Lillie: "What you all think bout that tale the Elder tell Sunday bout his Great Uncle and the snakes!"
Stella: (To Uncle Ben) "What you tink bout it? You tink a ma truss to go in cypress hollow wid rattle-snake?"
Uncle Ben: "Let me see how was it!" (Deep thought as he rubbed his face in his palm; smile as recollection came) "On Rutledge Plantation[5] a man wouldn't take no beating. Found a large hollow cypress tree been rotten out long years. Gone in. Lie down sleep. Fore day wake up! Feel something crawl over him. Nother one crow like game chicken!" (Negroes all say rattlers crow!) "Smell him. Crawl over him. Crawl out. Get out."
Stella: "Revents had it wuz a man in a cypress tree and seven—how much wuz it? Twelve? These twelve monster snake crawl over him. If you move, he strike."
Uncle Ben: "Right there where Dr. Ward[6] stay had a big old stable—see these two hole in my jaw. Had a stable high as that tree. Big Jersey bull gone in there eating that straw like we thrashing. Big rattle-snake pop 'um. Fall dead."

"How doeswemark shoat? Under-bit; upper-bit. Swallow fork in the right year![7] And a square crop in the left!

"How much been task? A quarter (acre) if you mashing ground. Ten compass digging ground. Cutting rice one half acre a day." (awful job.)
Stella: "Plow; harrow 'em."
Ben: "Ain't you mash 'em?"
Stella: "Mash a bed a day three task deep."
Ben: "Mashing raw ground half acre—some quarter. Mash 'em—take hoe full up them hole, level dem, chop dem big sod!"
Stella: (age 65) "You got a mis-sheen (machine). Ox pull dat mis-sheen!"
Ben: "Dat mis-sheen come in YOU day, darling! My day I trenching hoe trench dat! I done dat, Stella. You come on sow in trench lak (like) dey sow turnip. YOU day got mis-sheen! Ox pull 'em. Great I AM! Missus, fifteen to old

5. Plantations owned by the Rutledge family.
6. Dr. Ward Flagg.
7. Probably "Shallow fork in the right ear!"

Stella Horry at her home. *Photograph by Bayard Wootten. North Carolina Collection, University of North Carolina Library at Chapel Hill*

islant (island), twenty silver islant, (I been Silver Islant. Cross old islant go Silver islant.) Josh Ward one some four or five hundred acre. Something been here, darling! Something been here! Left Brookgreen go Watsaw; left Watsaw gone Longwood. Plant ALL DEM plantation. I work there. Cut rice there. Cutting rice task been half acre a day. "Squirrel creek? Cedar tree and cypress hang low. Squirrel love dem ball. Tree work up wid dem. Good place for go shoot squirrel. Give 'em name Squirrel Creek.

"Bury live? I did hear some talk o' that. I didn't know whether they bury 'em to scay 'em (scare 'em) or what. I DID hear tell bout it. I most know that man name. Some these white people that day something! They either manage you or kill you."

Lillie: (To Primus who was a listener to Uncle Ben standing propped by a post of the proch where Uncle Ben, Aunt Stella, and the white visitor sat) "Prime! Why you keep that church door lock Sunday and not let the Missus out?"

Primus: (Grinning—and he hadn't grinned Sunday but steadfastly shook his head when, after a three hour service, guests thought it time to go) "Second man next to me, Asham, Secretary, tell me keep door shet through sacrament."

Ben: (Who is quite deaf—ignoring interruption—when asked about Oregon Plantation which was owned by a family who, from all accounts, had a cruel overseer.[8])

"I didn't have to much to do to Oregon in them dark days. If I go from Brookgreen, I go Cap'n Josh git my mittment.[9] Anybody bother me I say, 'I not a run-way nigger! I got mittment!'

"Very FUSS girl—FUSS one I go with name wuz Teena. How many girl? Great God! I tell you! FUSS one Teena; next Candis. Candis best looking but Teena duh largest! Go there every Sunday after school. (Oatland Plantation—blong to Marse Benjamine Allston.) Stay till sunset. Got to have paper. Got to carry you paper. Dem patroller put you cross a log! Beat you to death. I see them beat Ben Sharp. Beat 'em till Ben kin hardly git cross fence. Jump over fence give 'em last chop! Patroll jess like road men now! (Stella! That man ain't coming! I got to go! Got to cook my supper Cook dem crab—) Blood! Christ! Yes, man. Listen me. Lemme tell you what I see wid my eye now! (here he prised both eyes wide with his ten fingers) If I much of age reckon they have to kill me! I see gash so LONG (measuring on fore-finger) in

8. Oregon plantation was owned by John D. Magill.

9. The exact term invoked here is not clear, but the meaning is certain. Ben Horry is talking about official papers given to a slave by his master that guaranteed safe passage between plantations.

my Mama—my own Mama! (aside to Lillie) I shame fore Miss Jinny! If one them driver want you (want big frame gal like you Lillie!) they give you task you CAN'T DO. You getting this beating not for you task—for you flesh!"
Lillie: "That why nation get mix up so'" (Races)
Ben: "Susan wuz a house woman, to buckra woman like a you to Miss Jin. (Susan worked in the house—no field hand—like Lillie works for Miss Jin) To my knowing she had three white chillun. Not WANT 'em. HAB 'em. Boy (you know 'em Lill) near bout clean as them boy of Missus! Tief chillun show up so! Woman over-power! My mother nuss (nurse.) Get up so high—natural nuss for white people.

"Place they call duh 'Bull Pen.' In 'Bull Pen'[10] thing they call 'PONY.' Got to go on there—on the 'PONY.'
Lillie: "RIDE you on it, Uncle Ben?"
Ben: "Ain't going ride you on 'PONY'; going RIDE YOU! I stay there look wid DESE HERE (eyes)! Want you to know onw thing—MY OWN DADDY DERE couldn't move! Couldn't venture dat ober-sheer! (Colored overseer) Everybody can't go to boss folks! (Meaning only house servants could contact Missus and Massa). Some kin talk it to Miss Bess.[11] Everybody don't see Miss Bess. Kin see the blood of dat ober-sheer fuss year atter Freedom; and he blood there today! Atter Freedom mens come from French Broad and you know the colored people—we go there whey (where) they music. Agrippa[12]—daddy name Parrish—Redmond one he child outside. (Outside chillun are those not born to a man's legal wife) He say, to gal. 'Go that barn!' YOU GO. You could yeddy him SLAP cross dat creek! When fowl crow (daylight) and you yeddy him SQUALL, you best git to flat! I stand dere and my Daddy HAVE to stand dere and see! Josh Ward from French Broad—hundred mile away. (Boss Massa 'summering it in mountains) and negro over seer—just fresh out of Africa TURNED LOOSE. White obersheer a little different for one reason! White obersheer want to hold his job. (On Waccamaw—and same true of all south as all know—white overseers worst kind of 'White trash'—respected less by negroes than by whites) Nigger obersheer don't care too much. He know he going stay on plantation anyhow.

"Now, dater, I tell you bout the loom and weaving next time!"

And we left Uncle Ben Horry—age 87

Murrells Inlet, S. C.

August 1937.

10. See page 47, note 7.
11. Elizabeth Ward, Joshua Ward's wife.
12. Agrippa Knox.

to go on 'to the Schoolfield house and cook supper for a house-party. This week he stepped up to Con-o-way. Says he had to walk it twice a week—formed the habit when he was on old river Steamer Burroughs and had to walk up to Conway Monday and back home Saturday. About thirty miles (or more from his place) to Conway. At 87 he still takes this little exercise almost weekly. Having such a struggle holding on to his land! All the lawyers saying 'sign here' and trying to rob him! Poor Uncle Ben needs desperately a Massa to help him out with his land. Not many Uncle Ben's left to be robbed—

(told that the cruel negro overseer was shot down after Freedom—blood still on the ground (accordingly to Uncle Ben) because he led Yankees to where silver, etc., was buried. Have heard story from other old livers.)

Uncle Ben Horry

Uncle Ben and his wife, aunt Stella, live in their two-room , white-washed cabin that sits sideways to the King's Highway, which Uncle Ben always calls ' the King Road , ' near Murrell's Inlet, S.C. Paving and straightening this old King's Road, now U.S. 17, has put the two old people in the world. Around the cabin lie the fourteen and three quarter acres that were paid for by Uncle Ben and his father, six or eight acres cleared, the rest woodland. Uncle Ben earns a living by gathering oysters from the Inlet's waters, opening and roasting the oysters for white visitors. Uncle Ben is a great walker. He walks to Conway, the county seat of Horry (Murrell's Inlet is situated on the line between Horry and Georgetown counties), a distance of approximately thirty miles depending on whether one sticks to the paved highway or takes short cuts through the woods , in preference to riding. One day he had walked to Conway and back by eleven o'clock in the morning. Uncle Ben's scrappy conversation will tell how he earns his bread, fears and fights 'the Law' , provides for Stella's future and works for and honors white folks. Brookgreen, which he mentions as the plantation on which he was born and raised, is an open-air museum, donated to South Carolina by A.M. Huntingdon,[13] and visited by thousands of tourists. (See S17, Tour 1).[14]

13. Archer Milton Huntington; see page 83, note 33.

14. A reference to another WPA project. "S17, Tour 1" is shorthand for "South Carolina, Volume 17, Tour #1." Around the same time Chandler was interviewing, WPA workers were inventorying and documenting sites of interest throughout the state. These records were ultimately published as *South Carolina: The WPA Guide to the Palmetto State.*

"I the oldest liver left on Waccamaw Neck that belong to Brookgreen, Prospect, now Arcadia), Longwood, Alderly Plantations. I been here! I seen things! I tell you. Thousand of them things happen but I try to forget 'em. Looker!" He pointed to what appeared to be primeval forest in front of his battered little porch. "That woods you see been Colonel Josh Ward's taters patch. Right to Brookgreen Plantation where I born. My father Duffine (Divine) Horry and my brother is Richard Horry. Dan'l and Summer two both my uncle. You can put it down they were Colonel Ward's musicianer. Make music for his dater (daughter) and the white folks to dance. Great fiddlers, drummers. Each one could play fiddle, beat drum, blow fife. All three were treat with the same education. You know, when you going to do anything for them big people you got to do it right. Before time (formerly) they danced different. Before strange city people fetched different steps here. But , then, they could use they feet all right!

"My father fore he dead been the head man for old Colonel Josh Ward. Lived to Brookgreen. They say Colonel Ward the biggest rice man been on Waccamaw. He start that big gold rice in the country. He the head rice Cap'n in dem time. My father the head man, he tote the barn key. Rice been money dem day and time. My father love he liquor. That take money. He ain't have money but he have the rice barn key and <u>rice</u> been money! So my father gone in the woods (he have a head, my father!) , take a old stump, have 'em hollow out. Now he (the stump) same as mortar to the barnyard. And my father keep a pestle hide handy. Hide <u>two</u> pestle! Them make pestle outer heart pine. When that pestle been miss (missed) I wuzn't know nothing! The way I knows my age, when the slavery time war come I been old enough to go in the woods with my father and hold a lightard (lightwood) torch for him to see to pestle off that golden rice he been tote out the barn and hide. <u>That</u> rice he been take to town Sat'd'y when the Colonel and my father go to get provision like sugar, coffee, pepper and salt. With the money he get when he sell that rice, he buy liquor. He been hide that sack o' rice fore day clean(daylight) in the prow of the boat and cover with a thing like an old coat. I members one day when he come back from town he make a miss (step) when he onloading and fell and broke he jug! The Big Boss see; he smell; and he see WHY my father make that miss step; he already sample that liquor! But the Boss ain't say too much. Sat'd'y time come to ration off. Every head on the Plantation to Brookgreen line up at smoke-house to draw he share of meat and rice and grits and meal. (This was fore my father been pint (appointed) head man. This when they had tight colored man in that place by name Fraser. They say Fraser come straight from Africa). Well, Sat'd'y when time come to give my father he share of rations, the headman reach down in the corner and pull out a piece of that broke whiskey jug and put on top my father rations where all could see! Colonel Ward cause that to be done to broke him off from that whiskey jug. My father was a steady liquor man till then and the Boss broke him off.

"Slavery going in. I members Marse Josh and Miss Bess had come from French Broad (Springs) where they summered it. They brought a great deal of this cloth they call blue drilling to make a suit for every boy big enough to wear a suit of clothes and a pair of shoes for every one. I thought <u>that</u> the happiest 'set-up' I had in boyhood. Blue drilling pants and coat and shoe. And Sund'y come we have to go to the Big House for Marse Josh to see how the clothes fit. And him and Miss Bess make us run races to see who run the fastest. That the happiest time I members when I wuz a boy to Brookgreen.

"Two Yankee gun boats[15] come up Waccamaw river! Come by us Plantation. One stop to Sandy Island, Montarena landing. One gone Watsaw(Wachesaw landing). Old Marse Josh[16] and all the white buckra gone to Marlboro county to hide from Yankee. Gone up Waccamaw river and up Pee Dee river, to Marlboro county, in a boat by name Pilot Boy. Take Colonel Ward and all the Cap'n to hide. from gun boat till peace declare. I think Pilot Boy been a rear-wheeler. Most boats like the Old Planter been side wheeler.

"They say the Yankee broke in all the rice barn on Sandy Island and share the rice out to colored people. The big mill to Laurel Hill been burn right den. That the biggest rice mill on Waccamaw river. Twuzn't the Yankee burn dem mill. Dese white mens have a idea the Yankee mean to burn dese mills so they set 'em afire before the Yankee come. Nothing left to Laurel Hill today but the rice mill tower.[17] That old brick tower going to BE there. Fire can't harm 'em.

"The worst thing I members was the colored oberseer. He was the one straight from Africa. He the boss over all the mens and womens and if omans don't do all he say, he lay task on 'em they ain't able to do. My mother won't do all he say. When he say, 'You go barn and stay till I come,' she ain't do 'em. So he have it in for my mother an lay task on 'em she ain't able for do. Then for punishment my mother is take to the barn and strapped down on thing called the Pony. Hands spread like this and strapped to the floor and all two both she feet been tie like this. And she been give twenty five to fifty lashes

15. See page 46, note 2, on Federal gunboats in the Waccamaw River.

16. Though Horry refers here to his former master as "old," he must be talking about Captain Joshua Ward who was in his thirties at the time. Colonel Joshua John Ward died in 1853.

17. The tower still stands. Surrounded by mammoth trees, it is barely visible from the river.

till the blood flow. And my father and me stand right there and look ain't able to lift a hand! Blood on floor in that rice barn when barn tear down by Hontington (A.M. Huntingdon). If Marse Josh been know 'bout that obersheer, the oberseer can't do 'em; but just the house servant get Marse Josh' and Miss Bess' ear. Them things different when my father been make the head man. What I tell you happen fore Freedom, when I just can remember.

"Father dead just before my mother. They stayed right to Brookgreen Plantation and dead there after they free. And all they chillun do the same, till the Old Colonel sell the plantation out.[18] Where we going to? Ain't we got house and rations there?

"How many chillun I got? Lemme see. Lemme see how many head of chillun. You, Stella! Help me now! Don't let me tell the Missis wrong. Charles Henry, thirty eight, dere in New York. Ben Horry—I gie' 'em directly!" (Lifting cap and scratching high forehead and gray wool). "Twenty four. I going to give you all I got! All I know about! Bill Horry, that's a boy, he twenty. Dinah, that's a gal, twenty five. Christine, she bout twenty. Mary Horry, I would say fifteen. When the last war come, the last war deputize them boy and take 'em way up North and the gals follow , trail 'em on to New York.[19] That the war when you can't get no sugar and have to put candy in your coffee.

"How old I is?" Slowly and deliberately "December 13th., 1852. Eighty five years or more. When my mother dead to Brookgreen. I would say I 'bout thirty three year old.

"After Freedom, from my behavior wid my former owner, I wuz pinted (appointed) head man on Brookgreen Plantation. By that put drop in my hand (getting the drop on others). When kennel been dug out (canal dug) from the Oaks Plantation to Dr. Wardie Flagg house, I wuz pint (appointed) head man. Take that down. Missis. Kennel (canal) cut 1877. Near as I kin, I must task it on the kennel (canal) and turn in every man's work to Big Boss. That kennel(canal) bigger than one Mr. Hontingdon dig right now with machine.

"Missus, slavery time people done something."

Uncle Gabe Lance, born on Sandy Island the first year of the Civil War, a visitor at Uncle Ben's : "Yes sir. All them rice field been nothing but swamp.

18. Upon his death in 1853, Joshua John Ward left Brookgreen to his son Joshua Ward. After Joshua Ward's death in 1869, his father's will was contested and the central portion of Brookgreen went to Joanna D. Ward, who in turn sold the property to her former son-in-law Dr. Lewis C. Hasell.

19. World War I.

Slavery people cut kennel(canal) and dig ditch through the raw swamp. All these fields been thick woods. Ditching man task was ten compass. "

Uncle Ben continues: "Storm? Ain't I tell you I BEEN here? Yes, sir. More than one storm I live through! Been through the Flagg storm. Been turn over twice outside there in the sea. One time been have the seine. Been rough. Have weather. And the breakers take the boat. I swim till I get the rope hold. Two men on the shore have the rope end of the seine rope and I hold to that and that how I save THAT time.

" Member another time. Had a boat full of people this last go 'round. Wuz Miss Mary, he aunty and the lawyer. I take them fishing outside in oshun. Been in the Inlet mouth. Come half way to Drunken Jack Island. Breaker start to lick in the boat! I start to bail! Have a maters (tomatoes) can for bail with. And that been danjus (dangerous); have too much women in there; dey couldn't swim like a man. And it happen by accident, when the boat swamp and full with water, our FEET TOUCH BOTTOM. When he (the boat) turn over, I didn't aim to do no/thing but swim for myself. Wasn't able to help nobody. But here out feet touch bottom. Only an accident from God!

"One time again I swamp outside, 'tween Georgetown and Charleston. Try to bail. Swim with one hand, hold with the other. Roughest time I ever see 'cause it been cold wedder (weather). Old before-time yawl boat, carry eight oar, four to each side. Young man then ; 1877. After the wedder (weather) surrender, we we gone back in dere and find cork going up and down and save us not and all!

"When the Flagg storm been, 1893, I working for Ravanel and Holmes.[20] I was taken up in that storm in a steamer boat. Leave Charleston generally about five in the morning. That trip never reach Georgetown till nine that night. Meet a man on that trip got he wife hug to a mast in a little kinder life boat. Had he two chillun; rope wrap 'em to that mast. Serve man and wife and chillun and gone back and save some of he trunk. After that they quit call me 'Ben' ; they call me 'Rooster.'

"After Flagg storm, Colonel Ward take me and Peter Carr, us two and a horse, take that shore (follow the ocean shore line) to Little River. Search for all them what been drowned. Find a trunk to Myrtle Beach. Have all kinder thing in 'em; comb for you hair, thing you put on you wrist. Find dead horse, cow, ox, turkey, fowl—everything Gracious God! Don't want to see no more thing like that! But no dead body find on beach outside Flagg family. Find two them chillun way down to Dick Pond what drowned to Magnolia Beach; find them in a distance apart from here to that house. Couldn't 'dentify

20. A Charleston shipping company.

wedder Miss or who. All that family drown out because they wouldn't go to this lady house on higher ground. Wouldn't let none of the rest go. Servant all drown! Betsy, Kit, Mom Adele! Couldn't 'dentify who lost from who save till next morning. Find old Doctor body by he vest stick out of the mud; fetch Doctor body to shore and he watch still aticking. Dr. Wardie Flagg been save hanging to a beech cedar. When that tornado come, my house wash down off he blocks. Didn't broke up.

Religion? Reckon Stella got the morest of dat. I sometimes a little quick. Stella, she hold one course. I like good song. One I like best? "

> 'Try us, Oh Lord,
> And search the ground
> Of every sinful heart ! (Uncle Ben stopped to think).
> What 'eer of sin
> In us be found
> Oh, bid it all depart!

"Reason I choose that for a favorite hymns, I was to Brookgreen doing some work for Dr. Wardie Flagg and I had to climb as high as that live oak tree, and I fell high as that tree! I lay there till I doze off in sleep. And I tell you what happen to me curious. While I was sleep I seen two milk white chickens. You know what them two white fowl do? They gone and sit on my mother dresser right before the glass and sing that song. Them COULD sing! And it seem like a woman open a vial and pour something on me. My spiritual mother (in dem day every member in the church have what they call a spiritual mother) say, 'That not natural fowl. That sent you for a token.'[21] Since that timeI serve the choir five or six years and no song seem strange to me since that day. God ain't ax about you color; God ax about you heart.

"Make my living with the ister (oyster). Before time (formerly) I get seventy five cents a bushel; now I satisfy with fifty cents. Tide going out, I go out in a boat with the tide; tide bri g me in with sometimes ten, sometimes fifteen or twenty bushels. I make white folks a roast; white folks come to Uncle Ben from all over the country—Florence, Dillon, Mullins—every kind of place. Same price roast or raw, fifty cents a bushel.

"I bout to quit up with sell. All the lawyer. Turn all my papers over to Mr. Burris.[22] I got too much of paper in that Con-o-way. Court House,. Got more paper in there than the house worth! Have to step to Conoway all the time. Struggle and starve myself out for these fifteen acres,. Thirty miles to

21. A token is a sign of supernatural significance.
22. Conway lawyer Franklin G. Burroughs.

Con-o-way. Thirty miles back by the course I travels. All them tricky mens try to go and get old Ben's land sign to 'em. That's the mainest thing take me to Con-o-way every week. They all talk so sugar mouth till my name down; then when my name write is another thing. When I in to much trouble, I just has to step up to Con-o-way and see Mr. Burris. He's a good man.

"They try to mix old Ben up in this whiskey business. It look too brutish to me."

"Missus, I want to tell you all I kin but the old man punish with this bone felom (felon) . Worse'n I ever been punish in all my eighty five year. Crab bite' em and ister (oyster) cut 'em (hand). Woman die and bury Sunday have hand just like this. If you say so, I'll go to the doctor. Don't want no blood poison. He (bone felon)[23] did act like he trying to dry up. I tie pea leaf on 'em. Can't put my hand to my head.

The next day Uncle Ben was found with the doctor's white bandage very muddy. Uncle Ben had gotten out of bed to go get oysters and even the bone felon did not stop him. Uncle Ben is still hale and hearty, having triumphed over the bone felon, and is one of the noted characters of that region.

(Uncle Ben Horry (Reb's Time Nigger—over 80)
(Uncle Ben and visitors)

Uncle Ben: (To white children) "Go on see if you can find one or two plum on duh tree. I been want to go to town wid you—dat all right daughter. (He pronounces it Dater—long Italian 'A') Chillun, ain't find duh plum, enty? Dem Sandy Island people come and clean the tree. Too sorry wonneh ain't get them plum!

"Stella gone in creek fishing. Him and Lula gone—Lula McCoy. You say me?" (To neighbor walking up) "Four men been here load they car up wid hand. How come you ain't gone to the bacco?" (To work in the tobacco fields in truck sent to find hands)

Pauline Pyatt: "If they ain't pay my price, I ain't going leave home. I ain't gone for 75¢ a day. Feenie Deas gone yestiddy."

Uncle Ben: "Near bout blind. Couldn't see out no eye nor nare (neither) one o' my eye. Doctor put sumptin in 'em do me too much o' good. How I is? Fall out? Deth come I fix![24] Don't know bout you!"

Pauline: "I fix!"

Mary Gary: "You fix, Uncle Ben?"

Uncle Ben: "I gwine fix!"

23. Bone felon, an abscess caused by a serious infection, usually located in the fingers.
24. Ben Horry is certain that his soul is fixed, or saved.

Pauline: "You ain't fix?"
Uncle Ben: "I fix all right! I going fudder dan duh grave!"
Pauline: "I been Tarbox." (To Mr. Tarbox)[25]
Uncle Ben: "Down by Gallie?" (Gallie's house)
Pauline: "I ain't see nobody. What you see?"
Uncle Ben: "Ain't see nobody tall—tall-."
Pauline: "Alice! I see Alice!"[26]
Uncle Ben: "Ain't see nobody else?"
Pauline: "Nobody else!"
Uncle Ben: "Nobody else?"
Pauline: "Nobody else. She by herself!"

Uncle Ben Reminisces

"Fore freedom? Fore freedom? Well now, fore freedom we were treated by our former owners I will say good—cording to situation of time. Every year when Massa and Missus gone mountains,[27] they call up obersheer (overseer) and say, 'Don't treat them anyway severe. Don't beat them. Don't maul them.' (Mr. Hemingway[28] been severe.)

"Anybody steal rice and they beat them, Miss Bessie[29] cry and say, 'Let 'em have rice! My rice—my nigger!'

"Brookgreen and Springfield every Sunday morning, every gal and the young one must dress up and go to the yardand Miss Bessis give 'em candy. Don't want too much o' beating. Glad to see young women dance. But some cruel to the colored. Some on 'Prospect,'—'Hermitage'—and 'Woodland' treat all right.

"I know Yankee boat came to Inlet and went to Oaks sea-shore with load of cotton. Band of our sojer gone—(Rebs—'OUR sojer!), and Yankee sojer come off in a yawl boat and our sojer caught two of them men and they hang that man to Oaks sea-shore. And when the Yankee find out—do my Lord! A stir been! A stir here! Shell clean to Sandy Island! Knock hole through the sick-house (at Brookgreen!) Pump! Well, ain't it? Brick work pump. Well. Handle. You turn! Turn. One bucket gone up; one gone down. Ward take

25. Frank G. Tarbox.

26. Alice Kinloch.

27. During the malarial season, the wealthy planters sought refuge from the mosquito-infested rice fields.

28. J. A. Hemingway and Thomas Hemingway were two of Robert F. W. Allston's white overseers.

29. Elizabeth R. Ward.

care of his nigger, sho! Best man own slave! Ward and Ploughdon[30] sho treat they nigger right! Live 'Laurel Hill.'

"Ward had on Prospect and Brook-green. You know what I see? Right there in Oaks sea-sho after them people done that murdering with that man? Take all the slave, get on flat and gone out way of shell. Gone sand hole.[31] Take all the people from Brookgreen and Springfield—and carry dem Marlboro. Boat tow flat. Carmichael[32] came through and established the freedom through here. They come back from Marlboro where they refugee to and Maham Ward come back on the flat. And this Ward, share out the rice—broke open barn. We people? Anything like a silver, bury right there in that garden! Right to Brookgreen garden, what Hontington got now. All Ward thing bury there. Them old time people kill you—you meddle them thing. Cry out, 'Massa Ting!' You better let 'em stay there!

"After Freedom Miss Bessie gone to she house in Charston—Rutledge Street Charston. And you could see way out in ocean.

"My fadder—him and Uncle Dan'l and Uncle Summer uster been fiddler. Gone all round when the white people gone to Prospect to ball and sich as that. Dem white people didn't treat you so brutish! Dem obersheer!"

(Aside) "Wonder Christ sake why Lula stay out that creek so long!"

Pauline: "Fine season for corn!"

Ben: "Sho is!"

(Uncle Ben keeps a little grocery and fruit for sell. Customer comes)

"Missus, Take twenty cent out of dollar."

Pauline: "My grand-mother in that storm. They leave that Thursday. I been to Oaks. When Flagg storm wuz. Richmond come off Magnolia beach to Oaks Plantation and get the washing—the missus clean clothes. Had to swim the horse off the beach to get the clothes. I been on the beach Thursday—and cousin Joshua-way. Pony Myers daughter born in Brookgreen street day of the storm. Pony Myers wife name Adele. Marsa Arthur had one little twin.[33] Joshua Stuart and Ben find dem to the end of Myrtle Beach. Arthur twin baby—bout that high—little walking chillun. Look how curious thing is! Them two chillun drown and find to the foot of Myrtle Beach! (fifteen

30. Plowden Charles Jennet Weston (1820–1864) owned Laurel Hill, Hagley, True Blue, Waterford, and Weehawka plantations.

31. Sand Hole Creek.

32. This was probably the Union officer who oversaw informing the slaves of their freedom.

33. Arthur Belin Flagg Jr. and his wife, Martha LaBruce Flagg, had twins who died in the Flagg storm.

or twenty miles north). Find Tom Duncan mother. Find Francis mother—Francis Gadsden. Doctor Ward pa[34]—find him by duh vest. Vest sticking out duh mud. Watch going. My grand-mother was keep a walking from door ro door.

"Find a mer-maid and kept to magnolia." (Pauline said, !mere-maid') "Doctor Ward and dem shut 'em up a month. Mer-maid. Had a storm ball. Keep a turning round. Keep a telling him (Dr. Arthur)[35] storm coming. He wouldn't b'lieve 'em. (Barometer—called by Uncle Isaac's wife, gatekeeper at Brookgreen, chronometer.) He wouldn't b'lieve. And a cussing man! All the time cuss! Mere-maid got a forked tail just like shark. From here down (illustrating by pantomime) all blue scale like a cat-fish. Pretty people! Pretty a white woman as you ever lay your eye on."

Ben: "Pretty, enty?"

Pauline: "Dem stay in sea. Dey walk—slide long on tail." (twisting from her waist to illustrate.) Pretty. From they waist down to tail blue scale. You got a bathing house on beach. Leave bread in there. They sho eat bread.

"Marse Allard say top of the barn fly off. Cat jump and on it! And horse too. And he jump too and tide bring 'em to Brookgreen.

"Joshuaway Stuart been plantation carpenter. He made one box for the twin what drown and Colonel Mortimer bring one from Georgetown."

(Aunt Stella and Lula arriving from fishing trip)

"What ketch?"

Lula: "Get some catty!" (cat-fish) "Mary, you dress down!"

Mary: "I gwine ketch me a fellow! (Looking in bucket)

Gosh! Did got a good mess!"

Lula: "Little fellow."

Mary: "Rather eat them large one."

Pauline: "What yinnah nuse for bait?"

Lula: "Swimp."

Pauline: "How you catch 'em?"

Lula: "Take a crocus and dip 'em up."

Pauline: "I gwine try to-morrow."

Lula: "To-morrow been Sundy! How old I is? Have to put a guess on 'em. Bout fifty I guess. Flagg storm? That big one? When the storm wuz, I wuz seven year old."

34. Joshua John Ward Flagg's father was Arthur Belin Flagg.

35. Arthur Belin Flagg.

(Discuss Reb time and Flagg storm.)

Pauline: "Yes. Wind bring young Allard in to Uncle Joshua-way Stuart field right down there where Cindy Poinsett now. Joshuaway been Cindy Pa.

"Doctor Ward shut that mere-maid up. He been in that! When that storm wuz, he wuzn't old. I go there now and talk bout that storm and he eye get full o' water. Looker his Papa clothes. Got 'em all pack in trunk. I never shee 'um court myself. Every time I shee 'um with a crowd o' man.

"Long as he have mere-maid shut up, it rain! People gone there to look at 'em. Long as keep 'em shut up it rain. That time rain thirty days. That just fore Flagg storm." (Looking toward creek) "Yonder Stella, wonneh, now!"

(Uncle Ben gave each white child a little cake—then gave from his hand, hunks of corn bread to each colored woman.)

Conversation taken down on Uncle Ben Horry's porch where he sat awaiting the return of Aunt Stella who had gone 'in the creek' to 'catch a mess o' fish.'
Murrells Inlet, S. C.
June 15, 1937.

(Verbatim)
Miss Georgie at Woodland
Ex-slave Story

"He was a full-blooded man—the Cap'n. Didn't disgrace. He put goat on Goat Island.[36] Money was bury to Goat Island. People after people been sent. I dinnah know wedder they find or no.

"Mack McCosky was sent by the State to fetch molasses, meal and hominy and goat on Goat Island. He can't tell you! People can't know sumpin when they ain't born!

"After de war 'e come back and take into big drinkin' and was'em (waste them) till 'e fall tru. He been fell tru wid his money (lost his property). Didn't bury so destent (decent).

"We smaller one didn't have chance to go to war. My Daddy have for go. Have to go ditch and all and tend his subshun. His subshun was waste and steal. Paris! He the man control all the Buckra ting. And, by God, he go and show Yankee all dem ting! Ole Miss git order to have him kill and don't harm none! She ain't one to see him tru all that thousand head o' nigger for get 'em.

"They come have big dinner. Cap'n come from Maldro. (Marlboro). Drum beatin' little one dancin'. Gone back to Muldro. (Maham Ward and these udder come from Muldro.) And they leave ting in Uncle William Baillard

36. Goat Island was at the mouth of Murrells Inlet. The hurricane of 1893 killed all of the trees, leaving it little more than a marsh bank.

hand. And he carry on till everting surrender. And then the Cap'n come home from Muldro and they try give you sumpin to make start on like cow and ting. They ain't treat you like a beast. Ain't take no advance o' you. What the Cap'n do he do for you good. I b'long Dr. Ward.[37] I entitle to bring him two string o' bird. Rice bird come like jest as tick as dat (thick as that) Sometimes a bushel one shot.

"They put you in the flat and put you over there. When they tink Yankee comin' you take to Sandhole Crick for hide. Mr. Carmichael sent by the state. Go to Brookgreen, Longwood, Watsaw. Tell everting surrender. Go to any located place. He's a Gineral. Go open the barn door and give us all us need. He better to we nigger boy dan he Daddy been! Wouldn't beat you 'thout the lil' boy really fightin'.

"Time o' the war the colored people hear 'bout Yankee. Not a one eber understand to run way and go to Yankee boat from WE plantation. These Yankee people wuz walkin' 'bout on the beach. And while they come in to the hill, the Reb have a battery to Laurel Hill and they cut off them Yankee from the ocean. These they cut off they carry dem to Brookgreen barn. Hang one colored man and one white man to Oaks Seashore. White man musser be Sergeant or big Cap'n. Just as soon as the sun go down you see a big streak come over and they BUSS (bust) Duds. Woman in the street killed. (Street of negro Quarters—Brookgreen) Blacksmith killed. Cut off he brudder-in-law (Judy's) and kill Judy. Dem shell go clean to Sandy Island. Pump make out o' brick to Brookgreen. Dat boy (shell) come and hit the pump. De horn blow and they make for flat and gwine on to Sandhole down that black crick. There a man for dat—dat flat. Get everbody line up. Ain't gone there for PLAY. Gone for wuk (work). I wuz big 'nouf to do diss—go wid my fadder and hold light.

"It this way. You ain't LOW to eat the whole rice you kin make money outer. Beat dat rice. But my Daddy been a great whiskey man. Liquor. Didn't have 'em less he go to town. Money scase. ('E wuz a kind of musicianer for the Ward fambly). But he break he jug. He break he whiskey jug. En when de obersheer (overseer) git out de ration and gib'em to mah Ma and us chillun he hand mah Pa a piece o' dem break jug! That keep him in mind o' that whiskey jug.

"Yankee come here and butt us colored people. I 'member we youngun's just could 'tote up dem gold pitcher and bury dem in the garden. Not far from the flowers tank. Tank have on 'em a woman head (Flowers' tank was a fountain). All the master fine ting way down there bury! De Ward didn't lose nothin'. They move us out the plantation. Col. Ward took 'em in a flat to Mulbro.

37. Joshua Ward.

"Dr. Heriot[38] after the war took into big drinkin'. Didn't bury so decent. Fell tru wid all he money. Not bury so decent."

SOURCE: *Told by Uncle Ben Horry, Age 88, April 1938, Murrells Inlet, S. C.*

Uncle Ben Talks 'bout the Old Doctor

Questioner: "Uncle Ben, how long did you know the old Doctor?"[39]
Uncle Ben: "I been wid the doctor. I been wid he Daddy 'fore he born. And when I fetch rice-bird he just old enough to take'em outer my hand. I goin' tell you what God please wid and the Debbil hate. I nebber know him to bodder wid no woman since he old enough to know what woman was. But he brudder?[40] Glory to God, he catch at he own shadow. Glory to God take'em all long he path. Didn't pass none. The old Doctor got a life time character with the people he gwine long with.

"You hear 'bout the Big Storm? I take thought in 1893 storm. Doctor he have enough to make a man study and stop. There all his family—thirteen head—drownded and gone right out to sea. And him and little girl two leave hangin' on bush of beach cedar.

"After that all bury and gone and Doctor stay in that house a year and don't come out. And I tell you God's truth, that right when the Doctor turn to he toddy. The whiskey keg what he buy would full this place up to the top! Long as you there, white or colored, he say, 'Take a little toddy!'

"If we get to Heaven, white or colored, and the old Doctor not there, I say and John Bunyan say: 'It a great wonder!' (John Bunyan say that out the Bible) If I get there and I begin to look 'round and Doctor not there I think I land the wrong place!

"Daughter, you got what I say set down? When old Ben gone, if anybody give you that good testimony I tell you"bout Doctor 'bout ME he tell what not so! When you goin' talk 'bout God's departed man, tell God's truth!

"Doctor and these neighbor ladies, them visit. Doctor and he two brudder in they noung day had visit them ladies. And one noung lady seem to catch on to the Doctor. They does right them day. Doesn't have car; have horse. Drive out to the Chapel; drive out to beach. No spotted character.

"Colored people watch white people, but they don't tell on they Missus and Maussa. They see and they know. They tricky, Can't be fool!

"The Preacher tease the old Doctor way back yonder to gone out with girl but I don't think my Doctor been study girl.

38. Dr. Robert Stark Heriot (1830–1859), son of Dr. Edward Thomas Heriot (1793–1859), owner of Mont Arena plantation on Sandy Island.

39. Dr. Ward Flagg.

40. Arthur Belin Flagg or Charles Eben Belin Flagg.

"Clarissa—Clarissa Horry—hang on that same beach cedar in the storm. Clarissa a waitin' gal to he Mama. The other day when the Doctor bury, like the old Doctor gone and bury today, Clarissa who was with him in the storm die and bury tomorrow. He and Clarissa catch on the same tree. Here the doctor bury today, this gal gone tomorrow.

"Tom Ma, Adele, didn't save on that same tree. Tom little brudder drown. Francis Gadsden have sister drown. Old lady Adele gone out! Clarissa, the little waiting girl, come home live. No chance for a boat. First breaker so strong wash up big, strong oak by root. Breaker LICK off roof! And Marse Allard get on that. He servant get on that. Horse and dog get on that. "(White people tell it horse swam along behind in wake)" I didn't gone myself but Brook Green have hundreds of man. Fetch him and carry him home. Carry Marse Allard home too. Old Doctor not stay to he house. Not stay to he house all night. Gone to us street where he not grieve hisself for company. Two little girl gone out so far two body wash up to middle of Myrtle Beach. Ribbon on they hair—Yaller ribbon. When me and Peter Carr gone to body, Morty Ward, the Senator, gone with us. After the storm I gone over there in boat 'cause they goin' deputise anybody they got belief in, anybody with character to look out for box and trunk and thing. I and Peter Carr even get the bracelet!

"You got Doctor Ward now 'cause ain't a soul can 'spute dat!

"I got a wife home all right but if I tells you what God love and the Debbil hate (You ain't want what the Debbil love?) I DOES like the Missy folks. My Ma been one, you know! And ever since I know my Ma, I been runnin' after the womens."

SOURCE: *Uncle Ben Horry*
Murrells Inlet, S. C.
Age 88 years. 1938

Uncle Ben Horry
Ex-slave

Nothing about slavery.

Description: Mr. Baruch[41] shot Ben—on grounds of trespassing; tells physical effect and injustice. Being land owner has caused Ben great suffering; apparently victim of unethical lawyers; unbalanced now from fear of losing land.

Negro neighbor says Ben tried to sell land owned jointly by self and sister without paying her; she had lawyer make him pay her.

41. Joe Baruch, cousin of financier Bernard Baruch who owned 17,000 acres of plantation land at the foot of Waccamaw Neck.

Also accused of bootlegging—turned out of church. White competitor ruined business; penitent (wept) , Ben was welcomed back by preacher.

Uncle Ben Horry
Ex-Slave

Uncle Ben was seeking light on a dull day with the wind north-east. Hanging on the wall of his front 'proach' (porch) was a mirror in a quaint oval frame, and seated before the mirror with one leg of his chair precariously near a big crack, was Uncle Ben.

"Where you going, Uncle Ben?"

Uncle Ben smiled his quick, sly smile and still facing the mirror, razor poised, cut his eyes side-ways.

"Ain't gwine no-whey (where). Just take so much o'hair off my face!"

Visitor: "Tell me about why you were shot?"

"When I shoot? All that shot go from here to here!" (And Uncle ben started at his waist line and carried his two wide spread hands to his feet.)

"Dr. Dick[42] count 'em! He got 'em in he book and got 'em to the law office in Georgetown! Dr. Dick get eight man and counted fifty-two shot in me! Thirty-two in the bucket and fifty-two in me! He didn't have nothing to kill my flesh, so he could go down fudder—probe down in dere. He want all dem shot out but I take a risk. He give me two dost o' medicine. And then five more shot worked out! That sho been strong medicine. Musser been strong. One day I went long and something keep eeching and eeching me! (itching) And I loose my pants and take my knife and scrape it a little and shot drop right out. I take 'em and look on 'em and say, 'Tank God!' Lot o' white people fraid I'll blood pizen. I say, 'He (the shot) won't blood pizen!'

One day bucket been in my hand. Going to Miss Mary[43] house. Boy come here tell me somebody been break in Miss Mary house. I rush by Mr. Baruchs proach, And when I git to Miss Mary house, trunk broke open and silver took! I come on back and Mr. Baruchs say, 'Ain't I tell you stay off my land?' And I tell 'em where I been rush to when I hear tief gone in Miss Mary house, and I in charge of she plantation in the winter time. He have he gun on front proach.

And he say,'I tell you keep you foots off this land!'

And I tell 'em he ain't never pay me for the land no how.

42. Dr. Dick Willcox.

43. Mary Buck, a woman who owned a house near Woodland. Ben Horry occasionally watched this house.

And he raise he gun and I ain't know what hit me. Quart or two quart o' blood in the bucket. Have bucket in my hand. Stella hear shot. She been hail. She know I been in the jam with Mr. Baruchs. He wife been make 'greement to pay Stella for two weeks work with a overcoat—and she move the buttons and all so he kin fit Stella but after that shooting that overcoat forgot 'bout.

"Every time Doctor cut a shot out, some them eight men hold me! Bone felom hurt me and hurt me hard, but when them shot been take out o' me I ain't know wedder I been in hell or Heaven!

"Then he (Mr. Baruch) do that ditement! (Indictment) Next thing Cap'n Oliver come down here wid he pistol. I right dere standing up. He say,

'What you and Mr. Baruchs fussing 'bout?'

I say, 'right been right, you know! You duh sheriff?'

He say, "'I talk to Baruchs and tell 'em he could get on better wid the colored people than dese darn po-buckra!' I tell 'em (tell Mr. Oliver) Mr. Baruchs tell me, 'Uncle Ben can't go on beach shore for roast he ister (oyster) and can't walk cross he bridge.' That make Stella and me wade in deep mud to hit the stream. Phone sheriff. He come. Say,

"'Uncle Ben, move you ister! Ain't want Mr. Baruchs to shoot the old men!'

"And now Mr. Baruchs got that beach, and that lawyer got that point yonder! No principal white person wanter go to that point now! Man there selling liquor. Take all Uncle Ben beach but I got my yard! When they call, I tell 'em 'Come right to my door! Stella, help me start fire round these ister for the Buckra!' White people come to Uncle Ben and Stella! But they got me BEX! Fust Baruchs say I sign that land way to him; I get lawyer; he take mortgage on me for straighten out Baruchs and now lawyer say I sign way to him! I tell you Missus, I got more paper to court house than the building worth! Mr. Burris take charge! I quit wid lawyer.

"How many mile to where I get ister? How much mile to Drunking Jack? Bout a mile if you go straight. But then you can't go straight! Far as I can guess it, must be bout two mile!"

(The neighbors, black and white, say when not hiking to Con-o-way to straighten out his legal affairs, Uncle Ben walks for miles and miles and miles in the woods and along the isolated woods' roads. Sometimes he carries a gun and is supposedly squirrel hunting. It is the accepted theory that fear of losing his land has him worried until he is a bit unbalanced—not able to stay put. He tried various lawyers, and Uncle Ben's land having been put on the map, and becoming of value when the new highway came through, seems to have been a bait lawyers found it hard to resist. Each one he consulted affected his faith in the 'law' till now he's just quit off with the law. Worry has him with the wandering sickness.)

A black neighbor says:
Zackie:[44] "I tell you jest how it is. Uncle Ben try to sell it out from under he sister unbeknowst to HER and she jest wheel back and got a lawyer and make Uncle Ben pay her part. What he was after was getting it all—not letting her get no share.

"Nother thing bad—Uncle Ben nuster sell likker and it happened the Revents been there the day some people come to buy it. You know in US church always turn people out of church when you finds 'em selling liquor. Then Uncle Ben quit for awhile. (Had to quit. White man set up a liquor place by him and cut him out.)

And when he had to stop—gone on to Reb (the Revents) and cry and cry and he take him back. Reb stood up in church and give him welcome fore the congregation. Said, "'Here's the wandering sheep come back in the fold.'"

44. Zackie Knox.

Bobbitt Horry

Horry's interview, with its charming children's song in the middle and the overall variety of its discussion, presents her as a loquacious subject. Horry comments on her work as a wet nurse, the Flagg storm, her fear of hags, feeding her cow, and working in Charleston. According to the 1900 U.S. Census, Bobbitt Horry was born in December 1854. The same report lists Ben Horry's birth as September 1859. Bobbitt Horry claims, however, "Uncle Ben and me one year chillun'" (meaning, they were born the same year). In 1938 Chandler placed Ben Horry's age at eighty-eight. However, the 1930 census lists Bobbitt Horry's age as sixty-eight, which would have made her more than ten years his junior. Bobbitt Horry's maiden name was Pine. Her father was William Pine. Pine obtained his surname from his mother and did not know his father. Bobbitt married the carpenter Joseph Horry. They had six children together: Prissilla, Delia, Rosena, Gabriel, Joseph, and James. Census data from 1930 also indicates that Horry had her daughter Rosa and two grandchildren, Lisa (age sixteen) and Josh (age twelve), living with her at the time.

"Aunt Stella Aunty, Mom Bobbitt, is a sweet old soul. Make a nice prayer to Brookgreen Sunday.

'You better to us than we to ourselves. Ain't but me one! When I get down on my straw bed and the covering get too short—winding up time must come!' (The bed you sleep on sometimes too short after you die! Every nerve—every vein stretch!) 'When I stretch on the cooling board, I ax Master Jesus to stand by me!'

Mom Bobbitt's prayer reported by
Lillie Knox—age 35
Murrells Inlet, S. C.

Ex-slave Talks
Aunt Bobbitt Horry

Bobbitt: "To Bookgreen they have a large house in the middle of the street. Big house. Three chimbley to'em. Set right there for all the chillun. Call that the NUSS (nurse) house. In the mornin' all the chillun fetch to the nuss house.

"How old I is? Uncle Ben and me one year chillun.

"Old hag? I don't talk dem. I too fear dem! I did been Bobbitt Pino. William Pino[1] carry he Mammy title. She give him no Pa.

"Song 'bout the hag? I sing to chillun that I didn't put HAG in'em.

> 1. "Mammy, you see Bobbitt?
> No! No!
> Mammy you see Bobbitt?
> No! No!
> Every where Bobbitt gone
> He carry you bubby gone!
> (Note: Bubby—is 'nindy, titty'—breast milk)
>
> Papa, you see Bobbitt?
> No! No!
> Papa, you see Bobbitt?
> No! No!.
> Every where Bobbitt gone
> He carry you bubby gone![2]

(Note: Aunt Bobbitt was a wet nurse for colored children.)

"That boy look like he cripple. All hump up. My boy tell me 'bout see him. I tell my boy I hope he ain't laugh atter him.

"I 'member too good that storm.[3] Call dem the Doctor storm. We have a place we call a loft. Leak? Rain through like out doors.

"We hear a whooper and a holler. My old man he went to the door and lis'n! He say: 'The hollerin' say the BEACH GONE!'

"We get in the street and here Summer Horry streakin'! We come for see we self! Get to Clam Bank. Here Tom Duncan come crackin'. Say: 'I wanter see Ma and I can't see Ma! Ma wanter see me and can't see me!'

1. Bobbitt Horry's father.
2. John A. Lomax made an audio recording of Bobbitt Horry singing this song.
3. The Flagg storm.

"Foggy! But you could see that time 'cross the marsh. By ten o'clock sun come cut TOO pretty. You could see the storm leave but one house on Magnolia. That Mrs. Hazel house.

"People was thick like marsh grass on that point. All was cryin':

"The old Doctor[4] gone! Miss Georgia[5] gone!'

"They had bring the young doctor[6] 'cross in a boat. All he clothes had wash off. They had take him to Mr. Hazel to put on him some clothes. He stand there and look. Not talk. Look. Seem like my heart wanter bust. To Clam Bank that day people stand like THAT," (Aunt Bobbitt laced her fingers together to show the people were so thick they were touchin').

"Now here young Doctor get tired and he gone too. Time come".

Annette[:][7] "Yes! I been there. Such a pretty funel! (funeral) I shake and hand with the people. All he people come to the funel. Marse Franz come from Newberry; Miss Florence, she been there. I talk one or two talk with dem."

Aunt Bobbitt: "Time of storm young Allard[8] come cross with he horse. All the people out the street collect up to Vettril Deas house. I tell new not what I SEE; this what I HEAR! They tell Miss Georgie been hang on a bush. She could save but she turn loose and gone to him—and they hug up. He call: 'My dear, come where I is!' The young doctor hold on to what he got. And he say: 'Lord, have mercy!'

"He oldest daughter didn't been there. Him save! Him save! And the day she baby born she get tally-gram from the war she husband die!

"After the water gone back, they catch the servant body so here-and-there. Gone right out in the Gulf Stream.

"It was rice harvest time. I know we been-a cut rice. When Doctor Storm come we been a-cut rice. Marse Allard say he goin' catch someone take (Steal) he rice in he field. Say he goin' catch dem that same night. Storm come! Rice all mix up! Water float dem. We catch dem all 'bout and dry dem. They not rot.

"To beach, Mis Hazel one house save. Doctor house and he son house and all the rest house sweep out! He cat and he cook ride in on the roof with Marse Allard.

"They had read 'bout it, they read a thorolatercomin' in the sea! He have the chronometer[9] and he see it keep a-fallin'!'

4. Dr. Arthur Belin Flagg.
5. Georgianna Flagg.
6. Dr. Ward Flagg.
7. Annette Holmes.
8. Allard Belin Flagg Jr.
9. Barometer.

"When I stay to Bookgreen street, I have the cow and yellin' and a yoke o' oxen and two milkin' cows them time. No fence. They feed in woods. Now no place for keep cow. I sell all. Mr. G—— he have charge and what he say LAW. He come by see me pullin' down gray moss for feed cow. He say: 'That'll kill you cow. Pay me fifty cents a head and turn'em in the field.' I too glad. They get corn and peavine and all in the field and that fatten dem.

"Charlie? Not the Charlie in jail? That boy Mammy gone to Chicky-cago. This here Chicky-cago, I hear that another state!"

Annette: "Missis, Christopher Columbus, what did he discover? Row-boat or schooner? They all kinder how to go 'bout. All kinder how to go 'bout. All kinder animil."

Aunt Bobbitt: "I been to Charston workin' with some Germany descent. They want my picture with the baby in my arm to take 'cross the ocean. They say all they people where they come from think colored people just to hitch to plow!

"My mother been a warrant Granny. (Granny woman with a license) She hear that after Freedom there doin' to be JUDGEMENT. She say she not wantin' none of her grands to be Granny. Before time, if you a Granny woman and baby die, they hold you!

"Yes. Doctor gone. Come. Don't know WHO goin' look at the tax for me now. Doctor gone."

Annette: "You 'tend service this week to Gordon?[10] No? You hear 'bout that woman holdin' vivry meetin', ain't you? A PREACHIN' 'oman! Been preachin' all week. I ain't hear 'bout the convert. Been two come through to Heaven Gate last week."

SOURCE: *Annette Holmes visits*
Aunt Bobbitt Horry
Sept. 15th., 1938
Parkersville, S. C. (Georgetown County)

10. Gordon Chapel.

Alex Johnson

IN HIS TWO BRIEF INTERVIEWS with Genevieve Chandler, Alex Johnson discuses the economic injustices of life in the Jim Crow South. Johnson also offers his account of the 1893 hurricane.

Johnson was seventy-two in June 1938 according to Chandler. U.S. Census documentation for 1910 cites his age as forty-three, which roughly confirms Chandler's assessment. The census also reveals that his first wife's name was Elizabeth and that they had several children: Alex Jr. (age ten), Hagar (age ten), George (age eight), Wattis (age four), and Abie (age one). When the 1930 census was taken, Johnson had a second wife, Sarah, and lived with her and her two sons, Matias Allston (age twelve) and Joseph Allston (age nine). At this time Johnson is listed as owning his own home in the Murrells Inlet / Waverly Mills area, as being literate, and as employed in public works labor.

Baptisin' to Chapel Crick, Waverly Mills S. C. June 5th., 1938.

"Twenty-head! Twenty-head due to baptize. Doan know wedder dey all been in readiness or no! But the best part! The best part'll be here!

"The upper store been name 'Grab Some.' The middle store been call, 'Grab all.' And Cap'n Nesbit own been call 'Take Some.' One nother lil' store have the name 'God Save My Life!'

"Way back after Freedom they try the men with forty cents a day. The women work for thirty cent a day. And they run'em like that till the World War come long. The World War[1] come long 'fore that thing banish from here. Done so well on that thirty cents and forty cents till it been the World War 'fore that thing banish way from here. Livin' on that system more'n thirty year. See nigger done so well on that system. Take that CARD business! The man start that CARD business work that same proposition and he leave here MILLINERY! (Millionaire) I tell you the truth God love, they have you BLIND dem days. The store man low himself ten cent and the clerk ten cent and take

1. World War I.

out so much ten cent 'till you get eighty cent. All you get been eighty cent out your dollar.

"Eagle? You talk EAGLE? He the rulin' bird o' the element. Take the WHALE he the master fish o' the ocean.

"Story say lion holler 'Me and GOD rule the world!'

"Now man wuzn't stayin' very far off. Man have a good gun. But a load o' buck-shot in'em. Man say:

"'You IS?'

"Lion holler out:

"'Me and MAN and God rule the world!'

"Take the BEE. A swarmin' 'bout a quart. And every swarm got a MASTER BEE."

SOURCE: *Given by: Uncle Alec Johnson (Age 72)*
June 5th., 1938
Baptisin' at Chapel Crick,
Waverly Mills, S.C.

Flagg Storm
(Verbatim)

"Tink dat was Tuesday. I have rice cut down, stack, tie, ready to go to yard. And that night wedder make up. Take me and my wife. We had to brace 'gainst'm. Had to hold the window back to hinder the storm from blowin' em in.

"When it carry the old man and his wife,[2] the wind nor'east. He wuz on one beach cedar limb. Wife on one. Old lady give out. Sea a-bussin'! He turn loose he holt to get her, he had turn HIS holt he'd a-gone.

"Thirteen head gone in one house. Gin to screen and holler. Pa get up and lock the door. House and all take out to sea and broke up in the sea. How come they get the name o' Flagg Storm.'

"Road was lined wid casket. Huntin' up them people! Three weeks 'fore all fin."

SOURCE: *Alex Johnson*
Waverly Mills, S.C.
(Parkersville)

2. Arthur Belin Flagg and Georgianna Flagg.

Andrew Keith

Andrew Keith was twenty-seven in 1910 according to the U.S. Census taken in that year. While that record cannot be considered authoritative, it suggests that Keith was definitely still a young man when the census was taken. Based on data from the 1900 and 1920 censuses, we can surmise he was born in the early to mid-1880s and married his wife, Emma, around 1909. Andrew's father and mother were Murphy and Eliza "Bina" Keith. He had numerous siblings, including Lea and Joe, who were older, and Emeline, George, Mary Jane, Marlina, and Melvinah, who were younger. In 1938 Keith was probably in his midfifties. Keith owned a team of oxen and a wagon by which he derived his income. He hired out the team along with his own services for breaking ground and general heavy hauling. In the 1930s the Waccamaw River still served as the primary transportation artery for the Murrells Inlet area. The Wachesaw landing served as its distribution point. Keith delivered goods ranging from construction materials to fine furniture from Charleston.

Superstition Regarding the Eagle

"Peter Reed was a real hunter. He always say at the first accident of destruction of the buck know from the smell and he race backwards and fowards and not leave the bay till the noung deers and the does all out. Then he lay his horns on his neck and leavin' from there.

"Just the other day some men come to my house and tell me 'bout a eagle nest they had find down to McClennanville. Must -a been real. They run up on that eagle nest in a bay one day. They could see two young there in nest. They said they cut all the tree round about and leave that one with the eagle nest and say 'Tomorrow we'll come and get the noung eagle.' Next mornin' they come early. Eagle gone, nest gone and not but one noung eagle leave.

"They wantin' to cut that pine cause they interested in that stone.[1] Very fortunate stone. Of course all Bankers have it. Some say it'll protect in court. Has very powerful influence on judge and jurors.

1. According to Gullah lore, bald eagles keep a stone in their nest that has conjuring properties and confers good luck on the possessor.

"I have a book that advertise these wonderful charm and stones. From Louisiana. One called 'John the Conqueror.' Seem to be very powerful stone."

SOURCE: *Andrew Keith, Supt. of Gordon Chapel Sunday School (negro)*
Trustee of School (colored)
Murrells Inlet, S. C.
August 24th. 1938.

Addie Knox

IN MANY WAYS ADDIE KNOX was the great matriarch of the Knox family. Local reputation presents her as the center of a complicated nexus of relationships —a reputation confirmed by U.S. Census records. In 1900 she appears as the wife of Gabriel Knox, who was then eighty. Sharing her household at the time were children young enough to be her own and young adults who were most likely the offspring of Gabriel's previous marriage: Isaac (age seven), Gabriel (age two), Julia (age eleven months), Quimby (age twenty-four), and Silvie (age twenty-five). By 1910 Addie Knox had married Frank Ladson (a fisherman), who was several years her junior. At this point Addie worked in a "fish factory," probably a cannery. She seems to have brought five children with her into the Ladson marriage: Isaac (age fifteen), Richard (age ten), Julia (age nine), Douglas (age eight), and Mary (age four). She also had several children with Ladson, including Minnie Ladson Knox, and raised as her own some children who may have been more distantly related (Zackie Knox being a prominent example). At the time she sat for her interviews with Chandler, Addie Knox seems to have been utterly exhausted by a demanding life. Chandler's physical description is less than generous: "Cross-eyed. Cock-eyed. Face wrinkle and nose crinkles when she talks. Gums blue. Pizen if she bites. Face works convulsively with the effort make when she puts hersef in words. Constantly exspectorates." Appearance and carriage aside, Addie Knox managed to raise a great number of children and grandchildren. Like so many of her relatives and peers, she was fascinated by encounters with the supernatural. In fact she claimed to have met a plat-eye in the graveyard.

Truss Gawd or Ad's Plat Eye

Her house has one room. Smoke dried inside and out. Stove pipe perkily protrudes from the left side. Squalot. Filth. Something broken every where. Children's treasures. Play-house under live-oak. Four sticks and a board-table. Clam shells-plates. Blue magnesia bottle-vase. And that's a chair and that's a bed. . . . To the child all beautiful. An escape from reality. Aladdin's Lamp. The magic carpet. To us- car tires. Broken bycycle. Bunged up body of a car. Wheelless wheel-barrow. Pump that protests. Open door. Dark within on the sunniest day. Why? Simple. No window. Some boards still show signs of white-wash. Dingy white-wash. Smoky white-wash.

Now Ad. Cross-eyed. Cock-eyed. Face wrinkle and nose crinkles when she talks. Gums blue. Pizen if she bites.[1] Face works convulsively with the effort make when she puts hersef in words. Constantly exspectorates. Between each sentence. Punctuates her remarks with exspectorations and convulsive contortions. Hair plaited down tightly wrapped with white twine. Nondescript garments hand loosely from her space frame. Perfect scare crow. Splay feat unshoed. Never clean. Rarely washed. And yet? My hat off to her. Why? She raises gran. She feeds great-gran. I'll have to count'em. May be I'll get'em. Capers,[2] Adeline, Maude, Ester Lee,[3] Betty Jane, Julia Lillian, Nellie, William, Adele, James, David, May Ethel,[4] Eloise, Elinita Grace, and Lillie May. Fourteen. Fourteen human sould she keeps alive with her two hands. Under norished. Half naked. All in one room. Unmoral. Once a dead baby lay hidden under its sick mother's bed for a week. In a civilized country. And we are Christian.

Yet in that yard crepe myrtles make gay color and red-birds visit and sunflowers turn their faces to Lord sun. Behind that shack and to the right and to the left green corn waves and gives bright promise. Wild plum trees hug the house and hand heavy. A bantam rooster struts and his the heart to crow.

One neighbor says, "Heathern". Another, "Barbarians". Listen to her. Let Ad talk.

"Plat Eye?[5] Yas'm? De ole folks is talk bout Plat Eye. Dey say dey takes shape ob all kind de critter-dawg, cat, hawg, mule, varmint and I is hear tell ob Plat Eye taking form of gator. I aim see dem scusing wan leetle time. You know dat leetle swampy place hind de Parsenage?[6] Dem does call dat Parse-

1. According to Gullah lore, bluish gums indicate that their owner has a venomous bite.

2. Capers Pickett.

3. Maude Ester Lee Pickett. The comma setting the name Maude off from the name Ester Lee was probably a error made in Washington by the typist responsible for transcribing Chandler's early handwritten work.

4. May Ethel Pickett.

5. Plat-eyes are disembodied spirits of the murdered. They characteristically behave like shape-shifters, tending to harass lone travelers who inadvertently trespass on the site of their death. A plat-eye may be distinguished from the creatures it imitates by its glowing eyes, which are the size of dinner plates. Plat-eyes are often used to guard buried treasure. In fact it is alleged that murders have been committed on the site of many a hiding place solely for this purpose.

6. Mission swamp lay behind the Belin Church parsonage, which was called Cedar Hill.

nage Branch. Well, wan time—I hab med bloom on me on wuz clam-ming dem days—en de tide been berry late in de ebening. Hit wuz dusky dark when I hit de Parsenage lane—light dusky dark. I wuzn't feared none tall. You see, ez I say, I hab meh bloom on me in dem days. En I pass de Cap'n barn en stable. Dere he wuz wid Allan son Milkin. En I say "good eben, Cap'n Bill!" En he gin me back ma word. En I barg thru dat deep white sand en I passes de grave yard[7] entrance en I leabes de open en enters dem dark woods. Whey de moss wabe low en bresh in your face. En I bin think bout Plat Eye. De mind come ter me it wuz good time ter meet'em. Den I bresh dem weopin moss aside en I trabble de wet mud in make bare feets en my shoe bin tie ter meh girdle string. En, Miss Jin, when I bin come ter de foot lowg I could see same ez I see you now. I could see de foot lawg—dat same old cypress what been dere now. He blow down in dat las big September Gale. En I bin see Mr. Bull Frowg hit de water—"ker-plunk!" En a cooter slide offen de lowg at my feets. En, Miss Jin, clare ter Gawd, I bin fer look up at dat cooter en den I turn mah eye up en der wuz a cat-black cat wid he eye lak balls ob fire en he back all arch up en he tail twissin en er switchin en he hair stan on end. He has move backward front ob me cross dat cypress lawg. En he bin big. He bin large ez mah leetle yearlin ox. En I talk ter'em en try fer draw close. En I say ter'em, 'I ain't fer fear nuttin. Ain no ghos! Ain no hant! Ain no Plat Eye. Ain no nuttin!'

En I'se try fer sing' He carry me tru many ob danger Because he fust lube me. He guard gainst hant en Plat Eye. Because he fust lube me.'

En dat Plat Eye ain gib me back mah word. He mobe foward en he tail swish en swish same lak big moccassin tail when he lash de rushes. En de send come to me, 'Child ob Gawd Doan you show no fear'

En I is brace up. En mah short handle leetle clam rake been in muh hand en I sing, 'Gawd will take care ob me. Walkin tru many of dangers, Gawd will take care ob me'

En den de min come ter me, 'De Lawd heps dem what heps demsedl' En I rais up ma rake en I come right cross dat critter hed. Ef dat had bin real cat, I'd er pin him ter dat lawg. My rake bin bury deep in de lawg hold em. En I clare ter Gawd, Miss Jin, he up en prance right onder mah feets dem eyes burnin holes in me en he tail swish, swich lak ole Sooky tail when de flies bad. En meh ire bin raise. I fer struggle wid mah rake en de lawg loose'en he grip en I fer pray, 'Gib Addie strenght, O Gawd!'

En down I come straight tru dat critter middle. He stummick ball up sam lake de lettle puffer toad-fish. But dat criter ain feel mah lick. En I'se rassel lak Jacob wid de angel. I bin strong en hab mah bloom on me. It ain't nuttin.

7. Belin Church cemetery.

No man! Mr. Plate Eye jest ez peart en frisky ez fore he bin hit. En I buss'em en I cuss'em en I say, 'you debbil! clare mah path!'

En ef dat critter didn't paw de air en jus rise up dat big bamboo vine en me fer hit'em ebey jump! So, Miss Jin, I tink, 'Sinner, leble dat lawg? Mah mind come teh me, ' child ob gawd, trabbel de wood's path!'

En I turn back en meh haste. En I hit dat path. En I ain bin tarry en jes ez I wuz gibbin Gawd de praise fer deliver me, dere dat cat! Dis time he big ez mah middle size ox en he eye bin blaze! En I lam en I lam. En dat rake handle bin wire en bin nail on. En jes ez I mek mah las lam, dat critter rise up fore my eyes en did time he bin big ez cousin Andrew[8] full grown ox. En he vanish up dat ole boxed pine ez you quits de deep woods. Yas'm. I ain bleeve in Plat Eye 'twill den, but I minds mah step since dem days.

En when I trabbles de deep woods whe de moss wabe low en Mr. Cooter lib en Mr. mocassin crawl on de fire fly flicker—mah packet fer load.

Yas'm. I'm ready fer'em. Gun-powder en suplhur. Dey is say Plat Eye can't stan dem smell mix. No'um. Dey ain fer trubble me sense dat wan time. Uncle Murphy he witch docrer en he bin tell me how fer fend'em off. Dat man full ob knowledge. He mus hab gawd mind in'em. So I totes mah powder en sulphur en I carries stick in mah han en puts mah truss in Gawd."[9]

(Submitted: May 25, 1936)

8. Andrew Keith, said to have owned the only oxen in Murrells Inlet at the time.

9. The variety of precautions Addie Knox takes against evil provides some insight into the complex belief system that Gullah culture sustained. Religious views that are in some ways incompatible find a peaceable common ground in Gullah culture and in Addie Knox's mind. She brandishes as many weapons as she holds explanations for aberrant phenomena. The charmed powder and sulphur are a tangible nod to the West African animism that lived on as a vestigial feature of the Gullah worldview, providing protection from plat-eyes, hoodoo, conjure, and the like. Her "truss in Gawd" is an obvious reference to the Christian faith that was also strong among the Gullah. The stick is a practical answer in case evil presented itself in a purely physical, rather than supernatural, form.

Lillie Knox

LILLIE KNOX (A.K.A. CARRIE NATION) is easily the most significant of Genevieve Chandler's informants. As the Chandlers' housekeeper, Knox was constantly accessible, and this accessibility made her an obvious and frequent choice for Genevieve Chandler's sittings. By fortunate coincidence, Lillie was an ideal subject, so ideal that the matter of her accessibility becomes incidental.

By her own report, Lillie was a large woman. She had an affinity for singing and a tendency to talk to herself. Many of the snatches of dialog and song that follow were recorded candidly while Lillie performed her daily rituals. As a result a large share of the interviews are set in the context of Lillie's domestic responsibilities. Other formal interviews are also included. Many interviews include cameos from Lillie's intimates, most of whom are popular subjects in their own right for Chandler's lens.

In conversation, Lillie was a gossip, a joker, a moralist, and a spinner of fantastic stories. She was a loyal, tolerant wife to Richard Knox and mother to Rich Jr.—both of whom, as she was quick to acknowledge, gave her lots of trouble. As a friend, she was benevolent. As a businesswoman, she was shrewd and fair but somewhat cunning: see, for example, the story "Zack! Oh, Zack!" told by Zackie Knox (p. 261–64).

Lillie Knox was born September 2, 1902, to Liza and Henry Cogsdell.[1] Her mother did laundry work for the Willcox family, and it is through her that Lillie came to know and later work for the Willcoxes. Lillie's maternal grandparents were Kit and Washington "Wash" Farewell from the Ark plantation. Her paternal grandmother's name was Venia Cogsdell. Lillie had several siblings, including Geneva, Henry, and Elijah.

Lillie was troubled with misfortune for much of her life. Although astonishing to a present-day reader, sudden death due to seemingly simple illnesses, as well as gross inequalities, were common to the lives of poor southern blacks during the Depression. In 1914 Henry Cogsdell, Lillie's father, died of

1. We have elected to use the spelling "Cogsdell" although Chandler also uses "Cogsdale" (in "Papa's Knife") and although the census takers for 1910 and 1920 record it as "Cogswell" and "Caswell," respectively.

unknown causes while fishing. Lillie was only twelve years old. In 1918, at age sixteen, she had a son she named Paul. Shortly thereafter Lillie's mother, Liza, fell ill with a fatal pneumonia. Orphaned, Lillie had to raise her own son, Paul, and her younger siblings Geneva, Henry, and four-year-old Elijah.

Knox had followed in her mother's footsteps and worked as a domestic employee for the Willcoxes. After Liza Cogsdell's death, the Willcoxes moved Lillie and her dependents into the old servants' quarters on the creek side of the Hermitage. Not long after the move, Lillie's sister Geneva drowned in the salt marsh behind the Hermitage.

Mrs. Willcox persuaded Lillie to marry Richard Knox (the father of Lillie's son, Paul, and the son of Addie and Gabe Knox). They were wed at Heaven's Gate Church with Genevieve Chandler standing in as Lillie's maid of honor. Lillie wore a blue satin dress that Mrs. Willcox had made for her.

Richard Knox farmed and fished for a living. Lillie continued to work for the Willcoxes. After Tom Chandler's death, she began to work for Genevieve Chandler. She and Richard raised several children together (Paul, Richard Jr., and Mary Knox Moore). Knox also gave birth to a son she named David, who was asphyxiated by his own umbilical cord and died in his mother's arms soon after birth. Lillie's daughter Julie was born with severe birth defects and lived only a few months; she too died in her mother's arms.

Lillie was some ten years Genevieve's junior and had known her all of her life. Lillie's move to the Hermitage facilitated familiarity and friendship between the two women. Ultimately Tom Chandler's death and the demands of the Depression bound them to one another. Chandler found herself a pregnant young widow with the responsibility of raising her four (soon five) young children. Writing for the WPA paid Chandler approximately sixty dollars a month, which provided needed financial support. For the care of her children and the running of her household however, Genevieve turned to Lillie. Lillie only earned twelve dollars a month working for Genevieve, but the job also provided milk from the Willcox's cow as well as food for her family's dinner table. When Lillie cooked, she cooked for her own table as well as the Chandlers'.

Knox was naturally talkative, a gift she accentuated for Genevieve, knowing that both of their incomes depended on Genevieve's writing. When Genevieve was writing or traveling to visit other informants, Lillie cared for the children. This partnership made the interviewing possible, and in this respect, as well as others, Lillie was crucial to the work.

Lillie continued to work for Chandler until further mischance forced her to move away. Lillie's husband, Richard, accidentally shot a woman in his nightclub. He was found guilty of manslaughter and sentenced to time on the chain gang. Lillie was forced to provide for her children without Richard's

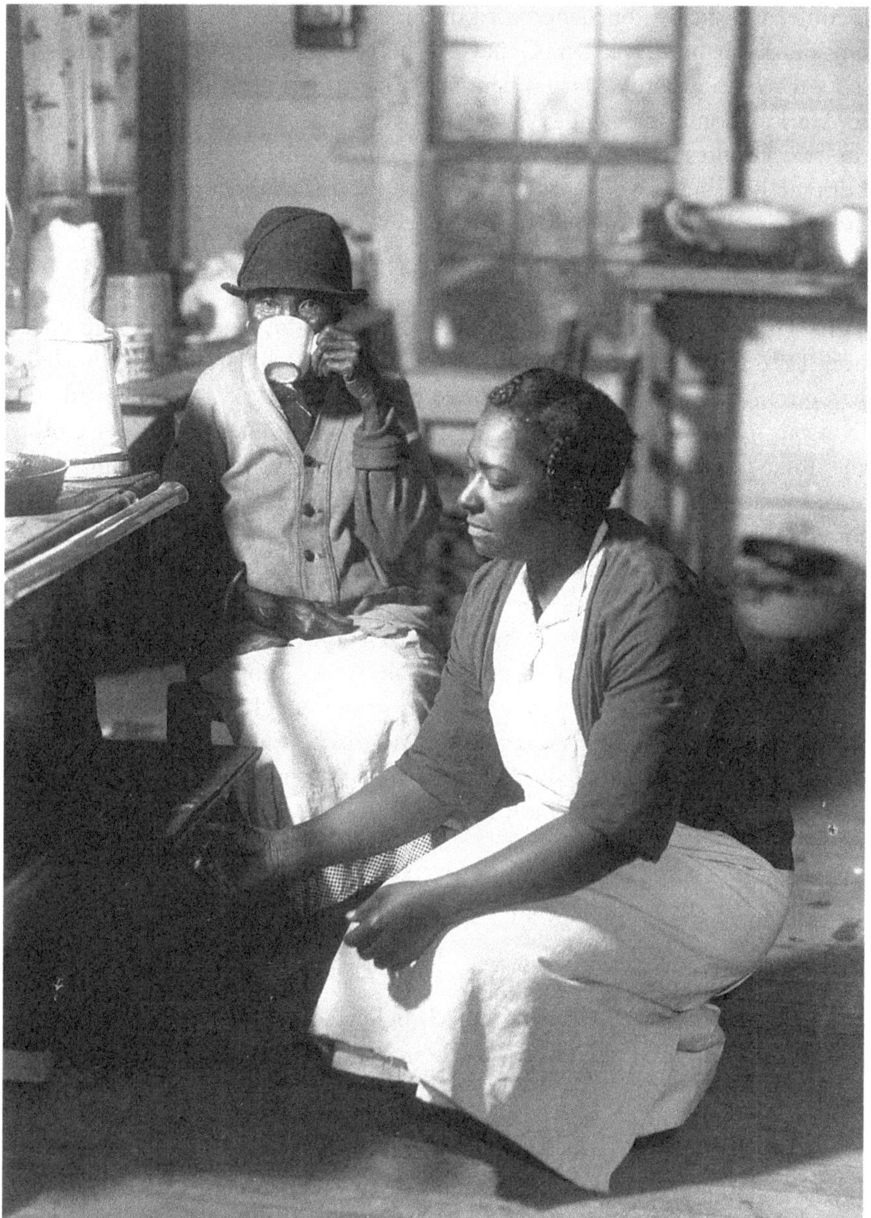

Lillie Knox (front) and Hagar Brown in the kitchen of the Chandler home.
Photograph by Bayard Wootten. North Carolina Collection, University of North Carolina Library at Chapel Hill

income, and she was burdened with trying to come up with enough money to buy her husband's freedom. Genevieve helped arrange work for Lillie with Bisco Davis, a wealthy Marion dentist. Lillie moved her children and herself to Marion, some forty miles away. Although the physical distance between the two families had grown, the Knoxes and the Chandlers remained close. Ultimately Lillie moved back to Knoxville, where she remained until her premature death from cancer in 1959.

Hag

Aunt Kit[2] was more than half Indian as her straight, black hair, high cheek bones and light reddish skin testified, but Uncle Wash Farewell, her husband was pure African. Before her death a quarter of a century ago, she made her living in summer doing the washing for summer people. To get her clothes she walked five miles down the sandy hot "Kings' Highway," returning home with the heavy burden balanced gracefully on her head. Once seen this barefoot figure was never forgotten swinging smoothly and rhythmically along, heavy gold rings like ear-bobs dangling and jangling with her every step, grey eyes straight ahead.

One WPA worker wanted a hag story. For some reason Aunt Kit and hags were stored together in her mental art gallery. As Aunt Kit had gone to her reward and only a grand-daughter left, the grand-daughter was questioned. In appearance, this "grand," short and fat and black, was more like her African forebears. From Aunt Kit she inherited the stoicism, loyalty and caution of the Indian. Her name is Lillie Bug. The following conversation is given verbatim:

"Lillie Bug," you believe in Plat Eye"?

"Oh, no, Miss Jinny. Dey ain't no sich thing".

"How 'bout Hag?"

"I ain't believe in dem things."

"Didn't your grandmother, Aunt Kit believe in them?"

"Oh, yas'm, She did been tell me bout hag."

"What did she tell"?

"One time de wuz two men grewed up as frens, jest like Cap'n Tom[3] and Cap'n Joe, and dey marry two omans jes de same time. Time pass, bout tree weeks and fren ax de other fren "When you wake up in de nite is you wife wid you?" "Yes man, why?"

"Well, I goes to bed and lays down. Dere she is. If I wake up bout one o'clock, dere she ain't. When I wake up later, dere she be agin."

2. Kit Farewell.

3. Thomas Chandler, Genevieve Chandler's husband.

"Man, man, you must be marry wid a hag."

"What dat? How de do?"

"If you is marry wid a hag, she gits up and slips out'n she skin and hide it under the stair-steps or back door steps, and when she come back she gits back in and lays back down. Now, when you wife go, you git up and look under the staircase. Ef yo find she skin, you salt and pepper it good same lak you salt and pepper fish what you goin fry. Ef she gone haggin, she sho left it, and if you salts it, she caint get back in.

"Dat nite sho nuf bout one o'clock, out she sneak en off she go. Dey mans mek out lak he sleep but soon as she is gone and he hear de do shet out he go and sarch ondor de stair case en de do step en sho nuff dey he fin he wife's skin all ball up in de corner. Den he salt it and he pepper it, en he go back ter bed. Den he lay dere. When he wife come home by-en by, he hear:

"Skin, skin, you know me?
Skin, skin, dis me.
Skin, skin you know me?
Skin, skin, dis me."

But she caint get back in because it smart her same like salt do when you cut you finger. So she wind up in a sheet en lie down. When de sun rise she don git up. Time come for brekkus. (breakfast)

No brekkus. She talk onder de (sheet.)

"I gwine for de doctor." But she keep on talk onder de sheet. She doan need no doctor. Doctor cost too much. Caint spare de money. She sist and sist doan he git no doctor. So the mans mek lack he gone to hoe dem taters but sted o'that he hide en peep troo de shutter en he hear,

"Skin, skin, you kno me?
Skin, skin, dis me.
Skin, skin, you kno me?
Skin, skin, dis me."

But she skin ain kno she and won't come on no how. So she wrap herself back up and go back in der bed. Bi-en-by de sun in he stummick say it goin on twelve so de mans come in fer bittle, but for he come he go git de witch doctor. Dey come in and find de omans still twist all up entalkin under de kivers. So de doctor, he say,

"What ails you, oman?"Den she low dere ain't nuttin wrong. En de talks backards and forwards twell de doctor done lose patient en fuss news you know he jerk off'n de sheet en dey she wuz jess as red en raw as er beefsteak. En de doctor he say,

"Man, man, you is done marry wid a hag."

Den he puts her in a barrel er tar and burns she body alive. Ain't nuttin else ter do."

"Lillie Bug, asked the seeker after knowledge, where did that woman go that night when she left her husband?"

"Well, Miss Jinny, hits dis way, hag rides you. She wuz ridin somebody. Dey say hag sperit can go troo de key hole of de do en ef dey lak you de goes in an sucks yer blood troo yer nose. Nobody scusing a hag lak dat kin a diet (eatin) but dey eats dat for de syrup on de bread. When hag ride you, you mek noise same lak er little shivering owl. You can't wake up en you won't wake up twell somebody tech you.

"Lillie Bug, I call that a nightmare."

"Yas'm you calls it er nightmare, us calls it de hag ridin we and ef somebody doan tech you, you sho goin die. Turrible, turrible thing.——————

"Now, Miss Jinny, I wonder if that kin be so."

N.B. An uncorked bottle with a new needle in it, or a Bible or newspaper under one's pillow at night will keep away hag.

(Submitted: May 21., 1936)

Hant House

"Maum Nellie,[4] she try'em. She fight'em seben year. Jes she wan. She ressel wid'em. How did she run 'em? Lord Jesus! I ain kno. I never has run wan. But atter seben year dey run she. She say she too old fer de hag fer ride. She say she too tired. She wuk so hard. She hoe. She plant. She harbest. En nite come en she crabe fer res. She doan git no res. Dem hant pure ruin she res. She ole bones bin gib out. Come fuss dark, she fer bolt she door. She eat she bittle. She bed down she fire, en she fall in she bunk. But she ain't fer out she lite. She lite burn low fer keep hag out. En de sifter bin hang ober de key-hole . Dat, too, fer keep out hag. When hag come tru de key-hole en get in dat sifter he hab de culiosity. En he stay right dere twell he count de hole in dat sifter. En he lose count. En he start ergin. En he count. En he git mix. En day light kotch'em. En he hab fer go. Maum Nellie she kno. She fix fer keep hag out. But when she hit dat bed, trubble bin fer start. De hag kaint trubble she. Hag jes human. But she ain't fer manage dem hant. De hant woorser at de full o' de moon. Maum Nellie fer testify it start way cross de fiel. It bark lak fox. It howl lak dawg. It hoot like squinch owl.[5] It soun' lak all de beas ob de woods.

4. Nellie Pickett.

5. Screech owl, *Otus asio*, distinguished by its ear tufts and a quavering, whistlelike call. Often thought to be a portent.

En fuss news it hit de house. It circle. It prowl same lak stray dawg. En while she hol she bref de door what she done bolt mube open. De pot lid lif. De rockin' chair rock. Now, Maum Nellie hard. Maum Nellie hab a strong heart. She bin fer stan'em seben long year. Den she gib out. She mube cross de road ter she son house. She say in-law gib'em mo res dan hant.

"Dat house wuz idel some time 'twell Zeke[6] gin'em ter he daughter Julie en she husban' fer use 'twell Mauser kin build he own house. Dey two bofe bin res quiet in'em. Hant ain fer trubble dem. Dem wuz not born wid caul. Dey res dere two, tree munt. Den when he gal mube out, he son George[7] mube in wid he bride. George jus' tek wife. She young gal. George just sebenteen hissef. He workin ter de mullets fishery ter Floral's Beach.[8] He late fer git home. He wife bin dere ter dat hant house—She wan. De moon full. She hear strange noise. She hear 'em way cross de fiel. Dey comin' tru dat pecans orchard. She kno dat hant. Dey hit de house. Dey mube all round de house. Dey prowl same lak stray dawg. She bin keep still so dey tink nobody fer dere. De mo she keep still de mo dey prowl. De do bin bolt. She watch'em. He creep open. De pot led riz. De rocker rock. Jes when dat gal good en scared, Zeks's boy come home. He say dey ain no hant but she kno what she kno. So de nex nite he say,

'I fix 'em.'

"En he git he gun en set. He set up wid'em. He doze en he chair. En come twelve o'clock de moon bin fer rise. En he wife fer hear dat critter howl. En she fer wake George en say,

'Hear dat! Hear dat!'

En he rouse up en tek notis. En dat hant prowl. He hoot lak a horned owl. He sound same lak leetle squinch owl. He bark lak fox.
He howl. He coo lak dove. He bellow lak gator. He mek all dem noise. En den he try fer open dat door. En when dat door open fer crack, George brace hesef en fire on 'em. Bofe barrels bin fer shoot at wan time. De gun kick'em down. He mos fer tear he fodder house do down, but he ain fer stroy dat hant. Den he frens come. De berry nex nite day come and dey all hab gun. En dey sits up en dey all bin shoot, but dey waste dey powder en shot. En dat pore gal grow so tin. She ain hab no res all day. What wid de washin, en choppin en totin' wood. She worry en all nite she lay wake. So dey talk. Zeke aks de vice ob de ole people. En he do what dey say. He mube dat house. Dey bin tek it down plank by plank en mube it cross de road. Dey is dem dat say if de hant dere dey gwine stay in de boad. But dats all he kno ter do—fer mube

6. Zeke Pickett.
7. George Pickett.
8. Sabe Rutledge's fishery at the Ark plantation.

'em. En den dey dig. Dey wuz talk ob mens ben murder on dat spot. So dey dig. En way down 'bout five, six feet dey trow out cedar lawg what bin burn en char and onder dat dey wuz bone. Some say dem critter bone. Some say dem ain't. I ain kno. But I tells yer what I am fer kno. Dat house been build on de berry spot whey de carpet-bagger en de Scalawag bin bury what de Federick[9] soljir shoot in time ob freedom.[10] Day my fodder tell me. I ain kno all. I jus tells you what I is kno.

You say why Julie[11] kin lib in dat house en George bride can't fer stay? Ain't I fer tell yuh Julie ain fer born wid caul but George gal Zena[12] is. Dat gal bin born wid caul. She can see what de ornary, common run can't see. Yas'm. I tell yer."

(Submitted: July 20, 1936)

In Lillie's Kitchen

"Rich[13] look lak a spring frog under a cooter back! On a wheel! I ain't see'em ride a bicycle in so long he look funny. (Talking about her husband passing on the Highway.)

"Wake up full of song this morning. Grab, 'Come On Sinner-man, Come Go With Me!'

Knox: "Gal, come gimme a cup 'o coffee, heah?"
Lillie: (Singing) "Sinner-man, come go with me!"
Knox: "I want my coffee. Want my coffee hot!"
Lillie: "Come On Sinner-man, Come Go With Me!"
Knox: "I ax you if my coffee hot!"
Lillie: "Sinner-man, come go with me!
Come on Sinner-man, come go with me!"
Rich: "Gal, you gone?"
Lillie: This world not my home!
Living on a borrowed land!
Come on Sinner-man!
Come go with me!"
Rich: "Well, good day!"

9. Confederate soldier.
10. Near the end of the war.
11. Julie Pickett.
12. Zena Pickett.
13. Richard Knox, Lillie Knox's husband.

Lillie: "Time I going! Eight o'clock. How come you telling me 'Good Day'? Must be going to dead!"
Rich: (Loud guffah) "Co! Co! Co! Co'
Lillie: (Walking down the road to work) "So strange!
(Resuming her singing)

So strange! He telling me 'good-day.'
1.
"Haul in your plank let us go!
Haul in your plank let us go!
Come, haul in your plank let us go!
Come, Sinner-man, come go with me!
2.
I didn't come to stay alway!
I didn't come to stay alway!
I didn't come to stay alway!
Come, Sinner-man, come go with me!
3.
This world not my home!
This world not my home!
This world not my home!
Come, Sinner-man, come go with me!"

Lillie Knox, age 35
Murrells Inlet, S. C.
April 16, 1937
(Submitted: Oct. 10, 1937)

Aunt Hetty Allston
(Deceased)

"You never aint see Aunt Hetty? She sho was funny. 'Well, daughter(Aunt Hetty said dater—Italian A). Take a dat now! Little ting jess (just) lak a mangy puppy! Aint no one to take him. Aint no one want 'em. But he human! I take 'em. No one to take 'em. I take 'em. I take little Mangy. Atter dat now, I mought (might) need her to bresh fly out 'er my face.' And she trim all the child hair off—(aside)—looker me here. Burn this waffle up talking bout Aunt Hettie!) Well the baby die. If one get sick and die Aunt Hettie say, 'By King and by Heaven! I done all I could for 'em. He dead. He dead now. I got that much off my mind.'

"Aunt Hetty raise Miss Rina, Aunt Marry, Janie, Becca (she marry Mom Hagar Grand) Julie, and Frank. One son. Frank die and left her one grand. Little sickly—puny! Atter it die, now Mattie get sick. Aunt Hetty say, 'Done all I kin for Mattie. By King and by Heaven get dat much off my hand.' Atter dat Sarah get sick. Sarah gone. 'By King and by Heaven, I got dat much off my hand!' Time come for Aunt Hettie to go. Us say we'll do all we kin for Aunt Hettie and she gone we lie in bed and laugh and say, 'Atter dat now, by King and by Heaven, done all I kin, got myself off my hand!' I gone to see her. I fan! I fan! I spend the day and I fan and I fan. And she say, 'Atter dat now, you jess lak you Mama. Got a heart, Lillie jess lak Lizzie! Atter dat now, you ain't got none dem book wid duh picture? Duh picture in it? I could muse me and lie here and see dem.pretty ting.' But, Aunt Hetty! If you ever make her mad! People! She'll never pass you. Never pass you on the road. Wouldn't want you to see her. Ain't want to pass you and not speak. Take the woods! Hold her head high as a crane. Board in her neck! She a pain! I couldn't magine sich a thing! You child dead and you say 'Got that much off my hand!' Them old slavery time people something else!"

Lillie Knox—age 35
Murrells Inlet, S. C.
June 1937.

Lillie's Prayer

"Good Master, you able to hew down the mountain; you able to make the crooked way straight; you able to make a way where there no way.

"Go to the Lord from the innest part of you heart, mean what y ou say, ax Him for forgiveness and he'll hew down the high mountain. Though you sin be dark as middle-night, he'll make them white ez snow. All power in His hand; he can defend and destroy. He can make a way out of no way. He can on-block the blocked road. He'll make it clear before you eyes. He'll move all them stumbling block. Everything is in His mind.

"I know my Redeemer live. I ain't know how YOU feel, but He's had His hand on me.

"Lord, YOU know all thing. All thing trust in Thy hand. You can defend and You can destroy. You can lay down in one hand and pick up in anudder—Lord, You can make the rugged road smooth. You can make the crooked path straight. You's able to hew down the high mountain; You able to make my sins whiter than snow. Lord, I trust You for all things, for You is the God of Hebben. And You will do right. Ed Lord, I'm so weak and You is strong. Make me be the woman You desire me to be. Guide me. Guide my feet in the path of righteousness, that I may live, so when You call me by my name I'll be able to answer."

("Where did you get that prayer?)

Lillie: "It just come to me after I converted.")

Lillie can neither read nor write. She had a few months of night school in the kitchen when she was twelve and was ambitious. Can still sign her name but did not use her learning si it went.

Lillie Knox—age 35
Murrells Inlet, S. C.
June 1937.

***Uncle Andrew*[14]**
(Verbatim Conversation)

"Poor old Uncle! He say last night, 'Oh, looker Lillie, what come to! Jess (just) O looker! I got all 'o you up here waiting on me!' He swoll up,[15] Lak (like) a drum, 'Oh, God, have mercy on me! I can't stand it!' (He smile!) 'Oh, how sweet the name of Jesus in true believer years![16] All us got to get us whipping! Take whipping to bring us to the fold! Lak (like) chillun mudder have to chastise. Do wrong-ful thing. Master have to chastise to get 'um to the fold!'

"Jess (just) bout four o'clock he say if he can't get ease he can't stand it. Jess can't swell no more. Poor old leg like a tree. Stommick like a bucket. Feet swell till every toe stretch! (But the sick man is thinking about his job which is to sell spring water for the boss man) Uncle say, 'Now chillun, carry the funnel! Go on to the spring with them people! Go on give the buckra the spring water. That man carry fourteen gallons? He owe you nother fifty cent. I aint going to do business that-a way! Give me the one dollar! I thank you! Thank you! Got a dollar for the doctor. Give it to him when he come tomorrow!'

"Everything split wide on 'em. Shirt all cut! Every pillow in the house under him. 'Lillie, don't try to lift all by yourself. You handle me so good. Don't hurt me. 'You see, Missus, by his flesh swoll so, it sore. His limb feel hard like a bottle. Never see a sight like that! Aunt Phillipa die with the dropsy, but didn't swoll so. Die one night bout four o'clock in morning. Sue found her fore she stiff and make the outcry. Call me. That day she call me—the day before she gone—'Lillie! You better come and see me Old lady no count now!' When I went back home all wuz dark and I thought they wuz sleep. Sue say she sot up on that bench looking for me till late—

14. Andrew Johnson.

15. Dropsy, an earlier name for edema, is an abnormal accumulation of fluid in the tissue or in a body cavity. This condition may be caused by any number of maladies, including kidney failure, heart disease, or diabetes.

16. Gullah for "ears."

"My little flicted girl wuz getting up fine from pneumonia. Had a relapse after fire. Fire didn't out in the heater. Jinks[17] is relation to me all right; he daddy and my daddy two fuss (first) cousin. Jinks 'ud come and cut wood and say, 'Lillie, you set still. Lemme get the medicine. You set there and hold that baby.' I nuss (nurse) sister two—and they die in my arm. And one born dead. That chile born not a soul in the house but me. I suffer over that child. Sweat drop on me lak (like) a bucket 'o water. I say, 'You aint going to sit down. You break that young 'un neck they'll jail us!' That child come he wuz twiss up in that cord! wrap three times round his neck. Come head fuss (first). Didn't know how to do it. Jess (just) wrap him up so he wouldn't get cold. Round that child neck three times and had his arm hitch up in it and around down to he leg. I name him David. Live long nuff we got back to that little thing. Missus give me a little sweater and little wool socks and one of Jane[18] dresses she out-grow. I put that on the child after she die. (Go on child! Put something on you leg! That sun'll blister you. No? All right, miss, All right!')

"Going out and drip[19] my cows now. Meet my old sweetheart on the road. I say, 'What you say?' He say, 'All right!' That car a Essex! Zack, aint you wish you have a car like that?"

Zackie: "No gal. Please don't get me no Essex. Me and Essex aint no friend a tall a tall. Essex carry me off from home one time bout twelve miles and stop 'bam.' Cut right off! I don't like a Essex—tall, tall. Oh, you say 'air-ship'? Rather have air ship—than risk Essex—Me and Essex aint friend tall tall!"

Lillie Knox—age 35
Zackie Knox—age 30
Murrells Inlet, S. C.
July 1937

Tar-baby Story

"I ain't know much of it. It just that bout, 'I slap the tar baby if he won't tell GOOD-MORNING.'

"One time duh rabbit ask—less see WHO Buh Rabbit ask!—Buh Rabbit ask Buh Wolfe, I blive! He ask Buh Wolf how come when he go at water in the morning, his spring does be muddy. (Buh Rabbit ask either Buh Gator or Buh Wolf or Buh Fox one.) NO! NOW I got it right! I think Buh Wolf ask Buh Rabbit! One o' dem ask him—Been so long—I'll say BUH WOLF!

17. Jinks Johnson, who worked for the Quantz family during the summers and cooked at the Clipper Ship Restaurant during the winter.

18. June Chandler.

19. A colloquialism for milking.

"Now you see Buh Rabbit' ud slip down dere and ketch duh jew.[20] Whichever one it wuz'ud say, 'How come my spring muddy ever morning?'"

Buh Rabbit say, 'I don't know!'

He'd drink all the water he can while it clean. So the Wolf say, ' wonder WHO muddy my water! I fix 'em whom-some-ever it is!'

So Buh Wolf make 'em a tar-baby and stand 'em up down dere by the water—by the spring. And next morning early—EARLY—Buh Rabbit went hopping down to the spring. Bright and early.

"Saw this little girl standing there. Say, 'Good morning, Little Girl!'

Little Girl wouldn't crack! (Wouldn't say a word—crack her mouth). He say, 'Good morning Little Girl' three times.

"You don't tell me GOOD MORNING I going slap you."

Little Girl wouldn't tell 'em a thing. So he haul off and slap her! 'SPI' (Claps hands together) 'Like that!'

'You can't talk?' Fuss hand stick! Buh Rabbit say,

'Turn me loose Little Girl! I slap you again!' Little Girl wouldn't turn loose.

Can't get loose! So he hauled off and slap her wid the OTHER hand. 'Turn me loose, Little Girl! Turn me loose Little Girl! Turn me loose, Little Girl! Don't turn me loose, I butt you!'

"Both hands stuck and yet wouldn't turn him loose! Kick with one foot. That foot stick! Wouldn't turn loose yet.

'Turn me loose!'

Little Girl still holding! So he hauled off and kick her with the other foot. Little Girl STILL wouldn't turn 'em loose.

"Turn me loose, Little Girl! Didn't turn me loose, I butt you down!'

Little Girl wouldn't turn 'em loose! He say he'll take he head and BUTT the Little Girl! He take he head and butt and he head stick tight! He beg and plead. He beg and plead! Little Girl wouldn't turn 'em loose!

"Wolf come! Come early—same time he always come! Saw Buh Rabbit all huddle up—all double over—buckle over. All he hand fasten, he head fasten, he feet fasten—there huddle over the Tar-Baby! Wolf say, 'Ah, hah! I find out who wuz muddying my spring! Buh Rabbit, what muss I do wid you I don't know whether to throw you in the fire and burn you up or throw you in the briar patch!'

Buh Rabbit make out like he wuzn't particular bout the fire—he wuzn't fear the fire but when it come to the briar patch, he beg like he thought that turrible.

And Buh Wolf say,

20. Morning dew.

"'I gwine throw you in the briar patch!' And Buh Rabbit plead, 'Please don't!'

So Buh Wolf take Buh Rabbit and jerk him loose from the tar-baby and pitch him over in the briar-patch just like he going to stave him gainst the thorns of the briar and punish him. And Buh Rabbit holler out, "Thank God! I right where I born and raise at! I raise in the briar-patch!"

Lillie Knox—Age 35
August 20th, 1937.
(This tale given Lillie by Mom Phillipa Knox—an old blind ex-slave long dead.)

Ill - Form
(Verbatim Conversation)

"Miss Trizzie say they send for her to come over and see the new baby but she warn't goin'. No use to ruin her baby 'cause that woman ruin hers,—lookin' at a lizzard catchin' flies! Baby got no palate. Mother done it payin' all her tention to a lizard out there in the sun catchin' flies!

"Talkin' bout ill-form chillun—I never see a sight like I see to Con-o-way Satdy! I see ill-form chillun all right—but that the first I see like that! That lil' girl was naturally—jest (just) like people in the face— just like any other natural people. Woman have her in a lil' waggin (wagon). Glove on her two hand. Get out and walk on those poor lil' hand. Lil' body and foots and leg swing clear—clear off the ground. Hurt the heart out you body! Foots look like lil' monkey foots. Woman pass 'round a lil' luminum cup with a handle on it. Child sit up there in waggin' and sing—then climb out and prance all 'round on her two lil' hands for foots.—So's people can see her walk! Woman pick guitar. Child sing,

"'I know the Lord'll make a way for me!
I know the Lord'll make a way for me!
If I live holy, and keep God commandment,
I know the Lord make a way for me!
"'Didn't he died to make a way for me!
Didn't he died to make a way for me!
If I live holy, and keep God commandment,
I know the Lord'll make a way for me!'"

"Every time I shut my eye that night I see that woman pickin' that guitar, those people crowd up, and that lil' thing pitchin' out that waggin and walkin' on her two hands, and her lil' bony legs swingin'. Then I turn and twiss (twist) in bed. Rich wake up. Say,

"'Gal, why ain't you sleep? ' I start in and tell him 'bout how I ain't close my eye. If'n I does close 'em I can't see nothin' but that lil' ill-form lil' thing. He say,

"'Gal, you best go sleep. Wish you hadn't sawed that sight! That child caught one dollar when you can't.'

"Had on a lil' green coat—cut off long here," (measuring on hips) "cut off short so's them lil' ill-form legs'll show.—Lil' baby rubber pants slip over the ill-form lil' leg and a white tam on her black hair—white tam with a tossel.

"A man was standin' there. He used to know Uncle Quinvy.[21] We got to talkin'. He give me five cents to drop in the 'luminum cup. He say ax Uncle Quinvy when I see him does he remember Lurenza Howe. He say tell Uncle Quinvy when they work together in the turpentine woods,[22] he never study anything 'bout dying and any here-after. Say them time he think it jest (just) 'Big ME.' But say his wife gone leave him. Now he lookin' for a better home. Say tell Uncle Quinvy he ain't the same man he work with in the loggin' woods.—

"He put fifteen cents in the cup—

"Every time I shut my eye I see that big ring—big host of people and woman pickin' that guitar and poor lil' thing—big old black eye—full eye—and long black hair. White tam—tam white with tossel on top—hair braided—lil' foots like lil' monkey foots—soles of her foots turned up—leg folded under her a-walkin' on her hands—"

SOURCE: *Lillie Knox—Age 36. November 17, 1937. Murrells Inlet, S. C.*

Superstition

"I ruin mine. Ruin my little girl—my only little girl.[23] Come here little arm and leg helpless. Little face so pretty. Prettiest one I had. Never couldn't a-walk if she had live.

"Help lift Uncle William wife.[24] I 'member that old soul leg broken. Have to roll her over on her side. Cun William would come after me spite of all. Have to help bathe her.

"Sue Belle and old blind Aunt Daddy went. They there a lot. Uncle William give his gold watch and chain to Sue Belle 'cause she there with his wife when she die.

21. Quinvy Knox, the father of Lillie Knox's husband, Richard. Quinvy Knox was a true patriarch of the Knoxville community—father, grandfather, or great-grandfather to almost everyone who lived there.

22. Turpentine is produced from pine tree sap.

23. Julie Knox.

24. Martha Oliver, William Oliver's wife.

"Yes, I sholy ruin my little girl helping turn and bathe poor old crippled Mom Martha."

SOURCE: *Lillie Knox—Age 36. Murrells Inlet, S. C. Nov. 17, 1937.*

Fire! Fire! (Verbatim)

Most sot (set) my little shanty, my little kitchen,—on fire this mornin'. Up there at four o'clock to get these boys off to the loggin' woods. Make a big fire in that old piece of stove. Pipe got red hot. Pipe full of soot. Soot get to burnin'. Roarin' like a car. I look up through the kitchen top. Didn't have to go outside,—see right through the roof. I grab my big gourd dipper and throw a dipper full of water on the fire. Onliest thing to do been to out the fire. Didn't burn so flourishin' after that. When it did blaze up. Thing scare me so bad I couldn't fix Rich bucket.[25] Put the bread and taters and fry fish on the table in the house and Rich say,

"Not goin' fix my bucket?"

I say,

"Man, I feel too bad!"

I was scared stiff, I tell you! I lie there and gone back to sleep. Sleep till day clean. Call Paul[26] and Little Rich. Tell 'em they best make haste. Tell 'em how I most to burn the house down. Paul say,

"What you do Mama, if you had-a burn this house down?"

And I say,

"Boy, I'd have to stay in the woods on a bark!"

Put me in mind of the time we were livin' with Mom Daddy. Aunt Jane would burn trash in the chimbley. Corner of the house pure rotten. She put a box of trash in and it blaze up and here everything burnin'. I had a new baby— Sent Henry[27] flyin' to the pump with a bucket. Here Henry to the pump, slow as if he goin' to church, have the pump handle goin',

"Chink-a-link!

"Chink-a-link!

25. Most laborers carried their lunch in a bucket, thus "bucket" became a metonym for the meal it contained.

26. Paul Knox, Lillie's Knox's oldest son.

27. Henry Cogsdell, Lillie Knox's brother.

"Chink-a-link!

"Chink-a-link!"

Uncle Quinvy come to see who at his pump that time of night.

Paul say,

"Uncle Quinvy," so slow like, you know how he stutters, "Uncle Quinvy, us house on—on fire."

Uncle Quinvy say,

"Boy, how the debbil you pump so slow here and so onconsand? I tell you chillun to notice that rotten corner by that chimbley! Then finally now I tell Jane that thing. I tell Jane 'bout burnin' trash in that chimbley." All the time he roundin' up that bunch of them Knoxes. Mother[28] come cross the field with her host and Uncle Quinvy come with his host. Rich gone at his best speed for the ladder. Rich tell me after all was safe and outed.

"When I gone cross that field towards the barn for that ladder, I feel somebody pass me when I comin' with that ladder. Don't know whether it was Mom Daddy or not. When that somebody pass me I feel the wind pass me like a V-8 Ford. Beings Mom Daddy blind and always go so slow I didn't think it was her."

"When I ax Mom Daddy if she took her clothes she say,

"Lill, I didn't study no clothes. I know I couldn't see and I had to get out the way—"

We had a good time to that fire! Her Mother say,

"Wrop Lill and the new baby up and take 'em to a safe place!"

But ME? It been too cold to go to a safe place. I wrap the baby up and gone in the shed room and stay there 'twill they had it all outed. We has a good time out to Knoxville![29]

SOURCE: *Lillie Knox. Age 37. Murrells Inlet, S. C. November 29, 1937.*

Lawyers
(Verbatim)

Lillie: "A lawyer? You able to pay 'em the money, they'll save you from the jail-house and gallows. Wasn't for a lawyer, they'd be many a people hang. Get in those seriously places, give all they got to get a lawyer! Know many a one give all they little land and get a lawyer clear 'em. Some does take vantage. Some'll strip you if they can!"

28. Probably Addie Knox, Lillie Knox's mother-in-law.
29. The Knox family community.

"When Miss Dot French Doctor[30] give me that treatment (he say 'just-ment')—I thought it was a-goin to keep on painin' me where he broke my neck. Mr. Johnson say, "Look out Lill! He goin' cunjur you!' Cunjur ME! People may can cunjur all right but I ain't goin' low myself to be bother 'bout nothin' like that till it falls!"

"Tell Miss Maude I thought one time I was goin' to leave these chillun—finger pain me too bad! Sometime ain't know where I at! But I must been too good for the devil; not quite good 'nouf for God. So He spare me a while longer to grow gooder. Thought my time had wind up here. You 'member in Con-o-way I tell you 'I goin' home! I goin' home!' I was willing to go right then—but then the Good Master know best! He know—"

"Poke-berry? Make good ink. Root pizen. But then pizen thing good in sickness. Aunt Bina[31] put poke-root poultice on sister breast when it riz and busted. I put that on my bone-felom. It would a riz and busted after a while but good thing I had a doctor lance that thing. Don't know whether I could a wait on that poke-root poultice and live or no."

SOURCE *Lillie Knox, Age 36. November 1937. Murrells Inlet, S. C.*

Cracklins
(Verbatim)

Lillie: "You hear 'bout Mr. Lenny in the hospital and Miss Mary Jones[32] lover? No?"

"Well I gone by there last night. (You know Miss Jones kill hogs this week. On the way home I had to pass her house, and I got to thinkin' how if I had some cracklins to go with my roast 'tators, I could make out for supper 'thout boilin' the pot. So I rapped on the kitchen door. She come to the door and I tell her, "'Miss Jones, I hear you kill hogs. I want a dime's worth of cracklins.'"

"She cackle out,

30. Most likely a chiropractor.
31. Bina Keith.
32. The Jones family was a poor white family.

"'Hah! Hah! Lor, chile, how much a dime's wuth?'"

"And she go on and measure out two cup full. She don't never have too much 'o cracklin. She careful to kill on a failin' moon and all the cracklin dry up to nothin' if you bile 'em on a wast'in moon. All fry way to grease. Well here she come with two cup full! And she say,

"'Take you dime chile! Keep you dime!'"

"And my mouth musser drop open. I think that woman must be goin' dead! Here she give me two tea-cup full 'o cracklins! But I list'n and she gone on to 'splain how she have a piece of jowl left—pretty near half a hog jowl—and just she and the old man, and they can't destroy all the jowls fore they'll spoil. So she say,

"'Lillie, stead of you buyin' cracklin', take you money and buy this hog jowl off me.'

"So then I see why she present me the cracklins and I say,

"'How much the jowl? This dime the last button on Abraham jacket! Money have eagle on 'em and fly from me on eagle wing! I can pay the dime and charge the nickel. Hope it won't be a 'charge to keep.'

"She weigh the piece of jowl and say,

"'I reckon fifteen cents 'll be enough! Take you cracklins! You can pay the nickle when you get it.'

"I take my cracklin and the little piece o' jowl and come on out. I say,

"'Thank you Mam! Thank you MAM! '

"I out do Mom Hagar makin' cutsy to Miss Jones for them cracklin! Nice to walk long the road and pick up 'nouf cracklins to grease you 'taters and not cost you a cent!

"'Fore I leave the yard I 'members to ax after her daughter. I say,

"'And how Miss Mary when you hear last?'

"'Hah! Lor, chile, Mary all worry up! Hah! Lor, chile! You don't know! Her boy friend 'bout to die.'

"I say, 'How sad that is!' And I ain't sad a tall! And I not feelin' sad! (Cracklins talkin', child! Pure cracklins!) Yessir! I make more cutsy for them cracklins this 'evenin' than Mom Hagar ever make for one us quart of milk! I come on down the road and had to laugh at myself!

"As I leavin' the yard Miss Jones hail me one more time.

"'Lillie, you all got plenty butter for Christmas?'

"And I tell her us cows give us milk for the chillun but not 'nouf for churnin' since it turn off so cold. Then she say as how she have plenty to spare if we happen to want some. When she get over-bound with it—over-flush—she don't give it to her daughter-in-law neither sell it cheap. She pickles it down. Make it up in little balls and puts 'em down in two quart jars and covers it with brine. Can hear her now. Kept right on 'bout her cow. Ever thing they have register and entitle to register! "'My cow! Payin' her way! Take care the family! Take care the chickens! And feedin' the pigs!'"

"Let me stop talkin' here and get fire under my pot! Cold? Oh, yes'm. It cold all right—but IT NOT COLD AS IT BEEN!"

SOURCE: *Lillie Knox, December 8, 1937. Murrells Inlet, S. C.*

Squinch-Owl.
(Scraps of Verbatim Conversation)

"Yeddy! Duh owl! Papa[33] fuss marry Mama ('e stole Mama, yuh kno. Tek huh out duh window. Drive huh tuh duh magister een Mister Burreen horses en buggy). Grand-pa[34] set by duh road two weeks. Keep gun loaded. "Kill yuh sho ez pot is iun (iron)." Papa stay shy uv him. Tell after uh mont uh so when his passion cool. Papa duh onliest wan 'e son-een-law 'e knowed. "Tek mah dautah! Nebber stan fuh hit!" Didn't want Mama tuh marry. She 'e bess wukker. Papa stole Mr. Burreen horse en buggy. Go tuh Ark.[35] Steal mama. Drive tuh magister. All 'e sister hide Mama. En leetle pole house een pine thicket. Squinch-owl on-nerbe Mama. Now they holler, they on-nerbe me. So ef I walkin lonesome pat en hear dem 'twell diss day when dark set een, I twiss mah apron corner, uh turn mah pocket wrong-side-outards. Uh man kin turn 'e cap wrong-side—. That'll stop'um. Missus gimme two water-millon tuh ca tuh duh chillun. Uh coo-coo owl, one whut got th' cat hed—kin sit en turn dey hed rite on roun—big ole pop-eye—uh settin ober mah pat. I hab tuh go onder dat owl. Root cot mah foot. Fling me wan way—million th' other. Buss'um. Put'em een th' sack en ca dem on. Mama say,

"Well suh! Yuh ain wuth nuttin!

"Mama, I too scared uh dem ting! Know dey ain nuttin but uh leetle bird, but I can't hep it. Starin after me! Turn on roun. Scared uh all. Big coo-coo en leetle squinch. Ain no differ tuh me."

Mister Burreen say fuss baby his'n. Dat cause Papa steal Mama wid'e horse. Allus did claim me. 'E say,

"I know yuh boy rascal! Yuh raise wid mah boys."

Lillie Knox(age 35—colored)
Murrell's Inlet, S.C.
(Submitted: Dec. 28, 1936)

33. Henry Cogsdell.
34. Wash Farewell.
35. Ark plantation.

Poor Rich
(Rich's Visitor Seed Loan Man)

Here the 'seed Loan Man' come. Ride up to my door and stop he hig car. I to the horsepittal. Horn blow! Mother[36] come lopin'! Man ask:

"Where Rich?"

Mother broke out:

"My Lord, Boss! He jest left here JISS now! Gone with he wife. Gone to horsepittal with he wife. She so sick. 'Bout to have the blood pizen. Most dead!"

And mother gone to cryin'—

Next time the 'Seed Loan Man' come he catch me home. Man say:

"Is Auntie YOU mother or Richs?"

I tell him:

"Rich's."

He say:

"Show me you sick hand."[37]

And when I undo my hand he say:

"You might-a die without good 'tention."

I say:

"Well, Cap'n, I live SOME any how. If I'd gone, it would-a been my time."

He ask:

"Where Rich?"

And I tell him:

"Cap'n suh, Rich ain' able to pay his doctor. Needin' treatment over week—just like my doctor GIVING me—and he can't get it 'cause he got a OLD doctor bill. Ain't able to pay doctor."

He say:

"Well, tell Rich I say son's he KIN have some money for me. I know 'bout sickness, horsepittal and all."

And next time the man come he meet Rich home. I was on the inside. I could hear ever word. Rich doin' the talkin'. (I have to laugh in there all by myself! You know I pay all my own expense. But you ought to hear RICH tell it!)

"Cap'n, I jest was thinkin' 'bout you this mornin'. Know I jew[38] you some money to-day! But here I just bring my wife home from the horsepittal—Big

36. Addie Knox, Richard Knox's mother and Lillie Knox's mother-in-law.

37. Afflicted with bone felon.

38. Due.

horsepittal bill. Borry all I can. Done strain my credrick—THAT on me. I ain't have no money to meet THAT. Come up here on my blind side—That the way sickness hit a man. And here I HOME. Ain't on no job. Can hardly put one foot 'fore the other!"

Man ask:

"What the matter with YOU?"

Rich tell him:

"Feel like I 'bout to die, Cap'n."

Man say quick:

"Don't you die 'fore you pay me."

Then Rich talk so pleadin'! He fix it:

"Tell you Boss, I got no money this mornin', but LOW ME a CHANCE! Low me a chance, Cap'n!"

And the man crank up and say:

"All right! All right! I'll cheat you right, Rich, I'll cheat you right.

Here Rich gone to worryin'. He don't do nothin' but mope 'round and look sad. Look like he goin' pass out sho' 'nough. Say:

"What I goin' do? Here come Satdy, I got to meet that seed loan man to the office Con-o-way. I jew five dollar on the car."

I say:

"You got till SATDY! This here Monday. Spit in you hand, grab a fresh hold and get down to it."

And this one time Rich pay me 'tention! He done it! He sho' did work hard last week. If he'd work like that all the time it wouldn't be no trouble to meet all them collector. Here Ricg out in the cold fishin'. Fishin' for bass and trout all night; oysterin' and clammin' on ever low tide. Scratchin' clam on HALF tide! And when it too high to find oyster, HAULIN' oyster! Beddin' down clam and oyster. Payin' all the white mans to town in OYSTER! Owe 'em a dollar—take 'em a bushel! Two dollar—two bushel!

Yes suh! Here the Seed Loan Man, The Grocery Man and the Car Man all comin' down on him! Time for TAX man. And here if he don't pay that FERTILIZE man we can't get no more for this year. Got to raise a few ear o' corn to feed us critter so he can plow and make more corn to feed another hog! Lord! Knox and his Visitor! It got so to our shack till little Rich'll run hide under the bed when a car stop to the door and mother say when a man call "AUNTIE!" she deaf, dumb and blind!

Now, take ME. Here Big Rich says:

"You goin' help me, ain't you old gal? Look here old gal, help out the old man! You got money stick down SOME where! Ain't you got none them bill hide in you Bible? Whey (where) you hidin' you money no how?"

I say:

"Who? ME? By the time I get four stummick full, my little bit GONE!"

Not ever woman would stand for Rich. But I endures it. Love is love you know—and as the good song say:

My trouble ain't gwine lasy alway!
My trouble ain't gwine last alway!
My trouble ain't gwine last alway!
AH! Ah Lord!

My trouble gwine to end some day!
My trouble gwine to end some day!
My trouble gwine to end some day!
AH! Ah Lord!

Tell me, the roll gwine call some day!
Tell me, the roll gwine call some day!
Tell me, the roll gwine call some day!
AH! Ah Lord!

How long the train been gone!
How long the train been gone!
How long the train been gone!
AH! Ah Lord!

Wonder if my mother on board!
Wonder if my mother on board!
Wonder if my mother on board!
AH! Ah Lord!

I'm goin' meet her when the roll is call!
I'm goin' meet her when the roll is call!
I'm goin' meet her when the roll is call!
AH! Ah Lord!

I wonder if my father on board!
I wonder if my father on board!
I wonder if my father on board!
AH! Ah Lord!

I wonder if my baby on board!
I wonder if my baby on board!
I wonder if my baby on board!
AH! Ah Lord!

Oh, God army gwine to march that day!
Oh, God army gwine to march that day!
Oh, God army gwine to march that day!
AH! Ah Lord!

I'm gwine to meet my sister!
I'm gwine to meet my sister!
I'm gwine to meet my sister!
AH! Ah Lord!

I'm gwine spend my time with Jesus!
I'm gwine spend my time with Jesus!
I'm gwine spend my time with Jesus!
AH! Ah Lord!

I'm gwine home some day!
I'm gwine home some day!
I'm gwine home some day!
AH! Ah Lord!

I'm gwine to live with Jesus!
I'm gwine to live with Jesus!
I'm gwine to live with Jesus!
AH! Ah Lord!

I wonder how long my trouble gwine last!
I wonder how long my trouble gwine last!
I wonder how long my trouble gwine last!
AH! Ah Lord!

My trouble can't last alway!
My trouble can't last alway!
My trouble can't last alway!
AH! Ah Lord!

I'm gwine be at rest!
I'm gwine be at rest!
I'm gwine be at rest!
AH! Ah Lord!

(And Lillie finished the last stanza and hung up her dish towel)

"Well, I sho glad us got cow feed! Goin' out yonder to the north pole. When Uncle Quinvy see that light last night he tell Paul:

"'Boy, better lay in wood! Cold wedder! When you see a clear red like that in the sky—up in the north—it a shore (sure) sign o' cold!" (Aurora borealis)

(Lillie ended:)

"Gone! I gone now to my cows!"

Told and sung by Lillie Knox
Age—36
Murrells Inlet, S. C.
January 26, 1938.

(Verbatim)

"Peas and rice all I have to cook. And thank the Good Master for the pea to put on the rice. Some ain't so much as have rice! Well I cook up a supply of peas and rice and come on to my job thinkin' them three men fix till next mornin' and when I gone home the pot pretty near empty. Pea pot been scrape. I tell 'em:

"'You all eat the pea too gentrous. Tell you 'bout goin' too heavy in them pea! '

"So I go on and fry meat grease to the rice and tell 'em, 'boutGo eat.' And I fall in my bed. Rich come in:

"'Lill, I taste meat grease in that rice. All I KIN taste. You must-a add butts meat grease to that rice and it been rusty. Ain't you call that peas and rice?'

"I tell him 'Next time come to eat; if I adds more meat grease, won't be nothin' but meat and grease. And ten grains o' rice.'

"Them two boys SCRAP over them cornfalkes I take home. Paul say:

"'Mama! This corn-flake too good for a nigger! Too good! This white folk ration. Yes SUH! White folk ration!'

"The way I situated if I keep life in they body that all I KIN do. And if they HONGRY they eat rice and peas pretty gentrous. Tonight Rich finish and come in. Say:

"'Lill, I find some rice in the pot.'

"I tell him: 'Oh, man, that hobblin' John.' (HOPPIN' JOHN)

"He say: 'I find about a dozen pea in the pot!'

"So now I gots to hurry home and put on another pot o' peas. Got to go by the store for a quarter wuth o' rice."

SOURCE: *Lillie Knox, Age 36, February 1938. Murrells Inlet, S. C.*

"They all supper-sticious me now. Malarial fever, eh? All right! What ain't dead I know he growin'. They know that a disease you can't hide but a certain length o' time.

"Here he come home tell me he been in the POST-office! My, My! He been there so much he don't mind! He don't mind the jail-house. He feel like he home there. 'Come out here with them lousy clothes! Bring them clothes out my house!' He 'umble as a lil' whip dog. Here I know he'd orter been kill and I too sorry for him. Too sorry.

"I gone in. 'Knox, what you doin' to town all the time? You been to Conway all this time jest so-so?' He say:

"'I send you word. I send you word. I tell Baby heart "One thing you can't tell Lill. You can't tell her I drinkin'. She ain't mind my ridin' the GIRL. '"

"I tell Noonie:[39] 'He ain't got no money Noonie. And 'rounoman ain't want man got no money, What they want wid 'em?' Here Knox talkin':

"'I wuz goin' long up on the hill. And here come five men clashin'. Clashin' out. Try to make me get out my car. I wouldn't do 'em. Throw them big word at me. I have to fight. There they put the war on me. One gone to get his gun. That why it all mount up to that $30. They charge you so much for the road. The LAW make you pay so much for TOWN LIMIT. Charge you more for TOWN fight. Fight in town.'

"I 'rounmembers he had knock a boy one time. I disremember all now. Been so long and he have it happen so much o' time. (Gosh! Rich knock that boy with a LOG tongs—irons you pick up logs with. He was on the GREEN DECK. He had to ride on the carriage. Calls that the 'Green Deck.' He had to turn them logs and TURN 'EM NOW. Can't wait. Go 'Zoon! Zoon!' Turn that log! Sumpin 'rounnother they 'rounspute 'bout. Somehow 'rounnother that boy was a relation to the Masons, 'rounblong to the Mason family. And the WHOLE TOWN upstirred. And the COUNTY too! Rich Mother wuz like a fish outer water. I had $2.00 I save up. That was what I save out my grocery money. Think I goin' have a dress. He had sent home $4.00 two Satdys before. Sometimes he would send home a little when he have a study (steady) job to the mill. And all I have wus that same $2. I didn't know Mother have no money. Here the white man runs the store stop he car to Mother house.

"'Aunt Addie, how you feelin?'

"'Not so much, Boss. Not so much!'

"'I hear to-day Rich in trouble. Got him in jail. Thought I'd let you know 'bout it.'

"'Where my boy been, Cap'n?'

"'He in JAIL!'

"'Knox in JAIL?'

"I in the house to the window. I hear. I lis'n. He gone on. I say to Mother:

"'Well, jail-house make for men folks! Well, mother, trial in the mornin'. No needs for us go till trial in the mornin'.' And we have a night.

39. Loney Heywood.

"Here Knox, he wuz jest as satisfy as a cat in the meat house. There he is to the window, neck tie up with a red hand-kercher, when we hit town in the mornin'. Me totin 'roun that big heavy boy o' his'n on my hip. He up there to the window and us down in the dusty hot road. I say:

"'What you doin' up there?

"'Who me? Got me here for safe keepin'!'

"'Come on down here!'

"'Not yet! Not yet! They gots to GUIDE (guard) me! Gots to guide me!"

"I so weak I couldn't hold the baby. Set right down on the ditch bank.

"After I resses gone on a back street and come out to the office where they goin' have trial. Oh, my Lord! Missus, when they tryin a man—My Lord. There sits Knox. He sit and look like, 'I don't know WHAT kinder sentence they goin' pass on me.' The boy he had knock been a spindlin', long-legged, biggety fellow. The kind you couldn't make him DO. Boy was workin' under Rich and wouldn't pile the lumber right. 'I didn't tend to knock him. He devil me till I knock him 'fore I know I goin' knock him.' Don't have no weepins. (weapons) Wouldn't went so hard. But if you beats him or he beats you you wears THAT. Rich have no witness. Boy have none. Boy say Rich knock him. Law axk:

"'Which pass the fust lick?'

"Rich tell 'em Boy cuss Rich. Boy pick up a piece o' scantlin'. Rich already have the iron tong in his hand. Law say:

"'Well, onliest thing for you is to pay the fine! It wuz 'foretempt to kill. Murder.' Rich ask:

"'How 'bout if he'd hit me with the scantlin'?'

"But it was this way. You bother a man in that MASON family seems like it a bad thing. Specially in town. TWENTY dollars and sixteen dollars over!

"I can see Mother right now. She worked ever day them times washin'. Wash, wash, wash. Wash all day for fity cents! Wash in the cold. Wash in the rain. Wash. Wash. And I ain't know she have ANY money and she pull out a roll o' bills! (Knox her HEART.) What? She cut it out and put it in the Magister hand.

"Goin' home she say: 'Knox, when that notion come on you, back 'foregainst it! Fight! Fight!"

"Yes, here I been down. Down in BED. Miss Hess and all come to see me and say:

"'Lillie, that not you Lill? What ail you no how?'

"'Lillie, what you doin' in that bed? Lill gone off! This must be some body IMAGE o' Lillie.' I tell 'em:

"'I have the malarer fever. Make you feel turrible! Turrible!"

"'Yea? Well Lill my Mat had that fever NINE long years! '

"I ain't say a word but I know this fever I have goin' last me nine long months!"

SOURCE: *Lillie Knox—Age 37. March 10, 1938*

DAMIEN AND PITY-US[40]

(This story was read from the Bible and pointed to with the Revents finger). The following is VERBATIM as reported by one of the members who heard the sermon.

Two friend boys in the olden time. Friend in need, friend indeed. But no friend now like in the olden day. Damien and Pity-us.

They went off together in the olden country. Pity-us had kill a man. And in that part of the country they'd put you in jail for a month or so with a death cap on you. And they set a date and keep tellin' you long and long to think up good what you wanter tell your people and they'd set it down on paper to tell your people after you dead. If you kill a man in that day and time you have to dead.

Just 'bout two week 'fore the date set come, Pity-us sent for his friend Damien and say, "Damien, I wants you to go my bond and take my place for a few days. I gots to go home and see my wife and child 'forefor I hang."

Damien say:

"All right, Pity-us. Take off you cap!"

Damien put on Pity-us death cap and take he stand. (Have a stand for him to stay on cap on he head.)

Jailer, ever time he come to Damien, say:

"Damien, you done as a foolish man. You know you'll be hang in that man place."

Damien give answer:

"I know Pity-us will come! Never told me a lie yet! Know Pity-us will come!"

Pity-us have count the days. And he know the day have come but time to leave he wife and chillun hold on so tight he couldn't get away. They hang on

40. The Greek story of Damon and Pythias. Pythias was condemned to death by Dionysius the Elder. Damon allowed himself to be held in Pythias's place while the latter arranged his affairs. When Pythias returned to accept his fate, Dionysius was so moved that he set both men free.

to him. They hang on to him! They hang on to him! WOULDN'T turn him loose!

Next day he was to be hang at twelve o'clock. 'foreLeven o'clock Pity-us not there. Jailer say:

"Damien, you better be thinkin' what you goin' to say. You got one hour 'fore you'll be hang,—for Pity-us not here!"

Damien answer was:

"I know Pity-us will come!"

Thats all he could get out o' Damien!

Time went on to TEN MINUTES. Jailer say:

"Damien, you better be thinkin' 'bout what you goin' say!"

"I know Pity-us will come," was all he say to the jailer.

And when not but five minutes left they look through the window and a horse comin' for all he could worth. A horse with a man on it. And before that five minutes was up, Pity-us was there.

"Come down Damien. Gimme the death cap! I low no man to die for me! I take my own death."

And he take he place on the stand.

Judge was there. He say:

"Jailer, turn 'em loose. Turn both of 'em loose!"

SOURCE: *Told by Lillie Knox as told to her by Uncle William Oliver as told to him by Revents Aaron Pinnacle from the pulpit. Heaven's Gate Methodist Church, Murrells Inlet, S. C. April 10, 1938.*

Lillie: "It Jailin[41] and Jeremiah[42] Daddy, Abraham,[43] that die. Mary Small his wife. She BEEN gone. Jailin the one the car run over Satdy. Look like goin' down in the ocean three times would-a warn him enough. That Jailin stay sweet all the time. His sister name Mary after her Ma but they calls her 'NINETEEN.' Ever did call her 'Nineteen.' Now why does they call that girl 'Nineteen'? She drink too. I know those chillun make their Ma turn over in her grave. The dead can see what you doin', you know. Their Pa, Uncle Abraham, was a black man—a full blood African. He did go way up Norf—to Ayden Norf Calina. He been all kinder place—(ever place but the RIGHT place!) He just come home to die. Say: I come home like the 'Prodical Son' I willin' to be one of His hired servant in the back of His kitchen.'

"So when Uncle Abe die they take that text and for his funeral they preach the whole text of that.

41. Jailin Small.
42. Jeremiah Small.
43. Abraham Small.

"They didn't tale time with that old man. Two of us and the preacher and his son-in-law had to stay and finish coverin' him up.

SOURCE: *Lillie Knox, Age 37, April 1938. Murrells Inlet.*

Sumpt'in t'Eat

Zack: "Listen to the roll
And the roll was callin'!
There nobody there to answer for me!
Lord, I have to answer for myself!

Listen to the grave
And the grave a-howlin'!
There nobody there to answer for me!
Lord, I have to answer for myself!

Listen to the sea
And the sea was rollin'!
There nobody there to answer for me
Lord, I have to answer for myself!"

(Entering kitchen)
Zack: "What you say Lill? What Rich doin'?"
Lill: Oh I don't feel like no spring chicken! Rich? The first thing Big Rich have to do this mornin' wuz to knock the top off the kitchen. It wuz a-fire.

"I wuz in there takin' the dinner rice off the stove. (You know how I does. Cooks them boys dinner same time I cookin' breakfast.) And I was gettin' ready to carry the rice for the dinner in the house. And here a big live coal drop down in my rice! I look up. Fire wuz blazin'! Then strip o' clap-board from the saw-mill wuz rotten on that roof till they wuz powder. Ever now and then they ketches(catches)

"I gone to the door. Hear the pump goin'. Sound like that pump saying: 'Suck me dry!

Suck me dry!
Suck me dry!
Suck me dry!'

I call: 'Rich! Come here and out this fire!' Pump makin' such a fuss—He come from pump 'round the corner o' the house empty handed. He say:

"'Where you bucket o' water?'

"I tell him:

"'Ain't YOU had a bucket and you pumpin'?'

"I always been the one to out the fire all the <u>other</u> time. He pendin' on me. I no fix now to fight no fire. I gone on totin' the sumptin' t'eat out the house. I know if the kitchen burn down they got to eat. And I leave him to outen it. I know this one time he got to do sumptin'—else the house goin' burn. Of course if he wasn't THERE I'd a out it. He know kitchen, house and all 'gwine go if he didn't out it. I tote in my breakfast. Step down on that block and carry in the dinner rice; come back carry the breakfast hominy pot.

"He had sleep late. Got up stand by the stove. I had already cook one hoe-cake. Has to do all my bakin'pun -top (up on top of) the stove. Old stove fallin' to pieces. All rust up and oven door off.

"And poor lil' Rich down in the bay field waterin' the 'foretaters they had done set out expectin' rain that never come. Poor lil fellow stretch he length. Onliest free time lil Rich have is when he sets down to eat his sumptin t'eat. I know he sorry school over. It take a man don't love work too much hisself to drive ever body else on the plantation!)

"I not wantin' to say much. Ain't wantin' to bother Big Rich. And here he throwin' water up over the stove to out the fire and I had carry in the hominy pot and fixin' to carry in the soup. Here he punchin' that rotten roof off. And 'bout that time a piece o' that roof fall down and catch me in the side. (If I hadn't a get that soup out it wouldn't a been fitten for nobody t'eat. I know I have no business in there!) I got out then and didn"t go back in there.

"Big Rich take a pitch fork and gone to cleanin' up—cleanin' it up. After he find out he HAVE it to do. I tell Junior:

"'Boy, wash your face and eat!'

"And Big Rich ask:

"'Boy, you finish water them 'foretater?'

"And I tell Lil' Rich to go to the store. And his Pa say:

"'What you wantin'? I tell him:

"'I wantin' Lil' Rich to knock off from that field time 'forenouf to go to the store and fetch me a twenty-five cent sack o' flour, twenty-five cents-worth o' rice and a can o' them big size sardines to get me by till to-morrow.'

"We have the rumble seat full up with wood. Carryin' stove wood down to a man house on the crick. I wantin' to ketch a ride with him but he seem upset. And I was thinkin'. I didn't cook no supper. I say when I gone in home last night:

"'Rich, you hongry?'

"'Not much. Why you late?'

"'I wait to walk 'forelong with Aunt Maria.[44] Where the boy?'

44. Aunt Mariah Heywood.

"'They gone to bed.'

"They is one o' Jule boy helps with the 'foretater planting for his three meal a day. He settin' there. I say:

"'James Junior, you boys cook?'

"'No'um.'

"'Why ain't you cook? You could-a fry some meat and cook a hoecake.'

"'Well, Miss Lillie, I have a piece o' bread leave from breakfast.'

"I TOO tired. Feel like I can't go no longer. 'I tell him:

"'Well, the other two gone to bed. If you ain't hongry and UnclenRich ain't got to eat, I'm not goin' to cook.'

"And I fall down 'forecross the bed clothes and all to rest a little Then I hear somebody to my pump. Adalaine.[45] I gone to window and say:

"'Adalaine, You tell Min[46] to lend me a pint o' flour till tomorrow. What kinder bread Min cook for supper?'

"'Muffin!'

"'Bring me one!'

"Here she come bring me two. I eat one. Put one on the table and gone to bed. Rich come in, eat that muffin, drink him a glass o' water and come on to bed. And you know I was ridin' long comin' this mornin' thinkin'. I reckon I had ought to cook that man sump'tin T'eat. You know mens. Button off. 'Here a button off this shirt! Ain't I got no shirt have button on? One thing I can't wear. That's shirt with button off!' Man! You talk MAN! Don't care how kind a man if he come in hongry and nothin' done cook t'eat! Let'em come in from work SWEAT DOWN and ax for a dry shirt and none ready! He madder than a vex sea-crab! I rather mix up with a rattle snake when he quile!

"And I not Injun rubber![47] When I gone in from my day I too tired to start another day's work. Food and clothes man two fightin' piece! Them two things make a man madder than a wild hog! Sump'tin t'eat! If he been so hongry why a in't he start fire in the stove? He scared o' that old smoky stove and old sooty kitchen.

"Here after I got out the car and leave him and walkin' here this mornin' I thinkin'. I know Rich was hongry this mornin' 'fore he have to fight that fire! And I blame myself for not cookin' him a hot supper. Men does like their hot sump'tin t'eat.

"There I was so full o' thinkin' I didn't know the kitchen top was blazin' and me standin' right under the blaze! The Lord fix it so that coal drop in

45. Adalaine Knox.

46. Minnie Knox, Adalaine's mother.

47. Lillie Knox claims to lack the resilience of India rubber.

that pot and make me look up. If he hadn't I'd a come on down here to my work and gone back and find nothin' but a bed o' coals.

"When I get that hominy and soup in the house I ask:

"'You want you breakfast?'

"Rich sound serious.

"'Breakfast hour past with me now.' (No supper but one muffin!)

"I bust out:

"'You big head you! Breakfast hour past! Wait till it comes again then! I gone on to my job!'

"He clean all that mess. Make the fire safe. Come and set down and full up on hominy and soup. And that when I say:

"'I want to ride a piece with you if you plannin' on goin' to the crick!'

"He ain't the same man! After he get full up he all right.

"I look up and see Rich Junior comin' from the 'foretaters patch. Say:

"'Oh, Mama, Daddy knock all the top off the kitchen!'

"'Yes. It were burnin'.'

"'I didn't see no fire!'

"'How you goin' see fire and you in the bay waterin' 'foretater?'

"'He goin' cover it up today?'

"'How he goin' cover it?'

"'Daddy kin take he trailer and go to the mill and get lumber.'

"'That Buckra Man not goin' to give you Daddy no lumber!'

"Little Rich look up.

"'Mama, plenty o' light can get in now: We can sho see better! But how you goin' to cook?'

"And I laugh and tell him:

"'Fool with me I gwine take some bricks and make me a lil' oven here in the yard. Won't be the first time I cook out the door! Here stedder ('stead of—instead of) he OUT the fire and stop wid that, he have to knock the whole roof off! And he couldn't make me CRACK! Wouldn't crack!" ("Not say a word") I gone on in the house with the hominy pot and get tickled in there all by myself. But I knows when NOT to talk!

"That fire had Big Rich straightened. He didn't have no chance to jump on me this mornin'. But if the hour wuz pass for his breakfast, when he done knockin' off that kitchen roof he sit right down and eat!"

"You talkin' bout a man and his sum'pin t'eat? I'm tellin' you!"

SOURCE: *Lillie Knox (age 36)*
May 10th, 1938
Murrells Inlet, S. C.

Plate (False Teeth)

"Here my plate go and break. Was bitin' a hard apple. I send it off to fix. Here it come back C. O. D. I get paid off and get my plate out the office. Go on home. Say:

"'well, I can chew now. I sho glad to have my plate back in my mouth.'

"'What it cost?' (Rich ax that!) I say:

"'It cost $5.08. That leave me eight cent and ninety cent to live on till next pay day.' Here Rich:

"'Can't get no where THAT-a-way! If you had leave off that hard apple—Settin' down there grumpin' on that hard apple. Five dollar and eight cent? Make no differ if you DON'T have that plate fix. That five dollar and eight cent spend onnecessary! You could-a get 'round that! Too much o'oman got no teet!'

"I say:"

"'Reckon they too triflin to work and make money and fix 'em. They goes with no teet in front 'forecause they 'forependin' on no count man!'

"And Rich have to laugh.

"'Yes. If I hadn't a sweat and make money I'd a never see a dentist!

"He say:

"'Oh all you spend always for onneccessary thing. Yes suh! You could-a leave that apple off! Five dollar and eight cents! You could a-get 'round spendin' that! You knows how to MAKE it all right but you don't spend wise.'

"And you know what he call spend wise? I tell him:

"'Ah—law! 'Lill, lend me a dollar! I know you got some bill hide way some where. A dollar all I needs but I sho needs one bad.' That the way you men does. We womens work and you all borry and spend.'"

SOURCE: *Lillie Knox (Age 36)*
Murrells Inlet, S. C.
(May 18th, 1938)

Rich say: "Lord place the law in MAN hand. Didn't place it in no 'foreoman hand. World is hold up by mens. One o' my rib makin' a WHOLE body. God give law to man."
Min say: "Dat one rib what ruin us!"

Lillie (Looking from kitchen window)

"Isaac and King Cribb goin' by."

Minnie:[48] "That the son o' the one what get shoot in he own yard and brains spatter on the ground for chicken to pick up?"

48. Minnie Knox.

Lillie: "No'um. That the son o' the Simon Cribb who die and leave a wife in bed and 'foreleven head o' chillun all down with the flu. Doctor say he take doctor's medicine and gone in the crick after oyster. There Aunty Mary[49] were stretch on her bed. All them chillum down too. All sick. One room and nowwhere else to lie. Them sick chillum lie on the bed 'forelong-side they dead Pa. When Simon die they do something I never see'em do to us church till then. They take a funeral collection.

"Reb[50] (the Revents—the preacher say:

"'I reckon it seem strange to yinnah. I not doin' this to help the dead body. This for the family. His wife down and all them 'foreleven head o' chillun havin' the flu. This collection fo the LIVIN'.' Was for the wife and chillum 'forecause all was down. And people what didn't go up at first march on up and put they last cent on the table. They reach over cross Simon box and put it on the table. I didn't know I had money and I scratch down in my pocket and find a dime tie up in mu hankercher. Thought I had put my last nickel in the poor collection.

"Simon youngest girl he leave growed now till she give her Ma a grandson. That child have a daddy some where in the world. Wish all them host o' girl would marry 'forethout stayin' home and fullin' Aunt Mary house full o' grand chillum for her to strain with in her old age."

SOURCE: *Lillie Knox (age 36)*
May 18., 1938
Murrells Inlet, S. C.

Noonie's Service

"Noonie[51] was one of the Committee's. Reb (the Revents)[52] pinted ten Committees. Mights as well say $5. You a Committee, you 'forespected to raise $3.98. So Reb was to put on a special service to help Noonie raise her collection. That the service she write you 'bout.

"I feel too bad when I gone out there last night. I wash all day and I too tired but if I 'forespect Noonie to help me out I got to brace her. I went to Heaven Gate Church. Mind you now, Reb car broke and he walk clean from Brook Green. If it ain't five miles it six. And he light up and here he and Uncle William[53] was a settin' on the front church step—them two.

49. Mary Cribb.
50. Rev. Aaron Pinnacle.
51. Loney Heywood.
52. Rev. Aaron Pinnacle.
53. William Oliver.

"He say: 'I'll give you air (any) night you want.' I say: 'You can't give me Friday bracing the first Sunday; That your regular Love Feast night.'

"I tell him I'll divide collection with him.

"The one raise the morest supspose to get a hand-some prize. All are to get a prize. Ten on Committee. Me, Martha Jane, O'Bertha, Noonie and Bell and all.

"They put a trustee rally on and they never hasn't paid out yet. Didn't all come up. This money raising now to put the finishing touches on Heaven's Gate. Got to have a lock. Need a double lock to front door.

"When we get tired waitin' for crowd and crowd don't come, start back and got in the church and meet Edna Holmes and Adeline. They ax:

"'You finish preachin', Reb?'

(Mind now. Nobody been there but me and Miss Mary two girls and

"Reb say: 'I can't preach to the pew!' He tell 'em he can take they collection. He say 'Noonie have this service to raise a collection. That the way she tryin' to raise money on her Committee.'

"We all hate to see Reb get in the road that time o' night to walk five miles. Take that jaunt that time o' night. He say:

"'(Gone off whistlin') Oh, it's just a few steps to Brook Green!'

"Rich pass him on the road. Rich walkin'.Rush on home and crank up and catch him and run him home. Rich say:

"'When you all 'forevite Reb on a club meeting up here, youn got business to fix a way to get him home when his car broke. Reb got good patient—good patient with yinnah. I wouldn't fool with walkin' way here to give you a service and nobody to hear him and no collection and no 'forerangement make to carry him home.'

"Reb meet them girls in the branch when they say: 'You finish preachin'.?'

"He say: 'Where Noonie? Nobody there! Couldn't preach to the pew! Now you girls so late give me your collection.'

"You ain't preach!'

"'I'm here tonight for the collection! Got this church to finish!"

SOURCE: *Lillie Knox*
Burgess, S. C. June 20th, 1938

Folklore
(Verbatim)

"My Mammy was mixed off her ancestors. My Daddy was a full blood African. Full blooded black man.

"Uncle Quinvy a jet black nigger. Isaac[54] mix on the MAN side. His Ma was a jet black. All the white bloods come on the MAN side. Onliest way white

54. Isaac Knox, son of Addie Knox.

blood can get in the colored race. On the man side. Colored mens can't cross the line. He a JET BLACK NIGGER—Uncle Quinvy.

"Grandma Kit[55] mix with white and Indians. She'd walk over five miles to Brook Green from the Old Ark every first Sunday to preachin'. Big knot o' straight black hair and gulla percha comb. Little sets—shiny lil' thing like diamonts. (Of course it wasn't diamonts) And the comb teeth was far apart. She must-a had that when she were 'forenoung people. She got so she'd just wear that comb on Sunday."

SOURCE: *Lillie Knox*
Age 36
July 18th., 1938.

Punishment
Just Half a Cut

One day Papa come in. Been cuttin' oats with a cradle for Mr. Henry.[56] Cuttin' to Woodlawn. Ride Daisy backwards and fowards to work. Leave Daisy to the well. Tell me (I the oldest):

"Feed and water that horse while I eatin'."

I gone right on and feed the horse and have'em water and tie back to the well so quick I have all done when Papa come out and he think the horse ain't been tend to. 'fore he know hisself or give me time, he chop me with that four-plait whip he always tote. Mama run in between me and the whip. Lick me here on the arm and cut Mama too. Liken to kill me! Hurt my feelings worse than it hurt me. Hurt my heart. I cry the whole evenin'.

Mama got fire mad 'bout he chop me that whip. She trow (throw) a gallon jug behind him! Toss it behind him. He didn't come back till dark. She say:

"Here you tryin' to cripple my depend! You goin' kill my child?"

Papa come back that night say:

"Gal, I too sorry I hit you that whip today. Didn't know you had feed the horse."

He tease Mama 'bout that thing. He say:

"Tell you 'bout the old hen! Hawk come bother them chicken she light on him!"

SOURCE: *Lillie Knox*
July 18th., 1938
Murrells Inlet, S. C.

55. Kit Farewell.

56. Henry Willcox, owner of Woodland plantation in Murrells Inlet and Clark Willcox's brother. Woodland was also known as Woodlawn.

Papa's Knife.

"Mr. John Simons was white washing Mr. Burreen store.[57] Was white-washing house and store. (The one what got burn down) Too far for him to go back down the country ever night where he live. Have to stay in the barn on a lodgin' (a pallet) like I spread a quilt down on the hay. He had brought a old quilt but they a pack of hounds had stay in the servants house and they have it all full of flea and not smell good.

"One Saturday Pa had went to the store and him and Papa make friends and Mr. Burreen say:

"'John, you know Henry Cogsdale?'

"'No, suh! I ain't know him. He have a Auntie down the road name Patient. She my neighbor and a fine woman.'

"'Well Henry a fine boy. I raise Henry how come he mischievous. 'fore-Cause I mischievous myself. I go out last night and stay late and come home daylight and 'forefraid to go in, throw my hat in. If Miss Lucy don't throw hat back out, I go in. She toss that hat back out, I stay way 'foretill Miss Lucy blood cool! You got a woman mad and her blood good and hot, better let her blood cool for she'll sho hurt you!'

"So that night John come home with Papa. Come home with him from the store. And he was to go back to the barn to sleep but him and Papa talk so late. Mama had a extry bed in the hall for company and two bed was in the room and cook and eat and all in the little kitchen built outside. Any company, Mama'd let them eat in the house. So she send Mr. John and Papa rations inside. Fix table and send me in there so if they need coffee or glass full up with water I can do it.

"That night moon was shining bright. Bright! They talk and smoke. And they talk such a talkin'. (Nuster call Papa Mr. Cogsdale 'foretill he got 'forenuster him then call him Partner) Mama come in the kitchen. She stretch her arm and clap her hand and shuckle. Shuckle. Shuckle.

"'Chillun, that man in there call you Pa 'Mister Cogsdale! Make him feel BIG tonight.'

"I say: 'Mama, first news hell be makin' us ALL call him Mister!'

"Papa say: 'Mister John, stay with us tonight! The old lady can fix you up a lodgin'.'

"He say: 'I hates to be trouble.'

"Papa say: 'No man! My old lady LIKES to fix for company.'

"(Mind now! Mama in the kitchen. She say: 'How he say I likes to fix for company? Where I get sheet? You hear you Pa? Where pillow slip comin' from? If I 'forepend on what HENRY bring here, I not READY for no company!')

57. Vereen's general store in the Freewoods vicinity.

"But Mama was fix for company. She wash her meal sack flour sack and grits sack (All the grocery them time come in CLOTH sack) And Mama rip'em up and take all that thread she ravels out and sew'em back up and bile all the letters out. Oh, Mama have clean sheet, all right. So Papa say:

"'Oh, John, my old 'foreoman'll fix you!'

"Here he come out in the kitchen:

"'Liz! Oh Liz! I hates for John to go way this time of night and sleep in that barn!'

"'Oh, man, how I goin' fix a lodgin'? When you buy me sheet?'

"Papa laugh at Mama. 'Oh, go long Liz!'

"Then Mister John say (that been Saturday night) he say: 'Well I fixin' to go Parkersville in the mornin'.'

"Papa tell him: 'Oh it Sunday. I'll hitch up the old nag and take you home.'

"When Papa gone Mama say: 'Ah hah! You Pa won't be able to drive Daisy home tonight.'

"Daisy a red horse with a white blazed-ed face. Pap keep that horse so slick a drop o' water'ud roll offen her back. Sometimes he'd go slow on rations and not buy full 'foremount <u>for</u> the <u>horse</u> but he'd never cut DAISY 'forelowance short!

"And Papa carry John to Parkerville and bring him back. They was 'Partner' from then on 'foretill they parted. John he'd sip; Papa he'd sip. Papa'd come home sweet but able to drive Daisy. Come home at night: say:

"'Well, old gal!'

"Mama say, 'Go way! Go way Henry! Go way from me!'

"'Gal, what the matter? What you want? Tell me! Any thing you want, I get for you! Mama say:

"'What you goin' get it with? You gots nothin' but youself and hardly gots that!'

"So he tell Mama Mister John want to stay again. Mama say:

"'You want him to stay, all right with me!' Papa say:

"'He'll pay you board! Mama say:

"'Yes? All right. That YOU business!'

"One night now Mister John watch Papa take he knife out he pocket and whet it sharp on he little long whet rock, and SHAVE with it. Spit on that little rock and whet that knife SHARP. (Papa so big and stroping. Never a sick day in his life. No failin' 'forecept he WOULD drink he whiskey and go behind the bushes.) So John stay two or three weeks and we get 'forenused to him and we chillun'd miss him if he didn't come. So this night more than all he see Papa take that knife and shave. Little cup and shavin' bresh. (He call Papa 'Partner' now!) Mister John say:

"'Look here Partner! You shave with you KNIFE?'

"'Yes.' Papa tell him. 'This all the razor I got. Liz, how long has I had this knife?' Mama say:

"'I disremember, Henry. My remembrance too short! I disremember how long you is had that knife. You had it ever since Lill here was crawlin'.'

"Mister John say:

"'Partner, you cuts 'forebacco with it and all?'

"Papa say: 'Yes Man! Cuts leather, whittles sticks, cuts tobacco, shaves with it and all!'

"He make a joke outer it. John say: 'Reckon you can get a man liver with it too?'

"Mama shuckle! Shuckle. She shuckle! Papa laugh: 'Hah! Hah! Hah! Yes, John, If I has to!' Mama say:

"'Henry have to be mighty mad! Don't think he do THAT!"

"John say: 'Well miss, sometimes we have receive '(deceive)' the wife!'

"Mama say: 'Yes. That what God hate and the Debbil love!'

"Papa cut a plug o' 'forebacco and hang his overhauls up and left his knife on the table. Now John always get up early and dress but he never leave 'foretill us get up. But that mornin' he get up early and leave 'fore we dress and he didn't come back that night nor any else night! Gone! And Papa knife gone too!

"Papa ask at the store and Mr. Burreen tell him:

"'John finish his job and gone way!'

"That hurt Papa. He say: 'I sho sorry that man take my knife! I rather he had AX me for that knife. I'd ruther gie it to him!'

"Mama say: 'Well Henry, you know, some of us Hagar race will do that! The same Lord help you to get that knife will help you to get another one!'

"And after that Papa had to buy a razor—one of them that shuts up like knife. He shave with a razor after that. Didn't get no more pocket knife whould shave him.'"

SOURCE: *Lillie Knox*
July 1938 Murrells Inlet, S. C.

"Uncle Simon lost two wife. Lost he first and marry Mary—Sarah Mary. She had one daughter for him and die and he marry Aunt Becky out the Free Woods. They got long together all right till one his sons marry and move in the home. And things change kinder critical. And she seen the best thing to do been to move out and gone back to the place in the Free Woods her first husband had leave to her.

"He the one gets up at funeral and excusses anything good or bad 'bout the decease. He'll say: 'I been knowin' this sister (or brother) since he was baby-hood. Know he Grand pa and he Grand Ma. Got good in'em. Know nothin' he done to get lost. And if any one know any thing he done to lost he soul and plunge torment, he mustn't do that same sin. We must live to shun torment. This brother preach he own funeral.' (Here Uncle Simon got he hand splayed open wavin' it 'round.)"

SOURCE: *Lillie Knox*
July 1938
Murrells Inlet, S. C.

Gilbert Comes By.

"This sevenin' Gilbert[58] come by. Ax me for ice water. I say:

"'Oh, man, how you spect me able to 'foreford ice?'

"He come on it. Sit down under the tree. I washin'. I say:

"'No nuse to ax you 'bout Bessie.'[59] After while he say:

"'I got mad one day and start to kill Bessie and her Mama and her Papa.'

"I say, 'You musser gone crazy! You didn't have a mind like that did you?' He say:

"'Well, I sho did. I know they'd be all three gone and I'd have my house in the penitentiary. Just one thing keep me from doin' it; my gal Goldin[60] and my son by my first wife. You know how my son gone?'

"I tell him, 'I ain't so much as know you have a first wife.'

"'I was to the hospital myself and was dismiss. I come on to town and meet my son in bed sick. He say:

"'Pa, that you?'

"'Yes! This me! Son, if I'd a get here two days sooner I could -a help you but I 'forefraid I too late.'

"And I lean down, touch he foot and he shiver and gone!

"Then I ax 'round how he was took sick. And they tell me he had start up town to buy a pint and a girl friend had a pint and give him a drink and he gone to bed. (She one the ones thinkin' he goin' marry her.) And he wake up with a fever and a chill and never get over it.

"Gilbert say he were too sick to 'foretend the boy funeral but he tell them to bring the boy to HIS house to lay him out. And he call Uncle Will to his bed and tell him to bring him a quart of water they wash the boy in. And Uncle Will done it. And he take that quart of water and lay it RIGHT SIDE OF

58. Gilbert Lee.
59. Sarah "Bessie" Lee, Gilbert Lee's second wife.
60. Goldy Lee, Gilbert Lee's daughter.

THAT BOY in the box! And he know good and well when that BOTTLE BURST them ones what poison his boy drink goin' to die![61]

"Sure enough THREE die—two girls and a boy. They die 'bout thee days after he gone. Gilbert say when the body burst, the bottle was gwine to burst and when it burst they'd have to go."

"Gilbert got off and I didn't give him ice water. He all kinds of a man. Susspose he goes home now and does sumpin'to me! He can fix people! He THINKS he can—and no tellin' what he CAN do!"

SOURCE: *Lillie Knox*
Sept. 8th., 1938
Murrells Inlet, S. C.

(Verbatim Conversation—and Spiritual "Plumb the Line"

"Poor ole Uncle Ben![62] In church after services he stay in. Tears just pour out his eyes. Th' pitifulest thing in this world. Pitiful! Pitiful? He make you cry. Realize he doing wrong and turn back. And they read the stripture bout th' prodical son have returned. Preacher say 'I haven't call him back! I haven't beg him to come back! What sent him back? God!' He hadn't turn loose altogether. Didn't hold like he shouldder (should have). Lord, just take me back and I'll be one of your hired servants."

Revents Calina wife[63] sitting by me. She say,
"Call Uncle Ben the ninety nine sheep come back to the fold!"

I wanted to get you another song but a man cut cross that Holiness preacher. This the one they sing first (she said 'fust')."

1. Plumb the line, Member!
 " " " "!
 " " " "!
 " " " "!
 Can't get to Heaven
 Till you plumb the line!

2. Deal right, Member!
 Plumb the line!
 Deal right, Member!
 Plumb the line!
 Deal right, Member!

61. An example of conjure in practice.
62. Ben Horry.
63. Ella Carolina.

Plumb the line!
Can't get to Heaven till you plumb the line!

3. Mourn right, Member!
Plumb the line!
Mourn right, Member!
Plumb the line!
Mourn right, Member!
Plumb the line!
Can't get to Heaven
Till you plumb the line!

4. Pray right, Member!
Plumb the line!
Pray right, Member!
Plumb the line!
Pray right, Member!
Plumb the line!
Can't get to Heaven
Till you plumb the line!

5. Class right, Member!
Plumb the line!
Class right, Member'
Plumb the line!
Class right, Member!
Plumb the line!
Can't get to Heaven
Till you plumb the line!

6. Oh, the Bible tells us,
Plumb the line!
Oh, the Bible tells us,
Plumb the line!
Oh, the Bible tells us
Plumb the line!
Can't get to Heaven till you plumb the line!

"Billy,[64] Put dat ax down! (Dats Corky!) Corky,[65] put dat ax down! Don't worry wid duh ax! Do Lord! Don't want no trouble here!"

64. William "Bill" Chandler.
65. Joseph "Corky" Chandler.

Lillie: "Aunt Hagar, Jake and he wife have that trouble bout a piece o' candy!"
Hagar: (Clapping her hand) "I yeddy so! God, I yeddy so! Debbil got the land. Debbil got 'em by the tail head gwine! Do God keep me! What duh matter? Shame! Shame!"
Hagar: "George come, Saturday night.

'Who dat?'

'George!'

'(Oh, Lord, help me do!) Coming!'

"Leven O'clock Saddy night. Baby come fore day clean. Got duh two gal, three boy. Got good help! Good help now!"

"Rev was a foot-foremost baby. He said Sunday at preaching his Mother say, 'Son, you'll never hongry. You'll never want! God will take care of you.' Our preacher foot-foremost baby. Fore he convert—like any other else man. Had to be borned again. A voice came to him, 'Go preach my gospel every nation.' When the hour pass for preaching, like a dog barking on a cold trail and rabbit pass."

(Mom Hagar enters)

"Cousin, you fine down! Fine down!"

Lillie: "No man. Aint fine down! How the children then?"

Lillie: "I member one song sing Sunday.

1. My dear old Mother sick and she can't get well!
   My dear old Mother sick and she cant get well!
   Oh, my Lord!
   Do, my Lord!
   What shall I do?
2. Send for the doctor, Doctor couldn't do no good.
   Send for the doctor; doctor couldn't do no good.
   Oh, my Lord!
   Do, my Lord!
   What shall I do?
3. Doctor tell the woman, better seek the man above!
   Doctor tell the woman, better seek the man above!
   Oh, my Lord!
   Do my Lord!
   What shall I do?

(Sung at Mothers Day service Heaven's Gate Church.
Murrells Inlet, S. C. May 9th, 1937)

Source: Song by Lillie Knox
Age—35
Murrells Inlet, S. C.
Conversation by Lillie and Aunt Hagar (Though 77 years old—born just before freedom) Aunt Hagar is still an active mid-wife.)

Poor Rich and the Collector Man

"O he goin'! Goin', honey, goin'! Night and day! Got somethin' HE want to meet. Payment got to be make on that little jit he bought on a credrick. I say:

"You had already owed that seed man a big bill. Now how you gone to town to range 'bout that and come home here with a car? Takin' more on your shoulder!"

"And 'bout the time he out of sight down in the woods where he cuttin' stove wood, here come the grocery man—the one Rich own for grocery he buy WAY last summer! I tell him:

"'You want the God's truth this mornin'? I got no money and my husband got not a penny!" And that man say:

"'Well, you got a good face!'

"'Well, 'I say,' 'where they's a will they a way.' But (God's truth I'm tellin' you) Knox will pay his debt all right but the boy not been able to work. Soon as he kin pay you, he'll scrap up all he kin and come to you in town!' So the man say:

"'Well, satisfaction mean a whole lot.'

"Now Rich come out the woods, I say:

"'That man was here!'

"Rich ask:

"'What you tell him?'

"I tell him, 'YOU BRING THE SHERIFF HERE TOMORROW MORNIN' AND MAKE RICH PAY THAT MONEY!' And I cackle out!

"That been Monday. Here Friday—no SATDY! Here I am on the job, Big Rich gone somewheres on the crick and Little Rich leave to home by hisself. Man come. Stop he car. Ask Rich. Say:

"'Boy, where you Daddy?'

"Little Rich tell him:

"'I dunno (don't know), suh!'

"'He been home to-day?'

"'Yes suh!'

"'Which part of the road he went?'

"'Dunno, suh!'

"'Who boy you?'

"'Rich boy.'

"'And you don't know where you Daddy?'

"'No suh!'

"Man crank he car and gone on. Here I come home. Rich Junior tell me 'bout a collector man come and ask for he Daddy. He tell me:

"'Mama, I didn't know zactly the spot where Daddy wuz—but I know which end of the road he went. 'foreCause I know Daddy gone next the crick 'forecause ain't he sellin' oyster? And I know he have to catch the tide. But Mama, I ain't know what that man want and I ain't goin' tell NO strange mans where Daddy! I didn't know that man from Adam house cat, and Daddy all the time owin' some man some big money, and that m'out a-been the sheriff comin' atter Daddy, for all I know! I ain't goin' tell no strange man I don't know WHERE DADDY. M'out a-carry my Daddy off to the gang.[66] That man say:

"'Boy you don't know nothin'? 'And I laugh. But Mama, I thinkin'

"'Mister Man, I knows 'forenouf not to tell all I does know!'"

Source:

Lillie Knox—age 36
Murrells Inlet, S. C.

(Snap Shot Humor and Caution)
(Verbatim Conversation)

"I can hear Miss H——[67] in the court room."

"'Now Sheriff,[68] you go on and swear Lillie Knox in! She know the whole stripture 'bout how that man treat me!'

"Sheriff say,

"'Lillie Knox, what you know?'

"I say,

"'All I know, what Miss H—— tell me.'

"Sheriff say,

"'What she tell you?'

"I say,

66. The chain gang, forced prison labor.

67. Mrs. Hewitt, wife of Garland Hewitt.

68. Sheriff Brourton.

"'What she tell me? She say—I member every word Sheriff—I has a good remembrance—.'

"Sheriff say,

"'Go on! Tell it! What she tell you?'

"I say,

"'She say he[69] beat her. She say he kicked her. She say she sored and bunged up. She say her shin most broke where he cut her with his old shoe. No bones broken—none tall. Not a bone broke in her body. Just sore! Sore! Have to limp ever step. (That is she have to limp when he ain't there.) When he there she can't limp then—or she don't limp! Say she ain't got no feelin' much in her right arm. Can't raise it to her shoulder. Warn't sure but that moughtn't be rheumatiz —.'

"And I can hear Miss H—— bust in and tell him,

"'Sheriff, I swear to God I haven't told Lillie Knox nothin' like that! I'd swear it on my dyin' word! Knox is the biggest liar walked on two foot!'

"Far as I concern I have to pass that door ever day.

"That woman'll never swear no warrant 'foregainst her husband—

"One time she tell me she have Mr. H—— under a peace bond, and if he tech (touch) her again all she have to do is tell the sheriff . Under a peace bond! He couldn't tech her! Sheriff tell her, "That man beat you one more time I'll swing him and his feet'll tech this here earth no more!'
And soon as Sheriff come—Lord! If you ain't got sense that woman'll mess you up! Get you in the BILBO fust news you know! (There was a building in New Orleans—used by Spaniards—the name was Spanish very like"BILBO." Still called by Spanish name. This building was in some way connected with imprisonment and punishment of slaves. More than once Waccamaw negroes have referred to the BILBO —when meaning jail.)

"I can hear her now"Lillie went on. "'I wish God would come right down from His Kingdom and stand right here on this porch and say, ' Gilland H——, won't you recognize I'm God and treat your family better?'

"I say,

"'Yes Mam!'

"Old Miss Smith[70] stop me. She ax me,

"'Lillie, What you think of Miss H——?"

69. Garland Hewitt.
70. Mrs. Gilmore Smith

"I say,

"'I don't think, Miss Smith. I don't live with 'em!'

"I have to stop Miss Smith one day from ax me too much question. Ever thing she ax 'bout somebody, (and that white woman want to know all happen from here clean down the Neck) everything she ax I don't know. (Since Lutella[71] left her kitchen she don't hear nothin'.) She keep on,

"'How 'bout so and so Lillie?'

"I don't know'm!"

"'They say Mr. H—— beat his wife?"

"I ain't see it. I don't know'm!"

"And old Miss Smith bust out and laugh. She say,

"'Well Lillie, my Lord child, what does you know?

"I say,

"'I don't know! I stays to my own lil' house and tend to my own affair.

"She cackle out. Didn't sound tickle. Sound like one of her own big hen when she tellin' you she lay a egg—

"Ha! Ha! Ha! Child, you right! Well you right! That the best way.!

"One day you been gone. A white lady come here. Say,

"'I come here from the office. Miss C——[72] home?'

"I say,

"'No'um. Missus gone to Sandy Island.'

"She say,

"'You been with Miss C—— long time?'

"I say,

"Yes Mam. I'll be these boy black Grand-Mammy when they grow up.'

"She say,

"'You sing a lot of song for Miss C——?'

"I say, 'Yes'm. I sing a lot of song for her.

"She ax,

"'Won't you sing some for me?'

"I tell her,

"'Tell you the truth, I have to sing a lot for Missus ever day and when I through my palate gone. It down. I too tired!'

"And I cackle out!' (Want to get her mind off them song)!

71. Lutella Lance, also known as Lucile, was married to Lucien Lance.

72. Mrs. Genevieve Chandler.

"Next she ax how old the house. Ax me 'bout the Storm Song. And I tell her that Mom Hagar gone. And that long 'fore my day. (Aunt Hagar tell me she meet one on the road one time have ax her thing. Say she tell her, ' Missus my membrance too short. Too old. Ain't know a God thing! All in my head 'foreblong to us Missus! Hers—already—'fore she ax for it!)' Mom Hagar! She can tell 'em."

Source: Lillie Knox, Age 36. Murrells Inlet, S. C,

Wages o' Sin.
(Not Exactly Verbatim)

"Old Miss Shecklefoot[73] been missin' chickens. So she pizen her fowl.

"It happen they put on a big feast to Sweet Water Baptist Church.[74] And some people will steal no how! Some of 'em can't help it.—Just a habit. They hand will stick. And this here woman name Janie, been helpin' Miss Shecklefoot on her farm, been have that habit. (Janie have fowl in her own yard! Why ain't she cook her own hen for the church feast?) I tellin' this just like it look to me. Yes suh! Some people will steal the soda out a biscuit!

"Janie have to pass the fowl coop ever evenin' when she goin' home. And you know a perfessor tief (professional thief) who know 'forezactly how to do, got it down so fine, he can go right out there and pick up a chicken and us right here won't know! Leave he track but what you gwine do 'bout a track? So here Janie gone by the coop. Reach in on the roost and pick off a big fat hen. Get her by the neck. Onliest way she could-a catch her—so she wouldn't holler, you know. Carry that fowl home and brown her down. Fat! Suh! Rolls of fat! Pure gobs! Two cups o' pure grease leave in the pan—fat grease! So fat she slick as mud! Corn bread dressin' and all! Janie have a basket fix up nice as any lady basket. (And here she walkin' down that Richmond Hill trail headed for the church and chucklin' cause it never cost her nothin'!) Brown down so good Janie had have to taste that dressin'—got to see if it seem right. And she eat the goozangle.[75] She goozangle it all right! Suh! She eat that goozangle 'fore she leave home and she just fall dead in the church all-way! (aisle way)

"Next thing Miss Shecklefoot miss her hen. . (She have a name for most ever fowl on her yard. That woman know how many fowl ought to come when

73. Genevieve Chandler has most likely taken the liberty of changing the names in this story to protect the guilty.

74. Sweet Water Baptist Church, on the road to Socastee, South Carolina.

75. Chicken gizzard.

she call.) When she miss 'Miss Smiff'(that been a big old yellow Buff Orp.)—when she see 'Miss Smiff' gone she up and say,

"'I give my hen ox vomit! (Nux Vomica[76]) you know ox vomit'll kill the hawk but not kill the chicken. But it'll kill you if you eat the chicken under a certain number o' days. I put that pizen in my own fowl. If I feed my fowl on ox vomit—that my business! I been thinkin' varmint or hawk totin' off my fowl. Janie the varmint. She the one eat 'Miss Smiff.' Now anybody else want to eat my hens they is welcome. A ain't fasten no 'hands off' sign on none. But my business not raisin' fowl for the community!'

"Now you can't well pizen a hog on strickland.[77] Not on strickland. Hog a hard creeter to kill. Strickland'll run out they heel string back here, and won't harm the hog none tall.

"Some people 'bout temptation like a deer the buck-shot hit; they fall ever time. Now Janie gone—fall dead in the church all-way and ever-body have they thoughts 'bout how she gone—and now the outcry come 'bout Josh.

"Josh the one feed the hogs. Workin' round Miss Shecklefoot pastor.[78] He have to slop them hog two time ever day come—not leffin' out Sunday. Hog so fat! Hog so pretty! Just look at 'em and you smell sausage fryin'—and see chitlin bubblin' in the pot. Make a man too hongry to look on them hog ever day—'specially when he eatin' dry hominy—So Josh he look at them hog and the more corn he give 'em and the more he look the hongrier he get. He think:

"'Just to look on them hog make me taste back-bone and rice. No nuse my tryin' to buy one. Miss Shecklefoot won't sell one no how. And I ain't got cash to pay if she would sell. So I'll just borry (borrow) one them shoat. I'll barrel it up. Salt it down. Too hot to keep less'n I salts it down. I'll kill it to-night and eat the first bait of fresh for breakfast. Hog haslet good eatin'. Haslet hash for breakfast! Then I'll have haslet on my rice in my dinner bucket tomorrow. Stew that haslet down to a low gravy, put in 'em a pod of red pepper, black pepper and a seasonin' o' onion! Nothin' better you kin eat! Cook that rice dry. Ever grain separate! I got to go in the woods and cut turpentine boxes tommorrow. Man needs nourishin' food workin' in the woods. Mustn't die in debt to his stummick!

"So that how come Miss Shecklefoot shoat went visitin'. She was loan out and that hog forget the way home. Josh had his haslet hash but you know it

76. The seed of an East Indian tree, *Strychnos nux-vomica*, which contains strychnine. It was once used in medicine and as an emetic.

77. Strychnine.

78. Pasture.

don't do to eat too much o' that green meat. Fresh'll kill you if you turn yourself loose. But when Josh Mama say,

"'Son, you better hold up! It ain't been too long since your cousin Janie let a hen take her off to Glory. Look out this wild hog don't do that to you!' (Josh feared o' his Ma. That the way he fix it—tell his Ma he kill a wild hog on the rice field bank.) So he talk back to his Ma.

"'Go on Ma! Please you self. Now take me. It takes more to full me up than it do for a woman like you. Takes a good mess o' fresh to satify Josh."

And he wouldn't stop till he satify. Eat a big bait. Take his bucket and gone on in the woods to chip boxes.

"You know, in the turpentine woods all the mens nusually hang they bucket on a tree and dinner time all come together. Eat at twelve! So when twelve come and no Josh the boys gone to callin', 'Josh! Josh! Josh! Oh Josh! Still no news! Then they pure take out a search warrant. Hollerin' 'Hey! Hey! Hey!' all through the woods. Searchin'! One man gone this way; one man gone that! Whoopin' and a-hollerin'! Finally one man tell 'em:

"'Last I see Josh he been headed down to that far corner with he tool on he shoulder.'

"And after they make search 'bout an hour they come up on Josh. Just had make start to box his first pine and lay right down dead. Look like he takin' a nap—Lyin' there so peaceful.

"Some say, 'Josh heart must-a gone bad on him!'

"Some say, It look like the digestion to me! Cute digestion!'

"Some say, 'Less us look in Josh bucket and see if he eat since he leave home.'

"And when they look they find that sure enough some body been eatin' haslet hash and rice. Some got to talkin' Josh must-a had his bucket fix! Didn't a grasshopper jump out that bucket when it was open up? Some body wantin' Josh job and gone and fix his dinner with some rattlesnake dust or something.'

"When old Miss Shecklefoot heard as how Josh had gone sudden like Janie, and heard what in Josh bucket, the old lady snorted and said, "'Well, there warn't no hands off signs on them shoats neither.'"

SOURCE: *Told by Lillie Knox, Age 36, Murrells Inlet, S. C.*

Manners Will Carry You

"You have meet a man. Man say:

"Where this road go?"

"Don't take time to say 'Good Day!' Them old timey people will call his manners! Like Minnie little girl come runnin' to me in the mornin', and sing out first thing:

"Aunt Lillie, where Paul?"

"And I tell her:

"'Well, good mornin'! 'You musser sleep with Aunt Lillie last night!'

"What I mean? Mean she musser sleep in the bed with me, so didn't have to speak to me. When girl and boy pass these old timey people, and don't pass the time o' day, I've hear Grandma say:

"'Good mornin' suh! You no manners rascal you! I just respect you for your Mammy and Daddy.'

"And when a boy show his manners they always say:

"That a mannersable boy! That good manners'll carry you where money won't carry you. Hongry, and got no money, manners'll feed you!"

"I' hear old Mam Crissia say the old slavery time people would go long, and tell her when she forgot her manners:

"'You go head! You won't go far! Go long with you low manners self! Them same low manners goin' put you where the dogs won't bark at you!

"I 'foremembers hearin' Grandma talkin' to one o' them boys:

"Oh, boy! If I fall on my knees, and pray to God for you! If I go to the Lord, and tell him how disobedient you is! (Grandma sound too seriously! Them chillun scared to death!) You mouth'll turn round the back o' you head! Go head—you no-manners rascal you! That no manners'll put you where the dogs can't bark at you! No good'll never follow you!'"

Lillie Knox—age 36
Murrells Inlet, S. C.s

Poor Rich!
(Rich's Mother and the Clam Man[79]*)*

One day the clam man come long and stopped his car to our shack. He see Rich mother and hail:

"Auntie,[80] where Rich?"

(Mother say she feel like teachin' that man manners. Here he hail and ain't take time to say "Good Mornin'". She most forgot and say "You must-a sleep to my house last night?"(In Georgetown county the old negroes tell any one "hailing"or requesting information before saying "Good mornin"or "Good even'in"—"You must-a sleep with me last night." One local authority called this "a modern impertinence"but the very oldest "livers"are familiar with this way of calling one's manners) So man say:

"Auntie, whey (where) Rich?"

79. Rich Knox harvested clams as one source of income.
80. Addie Knox.

And mother tell the man:

"Dunno, suh Boss! Rich leave home this mornin'. I dunno (don't know) which-a-way he gone!"

Man go on. Ax more question:

"Which way he wife?"

"Mother tell him:

"Who? Lill? She gone to her job down to the crick. And here you is wantin' to see Rich and I can't tell when that boy'll be back home!"

Man ain't stop wid (with) question:

"Well, he'll come home by night won't he?"

Mother talk so drawly—so slow—slow as cold molasses:

"No, suh! I can't say. He liable to be back most any time. He mout (might) be back tonight—and again he moughtn't!"

Man keep on. He look like he TOO anxious. Said kinder slow and sad:

"Well, I sho want to see Rich—"

(Mother know Rich all the time owin' somebody something. She too tricky! She want to keep Rich out o' trouble and she want to help the man! She think this must be the COLLECTOR MAN). Mother sound TOO sorry. She say:

"Well, suh, Cap'n Boss, I tell you zackly how it is—Rich didn't have no money to leave you DISS (this) time. Maybe he'll have some when you come NEXT time—"

The man look funny. And he act like he choking on cold potato or something—He say:

"Auntie, ain't you know me? Ain't you know who this is? I ain't come to get no money. I come to put some money in Rich hand! I the clam man. I run by to pay Rich for them last clam and to leave this sack o' change to pay off the clam diggers. Auntie, you Rich's mother? Well, here! You'll see he gets this sack o' change won't you?:

And the man make a big old shuckle and crank he car and rode off down the muddy road. Leave mother standin' by the road holdin' that sack o' money and her mouth drop wide open!

Told by Lillie Knox—age 36
Almost verbatim
(As told to Lillie by Minnie Knox, her sister-in-law an eye witness.)
Murrells Inlet, S.C.

Have Manners
(Grandma Kit and Aunt Maria Heywood)

"You could don't have manners, but you round Grandma Kit, and anybody come to bisit (visit) her, your size and sex NOT IN THERE! The old folks talk, and you don't know what they talk, and you stay in there, if you wanter, Grandma wring your ear, and pull you nose! Sometimes she'd take up Grandpa stick, and shake it at you. You better had catch that sign! That the way Grandma raise her crowd.

"Miss Heywood[81] was a 'slavery time' you know—(born in the Reb day)— She say when she a little girl they have to tote water in a pail. Have to tote water so far! Old people all cripple up. Walk on a stick in that deep, King Road sand. Old Reb time people all cripple up. Been through the hackles— them old people. All Aunt Maria mates gone! All dead and gone!

"Aunt Maria tell me 'bout how she totin' water, when she a little missy girl—totin' way from the spring to the Big House—and she'd meet one them old women, and they say:

"'Dater, (daughter) give the old woman a drink!'

"And Aunt Maria say the old person'd say:

"'Tank you, dater! You'll have long life!'

"She say she never couldn't refuse when the old people ask for a drink, not even when the sand deep, and the sun hot, and she know if they take the drink it mean she have to walk clean back down the hill, and up the hill, for another bucket. But some the girl wouldn't let the old people drink out their bucket, and Aunt Maria say they'd tell 'em:

"'Go long! You nasty no manners thing! You'll never live out you days!'

"And you know Aunt Maria say all them girls GONE and she one leave!"

Lillie Knox—Age 36
Murrells Inlet, S. C.

Trouble Reported
(Verbatim Conversation)

"Yonder go that man to the store to get something to eat for Miss H——[82] and them young'uns! He sho be surprise if he knowed what I know 'bout them young'uns! Yes SUH! She give me the whole inscription text! Miss H—— she un-burden herself on me this mornin'.

"Dogs was barkin' at me; two of 'em come out to road and I squall at'em and make 'em gone back in the yard, and here come Gertrude ——[83] the oldest girl to the door and ax me in. I say,

"'No, Lord, child! I late now. See the sun yonder and me got them cows to milk! Them cows 'forell think I'm done dead!' Then 'fore I can move on here

81. Mariah Heywood.
82. Mrs. Hewitt.
83. Gertrude Hewitt, Mrs. Hewitt's oldest daughter.

come Miss H—— to the door. Stick her head out. First she swallow and long her neck out like she choke, and try again to swallow and then she get out,

"'How you Lillie?'

"'Not much, Miss H—— how you this mornin'?' I say. And she start,—she put on a record—

"'Me? I tryin' to swallow a piece o' flour bread here—no kind of a lard in it nor no kind of a smitchin' of grease about it! Mix with the pure, plain water! But I'll not ax HIM for nothin'—No Not if I purrish—me and his passel o' young'uns!'

"'He says this mornin' afore he leff (left) and gone to the fish'ry[84]—he says, "God knows, you'd better not be draggin' these young'uns up and down the road!" Then he name a few o' my people and say, "I know your brother Jim's not goin' to take 'em, and I know your sister Marthy's not goin' have 'em, and your Pa's second wife ain't to lay hand on 'em." And the next one he name I up and say, 'I'm not axin' you THAT! I'm not AXIN' YOU who goin' to take 'em but if you think I'm for a settin' here and lettin' these young'uns eat bread that ain't had nary a smitchin' o' lard nor no kind of grease near it—you've got another think comin','—I says,

"'I took and took till I can't took any more. He's a free man! He's as free as 'fore me and him murried!'

"And you know when that woman down and I help bathe her—her lil' thigh up here absolutely purple—all purple streaks and just like a lil' squirrel thigh! Ain't no flesh on her bone tall—tall—"

(Verbatim Conversation)

"Miss Smith—the old lady—say Sheriff Brown say it a funny case. Sheriff say he GOES there and Miss H—— won't swear out a warrant.

"Poor woman! Her body all whale up. Neighbors full o' pity, try to help her. Call the sheriff! She do nothin'! Say it's a unknown truth!

"Then Miss Teeny[85] come long in her car. Pick me up! Say her Mother-in-law[86] tell her not to take nothin' to do with that! Onliest thing to do is to lodge complaint with Mr. H——'s boss man. So Miss Teeny, she so full of pity, gone to Mr. H——'s boss man. He ain't there! Miss Teeny say Miss H—— hail her own down three or four time and want Miss Teeny to carry her and that passel of young'uns to some body home for pertection. (I ain't tell Miss

84. Sabe Rutledge's fishery at the Ark plantation.

85. Teeny Oliver.

86. Mrs. Emma Limehouse Oliver.

Teeny she been wantin' to come to YOU for pertection! When Miss Teeny ax 'What Miss C——[87] say 'bout it?' I make like I ain't burden you none tall with that woman and her trouble!) Miss Teeny say,

"'Lillie, have she got a father?' And I say,

"'Yeah, I hear she have a father!' And she say,

"'I hear her say her Daddy want her to come, and I'll take her any day she'll come, but he won't take a young'un 'forecause they got their Pa blood in 'em! He'll take her and give her a bed and rations. No body ain't goin' to 'forecuse him of lettin' child o' his'n go hongry nor naked—but she best not bring any of G—— H——'s young'uns to his house!'"

"Of course Miss Teeny and I 'foregree no woman 'goin' leave her chillun with a man too mean to stay with herself. And to be sho he must be bad as the old boy hisself.—To hear his wife tell it!

"While ago I pass back 'forelong. She fixin' bread on the table. Hail me,

"'How you feel Lill?"

"I answer I not so much and how she makin' it. She say,

"'Not much,Lillie! Dear God, I'm as sore as kicks 'forell make me.' (Got her head stick out the door. She look back in over her shoulder—a man inside—one Mr. H—— fishin' partner! She fraid he'll hear what she say! Whisper—in a loud whisper), 'Lillie, I got a notice yesterday. Hear a storm on hand! God will pervide! '

"She go on and say if she just did have three cent for a stamp! Want to mail a letter to her people up in North Carolina."

(Verbatim Conversation)
Caution

Lillie: "Say George Sands got drunk Satdy and went home and didn't come back. Whiskey drown happiness—put it out like a rain-storm put out fire.

"Come by Miss H—— this mornin', got a BOOK. She come to the door when she seed me comin'—Start,

"'God knows—'

"Keep me there a hour. I sorry for the poor thing but I ain't goin' let her make no witness out o' me! Get me on the testify stand and tell the sheriff,

"'Sheriff you ax Lillie Knox. She 'forell give you the whole inscription text!' And when I say,

"'Sheriff, I ain't know nothin' but what Miss H—— tell me!' And when the sheriff say,

87. Genevieve Chandler.

"'Go on. Tell the court what Miss H—— tell you!'

"And when I no more'n start, I kin hear Miss H——

"'God knows, I didn't told Lillie Knox a thing—not a thing! She the biggest liar on two foots! '

"That woman 'forell make me out a liar right 'fore every body! No suh! I ain't goin' let her make no witness outer me. WHO? Not ME! "

SOURCE: *Lillie Knox, Age 37, Murrells Inlet, S. C.*

Mrs. Harland[88] *Again*

"Hello Lillie! (Mama, here's Lillie)"

"Lillie Knox, put yourself here! Let me look on you! God knows I haven't seen you in a coon's day. Best come and let me look on you for the last time. Garland's[89] takin' me and them younguns out in the woods—out in a cow's paster! A place out there they said had been empty. Garland tell me (he drunk as a jackass right then"(All this time she scratchin' way at her ankle) "I got a three months' womb[90] right here on my ankle." (Noise come from other room and she cut loose on the chillun,) "Stop that destent cussin' in there. I'll stop it or I'll run you all out in the bay. Yes, Lillie, we'll be out there in that cow's paster." (She was fryin' some bologna.)

"Well, child, tell me something 'bout that place! What you know 'bout it? (Shut up childs! I wanter hear something from Lillie. She knows something and you know nary a thing.)"

I tell her, "Well Miss H——, its got a chimbley!"

Miss H—— say, "I could take my younguns and go in that house cross the field, but seems like I couldn't sleep there no how! Seems like I'd be hearin' 'em saw the plank for that man coffin all night. Them two men a-standin' there a-arguin' and a-arguin'. Start to the office. Come back, one man have the gun! Other man say,

"'If you don't give me that gun, I gwine kill you!'

"And he gone lean 'foregainst that yonder big pine. Then he got in his car and drove home and got another gun and come back. Say,

"'If you don't give me that gun, I gwine kill you!'

"Gone to cussin' and had his mouth open. And the other fellow full his mouth full o' buck shot.—full o' bullets just like shootin' down a deer. I sawed

88. Mrs. Hewitt. This is another occasion where Genevieve Chandler invents a name to avoid damaging the reputation of one of her subjects.

89. Garland Hewitt.

90. A giant mosquito bite.

him when he fall. And the other man wife hoppin' up and down on that yonder porch a-sayin',

"'Goody! Goody! Goody! Goody! Goody! Goody! He's kilt him.'

"Seems like I can't move in there nohow."

SOURCE: *Reported by Lillie Knox, Age 37, Murrells Inlet, S. C.*

(Verbatim)
Bubber

Lille: "You know one time Henry[91] want a drink o' whiskey. Way back in the field plowin'. Got on he last coat. Cold. Freezin' weather. Come home in he shirt sleeve. (Now mind, now. Done spend all he money now. All his tobacco money done throw way. And his wife she work hard gradin' tobacco and GOT her lil bit.) Here Henry talkin' to Mary.[92] Call he wife Mammy.

"'Mamma, I gots to have two dollars. I owe a man and the man come down on me". (Cold Jinuawary weather!) Mary tell him:

"'Henry, the best thing you do is come here to this fire and warm.'

("Mary tell me she look at him and she think 'Boy, I wish I had a stick! I could knock him dead! I know what he wantin' money for! But then I not disgrace the church by takin' him in it!) Henry answer Mary:

"'No, Mary. I can't warm. Not time. The man holdin' my coat. Waitin' down to the road."

"'Where you sweater?'

"'What you have to 'foremember that sweater for? I leave that to Jinks[93] house.'

("Mary say she done hear he pawn that sweater for a pint o' whiskey.')

"And here Bubber go on so pitiful.

"Mammy, I don't want that man to sellmy coat. That coat all the over coat I have. You know what coat cost 'forecause you help me pay for it. Mammy, I does hate to lose that coat.'

"Mary short o' patient. She bust out:

"Let him sell it! Let him sell it! You gots no more sense than to pawn you coat this freezin' spell for $2.' And Bubba break down. Gone to pure cryin'. He wantin' that whiskey too bad!

"'M-m-m-m-m-m Mammy!.' (you know how Bubba does stutter.) I know you don't love me. If I could get to my sister she would let me have her last

91. Henry Cogsdell Jr., Lillie Knox's brother, named for their father.
92. Mary Cogsdell, Henry Cogsdell Jr.'s wife.
93. Jinks Johnson.

two dollar bill. 'Gots no Mammy, no Daddy, no sister no brother Lord I down here by myself.'"

SOURCE: *Lillie Knox, Murrells Inlet, S. C.*

Lillie-in-the-Valley (Verbatim)

"When you broke and got no money to go to doctor, you got to fall back on the old time remedy. I been makin' them chillun keep me in life 'forem' lastin' tea.[94] It bitter all right—bitter as gall. But not bitter as seasage. I makes mint tea. Makes that for them chillun. Then there's 'wild - physic - salts'—grows just like a piece o' grass—little brown roots like hair. And 'old-field-riglum.' Pine top[95] tea, sea-sage[96] tea and 'quinzy-light'[97] root all good tea. Old field - riglum[98] smell just like pennyriyal.[99] Steep the leaf for tea. Red root, white root[100] and wild physic salts—I pends on them. I don't trouble none with no doctor.[101]

"Had a visitor to our church last night. White man from New York. Said he glad to be in this beautiful world of ours. If we enjoy it much as he do we can get a great life out of it. ' Hope God will be with you all in this beautiful county.' Mr. E—— was there too. He grow so big I took him to be one of the guesses. (guests)

"Revents preach 'bout' the chaff will be winnow away.'

"Had a pretty good collection last night. The 'world service'money is a separate money. You pay a penny a day. Of course all the member don't pay it! But it got to go in any how. Preacher be move if collections ain't right. Preacher have to report paid up. Revents always 'foreport that.

94. Tea made from the life everlasting plant, *Gnaphalium obtusifolium.*
95. Probably longleaf pine, *Pinus palustris,* the most common form of pine in the area.
96. *Baccharis halimifolia.*
97. Queen's delight, *Stillingia sylvatica.*
98. Perhaps rignum, *Monarda punctata.*
99. Pennyroyal, *Hedeoma pulegioides.*
100. *Aralia spinosa.*
101. The slaves of the South Carolina lowcountry had some unique medicine ways that drew on African and European methods while remaining distinct from both. Slaves brought knowledge of healing and root ways from Africa but often found their new setting supported different flora and fauna than their homeland. They also encountered a host of new diseases in their new world. Over time the slaves synthesized new methods (some learned from indigenous Americans, some improvised) with what they already knew. The end product was Gullah root medicine, which is reported to have been highly effective in relieving maladies common to the area.

"Medicines? Bet you'd be surprise at the medicine Mom Melia[102] know in the woods to do her good. Ready for a plaster—no money to send to Drug Store—go out there on a country road where the wagon run over 'em all the time and make 'em show up—you can find pine roots—fat (must be fat!) Chip! Chip! Chip! Put 'em in a pot and bile 'em. Skim off that stuff come on top the pot—(Looks like skum that comes up when you makin' jelly.) Make a plaster that'll draw any sort o' pain out you. Missy goes in the bay all the time and gets white root to boil for Uncle Quinvy. Oh, Lord, they's all kind o' tea in the woods. Mom Hagar all the time Huntin' all the debblement in the woods—that how make she have all that host o' gran and great-grand. Chillun stumick runnin' off—(uster call it diary; call it colitis now)—Grandma'd go and get them runnin' briar roots and carry 'em in the house and get some sut (soot) out the chimbley and tie the sut in a cloth—piece o' soft rag—and she'd boil that briar root and sut in the rag and lil' chillun and big chillun on that for diary just a-long and a-long. And she had a lil' black-berry wine. And rice! She'd boil and boil and boil rice and sometime she put a lil' chicken in the pot too.

"That little stubby kinder myrtle (call it low-bush myrtle) and sassafas and shoe-maker (sumach)[103] makes good tea. You have the measles or chicken-pox the old Granny woman'll give you some o' them hot tea and cover you down and sweat it out you.

"For high fever, Grandma'd rub you with camphor and quinine and lard. Didn't have quinine she'd give you hoar-hound[104] tea. And she keep them Palma-Christian (Castor oil bean—'palma-Christi') growin' in her yard. You just let you fever go up and here come Grandma with her hand full o' peach tree leaf. She'd tie all them on the back o' you neck, and palma-Christian leaf on you wrist. Fever VERY high she'd wet collard leaf in cold water and bind 'em on your wrist and collard or palma-Christian leaf all tie on the bottom o' you feets and here she givin' you hot hoar-hound tea hot as you can drink it and coverin' you down and you'll sweat it off all right. You GOT to sweat.

"Now thyme! Grandma save that for seasonin'. Like she have the preachers or any big company. She'd want to do extry—put on airs! She'd put a lil' sprig o' green thyme in the oyster or fish and she'd put egg round the dish. When she have a brown baked hen, she'd put sprigs o' thyme and hard-boiled egg in all the little places on the dish where the chicken didn't full it. And let me tell you—chillun got no business in there till all the preacher through. And me? I must mind fly. She'd get a lil' gum stick or myrtle or youpon and

102. Emelia Holmes.
103. *Rhus copallina.*
104. *Eupatorium hyssopifolium.*

notch it up pretty and fold a newspaper like this' (illustrating over broom stick) "Lemme (let me) see here now. I can show you zactly how that think fix! Grandma'd say:

"'Come on gal! Got to make a fly bresh! Revents comin' to dinner!'

"And you can't crack! Can't open you mouth or move out you track. Keep a steady aim. And don't make no difference how long they sit to the table. And me so short and dumpy I have to stand on a block to reach over they head. Nothin' left but necks? Wouldn't be no neck go on Grandma table. They'd left the carcass and the neck in the kitchen. All the good liver and gizankle[105] cut up in the gravy. And Grandma goin' always have that company table-cloth and Sunday dishes. Certain dishes you not low to nuse ever day. Lord, Grandma hold her head high! I got the Grandma big old iron spider now she always bake her break on. Aunty Vick take mosto' grandma[106] old oven to Drumhill, North Calina. Grandma'd take that old oven and bake light bread and cake and rolls and all right down in the fire-place. She'd bake hen and all.

"Now Grandpa never didn't buy no meat. He'd have a bunch o' piney woods rooters and keep his good stock penned up. All the time he'd have a cow to butcher off and on. He'd kill five head o' hogs at a time. And when March come in he'd hold upp off the corn and buy grits and save the little corn left to run the creeters—the hog, chickens and horse. And he'd always figger so's he'd have one hog to kill in March. He didn't go to town much to buy. But in the spring he'd go to that mid way store and buy a big old hogs-git-barrel o' flour—and he'd make his own rice. Plant a little bottom (low piece o' ground) back there next the Big Bay in rice. That always carry them. Flour the most he'd hafter (have to) buy. Grandma so free-handed the lard would run out too sometimes. She never couldn't seem to enjoy nothin' too much when her neighbors hongry. But there was sugar and coffee. Sometimes she'd send me to the nearest Post-office for them. I'd go cross the big savannah and come o t there by that dippin' vat.—And walk the old Socastee road down for coffee, sugar, soap and gold-dust. Nusually she make her own lye soap. But she'd buy a lil' store soap to wash us faces and Sunday clothes. Wash! Grandma make you wash them clothes outer two sudzy water and must bile and wrench! (Rinse). You got to keep on wrenchin' (rinsing) till the water clear. If the water cloudy you just march back to the pump and tote another tub o' water. Pump! I pump water till my arm pure wore out. I can see Grandma right now smellin'! Smell 'em. Smell em! She wanter (want to) find out if they any soap left in 'em. She wouldn't low us chillun to tech Miss

105. Chicken gizzard.

106. Venia Cogsdell, Lillie Knox's paternal grandmother.

Min clothes. No suh! Wouldn't let us tech yinnah things. No,SUH! Take that oman clothes out there and dinge 'em? I can't trust yinnah chillun with Miss Min[107] clothes!

"I so low I have to stand on a box. There the tub settin' on a big old dead live-oak block. I was 'bout seven when Grandma learn me to wash. When I home nobody there when Mam sick but me. Nobody but me to do nothin'. Pick up scrange and thing to keep the pot boilin'. Corner in the kitchen pile up! I think I gettin' wood! Use no ax. Just ramble round the woods, find scrange and dead stuff, and broke 'em up with my foot, and come home totin' it all tie up in a ragged sack on my head. Mama lyin' in bed. Mama and Papa they'd praise me up! Here I'd pitch up in the mornin', start up a fire! Didn't need no kindlin'. Have all them lil' dry scrange. Here I'd sit down on the hearth and build a lil' fence out all them lil' limb and blow on the coal—(if they been any coal) and if I have match I'd set it to the bottom and watch that little fence go to burnin'. Then I'd go to cookin' breakfast. Aunt Jane and Mom Ella and all them old head come to see Mama. They'd look at the baby first,—the new baby. I can hear Mom Ella:

"“'Gal, my Lawd, you got a fine child!' Mama'd say:

"'Shucks! This here gal come she ain't know what ahead! Just come for see! Come for see!' (That how come we call Sister 'Come-for-see' till today).

"But you let a—BOY come, here Papa! He out front, the mens walk by Papa hail 'em!

"'Stop by! I'll make my boy wallow you in the sand!'

"Mans go look. Stand there by Mama bed lookin' down.

"'I tell you Cogsdell, you sho got a bouncer all right! That's a MAN! A MAN!'

"Papa laugh one them healthy laugh o' his'n:

"'A man SON! That a MAN son! '

"Poor old Papa! Old fellow didn't live to see his chillun get grown. Man is a funny creeter. They crazy 'bout they girl baby too. Love girl. But you just let a boy come! Take Miss Heywood to tell you 'bout a boy! She call 'em 'Thousand dollar' child. She say Slavery time girl worth her hundreds; boy sell for thousands. Say they rejoicing on a plantation when it come a boy.[108]

"When Papa gone, I know Papa was dead 'fore somebody come to house. Somebody had tell me in my sleep. Less see how old I wuz. 'bout twelve when

107. Mary Anna Willcox, Genevieve Chandler's mother.

108. As the Gullah people made the transition from servitude to freedom, certain traditions persisted. Male children continued to hold a privileged place in the collective Gullah imagination, partially because males had been a more valuable commodity than females in the slave trade.

Papa die. I join the church when I 'foreleven and I was workin' to Missus, 'bout a year 'fore he die.

"That night (Lijah[109] wuz three months old or less. That poor boy don't know nothin' 'bout he daddy. And Mama die when he four! He wasn't old 'forenouf to 'foremember her future (feature) nor nothin'. Mam wuz layin' down there. I been sleep too. Must'a been 'bout two or three in the mornin'. I wake up and start to cry. Mama hear me and ax what to matter I cry. I say:

"'Ain't nothin''!

"But I cry. I cry. I sit up in the bed and cry. And she keep on:

"'Tunk, (that her name for me) What you cryin' for?'

"And just when I fixin' to tell her I hear Miss Add[110] and Miss Hess talkin' comin' long the road. And they come on in the yard and call Mama:

"'Liz! Liz!'

"'Mam!' Mama answer.

"'Sleep?'

"'No'um. Wuz sleep but wake up now! This gal here wake me up cryin'. I ain't know why!'

"By this time Mama have the door open.

"'Liz, how you feelin'?'

"'Very well, Hess. How you?'

"'Not feelin' good.'

"'What the matter Hess?' And all the time Mama wonderin' what they want here in the middle night!'

"'Nothin' much! Nothin' much!'

"'Come on in!'

"And they come walkin' in and I lie there on the bed and I cry and I cry. I have see Daddy dead just as plain in my sleep and I know why they come—Nobody tell me nothin' but I wuz lyin' there listenin'. I know. I know!

"Miss Add say:

"'Liz, where Henry?' Mama tell her:

"Henry gone in the creek! Henry full up on water-melon and gone flounderin'. Take he gig and a cart o' fat kindlin' and gone 'bout sunset to fish till tide too high. This gal here say no where don't hurt her, but she keep right on cryin'. '

(Miss Hess get up go to walkin'. Walkin'. Go to bucket, take the gourd and get a drink and go back to walkin. Hate too bad to tell Mama. Go back walkin'.

109. Elijah Cogsdell, Lillie Knox's brother.

110. Addie Knox.

"'Liz, I ain't know how TRUE it is, but we come to tell you—Somebody say Henry mighty sick down to the crick shore—to Buck landin'. Don't know how true he is. This just what we HEAR—'

"'HENRY? MY Henry? He left here well this evenin'. Course he could-a took sick and die in this time—'

"And I cry out:

"'My Papa? He ain't sick! You can't fool me! My Papa dead!'

"Miss Hess sound too sorry:

"'No child! He just took bad sick—'

"And then I holler. I holler till the neighbors larmed. And here come Mr. Josiah to see what wrong.

"And Miss Hess and Miss Add never would say 'He dead.'

"Mama get up like she crazy,—and they throw a frock on her. Miss Min had give her a round velvet hat. Round hat. Reddish. Make up with a rim. Would pull down and keep you years warm. Wore skirts and waisses them time. And she had a worsted skirt lined from brown linin'. And Miss Add took a big safety pin and pinned it on. And Mama stepped in her old slides. Didn't take time for no stockin'. (She started bare-feet and they make her stop.) She goin' to Henry now—goin' down to the crick shore, to the water—

"Me there and all sleep. Other chillun know nothin'. Me one wake. And that dream have me scare. I call Sister:[111]

"'Sister! Sister! Papa dead!'

"Sister half wake. Tell me:

"'Oh shuc! Oh shuc! You all time 'foremagine thing!'

"Mama got to landin'. A big fire there.—Driftwood bonfire. Mister Joe there and a good many more. And she stumble and her hat gone in the fire. If they hadn't been quick on the trigger she'd fall in. That red velvet hat got burn up.

"And that whole four years she live behind him it was 'Henry! Henry!' She all the time talk Henry. Never stopped talkin' Henry. We'd have good fry fish and thing he love to eat. She'd say: 'Now if HENRY was just here!' and she'd stop eatin' and get up and leave the table. She fret so Lijah wasn't stribin'. Baby stopped growin'. Measley, weasley. Grandma talk to her:

"'Lizzie, that fretted milk goin' pizen that child.'

"And sho 'forenouf he didn't stribe like he orter.

111. Gineva Cogsdell.

"Here come Mister Joe bringin' Papa home. He was on a cotton mattress stretch out in a waggin. And when they got him to the house they had to rip down a piece o' the fence to the front gate. Took down a panel. Then they drive in and back the waggin up to the front door. I can hear Mister Joe say:

"'Right here!'

"I hear the waggin I say:

"'Wake up Sister! They bringin' Papa home!"

"'Papa dead show 'forenouf?'

"'Papa dead. Course he dead!'

"'Who tell you Pap dead?'

"'Ain't nobody tell me. I see him when I sleep. I KNOW. I know Papa dead.'

"Miss Hess had to nuse camphor and rub Mama and work on her.

"They bring body in. Had a lil' cot. Must-a bring that cot with them. Had to move the table and close the back door and let the cot go right 'forecross where the door. Big room and lil' bed room to side. I 'foremember how we shut our door. Two nails—one on one side; one on other. Had to tie string from one nail to other. Kitchen a separate lil' room off behind.

"Papa was swell till he couln't swell no more. And the water-melon gushing out his mouth and nose. Keep a-comin'. I 'foremember it good as A.B.C. When they got him dress and in the box that water-melon still comin' and he swell so he couldn't get in the box. They had to draw the nails. I couldn't stay in the room but I hear through the wall—I hear 'em talkin'—talkin'—They was talkin' to Papa.

"'Stretch you are out Henry! Stretch you arm!'

"Papa have his arm drawed up—but they kept on talkin' like that to him and he straighten out.

"Papa's Mama names was Venia—Mr. Red-Whiskered Wilson[112] what runs the mill made Mama Venia box and Grandma Kit box and Mama and Papa box. Fall. Carry Papa home that night. Wash him. Dress him. See after box that day and carry news round to everbody. Settin' up at Heaven Gate that night. Next day the funeral. Revents Heywood the preacher then. I 'foremember him startin' to cry. He start off:

"'Me and this man wuz like brother. We growed up together. We tramped the King Highway goin' to the Old Ark. We hunted, fished, played and tend school together.'

112. Local magistrate and owner of a gristmill. Wilson lived on the Wachesaw side of Mission Swamp.

"And the Revents broke down.

"Papa had a sad funeral. Wasn't sick. Just die right out.

"I 'fore member the Revents ask God to help the livin'. He say they the one to consider. Ask God help. Then they pass Lijah over the box. Done that so Papa wouldn't come back and carry the baby. That a old timey custom. One hold the baby on one side and pass him over the box to one on the other side.

"Then the four years Mama live to Mount Gilead[113] 'fore she die she say:

"'I took sick! I goin' home to my Lord and my Henry!'

"She had the pneumonia. And me sixteen. My first boy was here. Paul had come. And me the onliest one to take charge o' all that gang o' chillun—and my boy just walkin', and ever one o' the bunch gone down with the flu. Friday night she got up in a chair and tell me:

"'Tunk (she give me that name) hand me Lijah. Bring Paul here. And she take Lijah in one arm and she ax for the pillow and she "Peep-eyed"and played with them two babies, then she say:

"'I hates to leave my babies but I gots to go. Too sick. Take 'em now Tunk. Mama got to lay back down!'

"I 'foremembers how she got up and hold on to the rockin' chair and creep and pull long by the chair and fall back on the bed. Mama lay down there—look up and sigh.

"'Oh Lord,' she say, 'have mercy on me! Take care my chillun! Do, Good Master! For Jesus sake, Amen!'

"Yes I was sixteen. Tyler Carr come by. He been fishin' in the creek. I tell him tell Miss Rina Mama worse. To do come bring me some milk from Mr. Cause-er-way.[114] I want some for Mama and Mr. Cause-er-way the nearest white neighbor and he was milkin' then. Cow fresh. Miss Rina come and sit with Mama and I went to work that Monday. Miss Heywood got the news and here she come. When she gone she send Miss Hess. Miss Min say:

"'Let me hear but you don't leave you Mama, Lil"

"She 'bout gone Friday. She got up and gone on the back porch and pump herself a drink o' water. I was down to the crick. Thought I'd get a half a-dozen clams to make a lil' broth. She wasn't eatin'. When I come back in here she been to the pump. She say:

"'Missus goin' send you all sumptin' to eat. Some milk and grocery. Try to keep these chillun together and be a good girl. And above all things, Tunk, have good manners to all—'specially to old people. I'm goin', child! I'm goin' to my Lord!'

113. Mount Gilead is on the northern portion of the Murrells Inlet creek.

114. Mr. Causey, a white man in the area.

"Then she'd call Aunty Vick, She'd say:

"'Sister Vick and Brother Washie comin'!' (They had come from Drumhill sure 'forenouf and was to the Old Ark at Grandma house right then but NOBODY HADN'T TELL HER. We never knowed till next day.

"I 'foremember she slip way at sunset next day. I was the onliest one hold up. All the chillun in bed. And here you come. And you half full the glass with castor oil—the pure oil. And then you finish fullin' the glass with milk and shake it. And I 'foremember just as good you tilt my head back and hold my nose and I have to breathe and it gone down! When you gone Uncle Washie ax me:

"'She a doctor?' I say:

"'No, Suh. Her brother a doctor.'[115]

"Aunty Vick come. She look 'round. She say:

"'No doctor? Ain't nobody send for no doctor nor nothin'?' I say:

"'Auntie Vick, Mama sick, I sick, all the children sick. I done all I know to do.'

"Poor lil' Paul, the fever have him jest pantin', 'Huh! Huh! Huh! Huh!'

"And after Mama put away I take all them chillun and move to Missus' back yard."[116]

SOURCE: NARRATED BY LILLIE KNOX

Paul Tells a Story (Budder Rabbit and Budder Frog)

Last night all had finish supper and was settin' 'round. I was patchin'. Junior say: "Bubba, tell me and Sister a story." (Here he callin' Paul little thirteen year old wife SISTER! She nothin' but a child,honey. Nothin' but a child!) Paul say:

"One time there was Budder Rabbit and Budder Frog. They have some PEAS and they plannin' on swappin' the peas to Mister Man for a dog.

"You know Budder Frog does always be SWALLOWIN'. Swallowin' like he eatin' sumpin'. And Budder Rabbit he think Budder Frog was eatin'. And he think: "I better eat some MY pea too! There Budder Frog eatin' pea. So ever time Budder Frog swallow , Budder Rabbit HE swallow. Eatin' pea!

"Now here Budder Frog have he WHOLE BUSHEL! Both carry they peas at the same time to pay for the dog. Medjur (measure) up. Budder FROG have his whole 'foremount.—But Budder Rabbit was SHORT MEDJUR. (You see he had eat some his pea.) So the Man give Budder Frog a WHOLE dog. Budder Rabbit didn't get nothin' but a HEAD. A dog head.

115. Dr. Dick Willcox.

116. The Willcox's home at the Hermitage.

"Budder Rabbit stick he little dog head down in he pocket, suh, and come on. Budder Frog he hop long and his dog run ahead. He hit a trail. Went tootlin' off in the bushes and jump a deer! Big old buck deer! And he run him down and CATCH the deer.

"Budder Frog was makin' it to the deer and Budder Rabbit run and get there first! And he run Budder Frog dog way and put his dog head down there by the deer !'Bout that time Budder Frog come hoppin' up. Say:

"MY dog jump that deer !"

"No, Budder Frog. Was MY dog! My dog head was right TO the deer! See?

"Budder Frog say: "Dog head couldn't catch deer."

Budder Rabbit say: "Yes, My dog head catch that deer."

So now Budder Frog hop on off in the wood and call his dog and he get a stick and BEAT 'foregainst a tree! He BEAT 'foregainst a tree! Beat 'foregainst tree! And ever lick he give, he holler: 'Do Maussa! Do Maussa!Do Maussa! Tain't my dog. Maussa! Tain't my dog Maussa! Tain't my dog Maussa! Budder Rabbit dog catch you deer! (Ah VAM! Ah VAM! Ah VAM!) 'Tain't MY dog, Maussa; Tain't my dog ! Tain't my dog! Was Budder RABBIT dog! DO Maussa! DO Maussa! Do Maussa!'[117]

"Budder Rabbit listen! listen! He say:

"Hunh! Wazn't My dog! Who ever see a dog HEAD catch a deer before?

HUNH!'Stick he dog head in he pocket and gone on.Say: That sho was Budder Frog dog catch that deer!'

So Budder Frog skin he deer and gone on home."

When Paul had tell he tale Junior say:

"Now Daddy, you tell us a story."

Folklore
Todger Todd

"I'm late. Come by Miss Todd's[118] house this mornin' and I like to never got way. When I'm behind time it pays me to cut through the woods. I no more than come in sight down the road than that knee boy[119] they calls 'Hoot'[120]

117. Frog pretends to turn Rabbit in for poaching, thus outsmarting him and winning a rare victory for the other animals. The point remains the same, however, whether Rabbit wins out or not. The slave is intended to identify with the small, seemingly less powerful character who prevails, through wit and craftiness, over an obviously more powerful character.

118. Ola Todd.

119. Not knowing Ola Todd's children's exact ages, Lillie Knox refers to their relative sizes as descriptions. Hoot Todd is as tall as his mother's knees.

120. Hoot Todd.

beat it to the house to warn his Ma and when I hit their woodpile here was Miss Todd with her head poke out the front door. I'm tellin' you that white woman told me a book this mornin. 'Here she went talkin' right through her nose and not stoppin' for nothin' but to spit snuff:

"Well, Lillie Knox, how you feelin' this mornin'? Cold's got me all chocked up. My brongal goozles is pretty nigh stopped up. I gets hot over the stove and runs in and out a-totin wood and water.

"Lillie, did you hear 'bout my Todger? I thought I knowed him like I knowed my own name. Looks like any woman would a learnt a man when they been married to 'em goin' on twenty years. But here yesterday he took a new ridge of a plight! Put on his Sunday clothes that hadn't been took out the trunk since Pepper Todd's buryin' and made me dig up a outfit for the whole passel o' younguns and rig out the whole shebang. (Todger don't never miss a show in a tent.) And I said: 'Todger, to be sho they ain't havin' no tent show down to the village today? 'And he never said nothin'. He just piled the whole gang in that truck o' his'n and took the whole shootin' match over to that new Missionary or 'foreCiety or sumpin' ruther,"

And the waist high girl they calls Trizzie[121] went to 'foresplainin':

"Maw, that's Paw's KIND of a church. That's the kind of church he tended back in Norf Calina where we come from.
They started up a Missionary Baptist."

And Miss Todd went on:

"Well I donts know hits name and 'forenomination and I donts care but I'm shore glad to have Todger clear this bunch o' younguns out the house one day in the week so's I can fetch a breath and have room to stretch."

"Yes, he took'em ever one to meetin' on Sunday and he warn't drunk NEITHER. He was himself!"

And Trizzie said:

"That were a surprised church full of people when we piled in!"

"And Miss Ola went on:

"It was enough to give'em a surprise. Here Todger Todd
as had never darkened a church door since he come in the community marchin' in with all them younguns and fullin' up a whole bench!"

And Trizzie told her:

"Maw, little Hoot now, he made a miss step and went and set himself in the preacher's chair. He never so much as pulled off his cap but sot with his head dropped down on his
chist and his eye a-peepin' 'round seein' all there was to see and hearin' all he could hear through them ear flaps."

121. Trizzie Todd.

And Miss Todd she had to help tell it!

"And it seemed like they all had to praise Todger. Say he looked so nice they like to never knowed him! Even down to Miss Byrd[122] herself come and shook hands. They give my old man and the whole shebang such a welcome he's plannin' on not missin' nary 'forenother service. And now they gone to talkin' Christmas tree a yoke o' oxes couldn't pull my younguns way from that church Saturday night comin'! Todger come in and said:

'Ola, me and the younguns fulls a bench.'

And little Hoot said:

"I mean!"

And Cootsie[123] (she"s the one 'foretween Trizzie and Hoot) she said:

"Paw, has we gots to go ever Sunday after Christmas? That's the poorest show you took us to yet!"

George Washington (Verbatim)

"George was good to his Mama.[124] She say, 'I can pend on George!' Boy would drink! Shorten his days! Own worse enemy! Buy old stuff, drink it up, feel too rich for a few days.

"Miss Clara say, 'Oh, son, I brought you into this world, rock you from the cradle, and this mornin' I got to give you up. You leave Lennie and the three children.'

"Lennie[125] and Miss Clara think somebody put something cross George path. They think he been fix. He lie there and say he waitin' like Job till his change come.

"I had a half-brother like to been run crazy. Pain in the head! Fix! They took some kinder rattlesnake dust and fix him. Nobody didn't know how. Didn't know whether somebody lay something cross that man path or put poison in his cap or what been done. Uncle had to go to Florence and get the root man. Just did save him.

"Quimm[126] oldest boy gone off and got fix that same way by some girl mother to North Calina. Never didn't come back, dead or alive.

Get sick over to North Calina, Rich done that same thing. Got hissef (hisself) fix by some woman he run up with. Mother hadn't gone to root woman,

122. Wife of Ed Byrd.
123. Cootsie Todd.
124. Clara Washington.
125. Lennie Washington.
126. Quinvy Knox.

Rich would-a been gone long time. Mother just give Rich that root woman treatment and turn that spell in time."

Lilllie Knox

Rufus! Rufus!

I 'foremember a old slavery time story Aunt Sarah Gathers tell us 'bout Rufus. Talkin' 'bout Uncle Rufus Singleton and his slow horse must-a put her in mind of it. The way she tell it been this:

"Once they was a old man love to get up in the church and testify. He'd tell his 'foresperience to the church. When the preacher give them chance to tell their 'foresperience he the first one jump up and say:

"'Members, when the Lord call Rufus, Rufus ready for to go!'

"Now it happen they was a bunch of bad boys member of that church and they too tired of hearin' Uncle Rufus make that same testify ever 'foresperience meetin'. So they collect together in the church yard and plan together and when Uncle Rufus and all the old head come out the door the boys all done left. So Uncle Rufus give'em good-night all 'round an' gone hobblin' off on that old rattan stick he always walks with.

"It seem like there was a great big grand-father pine tree to the end of the church lane just where Uncle Rufus had to turn and when he come opposin' that tree here come a voice from 'forehind that pine tree callin':

"'Rufus! Rufus!
The Fadder call you home!'

"Come from 'forehind that big old pine. Sound weak the first time but come stronger the next time:

"Rufus! Rufus!
The Fadder call you home!'

"Here he gone! The old man ain't know he could-a walk at such a speed! And he move so fast he surprise himself when he look up and find he to the corner of the grave yard fence! And just when he 'bout to breeze easy, here come that same talk out the fence corner. Kind of sad little tune to it"

"Rufus! Rufus!
De Fadder call you home!'

"This time the old man so scare he don't take time to use no cane. He just bend over and plow throught that King Road sand and forgot he have a cripple leg. He ain't take time to 'foremember 'bout no rheumatism. And first news here the moon risin' and he see that big old sycamore 'front of that old shack where that wicked old Ham Deas passed out. That house a place nobody wantin' to pass at night no how and Uncle Rufus was scare 'fore he hear that voice comin' out tha t shack when he know well nobody in the shack"

"'Rufus! Rufus!
Your Fadder call you home!'

"The old man lit out! Aunt Sarah say he drop his stick! Say his wife find that stick next day. And he ain't stop till he hit his own front gate. The gate was hinge on and a piece of cow chain with a old iron pump swinging to it would always pull it to. They was a clump of wild plum bushes growing right outside the gate and as Uncle Rufus hand fall on the gate to shove'em open and he thinkin' 'Thank the good Master I home at last!' Here come that same little tune out them plum bushes:

"'Rufus! Rufus!
You Fadder call you home!'

"Uncle Rufus never couldn't 'foremember how he got in that house! Aunt Sarah say he fall in the front door and so tired he can't raise up so he just gone to crawlin' and he crawl! He crawl! He gone right under the bed 'fore he stop and leave nothin' showin' but his big foots. And he pant! He puff and snort and he get out:

"'Old 'foreoman! If anybody—come here—call Rufus—say—I ain't here!'

"And 'bout that time here that call come again and this time it to the front door! And Uncle Rufus wife hear! And she go and brace 'foregainst that door and she sing out:

"Rufus ain't here! He ain't home I tell you! Rufus to the church!'

"And that voice sing back:

"'De Lord say
Rufus not here to send he wife!'

"And you know what that 'foreoman done? She leave the door and run and grab him by that big old foot and she say:

"'Rufus! Rufus! Come out! Come from under that bed I tell you! 'fore-Cause I ain't'gwine! I ain't say I ready! I ain't ready for go! You all time say you the one ready! Come out!'

Aunt Sarah make me laugh that night. I laugh till I hurt. Here she pullin' chair out the way and makin' a break-a-way so he can crawl out. She actin' all that out and you can see his old brogan shoe poke out from under the bed—and Rufus not comin' when his Fadder call!

SOURCE: *Told to Lillie Knox*
By Mom Sarah Gathers
Parkersville,
Near Pawleys Island
South Carolina.

Calvin's Funeral[127]

"Warn't no use havin' things like they done. They knowed that was hard clay. Ought to set Calvin hour for twelve. Havin' the funeral preached at three! It'll be nine tonight 'fore they get that boy covered."

(The graves—mounds of brown oak leaves—were marked with articles loved or used by the departed. One had a clock on it; one, a bottle of medicine and the spoon last used.)

"Diggin' Calvin grave cross the world. He have to lie north and south. Make the grave north and south when a man drownded. He had a struggle! Never put them east and west. Anybody can come here and see that grave and know that person was drownded.[128]

"Was to put Calvin to Laurel Hill Cemetery but the new kennel (canal) cut the grave-yard off. Old Aunt Margaret wanted Calvin put to the church but nobody been put to the church yet; they haven't started off the new grave-yard. To start off a new buryin' ground, you got to dig a grave and bury a log—just like it was something. The old slavery time people say this must be done; if you don't do it this way the first one buried lie callin' for some one to come keep 'em company, and call so till they soon have the cemetery fulled up. Old Miss Blanton said she knew a man over in Horry, and he said wasn't feared to be the first. So when he died, they was a church to the foot of the hill he lived on, and they never hadn't started a cemetery, so they put him away there—the first one. In less'n a year he had called six members of his family.

"They warn't no use in makin' Calvin funeral so sad. If I'd a-preached it, I would not a-made it that-a-way.

"Satan try to steal my crown!
Satan try to steal my crown!
Oh, the sheep on the right,
And the goats on the left,
We'll never run to-gether any more!"
(Lillie's tune to this is a weird wailin')

SOURCE: *Given by Lillie Knox, Murrells Inlet, S. C.*

127. Calvin Bryant, who died seining at Sabe Rutledge's fishery on the Ark plantation.
128. Members of the Gullah community are traditionally buried lying with their heads toward the east. The drowned are the exception to this rule. They are buried lying north to south, so their spirits will not be restless.

Minnie Ladson Knox

Several of Minnie Knox's siblings figure significantly in Genevieve Chandler's collected interviews. Although their exact kinship is uncertain, Julia, Mary, Richard, Minnie, Zackie, Douglas, and Isaac were raised as brothers and sisters in the household of Gabe and Addie Knox. When Addie Knox married Frank Ladson, she brought a houseful of children with her. In addition Addie and Frank had children together. Minnie was one of these children. She apparently acquired the Knox name, not through the kinship ties of her mother's first marriage, but through marrying a Knox herself.

While she did not prove as voluble as her other siblings, Minnie did give Genevieve a good glimpse of her character. Her interviews suggest that supernatural mysteries held a special draw for her. Minnie's tales are filled with strange happenings, good-luck charms, and gypsies. The devil himself even makes an appearance. Her stories about the trickster slave John are also noteworthy. Unlike the allegorical Buh Rabbit tales found interspersed through the body of Chandler's interviews, these tales openly and boldly pit a crafty slave, John, against his powerful but utterly confounded owner. In Minnie's telling, John's success in the face of adversity has a providential character; as John puts it, "you can't hurt me Maussa. The Lord's for me Maussa!"

The U.S. Census records her age as sixteen in 1930. She would have been about twenty-four when Chandler interviewed her in 1938. Born in the Knoxville community around 1914, Minnie Ladson Knox lived eighty-two years. She died in Florida, where she spent her later years. Her body was brought back to the community, and she is buried at Heaven's Gate Church graveyard.

Lucky Bone

"Dey does say black cat has een'um uh lucky bone. Doan kill th' cat. Get yuh uh cat ain got on'um no white hair. Doan kill'um. Jess drap'um een uh pot uh biling (water) waututh en bile'um en bile'um till hit all bile tuh pieces. Wan leetle bone will stay on top. Dey does say yuh totes thet bone een yuh pocket fuh luck."

Minnie Knox (colored) 25 yrs.
Murrell's Inlet, S. C.

To Learn Black Magic
(Verbatim)
Minnie Knox

Minnie: "Go cross roads 'fore sunrise! Old King Highway. Right there near Heaven's Gate where us road crosses the old King Road. Go for NINE mornings. And ever mornin' make your wishes of what you want. And the ninth mornin' the Devil self will appear. You talk to him. He'll talk to you. The PURE DEVIL! (I'd run!)

Lillie: "I'd run till I fall! One time I'd get over ground fast. He'd have a time catchin' me! That a dismal lookin' man!"

Minnie: "Go back home and get a black cat. Mustn't have a single white hair. Put on a pot o' bilin' water. Bilin' hard throw the cat in there and BOIL HIM ALIVE. Boil him till all the meat and everything left the bone. Mustn't kill the cat. Must boil him live. Then take pot and all to runnin' stream. Runnin' stream o' water. And dump it in and all the meat and bone and water will go with the stream—all that is 'forecept ONE BONE! That the LUCKY bone. You can work any kind o' work with that bone. Any kinder magic. Can make a girl leave and follow you clean to the ocean."

SOURCE: *Minnie Knox—Age 22, April 1938. Burgess, S. C.*

(Verbatim)
(Another One Mom Phillipa[1] *Tales.)*

(Did this come from Africa? No lions here!)

'Nother Maussa have a man name John. Was something ruinin' Maussa mutton corn. Ever night was goin' in Maussa corn field. So Maussa call John and tell him.

"John, something eatin' up all my corn. And what-some-ever 'foretis John, I wants you to go down there and catch it."

"All right suh, Maussa."

Mornin' (Well, 'foretwuz 'bout twelve o'clock) John gone out in the field and saw a lion. Lion just BREAKIN' the corn. And the lion see John and stop breaking the corn and take right in after John. John know he'd a-over took him and John come to a big old oak tree. And John went 'round and 'round the tree. 'round and 'round the the tree. And the lion reach 'round the tree and John grab both he hands. And John feared to turn him loose. He hold and he hold. He hold and hold. And he hold all night and just when John 'bout give out here come Maussa:

1. Phillipa Knox.

"John!"

"Yes suh, Maussa!"

"What is that?"

"I don't know what is diss here but I got 'em!

"John, that's a lion! I wants that Lion in a cage."

"John tell him:

"Well, Maussa, 'fore you gets ready to put this thing in a cage you come here. Maussa hold right here till I come.'"

And John know Maussa had the lion all right and he know Maussa ain't goin' loose he grip. So John gone on home. Eat his dinner. Rest up. Then he come back feelin' strong.

"Maussa, do just like I tells you and we'll catch this lion!"

Then John started off. Now he was full up and strong and he took off 'forecross the field. He call to Maussa to loose the lion. And John run and the lion comin' right behind him and John come to the barn and he gone 'round the barn, lion right behind him, 'round the barn, 'round the barn and John make a scoop, he make a scoop, (he was head o' the lion) and he went under the barn. Lion think John gone IN the barn. Lion gone in the barn door. John make a scoop come out, lock and bar the barn door. Here come Maussa!"

"Maussa, I got him!"

"You is? John, you know what I wants now? I wants you to put the lion in a cage. I'll put the cage in the barn and I wants you to put this lion in the cage!"

John was a-quiverin'. Kinder fear o' that lion. He tell Maussa:

"All right suh. All right suh, Maussa!"

Cage put in the barn and John gone in. Lion begin to roar and raise his mange. 'foreGin to run John 'round the cage. 'round the barn! 'round the cage. John run 'round. He run 'round. John scoop down behind the cage. Lion thought John were IN the cage. Lion jump in the cage. John SCOOPED up from 'forehind the cage and locked him up. Then John call Maussa to come turn him out the barn. Maussa can't 'foreblive his eyes when he see John one put the lion in thecage. John TOO smart!

Later on corn come to gettin' ripe—dryin'. Maussa call John.

"John, I missin' my corn. Something carryin' ALL my dry corn. Breakin' my corn carryin' it." (Turn out it was JOHN breakin' the dry corn and carryin' it!)

Maussa set steel trap. John gone back in Maussa corn field. Step in trap Maussa come see John in he steel trap. Maussa surprise. Don't know what to make!

"Well John!"

"Yes suh, Maussa." (John sound too sorry)

"What you doin' in there John?"

Maussa I come out to get us mule some corn, and I step in this blame thing!"

"Well John, what I goin' do with you? What MUST I do with you?"

"I donno, Maussa. I donno! If you forgives me THIS time I'll not do this no more."

"John, you too good nigger to take a gun and SHOOT. I'll tell you what I'll do. I'll put you in a sack and tie a mill stone to the sack and throw you in the river."

So Maussa put John in a sack and left him on the river bank till he could go eat and fetch the mill stone.

John begin to sing. He sing. He pray. He shout. He begin to shout.

After while a poor old hungry woman come by. She say:

"Who is in this sack?"

John say:

"It's me, John. Maussa want to make me eat and I don't want to eat. I too full. And Maussa gone to fetch a dishpan full o' rice, ham, beans, pork, chicken, pie and I know if I eats all that I know I'll die."

"That what you cryin' 'bout? Well, John, I gots not a thing to eat in my house and I hongry."

"You hongry?"

"Yes, John."

"Well, I tells you what to do. You loose this sack and get in here and when Maussa come he'll give you all that good sumpin' to eat.

The poor old hungry woman loose John out and John tie her up in the sack and John gone on.

Man come. Maussa come. He open the sack to put the mill stone in and find the woman. He were 'forestonish. He say:

"Where YOU come from? How YOU get in here?" She tell him:

"John were here. He tell me you were comin' with a dishpan full o' sumpin t'eat—beans and ham and pork and pie. He tell me you'd give me a stumick full o' rations."

Maussa let the woman go. Gone on home and find John settin' on he step.

John Say: The woman say she want what you have for me! And you can't hurt me Maussa. The Lord's for me Maussa!"

So that night the man and he wife study. They study. Way behind Maussa plantation they were a great, big old desert back there full o' wild animil. She say:

"You take John and tie him back there and them animils'll eat him when they come."

Maussa call:

"John!"

"Yes suh, Maussa!"

"Come on!"

"Yes suh, Maussa."

Maussa take John way back behind the plantation where nobody travel but hunters and them dangerous animil. By and by here come some hunters by. They find John tie to the tree. Ask John:

"What you doin' here?

John tell'em:

"Maussa put me here to keep hunters off this property."

The hunters tell John:

"Well we goin' loose you and send you home."

John gone back. Gone back whistling. "Whee! Whee! Whee! Whee!

Maussa and his wife look through the window see John.

"John, ain'ts that you?"

"Yes suh."

"Who loose you?"

"Nobody suh!"

"How you get here?"

"Just walk Maussa."

Next mornin' him and wife study another plan. Maussa say:

"John, come with me."

"Yes suh, Maussa."

"Come with me."

Maussa take John to mill pond and tie big old rock 'round he neck. And he throw him over in mill pond. And John wuz a powerful swimmer. He feel himself goin' down and he swim out. Loose the rock from his neck and swim out. Swim out on the other side. Meet 'forenother Master. Say he'll give him a place to stay. But unbeknownst to John he advertise he have a run way nigger.

John Maussa come. Say:

"Well, Well! I try my best to kill that nigger. I shut him up in the barn with a lion, I tied him in a sack to drown him. I tied him out in the desert where the danjus animil and next I tied a mill stone 'round his neck and throwed him overboard. And here he is now!"

John tell'em."

"Maussa, I trust the Lord. Lord take care o' John." And John's faith turned them all to Christian. They all got to believin' Christian like John.

SOURCE: *Told by Minnie Knox*
Age 30 (?)
May 31st. 1938
Murrells Inlet, S. C.

Another Token (Negro)

"I know before Brother Isaac died they was a black snake come to car doorstep and raised up 'bout TWO FOOT on his tail and looked right in the door and WHISTLED. That was just two days 'fore he died. That was a token. Mama[2] said that was.

Minnie Knox (colored)
Age 30 (?) October 17th., 1938.
Murrells Inlet, S. C.

Gipsies
(Verbatim)

"Them gipsies took Rose Vandross[3] quilt. Took all o' Jane money. Took a silver dollar out my hand, Come to my house one time and I had a silver dollar in my hand and earnestly she tell me get her some COLD WATER. I got it from the pump. She say, 'Put it in a clean glass.' She give me a piece o' green weed. Look like weed grow on the beach dry. She say, 'I give you this, you give me a penny!' I go to my trunk and take Mama Da SILVER DOLLAR in my hand and a penny. I keep the dollar so she won't get it. She say:

"'UM-M-m-m-m-m!
Looga, looga,
Looga, looga!
Boil water boil!'

"And that water BOIL! Clean, cold water out the pump boil in the glass in my hand! And she got that silver dollar! How she done that I never couldn't figger. Couldn't figger that nohow. Got Mamam Da silver dollar out my hand and gone right 'forecross the road and got five dollars from Cun Missie!

"Poor Cun Missie had to place that money back! Uncle Quinvy[4] would-a flutter like a chicken with his neck off if he have miss that five dollar! Can hear him:

2. Addie Knox.

3. Rose Vandross taught at the school on Sandy Island. Much later she was a nurse to Genevieve Chandler in her final illness.

4. Quinvy Knox.

"'De finally now, got my house here now to let Gyptians[5] come in.' (He'll run 'em out that house now with the pure quarrel): 'De finally now, I have money here for you to let them Gypsum come here and carry? De finally now—Don't tell me nuttin''! De Debbil, Missy, de Debbil! I wuk so hard to get my money and debilish Gipsum come carry 'em! Misty, de DEBBIL!

"Them Giptian? Better not come back home there! I SHO take the ax! Yes! Went to the Revents house. Reb gone. Miss Ida one home. Took Mary plate her Mother die and left for her! Took it right 'fore Miss Ida eye! You see it in they hand and they GONE! Rose Vandross quilt—they get that too! Yes! She just have it quilt up so good. Lyin' on the bed foot and she never see 'em. Miss 'um when they gone.

"You hear what they done to poor old Uncle William?[6] Here he walkin' down the King Road headin' from Revents Pinnacle house and they met the poor old man and took three dollars and fifty cent out his pocket. He didn't know till they was gone!

"They too tricky! Come in in such a way you'd a-been sorry for 'em! Sorry till they GETS IN! First thing that woman say to me: 'I wants you to give me a piece o' bread for my boy! She have no breakfast. Any kinder piece o' dry bread will do!' Get in they take all you got! Took my cloth out my trunk! Talk Giptian to me!'

Minnie Knox—22 yrs.
Murrells Inlet, S. C.

5. The word "gypsy" is a corruption of the word "Egyptian."
6. William Oliver.

Richard Knox

Richard Knox was Lillie Knox's husband. Marriage to Lillie in itself would have brought Knox into frequent contact with Chandler and made him a convenient interview candidate, but Richard Knox was also a masterful teller of tall tales ("lies" in Gullah parlance). Knox told trickster tales with Budder Rabbit and his retinue, stories of the wily slave John, those of the supernatural, and those of his life as an experienced outdoorsman, hunter, and fisherman. His talent in telling tales made him a favorite in the Chandler home, especially among the Chandler children, who sat mesmerized as he spun his yarns. The children of course were not the only ones; Chandler sought out these tales from many of her sources.

The animal trickster tales and tales of the slave John have nearly vanished among the Waccamaw Gullah today, but even in the late 1930's they were becoming difficult to find. What caused the sharp decline in storytelling is a bit of a mystery. It is possible that, in a postslavery culture, the trickster tales had lost some of their relevance; maybe they were being supplanted by Christian allegories and stories; or maybe they were being lost in the slow assimilation of the Gullah into mainstream American culture. Whatever the case, Richard Knox proved to be a great repository of the genre, and without him the stories might have been lost.[1] Many of his stories went on to be published in edited form in the South Carolina WPA publication *South Carolina Folk Tales*.

Knox was born February 1, 1897, to Addie and Gabe Knox. He had many siblings: Julia, Mary, Zackie, Minnie, Isaac, and Douglas as well as an older half-brother, Quinvy. Sometime around 1920 Richard Knox married Lillie Cogsdell, and together they raised Paul, Richard Jr., and Mary.

Providing for his family was a struggle for Knox during the lean years of the Depression. Opportunities for a black man in Murrells Inlet, South Carolina, were limited, to say the least. The prevailing choices included hiring out

1. The stories told by Richard Knox as well as others as recorded by Chandler have witnessed a bit of a rebirth. They are told now by several individuals in the community thanks to Chandler's work.

as a farm laborer, farming one's own land (if one owned any), and fishing in the inlet. To put food on the table and provide for his family, Knox tried his hand at all of the above. To make ends meet, Knox often borrowed money for seed and supplies. Unfortunately he found himself in debt more often than not.

Sometime around 1940 Knox opened a nightclub in "The Hill," Myrtle Beach's African American community. One night a man attempted to rob the club. Knox grabbed his shotgun from behind the bar. The man grabbed a bystander as a hostage. Knox was already pulling the trigger as the robber swung the woman into the line of fire. She was killed by the shotgun blast. Knox was found guilty of manslaughter and sentenced to time on the chain gang.

Knox served his time. He and Lillie, who had moved to Marion, South Carolina, for the duration of Richard's sentence, returned home to Knoxville, where they lived until their deaths. Richard Knox died in February 1959.

(Verbatin)

"Lemme see what'll be the subject of this piece! The subject be
'THE GOOSE'—no—'THE RABBIT, THE FOX AND THE GOOSE.'[2]

"What started the thing off, they was a man have a garden of vegetable and have a little girl. Little girl was at home and the father he always goes to work.

"Now Budder Rabbit he was sorter tricky and cunnin', so he comes there and calls:

"'Lil girl! Oh, lil girl!'

"Little girl say,

"'Suh?'

"Budder Rabbit tell her,

"'Your father says turn me in his garden twelve o'clock; turn me out at one.'

"'All right, suh,' said the little girl.

"So the little girl turned him in at twelve o'clock, and when one o'clock come she went and turned him out. And next day, same thing again! Budder rabbit come,

2. This tale illustrates well the tension, common in trickster tales, between rewarding behavior that subverts traditional power relationships and punishing behavior that is morally irresponsible. Rabbit is often the protagonist in these stories because of his relative size and seeming vulnerability. His wit is what saves him more often than not. In this case, as in many of Rabbit's predicaments, Rabbit is also a victim of his own inordinate appetites. The morally ambiguous position that Rabbit finds himself forced to fill is a perilous one, where he often shifts between protagonist, filling an instructional position, and antagonist, serving as a negative example.

"'Lil girl, old man say turn me in at one o'clock and turn me out at two.'

"Next day little girl let him in at two; turn him out at three.

"Next day Budder Rabbit right back. (He do like that man vegetable.)

"'Lil girl! Lil girl!'

"'Suh?'

"'Old man say let me in at three; turn me out at four!'

"So now old man comein' home happen to go in the garden. Fine his stuff all crop down—bite off! Garden ruined! He say,

"'Who crop up the garden—ruin it all like this?'

"Little girl say,

"'Daddy, Budder Rabbit come, say you say turn him in twelve o'clock and turn him out one; turn him in one o'clock and turn him out two; turn him in two o'clock and turn him out three!' Daddy say,

"'I tell you what to do. When Budder comes here again, turn him in but don't turn him out!'

"Next day Budder Rabbit come. Call out,

"'Lil girl! lil girl!'

"Little girl turned him in. Budder Rabbit gone and he eat and he eat. He eat and he eat! Four o'clock come he went to get out. Come squinch up side the gate. Call out,

"'Lil girl! Ain't four o'clock yet? Ain't it four o'clock?'

Little girl say she got to bake some biscuit. Budder Rabbit wait awhile. She'll tell him when it time to turn out. Budder Rabbit tell her:

"'Gracious! It takes a long time for four o'clock to come.'

"So little girl says:

"'No, Budder Rabbit. Daddy says when you come this time, mustn't turn you out till he comes.'

"And Budder Rabbit gone to beggin',

"'Oh, do please lil girl, turn me out! Please lil girl! Do please lil girl! Budder Rabbit was fix that day! (Chuckling)

"So she didn't turn him out. She helt him. Old man he come home. He come home and Budder Rabbit still in the garden! Budder Rabbit squinch up by the gate so when man open the gate he can slip out! Man ain't open the door but a crack and slip in! He see Budder Rabbit squinch up in the gate jam.

"'Hey, Budder Rabbit, what you doin' in here?'

"Budder Rabbit ain't say nothin'.

"'What you doin' here Budder Rabbit?'

"Budder Rabbit ain't say nothin'.

"The man say,

"'I b'live I'll kill you! But you too poor! You too poor to kill. Tell you what I'll do. I'll let you stay here three days and get fat, then I'll kill you.'

"So man make a cage and full it full of feed. Budder Rabbit take all the feed and mumble it up. Mumble it up makin' out he eatin'. Last day come! Third day come! Budder Fox come long! Budder Rabbit sneeze!

"'Whee! Whee!'

"Budder Fox stop! Look 'round! Talk out loud!

"'Ain't I yeddy (hear) Budder Rabbit?'

"Budder Rabbit sing out,

"'Yeah!'

"Budder Fox ask,

"'Where?'

"Budder Rabbit say,

"'Right here in this cage! Got good things to eat! Keepin' me a store in here! Come on in! Don't bother to shut the door! Come on in Budder Fox! All kinder good thing in here to eat!'

"After Budder Fox goin in Budder Rabbit 'forecided he'd run and get him a drink of water. Budder Fox busy eatin'! Budder Rabbit gone on and say,

"'I'll be back terreckly!'

"Budder Fox eatin'! Budder Rabbit stay! He stay! Stay till time come for him to be kill! Man come! He ax:

"'Hey, Budder Fox! What you doin' in here?'

"Budder Fox tell him;

"'I'm stayin' here for Budder Rabbit while he gone to the Spring.'

"Man say:

"'Budder Fox, you ain't done nothin'! You ain't done nothin'! I'll turn you out if you'll go on down and carry a message to Budder Rabbit. Tell him if he don't come on back here and get in his cage, you gwine eat him!'

"Budder Fox agree. The man turn him out and he gone on down the road and here he meet Budder Rabbit runnin'. Budder Rabbit runnin' head down. Budder Fox say,

"'That a way for you to do!'

"And Budder Rabbit say,

"'I on my way now jest as hard as I kin go to turn you out.'

"Budder Fox tell him,

"'Man say I must tell you if you don't go back to that cage I must catch you and eat you.'

"And Budder Rabbit sing out,

"'Eat me! Don't eat me! I'm too poor to eat! I'll show you where they's a old mother goose and five head of goslin'. Eat them first then you can eat me! You eat me first, I can't show you the old mother goose and five head of goslin'.'

"So Budder Fox know the mother goose bigger'n Budder Rabbit, so he tell Budder Rabbit he 'foregree. And Budder Fox follow Budder Rabbit. Budder Rabbit say,

"'Go easy! Go easy! We don't want to scare that mother goose and them five head o' goslin'.'

"So they Slip! Slip! Slip! Slip! Till they come to a house. Then Budder Rabbit show Budder Fox the nest where the mother goose and the five head o' goslin. Budder Fox say he goin' catch 'em all. And when he spring over where Budder Rabbit point him to—he don't spring on no nest of gooses—he spring on a old mother hound and five head o' puppies! Old hound grab at Budder Fox, and she sing out,

"'Oh—oo"! Oh—oo! Oh—oo!'

"(Trouble in the camp now!) Fox runnin'. Hound in behind him!

"'You! You! You! You!'

"Budder Rabbit jump out the gate and get up on a big stump and call out,

"'E! E! E! E! Sick 'em!
'E! E! E! E! Sick 'em!'

"Budder Fox runnin' through the woods sing out,

"'I'll do for you Budder Rabbit!'

"Budder Rabbit sing on,

"'E! E! E! E! Sick—ey!
E! E! E! E! Sick—ey!
Do for me now Budder Fox!
Do for me now!'

"Budder Fox pass by anudder Budder Fox. 'foreNudder Fox call out,

"'Bear 'round! Bear 'round! Bear 'round! ' (He ain't wantin' them hound to pick up HIS trail!)

"Budder Fox call out,

"'I ain't bearin' round! I'm runnin' a John Brown bee-line to-day.'

"Budder Fox didn't have time to circle! Didn't have time to turn that day! Hound right in behind him!

"And here Budder Rabbit sittin' on the high stump clappin' his hand and singin',

"'E! E! E! E! Sick—ey!
E! E! E! E1 Sick—ey' "

SOURCE: *Told by Richard Knox—Age 25—30? December 10, 1937.*
Murrells Inlet, S. C.

Budder Rabbit and Budder Bear

("Budder Rabbit in one with Budder Bear.")
( )
( )
("A Lil' short tale 'bout Budder Rabbit and the Bear")

"One time Budder Bear[3] caught him a nice mess o' fish. Budder Bear meet Budder Rabbit and the fish make Budder Rabbit want some so bad! He think up a plan. He gone on through the woods head o' Budder Bear. He get in the path and lied down like he dead. Budder Bear come on 'forelong. He see Budder Rabbit lie stretch out same a dead Rabbit. He say,

"'My! My! Ain't that's a pity! There's a dead Budder Rabbit!'

"Budder Bear gone on. Budder Rabbit jump up, run through the woods again, get on the path, fall, lied stretch out again like he dead.

"Budder Bear come on long. He look and he say,

"My! My! Ain't that's a pity! Here another dead Budder Rabbit!'

"And Budder Bear keep on till he meet four dead Budder Rabbit. Then he lay he fish down by that last Budder Rabbit,and he think he'll go get all them dead Budder Rabbit. So Budder Bear walk. He walk and he walk. He walk. He walk to where he start from. And he ain't never see another dead Brother Rabbit yet! And Budder Bear suspicion where his fish gone.

"Budder Rabbit 'forefaid Budder Bear comin' to hunt he fish. He got a lot of turnips and collards he done ready steal out them people garden. So he put the fish in the bottom of the pot and the turnips and collards on top. And by that time here come Budder Bear. Budder Bear come and he hail:

"'Hey, Budder Rabbit! Hey, Budder Rabbit! '

"Budder Rabbit call:

"'Hey, Budder Bear! '

"Budder Bear ax:

"'Ain't you got my fish? You look like the same Budder Rabbit I lay my fish down by! '

"Budder Rabbit call out:

"'No! No! '

"Budder Bear say:

"'I smell fish cookin' ! '

"Budder Rabbit tell him:

"'No! No! Collards and turnips! See dere! See dere! ' (And Budder Rabbit stir the collards on top) ' Plenty meat in here! See! See the bacon? See? ' (Budder Rabbit got his old cook spoon stirrin'—stirrin'!)

3. In the trickster tales Bear usually plays the oaf—all brawn and very little brain.

"Budder Bear say,

"'Budder Rabbit, my nose ain't fool me! Lemme stir that pot! '

"And Budder Bear take the long handle cook spoon and turn up all the fish.

"And down the road Budder Rabbit have big business! Budder Rabbit straighten out! Straighten out! Right through the woods they gone!

"But Budder Bear never catch Budder Rabbit! No sir! "

SOURCE: *Given by Richard Knox, Age 40. December 11, 1937. Murrells Inlet, S. C.*

Mr. Man and Budder Rabbit and Budder Wolfe (Verbatim)

(Budder Rabbit gets the best of Budder Wolfe this time!)

Rich: "Budder Rabbit in ever tale they is. In everone! But this fellow got the best—no—Budder Rabbit got out of this one!"

"Mister Man bought some fish to the market and have them in his wagon goin' home. And Budder Rabbit see 'em and he say:

"'I want some of them fresh fish!'

"And he study! He study and he study! And he study up a plan. He run down ahead of the man and lay down in the road and stretch out. Mister Man come long. Say: (Talkin' to hisself.)

"'They's a dead Budder Rabbit in the road! I b'lieve I'll take him home to my dogs!' So he threw Budder Rabbit in the wagon. Budder Rabbit flutter. He flutter! He kick fish out! He kick out the fish! When he kick out all he can tote, he jump out the wagon, string he fish and gone on home!

"Man get home tell he wife all he fish fall out the wagon back.—

"Budder Rabbit bunch up he fish come long whistlin'. Meet up with Budder Wolfe. Budder Wolfe make 'foremiration over his bunch o'fish. Budder Rabbit tell him:

"'Man, you can have all the fish you want if'n you do the way I do.'

"Budder Wolfe say: 'How you does, Budder Rabbit?'

"'Go Lay down side of the road. Make out like you dead. Terreckly a man'll come long wagon load o'fish. Man'll say, ' I b'lieve I'll carry that dead Budder Wolfe to feed my dog!' And he'll throw you in the wagon. Then all you got to do is to kick out fish! Kick out fish! And when you got 'forenouf kick out, jump out the wagon back and string you fish and go long home.'

"So Budder Wolfe think that sound easy. He went and lay down side the road. Same man come by. Same man! But when he see Budder Wolfe lyin' down like he dead, stead o'puttin him in the wagon Mr. Man jump out, get a big old pine pole, come down:

"'A—boom!

"'A—boom!

"'A—boom!'

"And Budder Wolfe kick up dead! He dead now—sho nuff! And now man threw him in the wagon.

"Budder Rabbit miss Budder Wolfe. Meet Budder Wolfe partner! Say:

"'Where Budder Wolfe?'

"Budder Wolfe partner say,

"'Man kill Budder Wolfe! Man kill him!'

"Budder Rabbit say,

"'Now dere! He oughter have better sense than dat! I had ny eye open. Budder Wolfe have his eye shut! Dead Wolfe have open eye. Ought'n not to shet his eye! Oughter always to keep one eye crack so you kin see what goin' on.'

"So Budder Rabbit got the best o' Budder Wolfe that time! Budder Rabbit had the record that time! "

SOURCE: *Told by Richard Knox, Age 40 plus, December 11, 1937. Murrells Inlet, S. C.*

"Lemme see! How many that make? Two? Three? Lemme see now how that butter story go! This'n

'Budder Rabbit, Budder Wolfe and Butter.'[4]

That the subject o' this."

"They had bought some butter together. The way they buy they butter then, they buy it in a thing the form of a snuff box. They call that they 'barrel o' butter.' They jine in and throw in! Had it in that form so they can bury it. Bury it down to the spring. Day was to come they was to 'forevide it. Every day Budder Rabbit sample the butter. Gone there and dig it up.

"Now Budder Rabbit and Budder Wolfe had business together. First day they was to work, Budder Rabbit was be-lated. (He skimmin' the butter!) When he come Budder Wolfe say

"'Why you be lated?'

"Budder Rabbit tell him,

"'Man, man! I have a time last night! Trouble!'

"'What the trouble?'

"'My old lady had a fine boy last night! That how I come late. Had a time last night! Just me one!'

"Budder Wolfe ax,

"'What you name that fine boy, Budder Rabbit?'

"'Skim-the-Top! Skim-the-Top! Name that first boy SKIM-THE-TOP.'

4. A variation of this story is Lewis Small's "Buh Rabbit and Buh Wolfe" (pp. 339–40).

"Next day same thing! Budder Rabbit late again! Budder Wolfe want to know why Budder Rabbit late!

"'Budder Rabbit, how come you late again?'

"'Trouble! Trouble Budder Wolfe!'

"'Trouble, Budder Rabbit?'

"'Yes. Trouble, Budder Wolfe!'

"'What kinder trouble now, Budder Rabbit?'

"'Nother one o' dem boys!'

"'Nother boy?'

"'Nother one o' dem boys!'

"'What you goin' name him, Budder Rabbit?'

"'I name him One-quarter-gone! One-quarter-gone!'

"So it went on. Next day come same trouble! Budder Rabbit be-lated again Budder Wolfe ax the same old question:

"'What the matter now, Budder Rabbit? 'foreNother boy again?'

"'Gracious crown, Budder Wolfe! 'foreNother boy!'

"Budder Wolfe make a great 'foremiration. Budder Rabbit got another boy again!

"'What you name this boy, Budder Rabbit?'

"'Half-gone! Half-gone!'

"'Half-gone?'

"'Half-gone! Half-gone! Half-gone!'

"Night come and Budder Rabbit gone home. Next day same thing again! Budder Rabbit late again. Budder Wolfe say,

"'Budder Rabbit, how come you late again this morning?'

"'Tell you, Budder Wolfe. Same old trouble!'

"'What trouble?'

"''Nother boy again!'

"'What you name this'n Budder Rabbit?'

"'Most run out o' name! Name this one Three-quarter-gone! Three-quarter-gone, Budder Wolfe! Name him Three-quarter-gone!'

"Budder Wolfe laugh, 'Hah! Hah!' (All that time he ain't know Budder Rabbit eatin' up all the butter!)

"Well, next day come, same trouble! Ever day Budder Rabbit been late. Ever day late. Budder Wolfe ax:

"'What the matter, Budder Rabbit? Look like you can't never be on time!'

"'What the matter? Budder Wolfe, you don't never have the trouble I have! If you had to set up all night with you old lady, you'd be be-lated too!'

"'What's the trouble now?'

"''Nother boy! 'foreNother one of dem boy! 'foreNother boy this time!'

"'What you name him?'

"'Think he the last, Budder Wolfe! Name him SKIM-THE-BOTTOM! Yes suh! Skim-the-bottom! Think they won't be no more now!'

"That make Budder Wolfe think. He say,

"'Oh Budder Rabbit! We better go see 'bout us butter!'

"'Yes, Budder Wolfe,' Budder Rabbit tell him, 'You ain't see 'bout that butter? Time to see 'bout us butter. Less go share the butter up!'

"Budder Rabbit jump out! He the first one there. HE know where to go. They have the butter bury down there to the spring and they could see where the track and thing been 'round so regular. Dig up the barrel! They dig up the barrel, and Budder Wolfe see how the barrel been so light. Budder Wolfe say,

"'Oh, Budder Rabbit, where all us butter?'

"'Oh, Budder Wolfe,' say Budder Rabbit, actin' like he surprise, like it hit him hap-hazard,-like, 'somebody done eat all us butter!'

"Budder Wolfe look at Budder Rabbit.

"'Budder Rabbit, ain't you eat us Butter?'

"''Taint me! 'foreTain't me, Budder Wolfe!' Sing out Budder Rabbit.

"Budder Wolfe look solemn. He say:

"'Budder Rabbit, they tell me the sun'll draw butter! If it me eat that butter it'll prove; if it you, it'll prove. Lay down in the sun and stretch out! Which-some-ever one eat the butter, the sun'll draw it. The sun'll draw it out!'

"So Budder Wolfe and Budder Rabbit lay down and stretch out in the hot sun. Sun so warm, Budder Wolfe gone to sleep! Butter comin' out Budder Rabbit! Sun so hot! Butter jest a-leakin' out Budder Rabbit mouf. And Budder Rabbit take and wipe it off on Budder Wolfe! He rake it off and wipe it all round Budder Wolfe mouf! Take and wipe Butter all over Budder Wolfe! Budder Wolfe wake up and smell butter! He see butter on Budder Rabbit. He sing out:

"'Now, Budder Rabbit, I've caught you! See there? See there Budder Rabbit?'

"And Budder Rabbit sing out:

"'Oh looker dere, Budder Wolfe! You eat some too! You eat some too!'

"So Budder Rabbit had the butter and fool Budder Wolfe too! Make Budder Wolfe think he eat the butter! Poor old Budder Wolfe think he musser eat butter too! "

SOURCE: *Told by Richard Knox (Age 40?) "Rich out he thirties"*
Dec. 11, 1937. Murrells Inlet, S.C.

Bear and Rabbit (Verbatim)

"But one day Budder Rabbit catch up with Budder Bear.

"They make a out-cry Budder Bear dead!—Now Budder Rabbit glad he dead. Won't bother him no more! But he want to be sho' Budder Bear dead!

"Budder Bear lyin' up stretch out in the bed. (Ain't breathin'.)

"Budder Rabbit come squinch up by the door. All the other animal in the house. Budder Rabbit squinch up by the door and say awful sad:

"'My! My! So Budder Bear dead!'

"And all the other animal say:

"'Yes. Poor Budder Bear dead! '

"And Budder Rabbit stand to the door all squinch up and he study a plan to find out wedder Budder Bear dead or no. And after while he sing out:

"'They always tell me if a bear dead he'll turn over and groan three times.'

"Big old Budder Bear he turn hisse'f over and groan.

"Budder Rabbit stretch hisse'f up and ram he hands in his pocket.

"'Hah! Hah! Gracious!' he said, 'A dead Budder Bear can't groan like that.'

"And Budder Rabbit jump out the door and sell out the Budder Bear right in behind him! Bear jump up and follow him—sheet and all—but nothin' to it! Budder Bear can't run with Budder Rabbit! "

SOURCE: *Given by Richard Knox Sr. (Lillie's husband)"Age 40 plus—(Rich out of his thirties") Murrells Inlet, S. C. December 11, 1937.*

"Yes suh! Budder Rabbit in everything! Budder Rabbit play a trick on Budder Gator one time!"

Budder Rabbit and Budder Gator.

"Now Budder Gator he the fiddler—the music man. All the girls stuck on Budder Gator. Budder Gator thought EVERY day good. Here they have a dance. Budder Gator callin':

"'HANDS AWAY!
BALANSAY!
HUG ME DARLIN' !
TURN YOUR CONTRARY PARTNER!
AND YOU OBJECT DARLIN'.
AND YOU PARTNER AT HOME!'

"Such a time they have! Budder Gator have a steady.time. He say:

"'Every day good!
Every day good!
Every day good!
Every day good!

"He have no trouble in he life!

"The girls turnin'—they turnin' ! But no change in the music. He don't make no turnin' to the music. Budder Rabbit say:

"'Budder Gator, I'll fiddle a little and rest you! You dance awhile.'

"Take the fiddle. Jump up and play: He call out:

"'TURN YOUR CONTRARY PARTNER.

"'MEMBER YOUR PARTNER AT HOME.'

"Budder Rabbit play:

""'Some day good!
Some day bad!
Some day good!
Some day bad!

"That music suit 'em! Suit 'em so good!

"'Some day good!
Some day bad!
Some day good!
Some day bad! '

"Budder Rabbit fiddle off that piece!

"Budder Gator didn't like that so well. Budder Rabbit beat him at the fiddlin'. Girls dance so good—dance so good Budder Rabbit music.

"Budder Gator and Budder Rabbit talkin'. Budder Gator say:

"'TROUBLE? What is TROUBLE? I never see TROUBLE in my life! '

"Now one day, more than all, tide comes up in a stormy weather and blows up lot o' dead marsh. Dead marsh grass on the bank! One day Budder Gator crawl out there in the sunshine on that dry marsh and gone to sleep. Budder Rabbit gone there and walk 'round and 'round. 'round and 'round Budder Gator he walk and all the time he walkin' 'round Budder Gator, he stringin' fire on that dead marsh, just a-stringin' fire 'round Budder Gator. And when 'he get it all 'round Budder Gator Budder Rabbit yell out:

"'TROUBLE !
TROUBLE!
TROUBLE, BUDDER GATOR! '

"Budder Gator open he eye and fire comin' on him! Gettin' hotter and hotter! He raise up and

""'BOO-JOO!
BOO-JOO! '

" He gone over in the river. Gone over in the river out the fire."

" Budder Rabbit say:

"'Butter Gator, I'll tell you they IS trouble! I been tellin' you 'bout 'trouble' !

"'Some day good!

Some day bad! '

"'All day ain't good! '

"And Budder Gator knowledge they was 'TROUBLE' in the world."

SOURCE: *Told by Richard Knox, Age 40 and something. Dec. 1937. Murrells Inlet, S. C.*

John's Richness Page 1

"Goin' tell you a piece now 'bout this here fellow and the boss man thought he could tell fortune.

"Now you see here, this here butler in slavery time didn't have to work in the field. Just have to work 'round the house. He always know what the cook have cookin'. Always in the kitchen messin' 'round lookin' in the pots. So he go out. Gone where the boss man/ He say:

"'Boss, I betcha I kin tell you what you got for breakfast! You got hominy, you got eggs, you got ham, you got coffee, you got muffin'.

"Dinner time come. Butler meet boss in the yard. He say:

"'Boss, you know what you got for dinner?'

"'No, John. What I have for dinner?'

"'Boss, you got rice, you got chicken, you got biscuit, you got ice tea, you got pie, you got cake, you got puddin'.'

"'Supper time come he tell the boss:

"'You got fish and cornbread and this and the other.'

"Now the Cap'n study over that. He gone over and tell the other plantation boss—He say:

"'Bill, I got a fellow over yonder can tell fortune.'

"'No, you ain't! You ain't got no fellow can tell fortune! '

"'Yes! I bet you $500 dollar I got fellow over there can tell fortune! "

"'I'll put up my $500.'

"Then the Cap'n boss gone home and tell John:

"'John! I got up $500 on you you can tell fortune! You fail me I goin' kill you! '

"John took sick! Don't eat!

"Can't eat from one day to another! Got the doctor for John and John death struck. Doctor say John not sick! Bye and bye thing come to a close.

"Other plantation boss tell NO-BODY what he goin' do. He have caught a COON and put him under a tub. Send for John. Goin' test him. Boss come and bring John. Man say:

"'Well, John, what is under that tub? What is under that tub?'

"John, he fixin' to die any minute. He thinking 'bout dyin' any minute. He know he can't tell no fortune. He look 'round and 'round! He look up in the sky! Look 'round in the sky! Say, slow like:

"'I b'live you got the old coon[5] now! '

"John's boss run! Lift the tub! 'SEE JOHN!' He so happy! So happy! Hot deah! O—John jump up! He sing out:

"'Hot deah! I can tell you when judgement day comin'. I can tell you the day you goin' to die!'

"Here he won his Cap'n $500! Cap'n give him freedom, a house (the boss built it for him) a thousand or so dollars to live on and all that just for sayin',

"'I b'libe you got the old coon now!'

"And this happen right in the heart of FREEDOM!" (Rich meant SLAVERY)

"All John have to do atter that if any body talk sassy, was to jump up and pint his finger at 'em and sing out:

"'I can tell you the day you goin' die! ' "

SOURCE: *Told by Rich Knox, Age 40—(and something).* *December 1937, Murrells Inlet, S. C.*

"'I got that from some preachers. Goin' long seein' who could tell the best story."

RICH KNOX

Buh Ringo Hog[6]

"Oh, Budder Rabbit in some more of them thing yet!"

"Budder Ringo, he a fellow have some girls, and Budder Rabbit and Budder Wolfe goin' to see the girls. And Budder Wolfe had the finest lookin' girl out the bunch. Now Budder Rabbit didn't like that so, well—Budder Rabbit want to trap Budder Wolfe. (Dat's he buddy, now! Want to trap he buddy!) Budder Rabbit want to get Budder Wolfe girl! He have a girl but Budder Wolfe got the BEST LOOKIN' girl!

"Now it happen Budder Ringo—the girls' Pa—losin' he hog. Can't find out WHO takin' his hog! He ax all his friend to help him find out WHO takin' his hog.

"Budder Ringo girls havin' a party. Budder Rabbit and Budder Wolfe goin' to the party. Budder Rabbit gone to Budder Wolfe and tell him:

5. The use of the term "coon" in this case is a bit of wordplay. Knox obviously intends to invoke the racial slur, but according to Kato Singleton, the term also referred to eavesdroppers who roamed the plantation at night.

6. This tale showcases the dark side of the trickster's wit, his resourcefulness used for ill rather than good. Here jealousy and greed guide Rabbit to give false witness against one of his friends. Buh Wolf's subsequent murder by Buh Ringo turns the community against Rabbit. In the end this tale stresses its moral through negative example.

"'Budder Wolfe! I'll go and sing a song to the party if you'll bass it. '[7]

"And Budder Wolfe 'foregreed. Budder Wolfe 'foregreed.

"Gone to party! Girls all love Budder Wolfe! Havin' the best time! (That what Budder Rabbit ain't like)" (aside: "Oh, Sonny biy,[8] you must-a kill a chicken and let him die in you hand—make you nervous![9] That how come you drop that cup!) Yes, girls all love Budder Wolfe and Budder Rabbit got a jealous notion, and he gone to singing: He sing out:[10]

"'I wonder who stole Budder Ringo hog!

"Budder Wolfe sing back:

"'Nobody but me! '

"(You know Budder Wolfe promise to 'bass' for Budder Rabbit.

"Budder Ringo lis'n ! Budder Ringo lis'n! He lis'n! They had to sing it three times 'fore he understand! Here go Budder Rabbit:

"'I wonder who kill Budder Ringo hog!'

"Budder Wolfe sing out in his bass:

"'Nobody but me! '

"Then Budder Rabbit wink at Budder Ringo. Budder Ringo reach back and get out one o'them 'LONG-GO—YONDER'" (gun) " and pull down 'BAM!' Fire down on Budder Wolfe, right on the floor 'foremongst all the people. Gals all run to Budder Wolfe, so sorry, so sorry! So sorry Budder Wolfe get kill! Poor Budder Wolfe get kill.

"Budder Rabbit jump up and say:

"'Yes, that who stealin' you hog all the time. Didn't I tell you he'd tell you tonight who takin' you hog?! '

"Here Budder Ringo kill the innercent man ! Budder Wolfe know nothin' 'bout the plot!

"But the girls didn't pay Budder Rabbit no mind! All too sorry over Budder Wolfe! Lost his girl and din't get Budder Wolfe girl! Here he kill his partner AND lost his girl!

SOURCE: *Given by Richard Knox, Age "40 something—or-other"'. December 1937.*

7. A reference to the West African call-and-response tradition that appears in storytelling, preaching, and singing.

8. Addressed to one of Genevieve Chandler's children.

9. In this aside Richard Knox attributes an interruption (the dropped cup) to a superstition that connected nervousness and "kill[ing] a chicken and let[ting] him die in your hand."

10. Richard Knox would actually sing the following verses as part of his storytelling style.

Lill: "How old Rich? Forty something. He and Miss Rosa Parker come here the same week. Mother[11] gone to wash up Miss Cootie[12] after Miss Rosa[13] born and here Rich come and she couldn't go back!"[14]

Jack and Dinah

(Old slavery time story) (Second 'telling' of story sent in)
Told by Rich Knox

"One time a woman and a man—old slavery people—one was name Dinah. One was name Jack. Jack and Dinah.

"Jack and Dinah was stayin' with a 'Boss Man,' so Uncle Jack, he decided one day (he had got in sorter tough) he wanted some money. He study how to get that money. He say, 'Dinah, I GOT to have some money! I'se goin' get that money too!'

"Livin' on Plantation places! Jack have a 'Boss Man'! Wife have a 'Boss Man'! Different 'Boss Mans'![15] So Uncle Jack gone to his Boss Man. Boss say:

"'Well, Uncle Jack, how you feelin' this mornin'?'

"'Tough! Tough! Pretty tough, Boss Cap'n! '

"'What the matter, Jack?'

"'Cap'n, Dinah die last night! '

"'What! What! Dinah die?'

"'Yes, Cap'n. I come to see can I get $25 to bury Dinah!'

"'Twenty-five dollar? You can get a hundred dollar! You think twenty-five dollar enough? I'll put Dinah away myself? You sure twenty-five enough?'

"'Oh, yes, Cap'n Boss. Twenty-five all I needin'.'

"Uncle Jack take the twenty-five dollar, and gone on home. He show Dinah the money. He say:

"'Now mind, Dinah, you DEAD! I tell Cap'n you dead. Cap'n come here, you dead! You best is dead! '

"Aunt Dinah lis'n. Aunt Dinah study. Dinah study. She study. Then she raise her head. She say:

"'Ah hah! I can get money too! '

11. Addie Knox.
12. Mrs. Cootie Vereen, the mother of Rosa White.
13. Rosa White.
14. Addie Knox could not return to assist Cootie Vereen after Rosa's birth because she gave birth to Richard Knox later in the same week.
15. It was fairly common for slaves from different plantations, even slaves with different masters, to marry.

"Aunt Dinah Boss Man see her comin'. She say!

"'Mornin', Boss! '

"'Well Aunt Dinah, how you feelin'?'

"'Sad! Sad! Feelin' terrible this mornin'! '

"'How come that, Mom Dinah?'

"'Jack die last night! Lose Jack last night! And my business down here is to see can you lend me twenty-five dollar to bury Jack! '

"The Cap'n Boss say:

"'Twenty-five dollar? I'll not LEND you, I'll give you twenty-five dollars. I'll bury Jack myself! '

"'No! No! Cap'n, No! No! Twenty-five enough! '

"Then Aunt Dinah gone on home. Say:

"'Jack, I got twenty-five too! But, 'forememember, you DEAD! My Boss come, you better be dead! '

"Now they got the $50!

"By and by the two Boss Mans have a council together. Meet on the road. One Cap'n say: 'Looker here! They tell me Uncle Jack dead! ' Other Cap'n say: 'No. They tell me its Aunt Dinah dead! ' Then Jack Cap'n say:

"'Well I give Dinah twenty-five dollar to bury Jack! ' Dinah Cap'n say:

"'Spose'n we walks over and see 'bout them two old people: less us go see who dead! '

"Jack and Dinah look out cross the fields and see who comin! Uncle Jack say:

"'Gracious crown! Looker who comin'! We'd all better lay down and dead! '

"Here comes Boss Mans, talkin'. Comin' with the walkin stick. 'Now, now. Well! Well! Both the old people dead! ' Nobody to tell 'em to come in! Boss mans walk in. Stand 'round there, and look at this'n hand by his side! Look at this'n—hand cross! One Cap'n say:

"'My, my! aints that a pity! '

"One Cap'n say:

"'You know what's the truth? I'd give twenty-five dollar to know which one die fust (first)! Twenty-five dollar to know which one gone fust! '

"Uncle Jack Jump up.

"'Me, Cap'n! Me! I die fust! '

"Aunt Dinah jump up.

"'No. ME! ME! I die fust! '

"So both the old people die fust and both get twenty-five dollar and no debt! "

SOURCE: *Told by Richard Knox, Age 40—plus. December 1937.*
Murrells Inlet, S. C.

Tall Tale
Go-lias and the Devil

"Devil tell Go-lias[16] he was strongest. Go-lias tell devil HE was strongest. Devil tell Go-lias: 'Strongest man can FLING the furrest! Strongest man can fling the furrest! And I bet you so many thousand dollar I can FLING the furrest!' Go-lias bet the devil he couldn't. And the devil he up and shrowed (throwed) 'bout two, three mile. Go-lias told him he'd BEAT him: (Lot o' money up!)

"Now the devil done the first chunkin'. Go-lias said:

"'Well, my time to chunk, eh?' Devil tell him:

"'Yes. Your time to chunk.'

"Go-lias got him a flag and gone to wavin'. Wavin' and lookin' up! Wavin'. Wavin'. Devil say:

"'Go-lias, what you donnin'?'

"'I wavin' the angel to STOW WAY! STOW WAY!'

"Big old sledge! Big old piece o' iron! Wavin' the angel to move way! Stow way!

"Devil sing out:

"'Uh! Uh! NO! NO! You done win. You done win! You done win!'

"Devil didn't truss (trust) Go-lias after dat! Go-lias look like sech a strong fellow any how and after he find Go-lias was goin' chunk up in heaven and wavin' the angel out the way he GIVE UP. He done chunk TWO, THREE miles. Know he win. Wavin' the engel (angels) to move back out the way!"

SOURCE: *Told by:* *Rich Knox (age 40 plus)*
May 1938
Murrells Inlet, S. C.
tall story

Frog, the Squirrel, and the Rabbit[17]
By Rich Knox

"I don't know wedder I told you that thing 'bout the frog and the squirrel and de Rabbit! Sum'pin like that. Know the frog wuz de watchman. Now less see! Less see! The squirrel—they had him up. Less see! The Squirrel musser (must

16. Goliath.

17. In this tale Rabbit, who usually acts as protagonist, now plays the dupe. Despite the apparent role reversal, the story's structure is in keeping with other tales, as the characters' temperaments and significance are generally determined relative to those of the story's other characters. In this case Rabbit is the bigger, hence more powerful, of the characters. Squirrel is the smaller, wilier character here. Frog is just Rabbit's mindless henchman.

have) et Budder Rabbit mutton corn.[18] Budder Rabbit got at him and Budder Squirrel gone up a tree. They had him up and Budder Squirrel got way and got up the tree.

"Now Budder Rabbit he couldn't climb. Squirrel up the tree. So Budder Rabbit gone home to get he gun to shoot the squirrel down. Leave Budder Bull Frog to WATCH. Watch Budder Squirrel till he come.

"Now here Budder Squirrel up the tree CHAWIN'. Poppin' lil' stick. Chawin'.

"(Budder Rabbit had tell Budder Bull Frog, 'Watch dat tree!' and Budder Bull Frog say: 'Oh, all right. Budder Squirrel never come down by me!')

"Here Budder Squirrel chawin'. Budder Frog say:

"'What that you chawin' Budder Squirrel? What you chawin"?

"Budder Squirrel say:

"'I eatin' some ground pea up here!'

("Chatter up. Chatter up! Chatter up! Chatter up!)

"Budder Bull Frog so hongry. Say:

"'Hey Budder Squirrel, what you eatin' up there?'

"'Ground pea! Dem ground pea!'

"'T'row me some dese ground pea? All right! All right! Open your eye! Stretch'em big! Open you hand! Open you mouth WIDE! Eye big!'

Budder Bull Frog done just like Budder Squirrel tell him! Stretch he eye WIDE mind! Open he eye WIDE now! Stretch! Budder Squirrel let go that big handful ground up red pepper and black pepper and salt mix! Budder Bull Frog shet he mouth! Grab he hand to he eye!

"Budder Squirrel come right down by Budder Bull Frog and GONE!

Budder Rabbit come back.

"'Whey (where) Budder Squirrel?'

"Budder Bull Frog try to look up and couldn't do no business! Say:

"'He up dere!'

"Budder Rabbit say:

"'I ain't shum!'(See'um)

"'He up dere! He duh up dere. He up dere do!'

"'I ain't shum! Squirrel spit in you eye?'

"'Trash fall in'em! Trash fall in'em!'

Budder Rabbit get mad with Budder Bull Frog 'forecause he let Budder Squirrel gone and he haul back and lick Budder Bull Frog on he back wid he gun and Budder Bull Frog gone over-board.

"'Boonk! Boonk!'

18. Mutton corn is fresh corn. As soon as the ears have filled out, mutton corn may be removed from the ear and eaten.

("Red pepper and black pepper and salt all grind up together! Had'em in he pocket! Budder Squirrel all time tots that to fool people wid. He solid got away and just 'bout that time Budder Rabbit get back!")

SOURCE: *Rich Knox—(Age 45 (?)*
June 1st., 1938
Murrells Inlet, S. C.

Rich: "That one Mom Phillipa[19] story."

"Where Budder Squirrel, Budder Bull Frog?"

"Up dere!"

"I ain't shum!'(see'um)

"Up dere do!"

"What de matter? Budder Squirrel spit tobacco in you eye?"

(Pop-eye frog!)

"NO!"

"What de matter den?"

"Trash fall in my eye."

"I ain't see Budder Squirrel!"

"Up dere do! Up dere!"

"Budder Rabbit get sorter angry grab a stick, hit Budder Bull Frog. Budder Bull Frog gone in water to cool he eye:

"'Boonk! Boonk!'

"Water cool'em.

"Squirrel done eat the man mutton corn and dem get way!"

Sturgeon

Got a old water-jug corked up—a buoy. Anything'll swim. Marshes (meshes in net) that big! One get tangle up in the marshes (meshes) he'll stay there.

A buck[20] sturgeon'll fight pretty rapid, but a roe'll[21] not fight much. Sturgeon head'll weigh twenty-five pounds. Head got all kinder meat in'em. Chicken, beef, steak and pork. Hog meat fish and all! I cut the meat out the head many a time. Pure down leany steak! Every piece taste like itself. Sturgeon fishin' last until June.

Law on coons goes out in March.[22] April and May the laws on everything. Law is right. Law is right! April, May, June, July and August. Inside the

19. Phillipa Knox.

20. Male.

21. Female. The eggs, or roe, that the female bears serves as a metonym for the female herself.

22. State regulated hunting season.

length o' that time, little ones. Take a rabbit. She has little ones in April and May.

Put'em to the Law for huntin' out o' season.[23] I spent time on gang for it. Take'em up for oyster. Goat Island one time, Thompson, fish-ward man take up Zack.[24] Cap'n Arnold Brothers[25] had Zack was with'em. Mighter been a-takin' oyster to sell; mighter been pick'em to eat.

Grover Cleveland?[26] Grover Cleveland? Grover Cleveland? (Intently) Don't 'foreblive I know him. I hear the name. I hear tell o' him. Don't 'foreblive I know him.

Down on them preserve duck-ward man would sho pull you. They plants rice to South Island for them duck. Feeds'em. They HIS ducks!

When I was sent to supply the duck for them sturgeon hunters, I'd shoot on them duck while they settin'. When they raise up other barrel goes. Nine old hens. Nine head o' big old English black duck. And they just as fat as la rd. Morest I ever kill one time them nine head. So fat, so heavy I'd have to stop and rest with'em goin' back to the hill. Walk the beach down from South Island point. Walk nor'eastward. Good duck weather. Cold wedder they bunches up better. Bunches up in a swarm like. I was sorter new in the country. I was told to go out and get a mess o' duck. Anything go wrong they'll 'foretend to'em. Nothin' to do but put'em in the pot and bile'em. Couldn't bile but one at a time. So fat! We eat nothin' but the breast and thigh. That where the meat wuz. People never sees no duck flyin' thick as black bird. When they flies up like thunder! We all got fat that year eatin' shad and sturgeon and fat duck. I gone to visit to town and drink that water. Town not so healty (healthy). Give me the fever and the measles. Stay there three weeks. Nobody to nuss (nurse) me. Nobody feed me. Doin' the best I could. Doctor gin me one bottle o' medicine. We was livin' in a tent while we wuz fishin'. Tentin' on the beach shore. We'd cook (with water) right out the river. Mouth o' the Santee, we'd go three, four mile out there in the sea. And way out there we'd dip up water. River water stay on top.[27]

You talk 'Eagle Stone?' Eagle got lode-stone. In her head. Onliest way to get that been to kill eagle. Lode-stone. They know when fish hawk out fishin'

23. Knox was forced to work on the chain gang after killing a doe out of season.

24. Zackie Knox.

25. Captain Arnold was one of the earliest boat captains in Murrells Inlet. He primarily led fishing excursions.

26. President Grover Cleveland hunted ducks at the local Santee Gun Club.

27. Since fresh water is lighter than salt water, the fresh travels on top of the sea water for some distance after the river has spilled into the ocean.

They know when anything comin' to her nest. That man wore on he own place. Came Waard man TOO hurry!

SOURCE: RICH KNOX—*(Age 40 Plus)*
June 4th., 1938
Murrells Inlet, S. C.

Drum fish have a big stone in they head. Big old drum. Took two mens to tote. Scale him wid a hoe. Stand straight up and down and scale him like you hoein'. I disremember who net caught that big drum fish now!

Duck-ward man catch you don't take you to jail FIRST time. Say:

"Ain't you had know you had violate law?"

"No suh!"

"Don't be caught at this no more!"

Person don't know they CROSS THE LINE they 'forescuse you. Know you 'forecross the line they FINES you. Use the PINT o' the LAW on you. Place posted you got no 'forescuse. GOT to have a SIGN up to use the LAW on you. He can a-BID you, but not sign up, he can't do nothin'.

That man were on he own place. Came Ward man TOO hurry! Didn't look and find out. Kill him on he own place.

SOURCE: RICH KNOX—*(Age 40 Plus)*
June 4th., 1938
Murrells Inlet, S. C.

Duck Hunt
By Rich Knox

Oh, you can tie a 'foregator. You can take a fish hook and lead a 'foregator to Con-o-way. You can bend a nail and put in a stick and lead 'em.

I 'foremember down to Laurel Hill[28] Uncle Quinvy[29] huntin' cow and ever day thet jump over a big log. And one day more'n all a man call:

"Boy, this a 'foregator you jump over here!"

Uncle Quinvy say:

"What? Ever day I been jump over tha t log!"

"This a 'foreGATOR!"

"I goin' carry that 'foregator home!"

"Yeah man?"

"Yeah. Gwine carry that 'foreGator home! Make'em walk!"

And he jam that stick in he mouth and lead'em right on home to Laurel Hill street. Musser been tender in he mouth. Musser been. Lead him right on

28. Laurel Hill plantation.
29. Quinvy Knox.

to Laurel Hill street. Kill tha t 'foregator and cut off all the tail part and cook it and eat some and next day that 'foregator travel right back to that rice-field in man dinner bucket! Call it 'vengion.'[30]

'Gator meat health meat. I eat three messes. Three messes, I carry some to Woodstock[31] on my rice in my dinner pail. I done very well the FIRST day. And I done sorter very well the NEXT day. But I couldn't make it the THIRD day. She boiled it. Stew it down. Season it up with onion in it. The white lady cook it. Her husband had happen up on a 'foregator in the road and he say the tail too good to waste so she keep on cookin' till it all eat up. But three days finish me up. Say you never won't be sickly if you eats a mess o' 'foregator.

Now sturgeon a valable fish. Valuablest fish you find in water. Sturgeon fish 75cents a pound. Sturgeon EGG cost you $1.00 a pound—wholesale. Catcher gets $1.00 a pound. Me and Cap'n L.[32] catch one had in 'em twenty-five pounds o' roe. Get $25. for roe. $15. for the fish. Cut the head off. Cut off the tail. Cut off the fin. Sell him dress.

SOURCE: *Rich Knox*

Duck Hunt
Rich Knox

"I wuz down to Santee one time and a alligator like to scare me to death. Cap'n Leonard,[33] Joe Heywood and Doug B. and we four gone to get some ducks. We four wuz sturgeon fishin' in Waccamaw. Campin' on South Island. Ever mornin' we'd get out o' ducks, I'd go get us a new supply o' ducks. Never eat so much duck in my born days. White man furnish gun and shell. That place down on Santee nothin' BUT rice field. I was walking 'forecross the marsh. Walkin'. Had double-barrel gun walkin' long. Walkin' long. Walkin' long. Not a-lookin' down. Lookin' UP at the duck. BIG bunch o' ducks 'bout half mile ahead circlin'. And I walked up on a 'foregator eighteen foot long! Mought not a-been eighteen foot—but he look eighteen foot to me. Mought to been just twelve foot.

"I wuz all time lookin' for the white watchman[34] too. See this big log ahead. Ain't know 'foretwuz a 'foregator till he raise up 'BIM BIM!' 'Gator scare me so two barrel gone off! Shoot all two barrel and have two dead shell in my

30. Vengeance.

31. Woodstock plantation.

32. Charlie Leonard and Captain Arnold were the two earliest commercial boat captains in the area.

33. Charlie Leonard.

34. This duck hunt probably took place on South Island, a privately owned piece of land kept under watch to prevent poaching.

gun. Gator GROAN at me! Groan at me! When he groan wuz like a bull bellow! I look all 'round see nobody all them mile o' marsh. I'd a been most glad for a sight o' that white watchman. See no human. One mind tell me 'Load up!' Shoot'em!' I take that mind and gone back. He GROAN at me. I get him under his fore shoulder. Groan, bellow and shake the whole rice-field! Jump up and SLAP he tail! 'Bashaw!'

"I get him under the other shoulder. Some say shoot 'foregator on top knot—bump on he head. He look at me and open he mouth like THAT wide! I shoot right down he throat! (I was FEEDIN' him!) He not like that diet! He holler:

"'A—wah!' (I make him change he voice!)

"I study where I gwine shoot him again. Shoot him whey (where) he tail jine he body. That cut he speed! I study whey (where) I can shoot him next time. A mind tell me, 'Shoot he eye!' That weaken him a little. Here all my shell gone! Shoot him seven time. Not dead yet! I lay my gun down. Find a old pole like a cedar pole. I hit that 'foregator blow, 'woo! woo! woo!

"Gator put me in mind o' the woman the man hit when she call him louse. She say:

"'Old LOUSE!'

"He'd knock her! He knock her! Say she call him a louse again he'd souge her in a pail o' water. She raise up:

"'Old Louse!'

"Jam her head down in pail and gin to get lower:

"'Old LOUSE!'

"Voice lower! Voice lower! Voice weaker! Voice weaker! Jam her head down again. Near 'bout DROWNED! Soon's her head out:

"'You old LOUSE!'

"And that the way that 'foregator done me! He keep right on groan HEAVY. Groan lower. Groan lower. Lower. I had to leave him right there like a log. BLACK, ugly, roughy, and tough and I scared most to death o' him, too. I wouldn't a put my hand on THAT 'foregator!

"You never hear 'bout that man call the ('GATOR man?) Him and his wife comin' from church one night, and he seen sum'pin side the road he THOUGHT was a dog. He kick. He kick at the dog and he had KICK A 'FOREGATOR! Come to find out a 'foregator had throw the man down and got he leg and swallow the man leg jam up to he body! All he FOOT and shoe was down in the 'foregator belly! He'd a carry him and eat him! His wife were there! She study! She study! She just got and sot right down on the 'foregator back and he had he mouth WAY UP TO THE MAN THIGH! Had the man SWALLOW! And the other leg keep him stop. And she gone down in her husband pocket and take that big old hawk-bill knife and rake under that 'foregator throat and cut he throat and pull that man outer he stummick. That weaken the 'foregator. Under there 'bout the tenderest place they is. No more 'YOU' when your throat cut!"

SOURCE: *Given by: Rich Knox*
(Age 40 Plus)
Murrells Inlet, S. C.

Sheep Eye
(Verbatim)

Tell a little joke 'bout a boy goin' courtin'.

One time was a fellow didn't know how to court. He was young. Thought he'd ask his Daddy. Ask his Daddy how to court. Daddy say:

"Roll a sorter sheep eye at the girl. Cast a little sheep eye at her. Throws a little joke or thing. Be livery and merry."

Boy sorter mindless. Sorter short up-stairs. He thought he Pa meant real sheep eye. His Daddy have a lot o' sheep. The cow lot full. Boy gone stay there. Daddy pay no 'foretention. Come to find out boy gone and plugged out every sheep eye and put 'em in a paper sack. And he put 'em in his pocket!

Man gone out and all his sheep all bloody up. Eye all bloody. Come to find out!

Boy gone on to see the girl. Ever once in awhile the fellow take something out his pocket and roll down on the floor by her. She see somethin'. She couldn't know what it was. She got oneasy. She say:

"What that you rollin' over there?"

Boy say:

"Jest (just) a little sheep eye! I castin 'em by!"

Come to find out the boy have all he Daddy sheep eye! Come to find out the man have a pen full o'blind sheep all in misery! Come to find out have to kill all his sheep 'forecause they goin' to die and to put 'em out they misery!

People a long time ago ain't have the understanding they have now. Act cracky—silly like! A pen jam full o' blind sheep!

SOURCE: *Told by Rich Knox, age 40-plus. Murrells Inlet, S. C.*

Budder Wolfe fool Budder Rabbit[35]
(Verbatim)

"Budder Wolfe fool Budder Rabbit this time!

"Budder Wolfe was comin' long wid a good bunch o' fish. Budder Wolfe and a big bunch o' fish gwine home. Budder Wolfe meet up wid Budder Rabbit. Budder Rabbit say,

35. An etiology, or tale of origin.

"'Hello, Budder Wolfe! How you got all dem fish?'

"Budder Wolfe say:

"'You do like I do, you get all the fish you want!'

"Budder Rabbit say:

"'How you does?'

"Budder Wolfe tell him:

"'I goes down to the crick, set on a log and drop my tail in the water. Shake it 'round. Bob it. Fish'll bite.' One get on my tail, pull 'em up! String him on my line! Keep that up till I get my string full. So Budder Rabbit, you kin get all the fish you want that-a-way. You go right down there now (when the tide right) go down and stick you tail overboard. And the fish'll bite!'

"So Budder Rabbit gone and done what Budder Wolfe say. Budder Rabbit fishin'. Bobbin' he tail! Bobbin' he tail! Bobbin' he tail! No fish bite yet! Bobbin' he tail! Bobbin' he tail! Bobbin' he tail! Black frost come! Bobbin' he tail! Bobbin' he tail! Bobbin' he tail! So cold till he couldn't wiggle nothin' but he tail tip! Black frost freeze up all the water in the crick! Budder Rabbit 'forecide he better move. He set back. Couldn't pull he tail out! Set back! Couldn't pull he tail out! Budder 'Coo-coo Owl' up in the tree. Budder Rabbit holler out:

"'Hey! Come here, Budder Owl!'

"Budder Owl ax: "'What the matter, Budder Rabbit?'

"Budder Rabbit tell him:

"'Fish down here! Got my tail! Can't pull 'em out!'

"Then Budder Owl he come. Budder Coo-coo Owl come to help poor Budder Rabbit! Budder Owl fly down and grab. Fust (first) place he grab, he grab budder Rabbit by the two years! And he pull! (Budder Rabbit year gin to stretch!) - - - - - - - - - - And Budder Owl pull! (Budder Rabbit year stretch!) - - - - - - And he pull! (Rabbit year stretch!) Budder Rabbit year stretch and his eye gin to grow big! His eye gin to grow big! Grow bigger and bigger! Bigger and bigger! (That how come Budder Rabbit eye been big till to-day!) So Budder Owl stretch Budder Rabbit years and pull as long as he kin pull and finally through his strugglin' and pullin' he got Budder Rabbit out the frost by finally pullin' the tail off Budder Rabbit! By pullin' he years out long, poppin' he eye and pullin' off he tail - - - - - - he finally got Budder Rabbit out!

"so Budder Rabbit never didn't get his fish! Got a big eye, no tail, long years and no fish!"

Told by Richard Knox
(Lillie: "Richard in his forties")
Murrells Inlet, S. C.

Fightin' Fire

Gracious! I been in jail! I been there so many time! Bubba[36] put me there for settin' fire in my own field. All that burn was mine. He did have a row o' tater plant on my side, and the fire scorch off the leaves. Who was the man stood my bond? Lemme see. Andrew Johnson and Bill Oliver gone my bond on a $500 bond till trial at court. Neither one have witness but the family—the first startin' of it.

The first startin', one time my wife in the house with a child—one o' her chillun—Child just 'bout a week old, and she couldn't get out. And I got in hearin' o' the house, and I hear there cussin' and goin' on. And I know that nobody but Bubba and I think I best go back till he stop all that. So I gone on and don't come back till 'foreleven o'clock. And way here 'foreleven o'clock here he come, (bush ax over his shoulder,) dammin' and hellin'. Dammin' and hellin'! Dammin' and hellin' like he was 'Mister Big Jim.' And my old lady right in bed!

When I walk up, my mother she was there, and all the yard full up with chillun. And it made me sorter mad. So I gone on in my house, and when I come to the door here I have a pistol in my hand. And he offer the bush hook, and cuss all different kind o' cuss. He say:

"Here I come to find out, people tryin' to burn me out!"

And I tell him:

"I burnin' in my OWN field!"

And I throwed the pistol on him. I sorta aggravate. And here he drawed the bush ax on me! I say:

"I blow the heart out you body!"

Then he beg:

"Oh, don't shoot! Oh, do don't shoot me!" And he grab his bush ax and sail on back home.

Next day Boy come by, and see me grubbin' stumps. He say:

"Man, how you out here workin'? Ain't you know you Bubba got a warrant for you? Got out THREE warrant! Sault and battery, 'foretent to kill, and conceal weapon."

You know, 'fore they stop, they fine me $20 for puttin' out fire! I knocked all that out—and then turn 'round and make him pay half of ALL the fee! Make him pay five dollars more than I pay. I went to town and got me a severe, (surveyor) and that severe charge me $15 a day. Showed Bubba he LAWED me for my own things!

36. Not Richard Knox's brother Zackie. The man referred to here is more likely a neighbor who was called "Bubba."

How come the fire got out, I was burnin' up a snake in a hole. Snake run in a stump—hole. I sot the thing a-fire. Tryin' to burn him out. Wind was breezin' up. Fire got way from me. Burn over the whole field. Didn't get no where's on nobody else land. And here he lawin' me for burnin' my own land! Say I'm sottin' him a-fire and all that.

Tell you just what I done. I cross indite him, and tear the thing up. Put the place up for sale. And that make 'em all come to me to sqush the thing up. Drop the case. I had done find a man to buy the place in. Then Uncle William[37] gone to Bubba and warn him:

"You don't know what kind o' trouble this boy stirrin' here."

Next thing I hear, Bubba huntin' a lawyer! And next news, here he come. They all tell him he better compromise. Compromise the thing. It natural fire will get way with people some time.

I have one those water tanks on my back that time o' that big woods' fire. Had the fire all out but a little place on the shingle. And here they huntin' me, and huntin' me 'bout witness for that same fire. Man come to me, and try to make me tangle the thing up. Woods cot fire, surrounded the house, and I fought till it stifle me. Mr. Wilson[38] most fall in the fire. That day I learn a lesson o' fire.

The very next day I fight woods fire my last time. Man put a fire out at a stump. Then he gone and leave the stump burnin'. Come on through the bay. Cut it off from John[39] house and I secure Aunt Havillah.[40] Secure her that day. I fight fire! Fight! Help save all that man pine tree. I got enough o' fire fightin'. I come out the woods after dark, and all who see me say:

"Gracious Granny! You sho got red eyes! You look bad."

And I say, "I feel like I look." And I went home and tell fire goodbye. It burn Uncle William grape vine, sot his roof a-fire, burn all his kindlin', and burn his timber.

Why I through with woods' fire? That man what own all that big woods—all them big pine tree—told his fire-line man to pay all that help—all that gang o' men who fought fire. The watchman stopped me and give me a twenty-five cents. I say:

"What this for?"

He said, "Fightin' fire."

And I told him, "Mister you keep that."

37. William Oliver.

38. Local magistrate.

39. John Knox.

40. Havillah Holmes.

Rich Knox
Age 40—plus
Murrells Inlet, S. C.

Sumpin' t'Eat.
Big Rich Tells a True Story.

Big Rich say:

"Shucks! Yinnah done lie enough. I'll tell you a TRUE Story."

And he start:

"Once-pon-a-time was a 'foreoman.[41] She was out to the tub washin'. Tub was under the shade tree by the road where she could see everybody passin'.

"Was a peanuts patch and the hog had got out and root up some the peanuts vine and they stay out there in the sun two three days and them little green peanut had dry up and get SWEET in the sun. 'foreOman wash in' Hot August sun. She washin'.Say:

"'I think I'll not stop washin' till I done. I hongry I'll eat some these swiveled peanut. Won't stop to cook till I done.'

"So she full up on peanut.

"After while here come her knee high boy.'Mama, I hongry!'

"'Oman say: 'Come here eat some these peanut. Full up on peanut you won't starve.'

"Next here come the waist high boy:"Mama, I wants sumpin' t'eat."

"Oman say: 'Do like me and your Bubba. Full up on peanut. Ain't goin' cook till I done washin'.'

"'Bout two o'clock here come the 'foreoman old man, Husband gone in the kitchen, lift all the pot led (lids), come to the door and sing out:

"'Where the sumpin' t'eat?'

"Man too hollow. Empty till he sick. 'foreOman say:

"'Tryin' to finish washin' 'fore I cooks.'

(Rich tellin' this story! Didn't say LILL. He say ''Oman. Once-pon-a-time was a 'foreoman)

"Way that night 'bout twelve o'clock that 'foreoman rear up and say:

"'Get the soda quick! 'Quick! I got such a hurtin'.

"Man say: 'Uh HUNH! '

"In no time the knee boy sing out:

"'My stummick hurt me! 'And the first news here the waist high boy wake up groanin' :

"('My stummick! My stummick! Mama, got any sody?'

41. Lillie Knox.

"Here that 'foreoman make herself and all two both of the boy sick eatin' green peanut swivel in the sun. The man he SEE them peanut and they look sweet but he let 'em be. That 'foreoman thought she'd get by 'forethout COOKIN'. 'foreOman got business to knock off when twelve comes and cook for her old man and she wouldn't a been sick.—and make her two boys sick.

"Now what I tell you no lie. That a TRUE story."

And Rich look at me:

"If all three had DEAD, nobody wouldn't a know what kill yinnah! Too sick to tell me what you eat! All three with a colic to suit the comman meter!"

Rich: "Dat's a hoop-snake rolls! They don't hardly be 'round here much. 'foreNuster been long way back yonder.

"Was a woman wanted to finish her row. (She was Hoein' cotton) Tell me a coach-whip[42] tie her long time ago. TIE her! After the coach-whip get her tie UP take he tail and run up her nose to see whether she BREEZIN'! (She helt her bref!) Fust time he gone that she keep on Breezin'! He whip her again! And NEXT time she helt her bref. Then he slacked up on her—loosed up and she high-balled! Make her 'forescape.

"Coach-whip tail look like a possum tail.

"One time Lill and I choppin' corn. A BIG old coach-whip watchin'! Watchin' Lill on her corn row. Gettin' a chance after HER. (They'll run a woman when they won't run a man.) I tuk (took) after that snake. I ain't never see such a runnin' snake in my born days. I grab a big old stick and come in range I crack that snake on the head and he stretch his length. 'foreStonish me! When I lick him on the head gone to turnin' and that the fastest turnin' thing stay in one place I ever seen. I musser just addled him. Coach-whip? I don't truss 'em. Coach-whip comes from a black runner. A black runner gets old he turns to a coach-whip. Then he just grows older and older. Older and older. And the black all comes off and his tail grows and grows and grows. And the tail grows right on and on till tail grows nearly to the head. Grow long tail like that you scared to tamper them. There 'forenuster to be one to Grassy Bay[43]—Lovers Lane.[44] Was one in Lovers Lane and it run from Isaac and hit the wire 'BOOM!' In April and May they're sassy. Won't run from you THEN. Coach-whip meet you in May they'll sho whip you. Pow! Pow! Nuster

42. *Masticophis flagellum*, a nonvenomous snake falsely reputed (most likely due to its markings, which resemble a braided whip) to seek out human victims and thrash them with its tail. Coachwhips are said to travel in pairs. One is said to restrain victims while the other whips them.

43. Mission swamp.

44. This lane ran between the Hermitage and Belin Methodist Church.

tie up people pretty often. Reckon people 'bout got 'em kill out. They catch you they got partners and when they WHISTLE you better run! One'll tie you up and 'forenother partner'll come and they'll double bank you. One'll tie; other'll whip.

"Rattle snake travels in partners too. You see a rattle-snake pilot go through this yard in three days or eight days—pilot goes ahead to guide the rattle-snake. Same direction. Pilot killed, rattle-snake 'forell drill right'round that place. If they bite you and not get to that WEED they has to eat, they'll die. Rattle-snake weed. You pisen rattle-snake same as they pizen you. Mr. Howard[45] try and show me that weed. Rattle-snake is the baddest snake they is but they harmless. You w on't worry dem, they won't bother you.

"One time a man and he wife come in to go to bed. Was a old king snake round—is king of ever other snake. And this big king snake crawl up the steps. Pull out the biggest rattle-snake ever been. Pull him out from under the man bed. Drag him out from 'foretween the mattress and the spring. Kill him. Broke him up. That king snake broke ever bone in his body. And crawl right out. (Them people must not a done much turnin' o' they mattress!)

"I have kill snake with three eggs in'em. I busted dem ever one and they runned out he mouth."

SOURCE: *Given by: Zackie Knox.*[46]

45. Drew Howard, recorded by John A. Lomax.

46. Though the source of this interview is listed as Zack Knox, it begins with a citation from Rich that seems to be an unbroken narrative. Hence its inclusion in Richard Knox's chapter.

Thelma Knox

Thelma Knox was the daughter of Quinvy and Katherine Knox. She was fourteen years old when Chandler interviewed her in 1937. According to the 1930 U.S. Census, she shared a household with her parents and nine others (Isadora, Gabe, Rosa, Quinvy Jr., Catherine, Mattie, Elizabeth, King, and Herbert). In the one interview she gave Chandler, Thelma Knox distinguishes between two different types of supernatural phenomena (hants and ghosts). She then enthusiastically relates the tale of her sister Mattie's encounter with the former, also known as a "plat-eye."

Hant and Ghosts
(Verbatim Conversation by Thelma Knox—)

"They's hant then they's ghost. Hant is a plat-eye. And a plat-eye some those old timey people what been dead a long time. Ghost just uh evil spirit.

"Mattie see 'um. Well first she saw uh (let me see what color the cat was now!), she saw a white cat and next thing she saw was a big old white dog with red eye. Then after she saw all this, she leave out the house and was going next door to people she had farm with; and when she had step down the step and came out the door, she saw a woman dressed in white and aint got no leg and had 'foree arm fold up—to the corner of the house. Then as she was going off to Miss Jane house, she had the baby in her hand and the boy was walking and when she get a little piece down the road, she saw a woman standing up side the pump and it followed her and and walked between the little boy and her. And she told the little boy, 'Looker there Junior! Look at that ghost!' The little boy couldn't see it. And it follow her right on till it got just (she said 'jist') about ten steps from the house. Then he turned round and went back. (Almost always low country negroes get sex mixed, the old ones always saying 'he' for she.)[1] Mattie gone on to Miss Jane. She see that woman again. She and Gabe[2] can see 'um and Alice Knox. She can see 'um better than all.

1. See page 5, note 5.
2. Gabe Knox.

"She see that same woman and a man too. Somebody had got shot to the gate of that house. They called the place 'Jack Place.'"

Thelma Knox—age 15
Murrells Inlet, S.C.
May 12, 1937.

Zackie Knox

Like Lillie Knox, Zackie Knox began working for Clark and Minnie Willcox at the Hermitage at an early age—most likely when he was still just a boy. At first he worked in Clark Willcox's farming-sales operation. Zackie's responsibilities grew over time however. After Tom Chandler's death, Lillie Knox went to work for Genevieve Chandler full-time, leaving her position as housekeeper at the Willcoxes. Soon thereafter Minnie died, leaving Clark alone in the home. Zackie worked for Clark in several capacities—farming, repairing, chopping wood, performing tree surgery, and keeping house. According to Knox, Willcox did not compensate him in proper proportion to his responsibilities.[1] Knox was married to Evelina Carolina Knox, the foster daughter of Albert and Ella Carolina. Together Zackie and Evelina had three daughters—Blondel, Mary Ella, and Evelina—and one son—Zackie Jr. Their home was with those of the other Knoxes in Knoxville.

During the Depression most African American men in Murrells Inlet acquired provisions through occasional odd jobs that paid cash or through barter. Jobs that paid cash were extremely difficult to come by. Zackie's job therefore put him in an enviable position. On the other hand, the job did not allow him much free time to farm, fish, and hunt—all significant local sources of subsistence. Zackie expresses his family's want of food in a doleful refrain that stretches through many of the Chandler interviews.

Although Zackie Knox and Richard Knox behaved like brothers and were considered brothers in the community, it is most likely that they were more distantly related. Zackie does not appear in U.S. Census record for the area until 1930. According to his own report, his mother's sister moved to Virginia when he was still a child. His birth mother's whereabouts at that time are uncertain. Although Zackie is not recorded as a member of Addie Knox

1. Willcox family tradition holds that Clark Willcox was indeed fiscally conservative or, as they say, "chincy." Although not recorded in these interviews, Zackie used to joke that Willcox carried the whole world in his pocket. When asked for money or a loan, Willcox would turn his pockets inside out and say, "I don't have a cent in the world."

Ladson's household in the 1910 census, he may have joined the family shortly thereafter.

Like Richard Knox, Zackie was a master storyteller. Like Lillie Knox, he was a wonderful singer. John A. Lomax recorded Zackie singing several times. As a devout Christian, Zackie refused to sing any "fiddle songs."[2] Knox provided a dose of comic relief to many of Lillie Knox's interviews with Chandler and continued to play the jester when Chandler interviewed him alone, but Knox was a clown with a degree of depth. By turns goading his family members, singing songs, and making jesting complaints, Knox often managed to hint at some of the unpleasant realities in his and his neighbors' lives. He did so with a subtlety that made his complaints seem almost unselfconscious.

Fiddle Song
(Zackie and Blackie the Ox)
(Verbatim Conversation)

Zackie: "That piece you put in there belong to a fiddle song. I'll sing anything for that's fitten to sing. I can't hinder other people, you know."
Missus: "Is it a disgraceful song?"
Zackie: "Don't know its so disgraceful. Its sufficient for me. I know its gainst my religion. My religion don't low me to handle such language.
Lillie: "Jimmy uses bad language—fore the preacher too!"
Zackie: "Jimmy chuckle! Jimmy chuckle! Reb (Zackie's pet name for the Reverend) say 'Woman's religion laid on a stump till they get through talking. Go right to church, take the sacrament and go right on off and wash it down with corn likker, moon-shine and monkey rum! God going get tired of you foolishness some of these days. You can't play with that TABLE! Mustn't drink that whiskey behind it. Some woman's burn most as much of it as a man.'"
Lillie: "Zackie, they is worser things than drinking moon-shine!"
Zackie: "Town girl I wuz messing up with ax me where I can get some likker. I tell her I'd go get her some—and I take my pay and gone RIGHT ON to Mr. Tom[3] store and buy my grocery! She say, 'Mister, you ain't marry, is you?' I tell her, 'Yes. I got a raggy wife and five raggy chillun waiting on me!'"
Lillie: "Sing the bestest verse for the Missus!"

2. The "fiddle song" is a variant of the blues tradition in other African American communities. Officially the church considered both sinful. Obviously the traditions survived the religious prohibition against them, but singers like Zackie Knox were guarded about performing unsanctioned material too openly.

3. Tom Jordan, owner of the grocery store on Highway 17 near the Mount Gilead neighborhood in Murrells Inlet.

Zackie: "I ain't going to sing that! Ain't going to sing no fiddle song! Reckon part come off a record nohow. I not particular bout learning fiddle songs. Sometimes I get to rambling off and get myself tangle. Best go plow you yard and plow them peas under!"
Lillie: "Zackie, first thing you know Missus gwine tell you to carry that calf hindquarters home and leave the head here! If you ever tell Missus the first item of anything, you mights as well give ALL!"
Zackie: "I ain't going sing that fiddle song! Missus have me put in gaol!"
Zackie: (Going back to his plow where Blackie ox is restless)
"Man, a ox start to tie up, he kin tie up his heel string!"
Lillie: "Zackie, bring the cow some of them cornstalks!"
Zackie: "Gal, you can't tangle me up here now! Got them pea to plow under! (To ox) Come on Bubba! Come on here! Gee boy! Whoa! Get up there boy! I'm going to take a stick here terreckly and hot you up. Come on here, old man!

(Singing) Come on, Bubba!
Come on, Bubba!
Come on here!
Halleloo!"

Lillie: (Looking out at Zackie from the window and grinning) "Lena[4] say sometimes Zackie go on that a way at home and she say, 'Go on boy!' and make out like she going to knock him! Zackie run off laughing."
Zackie: (Warming up to plowing and gone to singing)

"Come on here!
I know you getting old!
Come on anyhow!
Come on here!
Halleloo!"
Ho—Brek—Haw!

Lillie: "What that mean?"
Zackie: "That just mean for him to go which ever way you want him to."
Lillie: "Why didn't you sing that plow song when the boss was here?"
Zackie: "He oughter'ed a strike Myrtle Beach when they digging that highway! He'd a got 'water calls' all right.
(Calling)
Wautah!
Ah Wautah! Boy!
I'm going to tell your Daddy on you.

4. Evelina Knox, Zackie Knox's wife.

I'm broke! Jam busted this morning! Busted and disgusted. (Singing)

> "Come up old man!
> Come up old man!
> Come up old man!
> Come up old man!

"You want the whole world to turn round in. Whoap!" (This 'whoap' is high and shrill—tenor)

> Come on in!
> Come on in!
> Come on in!
> Come on in!

(Talking) "Come on take it easy! Whoap!

> Come on in!
> Come on in!
> I know you getting old
> But come on anyhow!
> Whoap!
> Come on here!
> Come on rounder.
> Take it easy.
> Easy, old man, easy!
> Take it easy now!
> Whoap!
> Ho! Beck!

(Talking) "You better hear me this morning!"

> Come on you chain three pound and a quarter more!
> My old man!
> Come on black boy!
> Whoap!
> That's all right.
> Come on here. (Clicking teeth)
> (Singing)
> "Take it easy!
> Take it easy!
> Take it easy!
> Take it easy!
> Easy man! Whoap!

(Talking) "You better look!
You broke this plow here!
Come on boy!
Easy here!
Ho breck! (A signal like 'Gee' and 'Haw.')
Whoap!
Come on here!
Oh— (Hit a root.)
Whoap!
Come on boy!
Come on anyhow!
Whoap!
Come on here!
Whoap!
Come on black!
Whoap!

(Talking to Blackie) "You getting kinder slow this morning!

What the trouble?
Come on here!
Come on here old brother!
Come on see!
Whoap!

(Talking) "Gracious Goodness! Whoap!

"Move that log! Yonder nother one! That what I hate bout burying can where I got to plow! Wonder that ox didn't kick that boy! He kick you he think you going to hit him."

(Friend approaches)

"Boy, what you say?"

"Gwine give you a ceegret!"

(Zackie) (Looking his friend over)

"Must been hit a spot up yonder! Wearing you best hat every day!"

Lillie: "He ain't need no lunch! Looker how he bread basket set over his belt here! How Uncle? Uncle ain't swell none?"

Zackie Knox—age moved off when family moved to Virginia, taking Bible. Thinks he's 28.
And his sister-in-law.
Lillie Knox, age 35
Murrells Inlet, S. C.
July 24, 1937.

(Verbatim Conversation)
Zackie and the Yaller Gal

"She say she don't know but she think God intend her to be a teacher or something for one night God keep showing her things in her division. (vision) One night she saw a man sitting on a bale of cotton. Had a pitch-fork. Nother man give her a book and she wouldn't take it. That why she think God intend her to be something good—to do His good work. Her first cousin grandma came to die, call her to her and tell her her God intend her to be something—good for Him. That why he give her that book in her sleep. One night she sitting by her ma in the kitchen. Kinder squinch herself together. Nother shower come shake her. She squinch herself together again. Pa say,

"What the matter?"

Pa say, 'Sick?'

Not sick. Church sisters come pray for her. And when she done wallowing like that a pile of stuff that high (measuring about two feet) come out o' her chest—pile that high and look like white of a egg beat up. She say if she go to church and get two more sermonts like last night, she'd be all right. She halting tween two opinions. Want to do what right. Can't carry fire in one hand and water in the other. Either the fire will out the water or the water will overcome the fire! Cut out for a good girl, but dog eat the pattern. Vulgarity!—Call that a 'no harm' sin.

"Uncle Calina[5] ketch holt fore I stop good. 'A charge to keep I have, A Gods to glorify!'"

Zackie Knox—

"Now, Miss Jin, bout my age, I ain't zackly know. Mama sister put my age down in the Bible and her sister took it off to North Virginia. Now I think it bout 28."
Murrells Inlet, S. C.
July 1937.

Murder Reported

Zackie: (Entering the kitchen)

"Zekel kill a man."

Lillie: "Where?"

Zackie: "Somewhere in Horry."

Lillie: "What!"

Zackie: "Yes, gal. A white man."

Lillie: "How come?"

5. Albert Carolina.

Zackie: "Whiskey. Whiskey cause devilment and death of people concern and death of them not concern. You know Mr. Bob?[6] He the one pay him out the gang.[7] Zekel drinking. Pick up the ax. Haul back. Buss (bust) he brains out.'
Lillie: "He be lectrocute if they don't done lynch him."
Missus: (Entering kitchen—note book in hand)
"What's that about Zekel?"
Lillie: "Kill a man Sunday."
Zackie: "Lill, she got the pencil. Gwine quit right now!"
Missus: "Zackie, how'd it happen?"
Zackie: "No 'um. I'm gone!"
Lillie: "Zack, go on. Tell us bout it!"
Zackie: "I ain't know! Ain't know thing bout it. Mout not even be so! Ain't you want a song?"[8]
Lillie: "Zackie tell us what you heard."
Zackie: "I ain't hear nothing. Ain't know nothing."
Missus: "Zackie what your name?"
Zackie: "I ain't know!"
Missus: "Zackie, was it a white man?"
Zackie: "Missus, mought a been blue by the time it get here. Green Sea[9] a far place!"
Lillie: "How you hear it Zack?"
Zackie: "Must not hear that thing. Must a sleep and dream it!"
Lillie: "Zack, go on tell us. Missus ain't going get you in no trouble!"
Zackie: "All you all got on dress. Me, I wear pants!"

Given by Zackie Knox—25
Lillie Knox—35
Murrells Inlet, S. C.
July 1937.

Fox

One time the Fox caught Buh Rabbit. He say,

"You been messin' me up all the time and now I b'live I'll make way with you."

6. Bob Watts.

7. Bob Watts paid Ezekiel's bail, thus releasing him from the chain gang so he could return to work for Watts himself.

8. Zackie Knox's reluctance to speak on this matter stems from its immediacy. He is afraid he might be called to testify.

9. Green Sea is a village in Horry County.

So Fox caught th' Rabbit and start to eat him. And Buh Rabbit he start in to plead. He say,

"Please Brudder, don't eat me and I'll show you where an old gobbler—(no—turkey HEN) and six P. Ps is."

So the Fox say,

"You goin' show me where a old turkey hen and six P. Ps. is?"

"Yeah, Buh Fox, "Buh Rabbit tell him," I gwine show you!"

"All right! I rather have them than have you anyhow! The old turkey hen will make me a big mess and I'll come back afterwards and get the six P. ps."

Then Buh Rabbit say,

"All right, Buh Fox, less go!"

The old Mama dog was down in a big harricane" (dead, hollow tree lying on ground) " in a nest with her six puppies—have buy one way to go in. So Buh Rabbit told Buh Fox,

"All right, Buh Fox, when we get there I'm gwine pint my fingers to place where the turkey and not say any more, 'forecause if I talk the old hen might get scared and run. Now you jump right over in there.

Fox say,

"Well we won't talk. But if the hen does run, maybe I can catch her."

(Buh Rabbit know if he went there talkin' the dog would growl)

Rabbit say,

"Follow me!"

They walk long. They ease up there. Buh Rabbit point his finger to the place (the place where you go in the hollow) and the fox (when Buh Rabbit point his finger) just sail right over in there and when he sail over in there he sail over a Mother dog and six head o' puppies. There him and the dog. Dog beat him up. Like to kill him. Dog run after him try to catch him. As they run out, run past Buh Rabbit. The fox was running by. Dog had him in a speed. As they pass by Fox say,

"All right, Buh Rabbit! Tha's all right! I'll do for you!"

Buh Rabbit jump up and clasp his hands and say,

"Sue Boy! Sue Boy! Do for me now!"

(Hound must-a-been name Sue.)

SOURCE: *Told by Zackie Knox, Age 28, September 1937, Murrells Inlet, S. C.*

Sheep Heads (Verbatim)

Zakie: "One time a man had kill some sheep and a old woman used to help him.—(Wasn't so old neither. Kinder middle age.) And she have a boy. And they kill the sheep on Satdy. They give her a piece of the meat. She want all the sheep heads. And they give her the heads—all the sheep heads and she carry them home and skin'em and clean 'em and 'fore she got ready to go to church she put 'em on. And they most done 'fore she left for church. So she put some dumpling in 'em 'fore she left for church. So she tell the little boy.

"Keep a good fire under the pot and don't let the pot bile over."

So she gone on to church and leave the boy home and the boy put a big fire under the pot and the pot went to boilin'. After it went to boilin' he see the sheep heads turnin' over and over in the pot and he thought the sheep was tryin' to butt the dumpling out the pot. So he thought to hissef,

"I better run on to church and tell Mama the sheep buttin' the dumplin' out the pot!"

And he run on and come to the church door and when he come to church door he saw his Mama sittin' 'bout middle ways the church on the end of the seat. So he call his Mama.

"Mama! Mama!" And he wave his hand to 'em and talk to 'em the same time. She talk back to him,—winkin' her eye all the time and wisperin.

"Go back son! Go back son!"

He get pervoke and call out so all in the church can hear,

"All right, Mama. You can stay there winkin' and blinkin' at me, but I tell you them sheep head buttin' all the dumpling out the pot."

SOURCE: *Give by Zackie Knox, Age 30, Murrells Inlet, S. C., September 1937.*

Green Savannahs

"You see that been Douglas[10] job—but then I with him. He scared out there in them lonesome savannah by himself. Time we find a good place we turn them three ox loose—have a rope tie on they horn so if notion strike 'em to run we kin wrop that rope round a tree. Then we bell 'Wary.' They name been like the month they born—May, July and 'Wary.' 'Wary' been for Jinuwary or February one of the two. Yes, 'Wary' the one tote the bell.

"Time to eat if we anyways near home we go on home and fry up some that thing we call scrambled corn-bread; if we too far off we'd sometimes cook in the woods.

"That May ox was way yonder bigger than that big black ox of mine—two times as big. 'Wary' would stay one place pretty well—but that May and July gone on from here!

"Mr. Oliver[11] pay Douglas 25 cents a day for watching them ox. You see that the cheapest way he kin feed critters. All the savannah full of deep grass

10. Douglas Knox, Zackie Knox's brother.
11. Probably Captain Bill Oliver, owner of Oliver's Lodge.

but no fence nowhere to stop 'em. They welcome to the grass but they can't be leave. Too much o' people got no fence tall—tall. Got to be watch.

"One Sunday we thought we'd fix things so we put a bell on Wary and gone on to church. He was a long, slim ox—May the heavy, thick one. Wary lean and slim and just had that walking position (disposition). He never wouldn't lie down. He'd just stand there and chew two hours. That same Sunday Mama had cook up some stew beef with onions and tomatoes. It smell so good we didn't hurt ourselves hurrying none and when we gone back out there that Wary ox gone! That July gone too. July gone way to Socastee to the man house he been buy from—and Wary gone the object direction. All we had to do was jump out and hunt them two ox. Finally we found his track in the woods and when he hit the road again we trailed him right straight to the river landing. He come from Sandy Island in the first place and here he getting ready to swim the Waccamaw and go back where he come from!

"Me and Douglas took and tie a big old hemp rope to the ox horn—a long rope so if he start to run we could wrop it round a tree and stop him—run 'round a tree with the end of it.

"Coming home from the landing a wild-cat[12] took after us. Right down the road that cat come and run us jam to the King Road!

"Mama sent me to Mr. Gillikin[13] one day for a box of matches and I seen another big cat in the King Road—right where the fork comes in from the river. I didn't move. Was behind a big pine. And that wild-cat brought a little black pig and bury that. Then he gone off and 'fore I move he come back with a redbird and bury that. And no sooner he rake the last handful of dirt over that bird than that wild-cat look after me! Little black pig 'bout that long! (measuring 'bout a foot). And no sooner the last paw ful of dirt on that pig and bird than he sailed in right after me and here I took out down the King Road! Here we went! What he was after he figger I might go back and get his pig!

"Member where they bury it? Who dat? I KNOW they 'foremember. Mr. Oliver 'forenuster kill cow and give his dog too much o' bone. And he'd tote 'em right to the wood yard and dig a hole and bury them. And if you get too near where he bury bone that dog come up and get your leg.

Zackie Knox—age 28
Murrells Inlet, S. C.
Oct. 26th, 'fore37.

12. A bobcat or, more likely, a mountain lion.
13. A local store owner.

Zackie Brings the Mornin' News (Verbatim Conversation)

(Knock on door—hesitant—questioning)

"That's Zackie!" (Louder) "Come in! "

"Morning Zack! What's the news?"

Zack: (Hanging up coat and hat and stripping for action—milkin' etc.)

"Well, Jinks[14] most get kill. His lil' ox run way with him. Ox didn't have no 'foretention of harming Jinks—none tall. Myrtle and Martha Jane was playin' in the road comin' from school like young 'foreuns does, and they run up behind Jinks' cart. 'Brandy' (the ox) start to run twice and Jinks stop him. And then when he did take a good notion and make a break, one cart wheel had to drop in a hole 'bout that deep (illustrated) and it throwed Jinks 'foretween the ox hind foots and took him on such a surprise he kicked Jinks 'fore he thought.—'fore he knowed who Jinks was! Give him such another cut cross his face—right 'foretween his eyes.

"Jinks already have his nose near 'bout broke two months ago. Sonny pick us up in his car one Sunday night. He was running fast. Road full of hole. Turn the corner fast. Hit a hole like he running on the Highway. Jinks hit the car top. Blood spew out like water out the flowin' well.

"And here now the ox kick him and split right 'foretween his eyes and laid it open to the bone! Whoever would-a thought a thing like that happen just a-haulin' a cart load of fire wood! Now when Christmas time come, you'll hear 'bout accident.

"There the Revents[15] car stoppin'. I does hope that car ain't gwine broke down here 'fore us door this mornin'! When I'm pushed for time, I does hate to have somebody car broke down to the very door. He must be waitin' to borry us trailer—He does. " (Head out door) "Revents, Missis say 'Help you self!" She say that trailer must been have a spell on 'em. Every time you hitch on that trailer and start in the woods for a load of wood, you car broke! Better watch!

"Satan a liar and a cunjur too!
If you don't mind he'll cunjur you!"

(Revents chuckles and hitching on the trailer makes a start.)

(Zackie continues)

"Revents make start. But he'll stop 'fore he hauls first load. Jest (just) a habit he has.

(Pourin' coffee)

14. Jinks Johnson.
15. Rev. Aaron Pinnacle.

"If'n I was Revents, you know whatI'd do? I'd stop at the first garage I come to and say, 'If you got anything in here will run,—even a old model T,—take this here 23 Chevrolet and give me something will run! (Looking through the window) "I likes that as much as I like anything in the world."

"What's that, Zack?"

"To see the cows when I get done brokin' corn just goin' where they please in the field gettin' all they wants! I don't like to see nothin' goin' hongry! When I don't have no rations to carry home,—I jest (just) naturally can't go home! I can't face twelve hongry eyes!

"Yonder go a un-washed lookin' tramp down the Highway. Put me in mind of Aunt Bess,—from Tip-Top. If you jest (just) don't mention to Aunt Bess 'bout washin' her foots you and her'll get on. But she jest ain't goin' low water to tech her foots. Her foots same like that iron stove. Black like that stove and rough as 'foregator hide. She been to us house one time,—cross over from Tip Top in a boat. That night time come to crawl in Mama[16] say, 'Aunt Bess! Do wash you foots! I done put white sheet and clean pillow slip on here! Do, PLEASE, wash you foots!' She stopped long 'forenouf to tell her THINKS 'fore she gone—but she gone all right! Gone cross the river and COLD! It was cold—and most middle night too!"

(Knock on door)

"Who that, Zack?"

"Uncle Will."

"Morning, Uncle Will![17]"

"Mornin' Missis! What time tis'm?"

"Clock's stopped, but I'd say 'foretwas eight o'clock to look at the sun—'Bout eight o'clock in the mornin'."

SOURCE: *Zackie Knox—Age 28. November 1, 1937. Murrell's Inlet, S. C.*

(Verbatim)

Lillie: "I tell you 'bout leavin' that barn unlock."
Zack: "Well you see long as Evie[18] up I had a lock. Evie she a good lock. I didn't have barn, corn, none to study 'bout. I went in there and somebody had jest went in there and LOADED UP. I jest (just) figger lock is only for honest man. No nuse for you to lock up from a thief. If there's anything here you don't want a thief to get you best take it long with you. But God give me this mouth. And I know if you got something I want I kin ax for it.

16. Addie Knox.
17. Most likely Will Deas, during his stint on the ditching crew in Murrells Inlet.
18. Evelina Knox.

"But here when Evie drop and gone down[19] nobody on the out side! Ain't even got a dog for night watchin'!"

SOURCE: *Lillie Knox—March 1, 1938*
Zackie Knox—Murrells Inlet, S. C.

"He struggle all the week pickin' them oyster. Left home this mornin' with a load o' oyster [illegible] 'fore day."

Snakes

"You talk black snake? They'll run you all right! Run the socks off'n you. But then they not so serious as coach-whip.[20] Now coach-whip'll tie you down and whip you. My cousin Jake knowed a man to Bucksport who had a Uncle who got run by a coach-whip. He was a elder in the church—or a deacon and it was October. You know how it is in October. Everbody a-fullin all the jug and keg fullo' scuppernong wine. And bullice wine. Muscadine? We says 'bullice.' Well, anyways this man call them wild black grape. Uncle was stayin' to Cousin Jake's house and Jake allus was a great hand to make wine. The Law never didn't stop you from makin' some to keep in the barn for sickness. And the deacon didn't refuse when Jake told him to sample his. Seems like he must-a been needin' some medicine. He sampled all two kinds. He must-a sampled pretty gentrous. And here he started home and walkin' by old Salem church on the old River Road, sleep just naturally over-powered him. Now coach-whip does they runnin' and lashin' in May. They not susspose to run nobody in the fall but the next thing he knowed a big coach-whip had him tie up to a big log and was whistlin' for another one to come lay on the lashin'. My cousin John[21] told us that Man's Uncle showed all the stripes that night. They was still red stripes. His wife had him in bed and was pouring black coffee down him. Beings he was a Elder he must-a told what God loves and the Devil hates.

"Snake egg? I don't know 'bout snake egg. Snake egg one kind o' egg I don't bother with. Now cooter egg—that's different."

SOURCE: *Told by Zackie Knox*
June 10th., 1938
Murrells Inlet, S. C.

"Ain't no animal story. 'bout a woman and a little boy and a man.

19. When Zackie Knox's wife falls ill, in this case probably due to childbirth (the usage "drop" commonly indicated birthing), there is no one to watch the barn.

20. See pages 234–35, especially note 42.

21. John Knox.

"Say a man wife gone off one time. Don't know where she go. (You can put it where-some-ever you want to. Say to the store!)

"On the way home she meet a little sawed off man like Simon Cribb. She thought he was a little boy. He sassed at her when she pay him no 'foretention he cussed at her. So she gone on home and tell her husband: 'I meet a little boy down yonder and he sassed me and cussed.

"So her husband said: 'I'll learn him how to talk 'round ladies.' And he gone on down where his wife pint him to.

"The little sawed off fellow jumped on the big man and cross-walked him and beat him up with he fist. Like a bantam rooster and a big rooster. Bantam rooster can run right up under the big rooster and he can't catch him.

"When the little fellow got through the man went on home. He tell his wife:

"'Give me sometin' t'eat!'

"'Did you beat him?'

"'Give me sometin' t'eat!'

"'You see that boy?'

"'I see no boy. I found a man.'"

SOURCE: *Zackie Knox Age 30 years.*
Murrells Inlet, S. C. June 11th., 1938

Zacks' Memorandance

"Your memorandance must be gooder than mine. I just gone to school three days and I learn three words like Brother Rabbit. 'B.D.P.' That mean; 'Be d—— particular.'[22] I gots no book learnin' but I understand tha animal all right.

"I was slopin' one side of that road under the cedars. I got hot and I sot down on the pile of lumber and I mopped my face and I said: 'Now I wonder if I fixed that road last year?' (And I was studyin' 'bout goin' fishin' and a crow came flyin' outer us fig tree. He was FULL of figs.) And he went flyin' off down to the woods sayin: 'Ah HAH! Ah HAH! Ah HAH! And I say, 'How you spell 'Ah HAH? I didn't go to school but THREE days and I learn three words. 'B.D.P' Mr. Crow, your memorandum must be GOODER than mine!'"

SOURCE: ZACKIE KNOX
Age 30 (?)
Sept. 1938
Burgess, S. C.

Zack: "Well, see now, I want Rich to SEE WHAT A LOAD IS. Mama let him go. Pa turn him loose. Lillie catch him holt. So he ain't never know what the

22. "Be damn particular."

weight of the world been. Lillie catch him holt and put the corner of the world on his shoulder and GONE ON."

Lillie: "Now Zack, Rich not well. You know, Zack, Poor Rich not well. I come to work and leave him holdin' his back and gruntin' this mornin'. Now take ME, I can't 'foreford to grunt."

Zack: "Well, I start to gruntin'! Evie not bigger'n a washin' o' soap. Ever night I go home she TIRED. Always WORE DOWN. I don't blame her. Don't blame Evie. Got a house full o' chillun. Take all her strength to wash them chillun and full'em. She wore plum out when night catch her. When I get home I find a cold stove. She come in from her Mama[23] house. Been pickin' pea all day. I say: 'I thought you'd have me hot supper ready! I hongry till I'm seein' ghosts.'

"Evie drop down. Groan. Pull up. Say: 'Well, oh Lord, I reckon I best get up and put fire in the stove.'

"I tell her: 'No gal. I done cook. I foolin' you.'"

Lillie: "You hear 'bout the wreck? He just drive the ox in the ditch. Ethel was with him. And that was Wardie ox. All a family to-do. Just had to pay Wardie for the ox. What you'd a-done?'"

Zack: "I know what I wouldn't done! I wouldn't give her the 20 in the first place! I'd buy clothes for her to marry me all right. I'd a-take her to the store and buy just 'FORE we marry. Yes suh! If she BAREFEET she'd have to wait till we on the way to the magister! That the safest way. See how she done him?

"I bought all my clothes and Evelyn own too 'bout a month 'fore we marry. But I ain't take 'em to her house till the time come."

"Rich? You talk Rich? I want to see him go out every mornin' six o'clock and come back in at six o'clock and bring in a sack of grocery Saturday night."

Lillie: "Mind, Zack, that your brother you talkin' 'bout!"

Zack: "Tell you what the truth! You die and leave Rich he'll get his pay! Gettin' what comin'. All these boy 'round here have these good wife—First two Satdy here they come:

"Well, us didn't get pay off tonight.'

"These 'foreoman 'round here don't study bein' sharp. But them town women sharp. Take lessie. She can do ANYTHING. Curry a mule; dig stump; Ditch. Plow. Split rail."

SOURCE: *Lillie Knox and Zack Knox*
September 1938
Murrells Inlet, S, C.

23. Evelina Knox was raised by Albert and Ella Carolina.

Alligator Tail

"Alligator tail? It tastes all right but I didn't eat the thing good. What I eat it for they say you can take a alligator tail and fix it up for you chillun so they eat it and they'll never be sickly. I eat three messes. Ma give me alligator three times. I never been what you call SICKLY. First piece I ever et Mr. Buck[24] comin' from Marion and this here 'foregator was in the road. And he caught the car wheel and Mister Pete Heywood shot him and me and Jinks and Jackson cook it. We say we cookin' it for the dogs. Night come Mama sent me over with a bucket and I full it. Mama say she want a little to feed to the chillun so they won't never be sick.

"Next gator I see Mister Dave[25] kill to Rum Gully Branch.[26] We got the tail. He tell us he kill a gator there to the Branch and want us to have a mess of gator to keep us helty.

"Then Rich[27] kill one in that same branch next home and we went down there and got the whole 'foregator and brung him to the house and got to playin' with him. He wasn't zackly dead. Not right off. Gator take a long time to die like a possum. We was tickling his back leg and he'd crawl. We cut his tail off and skin that. Season it up. Look like white salmon—when it done cook.

"This March gone, 'Gustus[28] 'forenuster go to the hole and call'em. Them pond there 'round Mister Pete.[29] That was all me and him 'forenuster do when us was boys. 'Gustus'ud go like any kinder little puppy or dog like that and they'd come to the top. They down in the hole. Pond so dry people could walk right up to the Hole right side the root of a cypress. I see twelve little fellows. Like kill them. High water come all the pond full up with water. Every where was water. Come a big rain you can't get in there. I see gator eggs bedded up in them cane brake. Put you in mind of an old sow bed. Put you in mind of that. Ain't 'round as a chicken egg. More square. Ain't shape like fowl egg. Kinder SQUARE like.

24. Henry Buck, a white man who summered in Murrells Inlet.

25. Dave Carr.

26. A saltwater swash on Murrells Inlet near Sunnyside.

27. Rich Knox.

28. A dog's name, presumably a shortened form of Augustus.

29. Pete Heywood. Though younger people in the Gullah community commonly refer to their elders as Uncle or Aunt (reserving Mister and Miss for whites), there are occasions, like this one, where a younger person will refer to another Gullah person, from a middle-aged group, as Mister or Miss.

"Aunt Jane had a big old sow down there to Laurel Hill[30] and a gator made a CHOP at her with his tail and cut her whole shoulder off."

SOURCE: ZACKIE KNOX—*Age 35 ?*
1938—Murrells Inlet, S. C.

Buh Patridge Gets Buh Rabbit

Buh Patridge met Buh Rabbit in woods. Was raining. Buh Patridge have he head onder he wing.—gone right on walking and he head onder he arm. Buh Rabbit say,

"Buh Patridge, what you doing out here in the rain with you head off?" Buh Patridge say,

"Buh Rabbit, when it raining, I allus cuts my head off and leaves it home! Then my head don't never get wet!"

"Buh Rabbit stand and drop he mouth open and look at Buh Patridge and then he gone running on home in the rain. When he get home he say,

"Old lady, I want you to cut off my head!" Mrs. Rabbit say,

"Cut off you head, you'll dead!" Buh Rabbit say,

"No, I met Buh Patridge in the rain today with his head cut off and he didn't dead ." And Buh Rabbit kept on pestering till old Mrs. Rabbit take the axe and Buh Rabbit put he head down on a block and she come down "Ker Whack!"

Here Buh Rabbit head cut clean off from the body! Kick a little bit. Flutter about. He dead!

Wife went to cryin'.

Buh Patridge off in bushes. He know what happen. Come out and sing out,

"Hey, old lady. Where Buh Rabbit?"

"Old Mrs. Rabbit show 'em.

Buh Patridge laugh and say,

"Great God! That old fool ain't know I had my head under my wing?"

SOURCE: *Zackie Know, Age 25, Murrells Inlet, S. C.*

Zackie Talks

"Mama used to wash and iron and spit on the floor and send me errand and tell me, 'Be back fore the spit dry!' She want snuff one day. I slow. Mama say, 'Boy, you don't feel like gwine? I'll go.' I tired. Just come from a five mile errand. Get back by Mama. Mama ketch my arm. Jest rake that peach limb down! Grab that limb! Seeme lak Carson store[31] no distant-! And I thought

30. Laurel Hill plantation, now part of Brookgreen Gardens.

31. Carson's Store was located near Rum Gully Branch.

that store over a mile! You value you hide, you best move Mama say move! Mama liked to send me. I can gone and come!"

"What's the deadest thing? 'Dead as a wedge.'[32] That dead. Piece o' simmon[33] or dog-wood—that what they uses to make the hardest wedge outer. Got to cut it down and dry out fore you can nuse the wedge. Take a old cow bone or deer bone, you know hits dead. That wedge, it'll have to be dead by time you get through driving it in a log or what-some-ever you going drive it in. If it had any life in it, it'll sho be dead! So many hard licks would knock it out! You take 'Dead as rushes round little Moses.'—Rushes don't never die! I figger three more things generally say dead. 'Dead as a nit,' 'Dead as a door nail,' 'Dead as a mackeral swimming in hot grease.'

"Lemme see! I know that song! I can't remember how it wuz! Rev. Calina,[34] Uncle William[35] and Uncle Sabe[36] always apt to be the grave diggers. They way they does if a person die, nobody kin to 'em don't touch the spade (ten dig the grave.) By the time we get it line out we dig awhile and those two nusually dresses the grave. That's one thing Uncle Albert Calina can do. He kin dress a grave on the outside till it look pretty much like a casket."

"I know one thing. If the bottom of your feet itches you, you either going to a strange land or a burying. Right hand itch you get more money' left hand itch you get a letter. Move your foots, Missus. I ain't wanting to sweep over your foots today. I ain't wanting you to run away."

"She he third wife. She got he water on and it still biling. She go to church and say, 'Old man, have dinner when I come from church.' He don't want that first wife chillun fed. He and his mother get thru eating, second wife eat what left. He eat rice; she get the cake in the pot bottom."

"Scar? I done that fighting with Lewis. Didn't know Lewis had a knife. All the boys round in a circle. They say, 'Lemme have you knife.' Throw it on and on and on till it come up nobody have the knife! Lewis and H. G. and Sonny had it last. They the one always urging somebody. I find Lewis had it and I hit 'em on the chin and he cut me and run. I got my knife. I forgotten how I got it back. Some of 'em brought it. But I ain't forgotten the cut. That boy cut me and run. Good thing he did run. He took the bay and woods to his home."

32. For splitting firewood.
33. Persimmon.
34. Albert Carolina.
35. William Oliver.
36. Sabe Rutledge.

"Ain't no better nor I am and I have to get up at six no differ when I go to bed."

Zackie Knox—age 25–27
Murrells Inlet, S. C.

Buzzard and Hawk

"One time they wuz a hawk and he met a buzzard. He ax the buzzard, 'How you getting on?'

Buzzard say, 'All right,'

Hawk say, 'How you eat?'

Buzzard say, 'I wait on the Lord!'

Hawk wuz catching sparrows. He say, 'See that sparrow? All right! Watch me!' Hawk make a dive at the sparrow. (You see that sparrow wuz sitting on a sharp rail) Stake - and - rider fence. Got stuck on a rail. (In the fence) Buzzard say, 'Ah hah, old boy! I'll let you stay there till you get stink and and I'll come and eat you! It's good to wait on the Lord!'

Given by Zackie Knox—age 28
Murrells Inlet, S.C.
August 1937.

Zackie: Uncle Sabe over to The Ridge[37] tell me that story.

Seeking and Comin' Through[38]

You know, the devil a busy man! 'fore Reb (Revents—Zackie has it shortened to 'Reb') 'fore Reb come over here, I didn't know what church was! Evelena say they going to run Revival to Heaven Gate next week and say she going to Mourners Bench. I say I ain't going—I going fishing myself—going in the Crick. My mind tell me, 'Go on in the Crick get fish and let Evelena get 'forenouf religion for me and her too.'

Monday come. Monday evening I gone in the Crick. I got back home people just gone in the church. I could a gone in but I ain't gone.

Tuesday night come. Evie say, "Ain't you going to church tonight?"

I say, "If I get out the Crick in time!"

I gone on. I know I wasn't intentionally to go. Gone dragging along. Come out the Crick good time. Know Evie not home to fry my fish. Don't feel like

37. The name given to Sabe Rutledge's home and the surrounding land, which Rutledge owned.

38. Seeking is a religious questing similar to the vision quests of certain Native American traditions. Coming through represents the consummation of this spiritual quest.

frying myself. Give my fish to Miss Holmes.[39] Know if they get cook to my house I'll have to cook 'em. Think I best gone on to Heaven Gate. Devil been have me blindfold, I sit down way back. Reb begin to call mourners. He say,

"Anybody want to jine this church or any of us church, come on!"

Evie gone Monday and Tuesday she just get started. She hadn't come through. Took her Monday night and Tuesday night and all day Wednesday. Took me Tuesday night and Wednesday night and all day Wednesday. Took all two of us two days and two nights. I had chillun. I didn't know nothing 'bout 'em. Had to haul some from church. Had to haul me home one night. Eat. You don't study 'bout eat. Gone on home. Put me to bed. I wake up middle night. Gone over to that old house by Bethel Church where nobody don't live. Gone in Aunt Jane old house. Prayed. Gone in that old empty Bethel church.[40] Prayed. Kept penetrating from Aunt Jane house to Bethel church all night. Prayed.

You feel like you got nobody in the world but you—you one. Things don't look changeable to you till you get over—come through. Some goes out in the middle night in the woods seeking.

Trees, leaves and all look different. Look like you been shut up in a box all you life and never seen things before!

(Isaac next one. He gone to seeking. Look like 'fore he die he lost it all.)

I gone right back to Bethel 'fore daylight and come to find out Isaac been all night praying in the back of the church! Whole bunch of us been seeking at the same time. Me and Lija and David and H. E. and Jinks and Isaac and Evie. They just had a regular young army. After that Reb holler, "Come on, Christians."

I got up from Mourners' Bench singing.

"In me! In me!
It is Christ the Lord in me!
In me! In me!
It is Christ the Lord in me!"

I got up with that song shouting. And Miss Sue sister child come through singing that. Most all come through singing.

Some'll fall out to the church like they dead. And maybe way middle night they'll wake up and whole crowd settin' round their bed.

Yes. The world a new world when I come through! All the tree leaves. (It was the fall of the year.) All the leaves look bright and now. Feel jest like you been shut up in a dark box a year and just turn out!

39. Havillah Holmes.

40. Bethel Church, north of Knoxville community, was a white Methodist church. It was abandoned when Belin Methodist Church was built in Murrells Inlet.

Jinks and H. E. nuster be together all the time. They carry Jinks home stiff one night and the next night he come back in the church door singing, 'Soon, ah soon"

Some seekers have vision. I had one. After I did go to sleep—well I wasn't zactly sleep neither—He (the Lord) took me down to a road—seems like a long row of oaks—what He look like? You've seen His picture! Light was coming off from Him everywhere. They was that thing on His head—you know how it is—and light jest rayed off from that—Well He took me down this road and seemed like they was a big saw-mill biler (boiler) bury with the top sticking out the ground—had on it a heavy, thick led (lid) thick as that zinc tub there—and the led had the smoke and sut (soot) and all was biling out all round the edge—and I stood and looked at it and seemed like after a while a little black and red boy come out—run out that biler (boiler) and he bade his hand to me and told me to come there! Then he run and sit right in that black smoke biling (boiling) outer that biler. I stood way off and looked at him then I turned and walked off.

I seen one more thing. I seen a train. A black and greasy train. Come along down the road taking its time, !

Slack - a - tack - a!
Slack - a - tack - a!
Slack - a - tack - a!
Slack - a - tack - a!
Slack - a - tack - a!

And it seem like Julie boy William hanging out the window and he call, 'Come here Zackie!

Come here Zackie!'

And seem like I answer, 'No, man!'

And I gone on. After while seem like I wake up.

The next year they got Henry down to the mourners' bench. They carried Henry home stiff one night. His wife tried to turn him Baptist. All the time trying to get round the Methodist. They think they going to Heaven 'forethout praying, but that's a mistake.

Reb done some wonderful work since he been here. Sent a lot of convert to Salem, St. Peter, Mt. Nebo, Gordon—besides all he took in the Methodist to Brookgreen and Heaven's Gate."[41]

Verbatim conversation
Zackie Knox—age 28
Murrells Inlet, S. C.

41. Salem, St. Peter's, Mt. Nebo, Gordon Chapel, Belin Methodist, and Heaven's Gate are all churches in the Freewoods and Murrells Inlet.

"I 'foremembers that time bee sting me. One those blossom bee—white headed bee. How come he bit me, I was catching him. I turn him loose too. Old Aunt Ellen have all Ma chillun in the cotton field picking cotton. She run to me. She say,

"I see you ketching that bee!" I was hollering long time, I thought if I holler long 'forenouf Aunt Ellen'ud give me a piece of bread. She give me something all right—but it wasn't a piece of bread!

"Then I did pick cotton! Them old timey people kin put it on you and you can't take it off!

"Never didn't hear 'bout BURNING chillun. Hear tell of SWINGEING chillun.[42] When they born get-up and have too much sense. Don't know how they does it. Mama talks 'bout that. She can tell you how they does it."

"Nobody 'round here ain't no poor kin for corn. See a man starving 'round here the Lord just meant that man to starve. People kin be on starvation every where else but not here."[43]

Zackie Knox—age 28
Murrells Inlet, S. C.

On Return from Funeral

Lill: "Chainey was there."
Zack: "Hear Chainey was."
Lill: "Looker yonder! Chainey goin' to do her washin' and Parker trailin' her."
Zack: "He best stay home and let that gal and her job 'forelone."
Lill: (singing)
"I'm goin' down to the river of Jordan
Some of these days!"
"Goin' tell my Mother ——————"
Zack: "Well, my conscion clear!"
Lill: (Lookin' up from tub)
"What say Zack?"
Zack: "Well, gal, my conscion clear."
Lill: "You best be glad you wasn't there! Sugar ever was a good girl. Babboon (ain't that boy the one fight his Mama?)—"
Zack: "Babboon the one. He muster been drunk."

42. Giving the child a slight burn to instill a fear of fire. Open fireplaces were a constant danger for youngsters.

43. A reference to the abundance of other food sources, such as seafood from the creek and game from the woods.

Lill: "I reckon the morest what it happen 'bout, Babboon come in drunk and she won't let him fight his wife. That ONE thing 'bout Sadie. Give the devil his due! She won't let them boys fight they wife!"
Zack: "You know Babboon in collegion with the devil. He say if you wanter learn to play a guitar get to a cross roads by a church twelve o'clock Sunday night. He'll learn you. Go there and set down and start pickin' a guitar and he'll learn you to pick.

"I knew a fellow named Jones learn that-a-way. He couldn't sleep by himself. I had to sleep with him to the lumber camps. He could get up any time he wanter. Four, three or five o'clock. He'd call me there and throw up a deck of cards and thay'd stick up there and he'd call which-some-ever card he want and it'd come down. Say he KILL a man. Didn't intentional do it. Man was beatin' his wife. She a yellin' and HE come over there and first news he shot the man. Couldn't rest. He'd just ride some night till day clean. He say to do cards like that, you have to will your soul to the devil."
Lill: "They say old man B—— will his soul to the devil. If you want to dig a well that man 'forell take a willow stick—forked—stick[44] and hold it straight out and if you can get water there the forks will turn down. You CAN'T HOLD IT."
Zack: "You ever see a man have a MONEY needle? Is make out a WHALE bone. There a little railway station call EVERGREEN seven mile from Chadbourne.[45] Man there had one. What ever kind of money you want to hunt—want COPPER, put copper on it. Get over the place where they money, it will pint down. Can't say a WORD when you diggin' for money! My Grandpa and some people went to dig money and SOMEBODY SPOKE and the money disappeared. Heard a roarin'. Three big black men. Didn't speak. Got the money and fell in the hole and disappeared.

"Grandma kept seein' a light on her dresser. So bright you could even count stitches on her quilt. Grandpa told her that was somebody's spirit wantin' to carry her where money was buried.

"Cecil Hardy, a girl over there near home married now, had a large patch of collards. She was standin' at the window. Looked out. Saw a old man cuttin' the collards down in the broad day. Looked good and it was her Grandfather. Went home and he was dead!

"Mama saw a light one time. Said it wasn't a weather light neither!"

44. Divining rod, used to locate the presence of water underground.

45. Evergreen is a small town on the way to Chadbourne, North Carolina—just across the state line from Horry County.

Zack! Oh, Zack![46]

Here I was headed down to the creek to scratch a few clam. It was fixin' to freeze up. A cold drizzle was a-fallin'. Christmas was comin' and I was in a tight. It was root hog or die. And I was plannin' on scratchin' a mess o' clam for Lina[47] and them chillun. They ain't goin' be on starvation long as I can handle a clam rake. Anybody is welcome to clam.[48] Cold hand and wet foots is all clam cost anybody here on us creek. And I was makin' ninety—and wonderin' if I gwine catch the tide. Tryin' to make it to the creek 'fore them mudflat and oyster rocks cover.

Now Lillie know I gots no job. She know rations scarce for them seven head o' chillun and she know I stay hungry. And here she fall on me! You see one them fishhawk fallin' out the sky on one them mullet fish? That just how Lillie hit me. Here I passin' her house and I hear somebody callin'. I look and there Lillie head stick out the kitchen door.

"Zack! Oh, Zack! Ain't you wants a hot cup o' coffee?"

Now I never couldn't refuse nobody nothin' so here I gone on in the kitchen out the cold. And that coffee not barefoot. Lillie have the cow cream and the sugar can full. And when that hot coffee done drink and I just gettin' stimulate, fore I can say "Thank you Mam!—here Lill Start!

"Zack, if I plant you, will you grow? Don't have to grow tall!

By that she mean she goin' ask me to do a little job. But I know Lill. Lill sho tricky. I know what she goin' to say 'fore she outs with it.

"Zack, 'fore you go boy, how 'bout takin' two little planks and fixin' a little pen for us little pig Abe? Won't have to board up but one side and two end. You can make it side the tool-house for one side. And, us'll help, Zackie."

That little Abe pig been bring there in a hat-box. He done spent one night in the kitchen. But they can't keep him in the kitchen. Got to have a pen. One thing always callin' another. And Lill, she have me hem up! I can't say "I ain't got time" 'fore cause I didn't say "I ain't got time" when she said "hot cup o' coffee". So I stand there rubbin' my hands and turnin' and a thawin' out by the stove. Can't seem to make up my mind to left that hot stove. And Lill go on:

"Zack, it ain't goin' take you long. Just two little planks. Abe so leetle. Poor little fellow just a-shivelin'. Took way from his Mammy 'fore he wean

46. This story provides a clear source for "De Wind and de Tide," one of Genevieve Chandler's published stories.

47. Evelina Knox.

48. In the thirties all the creek-front property was owned by whites. Nevertheless black members of the community were allowed free access to the creek. There were no public beds or leases as there are presently. Anyone who could find oysters was welcome to harvest them.

good. Just able to suck down a little mush and soup. Poor little thing-he'll freeze out there by himself if us don't fix him up a nice warm pen and full it full o' pine straw for him to snuzzle down in. If he ain't fix nice and warm I'll meet him stiff dead when I come here tomorrow mornin'. That'd sho ruin my Christmas. Zackie, us can't let the poor little fellow freeze to death."

Lord, Lill can talk. She tricky. Lill won't do.

I drink my hot cup o' coffee and I make Abe's pen. All I can do.

Now all that happen last December. Here December come round again and Christmas in sight. Every 'foretater eat out the hill. Eat up. One old Grandfather rooster leave on the yard. Not gettin' a egg. No meal. Corn gone—and you can promise your back but you can't promise you stumach. Little Evie[49] foots on the ground. Shoe sole gone. And here Junior[50] sayin' he just got to have thirty-five cent readin' book or he'll get whipped at school. And every day it's "Papa, I ain't got no tablet" or "I can't go to school 'forethout a pencil". Every day sumpin 'foreruther. And Big Evie askin' me "What I goin' boil for them chillun dinner?" So Ijust sold out. Had to get way from all them hungry eye starin' me in the face. That place too hot—I'd ruther go in cold creek. So here I been headin' down to the salt creek so I can get a few bushel o' oyster. The man don't pay but fifteen cent a pack—but fifteen cent been a nickle and a dime. And what he don't buy, us can eat. But that was a raw time. Sneakin' cold. The north wind pure freeze the marrow in you bone. Little cold rain hit you in the face like sleet. So cold I got on all my clothes. Got on all two pair o' my creek pants. I'm hopin' the hole in the bottom pair will be cover up by the good place in the top pair. The same way with sweater. All three so full up with moth hole I have to put all three on one time. My boots do look good as new. Big old hip boot. Not a hole in the top part o' them boot. Them would be good boot if it wuzn't for the sole. Water slushin' in 'em and ever step I take water spurts up like a artesian well. But if they hadn't gone to leakin' Cap'n wouldn't a never give 'em to me. So I has to be glad they does leak. Reckon leakin' boots better'n no boots a tall.

So here I was plannin' on goin' in the creek. Rushin' long to catch low tide. Got to make it 'fore young flood.[51] When she once turn don't take no time for that tide to cover them oyster rocks. I was thinkin' if I just hit the tide right I'd get five bushel, and if I hustle maybe I'd get six. And a peck means fifteen cent. While I plannin' how much fifteen cent I goin' walk out there on them rocks and pick up and how much meat and meal I goin' buy to full up them chillun for Christmas, I find myself by Lillie house and somebody hail :

49. Zackie Knox's daughter, also named Evelina Knox.

50. Zackie Knox Jr.

51. The turning of the tide, before the incoming flood tide.

"Zack! Oh, Zack!. Come by! Got you a hot cup o' coffee."

I been 'forespicious o' Lillie and her hot cup o' coffee. And I know how Abe done out-growed that little pen. I got a notion Lill plannin' on a new pen—and it been too cold to be workin' on no pig pen. But that cup o' coffee sound too good. I feel like it won't do nohow to turn Lillie cup o' coffee down. How 'bout the tide? Time and tide ain't goin' wait and if I don't get them oyster from Goat Island, where the money comin' from to put grits in them empty chillun? How I goin' get thirty-five cent for Junior reading book? And ain't little Evie foots on the ground? While I stand haltin' 'foretween two 'forepinions, Lill sing out:

"Coffee, Zack! Maxwell House. Cow cream and us sugar sack full."

When that coffee done drink, here go Lill:

"Oh, Zackie. 'fore you go, how 'bout fixin' old Abe a dry place to sleep? Us'll help. My,that pig's a hog now. Been a year since you make us pen and, Zack, her babies comin' and that pen is sho a muchy place. Got to be dry and warm for them little 'forenoung thing when they born in this cold world. If them babies come in that wet, freezin' up place in this winter weather, they'll be icicles fast as they're born. Us'll help, Zack. Us'll help."

Gracious crown! It settin' in to rainin' now. What must I do? I can't see Abe little baby comin' here in this winter weather and no bed make ready for 'em. They'll be sho to die. Poor little creeters got to meet a warm bed just same like little humans. If little December pig get too cold they tail'll freeze and drop off.

So first news I find myself totin' planks most half a mile on my back. Big, old, heavy, heart fat-lightard posties—like so much lead—have to be tote the same way. Then a roll o' wire have to come. Diggin' them post holes I 'forefraid my hand goin' to pure freeze to that post hole digger. While I cleanin' a path through them thick bush and underbrush and briar for my wire to run in, I keep thinkin' 'bout what all Lillie say:

"We gwine help you, Zack. Us'll help."

Cold mist a-comin' down on me steady and Lill, she in that dry, warm kitchen close by that coffee pot. I can pure smell that Maxwell House. Gwine help me. And after all them posties bury and that wire 'bout stretch—all done but a few more nail and makin' a gate—it was gettin' on towards dark. I can't see so I stop and think: I miss the low tide today. Didn't get one bushel o' them oyster. But I does know what I can do. I'll catch the low tide tonight and take my gig and go strikin'. Take my old Sinkin' Sally and go out night fishin'. Might get a bushel o' bass and trout. Trout fifteen cents a pound. Then I gone on in the kitchen. Think I'll see what in there 'fore I goes in the creek. Here Lill meets me:

"Zack, how 'bout a hot cup o' coffee? More in that pot. Some leave for you. Got us pen ready ? Reckon us'll have it for Abe to sleep in ? You ready for some help. Us'll help you toll her in the pen."

I listen. US pen. US'll have it. US'll help.I say:

"No. Got half a day's work to do 'fore that pen ready. Gate to make and trough."

Lill ask (she sound too pitiful):

"Zackie, you comin' back to finish us pen, ain't you?"

That"Zackie" sound too sad. Sometime it "Zack" then again it "Zackie. I tell her:

"Dunno whether I'll make it or no."

But I eat some o' Lill's hot hominy and bacon and drink my coffee and gone on in the creek. It happen I hit the tide right and sho nuff I did full my bushel tub with bass and trout. My foots froze up in them cold boots and no socks on and it a-freezin' but, man, I have such a time giggin' them fish I didn't know I was cold till I hit the house. And I have 'bout four dollars' worth. It's sho a pretty sight to see them spotted winter trout a-lyin' so still and cold down there in the oyster rocks and seaweed. And,Good Master, I so happy thinkin' this'll buy grits to keep them chillun quiet for a week.

After I pull off them boots and wet pants and get my-self snuzzled down in bed by Evie, I find out I was cold. Seemed like I couldn't warm up. First news I find myself thinkin' 'bout Abe's babies comin' and the more I study 'bout the cold and them babies comin', the more I know I ain't goin' have no peace o' mind till that pen finish. Evie wouldn' want her younguns comin' here and freezin'up. And little creeturs is like little younguns. Them little pig come here and not meet a warm pine straw bed their little tails'll freeze and drop off just like I tell you. Then my mind turn to Lill's kitchen. Some way or ruther, she always does manage to have somethin' hot on the stove—

Day clean that old Grandfather rooster started crowin'. Seems like he was sayin" "Get up! Get up! They'll Freeze! They'll Freeze." So first news I find myself pullin' on my sweaters and gettin' in my pants and pullin' on them boots and headin' down to the creek. The first soul I see is Lill. She puts me in mind o' one o' these little blue-darter hawks done got his claw clamp in a little biddy—and me the biddy. Here she got her head stick out the kitchen door and she grinnin' like a possum. She know the kind o' fish I is and the bait I likes.

"Zack! Oh, Zack! Ain't you wants a hot cup o' Coffee?"

The Elder

"I gone to church last night. You see Sonny come by in his car. I got a lift with him. And I don't like that Elder—that new elder. Make all the preachers come up and pay they quarter first. Say nobody can't go out that church door till they pay they quarter. Not a man go out that door till they come to this table. Not a soul laugh; all went up and paid. I don't care—elder or what-some-ever you is, dat seem like to me COMPELLARATION. Say he got nine ($9) dollars yestiddy; say he want ten dollars ($10) tonight. They'll never dreen (drain) me! Going to take my chillun what-some-ever they need. They get all my labor and tote it way and I go there they got a good deestant (decent) home—won't as much as ax me in.

"I so far back behind there I couldn't hear no text. Some start to sing. When-some-ever they start to sing, the elder stop 'em. 'Don't sing now!' When they start the collection Revents Calina pitch,

"I shill, I shill, I shill not be move!"

"And the elder said 'STOP!' Don't sing that song now! I want you to be moved! Don't like him tall—tall."

Zackie Knox
Murrells Inlet, *S. C.*
(After attending night service at the District Conference)
(Brown Chapel, Brookgreen, S. C.)

Cinchy Lance

ALTHOUGH THERE IS NO STATED SOURCE for the sole interview that treats Cinchy Lance's character in depth, the text does provide a reasonable sketch of the person she was. Cinchy Lance was married to Gabe Lance, with whom she lived in the Mont Arena community on Sandy Island. Apparently Cinchy Lance was a dauntless laborer. In fact, if the unnamed source is to be trusted, she was a worker of heroic proportions. Mrs. Lance was involved in rice farming at every juncture: from planting to harvesting, transporting, thrashing, and sacking. She was also a dedicated mother, who found relaxation in smoking her tobacco pipe. She was a member of Jerusalem Baptist Church. Cinchy Lance ultimately left her husband Gabe and moved into her son's house on the mainland. U.S. Census data suggests Cinchy Lance was also known as Nellie Lance. The 1910 census states that Gabriel (age fifty-three) and Nellie (age unknown) had been married for ten years, that she had given birth to three children, only one of whom was still living. Also in their home were two "sons," Benjamin (age seventeen), and another Benjamin (age sixteen). Gabriel and Cinchy are both absent from the 1920 census, possibly due to the remoteness of their Sandy Island home. In 1930 the census lists her as a widow, living with her son Lushen (referred to in the present interview as Laban) and his wife, Lucile. Interestingly the same census lists Gabriel as a widower as well.

Mom Cinchy[1]

"Missus, you say that old man[2] look like an angel?"

("That old man looks like an angel!")

"You can't always tell, Missus. Nothing can't be tell by the outside look. That old man! Look at he wife!

"There Mom Cinchy—Uncle Gabe wife. She do work. She work in the heat and rain; she work in season and out o' season. She plant the rice seed. Bog in the rice-field. Jump on the rice. Clean 'em. She hoe 'em two, three times

1. One of Genevieve Chandler's more literary productions, this "interview" is probably more of a composite based on true stories and real people.

2. Gabe Lance.

in the briling sun. Help h'ist the gate for the three flow. First the sprout flow; that to sprout the rice. Then the stretch flow; that stretch 'em—make 'em grow! Then come the harvest flow. That full 'em out—make the grain envelope. Mom Cinchy make a full crop. Harvest time come she stand there with them chillun and wave she arms and holler for scare way them rice bird what'll clean up the crop it they ain't keep off every day all day.

"Day come to harvest the rice. She take hook and bend she old buckles (knee joints) and cut 'em with she two hands. She bundle them; she stack 'em. Then time come to tote 'em down to the flat boat and flat 'em to the barnyard. And Mom Cinchy the one who take the pole in hand and help pole that hebby old flat boat to the home landing. She have to tote 'em on she back to the ox cyart (cart). And then she trail that ox cyart through them deep, hot, sand up hill and down hill to the thrashing yard. Then she thrash 'em. She handle frail (flail) same like a man. She climb the high step and stand on that platform and holds that big winnowing basket over she head. The chaff fly! She winnow them same like a strong mans. Mom Cinchy have the strong arm! She clean 'em! And when everything been take out scusing them little, black grass seeds, she sack 'em. Now that she money. Yes, suh, she sack 'em and drag 'em in the barn.

"And then what happen? Call come! Mom Cinchy onliest body child[3] took down. The chill and febers grab a holt on she boy Laban. She go. WILL go. (All she kin do) Mother answer she child call whether or no.

"Now, you all know, the barn on us islant ain't have no lock on 'em. Locks for principle man; on-principle man ain't notice lock nohow! And when Mom Cinchy nurse Laban and cool the fever with the sea-sage tea, she come home. Yes, SUH! She cross back over Wacam and she meet the barn door shut—but the half part of she trash out rice been tote off! It been fetch cross the river and done sell. And she well know the one what done that.' She ain't say nothing. But she know ain't no human dasen't do that scusin she own old man Gabe. That same old man you say look so good and got the angel name. Mom Cinchy ain't say nothing tall—nothing tall—she suffer. And she ain't crack she mouth!

"Mom Cinchy have fowl. Them little—have the look of the patridge. But them little patridge size been sweet bird. And them she cash. Them fowl gwine pay the Revents and buy the white church dress and shoe for the 'Turning Out.' When Mom Cinchy Lodge—'The Will Go'—turns out for the annual sermont, all member must been dress in white. Glove, shoe, hat, and dress white. And she wear the top shoe for keep she old foots dry and warm. And, too, she need cash for she tobacco for smoke. She like she pipe.

3. Laban Lance.

That the onliest pledger (pleasure) she have out-side hard work. Think bout troubleation and trial she have for smoke. That the way she take she pledger. She say she kin set and watch the live oak coals and think bout the old riginols (originals) she grand and great-grand and old Missus and she Ma and Pa what gone before. That she happiness.

"Yas'm. Mom Cinchy sho struggle. She rassel with she chicken for make a little change. She happy now she got the new shoe and she think when she sell them little fry size she kin pay the Revents and pay she lodge dues so she kin be put away right. So when Sunday come she strike out for Jerusalem Baptist. The day come for the 'Turning Out' of the 'Will Go' Lodge. That the only church on us islant; over two hundred member to Mom Cinchy church.

"This been the fourth Sunday. She travel that sandy path all dress in white and she new white shoe swinging in she hand. She tater and she bittle (victual) been in she pocket and she make tracks. Why she tote she bittle? She been cautious. You ain't truss you own color too much. Too much food been fix.[4] Musn't truss to eat with every somebody. Ain't know! Too much o' people been pizen and ain't know how!

"Up and down them boggy sand hill Mom Cinchy gone. She forgot the old theumatism and as she plow through the heavy path, the old lady sing. She sing a song she gwine pitch to the church. You know she one of the choirs; she one the main songster to Jerusalem. When she toss a tune the church grab holt. So Mom Cinchy come in hearing of the church and sat down on the pine straw and pulled on her new white shoes. She been most there! Brudder Si[5] from way out in the Free Woods gwine to preach, and she been hurrying so she kin catch the text. Musn't lose the text! Mom Cinchy shoe been tight but she allus could stand pain. God spects folks to suffer in this world; there'll be no rest till we reach our home in Glory and try on our white wings and feast on milk and honey. She ain't like milk none much and honey been too sweet but don't reckon when we change to another world we'll crave different kind o' rations?

"(She tell me) She just catch the text! When she gone in and sat down in the Amen corner, Cousin Sam was just sayin, 'Now Brudder Si Sparkman, he one the Baptist shooter. He a leading fort in Salem church. He won't turn back! Stick he hand to the gospel plow! He'll fight! He'll fight till the war been end!'

"And Brudder Si took charge. He preached the whole stripture bout Joseph. Joseph dream several dream. Been sell down to Egypt land. King have dream. Wuzn't able inturpentate. Joseph tell 'em turpentation and it come to

4. Hexed or poisoned.
5. Si Sparkman.

pass. King put 'em on golden chain. Joseph live one hundred year and ten. Bow his head and die. God move in a materious way His bundance to reform! Will Go! Fight that war till time ended! God will bring you out!

"And when Uncle Si sat down in the red velvet pulpit chair, Mom Cinchy pitched her song.

'Oh, what are they doing in Heaven today?
Where sins in sorrow is all done away!
And peace above like a river they say,
Oh, what are they doing there now?'[6]

"And this God truth! When Mom Cinchy start to the church she ain't no more than loss sight of the house, fore old man Gabe been get up! He been unable to so much as go to the breakfast table. Mom Cinchy cook it and take it to his chair fore she make start for Jerusalem. And he have the nerve to say 'ain't she know he ain't choose egg with a break yaller?' And his leg so bad he can't put no weight on 'em tall—tall. The pain been worser in all he joint. And he back! Oh, Lord, he have such a back! But soon as she lose sight of the house, that old rogue, that old dirty skunk, that old scalawag who been talk so Christian to the Revents and act so onderhand to he wife—pull heself out that arms chair! He look all around. He see through the south window. Mom Cinchy ain't leave nothing but she white track. He look out the west window. He see nothing but the garden been roast in the harvest sun. He peer towards the east and he eye meet the yaller rice-field stubbles and them white cranes fluttering. And when he cast he eye north, ain't nothing but that little windey path what 'foreud tak 'em through the prickly pear[7] and san-spur to the river landing.

"And soon as he throw on his clothes, that lost the course he travel. And when he take his rattan stick and make a start, you know what he tote on his back? Ain't nothing but! What he take? He have the crocus on he back—the crocus sack—and in that crocus been all he wife fowl. All Mom Cinchy fry size—all them little patridge size fowl in that sack! That old soul been wrassel all spring and summer for raise them. All she hope of cash to pay the Revents—all she hopes of Lodge jews so she can get put away right going off with Uncle Gabe! Mom Cinchy have wave her apron and yell at the hawk; she jump up at midnight with ice in the cow trough and holler at the owl; she lie and listen and when the fowl sqauwk she run in she bare foots to kill possum and mink and suck like varmit. And the Good Lord knows she made her share of corn pone to feed hound dog for chase way fox. Mom Cinchy struggle

6. Recorded by John A. Lomax.
7. The common cactus.

with them fowl. She have a hard fight. But ain't I tell you she old rigonal? She tough and she fetch them through. And here all she labor going down the hill on the old man back! That man she tell the preacher she gwine keep for better or worser and it all been worser!

"And you know where that ramskallion been gone? He take and sell he wife fowl and with the cash in he pocket from Mom Cinchy own hard work, he gone to visit that cunjur mans down to North Charston. Yes SUH! He slip off every chance to that man for get cunjur ball—cunjur for hold he wife! He all tiem fraid Mom Cinchy gwine leave him. He know that what she out to been done long time. And she so want to go! She pure craves to cross over the river Wacamaw and join hand with she son—she son Laban over on Wacamaw Neck. He stay where there's ister (oyster) and sea-ball and swimps and crabs. But Mom Cinchy can't go!

"That old man with angel face and angel name have a devil heart! He got a cunjur ball and got it hide but she ain't know! She ain't know why she can't go way! She try. But when she make start to travel that path through the pastor leading to she son boat, when she try to travel that course through the pear-pad and sand-spur so she kin row cross the river in she son little dugout—something grab her holt! She can't go. It pull back. It keep her right where Uncle Gabe been. She try for go to she own body child, Laban? She knee joint give way and she ain't able for reach the landing! She ain't know why! She ain't know!

"But God have His way! Sometimes we full up with puzzlement. We can't see. We ain't onderstand.

"Here Mom Cinchy been to church in the middle part of the islant and there she sets and waves her turkey tail fan. (You see that fan? Make out the wild turkey tail. Fox kill 'em and she meet the fedder in the path.) There she sets and sings,

"I got the key to the kingdom!
Satan can't do me no harm!"

(And how vivid it all is! What a study in black and white! White church, white turning out dresses, black faces. And the best in each soul shining out on these faces as, with rapt expression, each one keeps time in his or her own characteristic fashion to the beat of the spiritual. One old lady nods her head. Right! Left! Now right! Now left! One pats white gloved hands lying in her lap. Another pats with one white glove and one bare, black hand—pats while her shoulders twist now right, now left! Hands and arms, heads and bodies move and sway with the one two three of the song. The daughter of the old lady with one glove wears the other glove, and she too pats and accompaniment.

Uncle Tom Pryor, old sinner, cannot stay down. He stands and up and down the center aisle he goes shuffling—tossing his head and arms like a spirited horse the while telling the world that he too has "the key to the kingdom."

And while all, including Brother Si, mark time, Mom Cinchy in her Amen corner waves her tukey tail fan and pats her foot. They need no organ. Each member of Jerusalem Baptist is a time keeping instrument. Dear old Mom Cinchy has used both feet and during the entire sermon has tap danced—rat-a-tat-tat! Rat-a-tat-tat! God did not cheat His black children. When He was showering down His gifts they stood where fell the gift of song. They could not work without it; they could not play without it; without it, how could they live? They live the words and music of their spirituals. As they sing they improvise words and music. "God gave it to me!" they say.)

"And there set Mom Cinchy. She was one content human. She trouble slip off she shoulder like a sile (soil) garment. She have peace. Till she go home.

"When Sunday gone and Monday come, her house by the sandy path with the bad luck mulberry tree growing by the chimbly hold but one human and that been Mom Cinchy. She one. She see she fowl gone and the old man gone and then she know they two both trabble the same path.

"When the old man got back on the river boat Friday, he been tote a box tie up in much brown paper. He say nothing. Just hobble in and open that cow hides trunk that he keeps under his bed—that old trunk his Pa leave him from slavery time. And when he place that exspicious looking box in that trunk, the lid been drop and the lock been lock. And he ain't say nothing—nothing tall—

"And Mom Cinchy ain't say nothing—nothing tall. What been the nuse? Like water pour on duck's back. Ain't she fowl done sell? Ain't the money done spend? Be like locking the door when the house done rob. And she got a chance! Ain't she got she health. She have the two hen and the rooster leave for seed. She can raise more fowl. And she do so crave peace and quiet! (Then Mom Cinchy been here.) She know she mans. She ain't the one to cross 'em. She say, 'You can't make a straight board from a crooked tree!' And she think, 'I work. Make a crop. Scarce o' meat sometimes, but I have my bread! Thank the Good Master! Scarce o' drink sometime, but I have my bread. My time coming. This old soul will shake off this unworthy flesh what anchor it down and fly like bird straight into Heaven Gate.'

"Now one day Uncle Gabe visit Uncle Simon. That he brudder. He the oldest libber (liver) on us islant. Uncle Gabe gone in the ox cyart. He son Laban take him. That the onliest way us can travel on us islant less'n you foot it. He gone to stay all day. Laban hurry the old man to make start. He hurry him too much. He hurry him till Uncle Gabe forget. Yes suh! He gone out he room and he leave he house and for the first he leave 'em with he trunk unlocked!

"They ain't suppose to worry none with that bed nor neither that trunk. But, while the old man gone on, Laban wife[8] help Mom Cinchy clean house. And that gal too clean! She must sweep onder all the bed and thing. And she have the culiosity! And she try for lift that trunk lid—the trunk what old Gabe got from his Pa and keep shove onder the bed. And the lid lift! And the gal look in! There much o' paper and much o' clothes and the new shoe to put him away in when he dead—new shoe to travel on that last long journey. And under them two new shoe been a box—iron box. And that gal have too much o' culiosity. And she think one little peep ain't going to know bout.

"And she lift the lid! And she make out-cry! Clare to God, Mom Cinchy say you could hear that gal clean cross the river!

"When the old lady drop she hoe in the garden, it fall on she young collard plant and she been made so much o' haste, she tromple the plant. She ain't tarry. That gal sound too distressful. Mom Cinchy forgot she age! She take the two back step like he been one. She call, 'I coming! Hold tight! I coming!'

"The bed room shutter been open to the east. This been the middle morning part o' the day. And there stand Laban wife looking like she see hant—ghost—plat-eye! Her eye fix! It pop! She got 'em fasten in that trunk! They boring! She can't take she gaze off that box what got the lid raise! She don't crack! She act like a seeker in strance!" (trance)

"Mom Cinchy hobble! She make the grade. There she is. And she too been look and she too make out-cry! Fore she ketch herself she fall on her knee and call 'Help! God help!'

"When that gal hear Mom Cinchy knee hit the floot plank, she wake up. She lean over. She grab down in that trunk and come up with Uncle Gabe box in she two hand. And she ain't stop. She head for the fire-place where she been leave a big ironing fire. Big live-oak log pile up and there a bed of pure live coals! The fire like a furnish. And Mom Cinchy trail that gal like a little bird or squirrel follow a snake what have 'em charmed! And yinnah know what she see? That gal with she two eyes still pop have help from God to make way with that debbilment! She tell me she done the hardest praying right there she ever hasn't done before! And with Mom Cinchy two eye looking, she pour that thing behing the back log in that hot, furnish bed of live-oak coals! She testify it frizzle up like bacon frying in a hot skillet. And the fire turn all different kind o' color—red—yaller, green, purple! Color all mix up worser than Joseph coat. That cunjur ball do burn curious(?)

"Right then the old man Gabe loss he holt on he wife. She been left him seven year now. When trouble first come, they done like all the old timey

8. Lutella Lance.

people. They gone to the church. Church didn't settle nothing. Gone to the magister. Law can't fix 'em. Nothing ain't done no good tall till Laban wife have the power from Heaven and stroy that cunjur ball! Now Mom Cinchy under she son roof, and, poor old soul, she rest quiet for the first!

What that debbilment look like? Lutella say the first look she give that box the shutter open to the sun—the light fall on 'em. It was the terriblest looking sight she ever has saw! She say it been all mixing up! The thing been fuzz up like a baby head and working up and mixing. Have eye. Have nose. Have mouth. Red eye. Fuzz on 'em. And the mond come to Lutella, 'foreStroy that debbil work!' And she done what the spirit say!

"Now take me! I don' believe in no cunjur ball nor no ritchcraft. I hear tell bout 'em. I hear talk bout a man over the river who just looked in a cunjur bag and he died! Now me, I don't blive in no coo-coo nor hoo-doo nor voodoo nor nothing—but, if I had a been in Lutella shoe, to this day Mom Cinchy would have been rasseling with that old man with the angel face and debbil heart!"

No source given.

Gabe Lance

According to one interview with an unidentified source, Lance was a feckless husband to his wife Cinchy. Haunted by the notion that she might leave him, he was driven to steal from her in order to buy a spell from a conjure man in North Charleston to "hold her." However, his scheme backfired. Cinchy left him to live with their son Lushen on the mainland. Gabe's brother Simon was reputed to be the oldest person on Sandy Island.

Lance also seems to have lived to a prodigious age. Born into slavery, he spent much of his single interview with Chandler recalling his memories of the Civil War. The U.S. Census indicates that Lance was born in 1860 and married twice: first to Abbie around 1884 and then to Nellie (Cinchy) around 1900 or 1901. He appears to have had a daughter (Carrie) and three sons (Benjamin, Benjamin P., and Lushen). The 1930 census finds him raising a nineteen-year-old grandson (George Lance). As previously mentioned, the same census record lists his marital status as "widowed." The status of Cinchy, living some distance away with their son Lushen, is also listed as "widowed."

Ex-slave Story
(Uncle Gabe Lance—Born and Living on Sandy Island)

"Great Peace! Missus, have to study up that!"

Uncle Gabe had just arrived from Sandy Island at the country post-office, having rowed over for his month's supply of sugar and coffee and things he cannot raise. After the five or six mile row he must needs walk three miles to the office.

"I could remember when the Yankee boats come to Montarena.[1]—gunboats. Bout ten o'clock in the morning. Soldier all muster out and scatter all over the island. You know that cause-of-way? Gone over that two by two, gun on shoulder glisten gainst the sun! Blue-coats, blue pants, hat all blue. Come back to landing bout five o'clock. Have hog, geese, duck! Broke in barn. Stole rations from poor people. My Grandfather the Driver—slave Driver. Name

1. Mont Arena Landing, a Gullah community on Sandy Island.

Nelson. Maussa—Frank Herriott.[2] Maussa gone in swamp. Hid in woods. My Grandfather take old Miss Sally—Miss Sally Herriott[3]—count she couldn't walk with rheumatism—Grandfather took old Miss Sally on he back to hid 'em in the woods where Maussa. Yankee stay but the one day. Ravage all over us island. All goat, hog, chicken, duck, geese—all the animal but the cow been take on the Yankee gun boat. They broke in Maussa big rice barn and share all that out to the colored folks.

Some my people run away from Sandy Islant. Go Oaks sea-shore and Magnolia Beach and take row-boat and gone out and join with the Yankee. Dem crowd never didn't come back.

Any slave run way or didn't done task, put 'em in barn and least cut they give 'em (with lash) been twenty-five to fifty. Simply cause them weak and couldn't done task—couldn't done task! 'Give 'em less rations to boot! Cut 'em down to

1 qt. molasses
1 lb. meat
1 pk. corn for a week

Good Master all right. Give plenty to eat. Reasonable task. Task dem time one-fourth to one half acre. Ditching man ten compass. Got to slush 'em out. Got to bail that water out till you kin see track.

All dem rice-field been nothing but swamp. Slavery people cut kennel (canal) and dig ditch and cut down woods—and dig ditch through the raw woods. All been clear up for plant rice by slavery people.

Beat my Pa and Ma to death and turn me loose! Ought to take care 'foreo me! I send off my 35 ct. fust (first) time, next time twenty-five cents I put what little I have in it. Ain't hear no answer. Some ten or fifteen head round here send off blank and don't get no hearing! Take what little I have and don't send me nothing TALL! I tired with that now! Ain't had a hearing!" (Referring to 'old age compensation').

SOURCE: *Uncle Gabe Lance, Age* 77, *Sandy Island, Murrells Inlet, S. C.*

2. Francis Withers Heriot (1825–1873) the oldest son of Edward Thomas Heriot, owned Mont Arena plantation on Sandy Island.

3. Elizabeth Stark Heriot, wife of Edward Thomas Heriot.

Mike Maybank

In the 1930s Mike Maybank was employed in public works, and when Chandler interviewed him, he was apparently working on a WPA ditching crew (Chandler describes him addressing "one of his fellow ditchers"). These crews worked for long stretches in close proximity to Chandler's home. According to U.S. Census records, Maybank lived in Murrells Inlet. He was married to Celia Maybank, referred to as SeliAnn Maybank in the 1910 census. They raised at least five children, including LeRoy, Sallie, Jack, Joe, and Pearl. According to the 1910 census, Maybank was a literate carpenter, who owned his own home. The 1930 census lists Maybank's age as fifty-six and his wife's as forty-four.

Maybank's interview is recorded in a documentary style that features Chandler's literary scene setting as well as numerous peripheral descriptions and interruptions. Maybank tells a trickster tale about two "old slaves on the old plan" and their "old Maussa." In the process of delivering it, a conniving bartender exchanges the hog meant to be a gift from Uncle Billy to "old Maussa" for a worthless puppy. Maybank takes brief but significant note of the social relationships underpinning the narrative, curtly explaining the reverence Uncle Billy and Uncle Jimmy have for "old Maussa": "Them been old timey people."

Crooked Friend
or
Uncle Mike Tells a Story

Billy Boy:[1] (Aiming his toy gun) "I'm going to shoot a fish-hawk!"
Mother:[2] "Uncle Mike, its against the law to kill a fish-hawk, isn't it?"
Uncle Mike: "I see dem boys knock 'em off right often."
Mother: "How bout buzzard?"
Mike: "DAT gainst law; gainst law killing buzzard!"
Mother: "How bout eagle?"

1. William Chandler.
2. Genevieve Chandler.

Mike: "I don't realize that. All right boys. Have plenty time eat dinner and give you plenty story!" And pointing across the canal where his dinner pail hung in the bushes Uncle Mike addressed one of his fellow ditchers, 'Bees,[3] please suh, when you come back, bring me dat bag over in duh bush deah! Let me get a little feed; my strenthness come.' Putting down his bottle of milk which he intended sharing with 'Bees,' Uncle Mike continued to his partner, 'wait till I come back. Turn loose there first, you take my luck!' (Meaning that Uncle Bees must not take the first drink from the milk bottle.) 'Diss coat yours? Meet 'em ober dere and bring 'um fuh you. Get up here on the table here!' (And Uncle Mike sat down on an old slavery time line bank—earthworks thrown up between plantations in the days when jobs were manufactured to keep labor busy—and patted the earth beside him.)

Billy Boy: "Uncle Mike, will this lizard turn another color if I put him on a green bush?"

Uncle Mike: "Cording to course he trabble. Lizard have that color. Lizard put me in mind of a crooked friend. That what we call man whats friend when to you face and another thing when he on another bush!"

Billy Boy: "Uncle Mike tell a story!"

"This is once upon a time—Talking bout a crooked friend put me in mind of Uncle Jimmy and Uncle Billy and old Maussa. Uncle Jimmy and Uncle Billy wuz two old slaves on the old plan. And Maussa seem to have been very loving to them—he go round them to cheer them up and see how they getting along. They cause him get his heart full; he know time short—he getting old.

One day Uncle Billy said to Uncle Jimmy, "Jimmy, I haven't see Maussa in the Lord knows when!"

"Maussa coming! Maussa sho coming by see bout us," comforted Uncle Jimmy.

It was getting on noon. Onexspectable to them, (they been a old by-road coming close they house), and here Uncle Billy settin in the door in a shuck bottom chair—stick in hand and somebody hail, 'Billy!' Billy look up and see Maussa coming in his carriage or buckboard!"

"Gig! Gig!" prompted Uncle Bees.

"Dat's it ! Wuzn't no carriage been here dem days—four wheels drive four horse under slavery. Well Uncle Billy been too glad to see Maussa. Jumped up wid a great maze and started towards Maussa leaping. Old man wuz old; feeling den his time wuz short. He wuz glad to seen Maussa to mention a present he want to give to his Maussa to remember him. He said, 'Maussa, I was grieving to see you this morning.' Them been old timey people. 'Compliments you sent by Jimmy the other day, I get it. And Maussa, I haven't got

3. Will Bees.

any-thing but I always member you at night in my prayer. Den I have some nice little pig, Maussa. I want to pres'ent you to remember me I should die.'"

Maussa said to Uncle Billy, "I thank you highly for it!"

Billy said, "Well, Maussa, I'm old. I not able to bring this pig to you. I get my friend Jimmy. He can get round better'n what I kin. Don't trouble for send, Maussa. Jimmy will bring this pig to you. Will bring this pig to YOU!"

Maussa said "All right, Billy," and gone on.

Things went on bout a fort'nit (dem time we call a week—no TWO week a FORT'nit) and Uncle Billy said to Jimmy, "Jimmy boy, you ain't doing any-thing so very particular! Spose'n you get that pig from the pen and carry him over to Maussa for me?"

Uncle Jimmy greed to do it. He said to Uncle Billy, "I soon be ready. I get the bag and soon ready."

Uncle Billy wuz old, as I tell you. Uncle Jimmy creep up to the pen, stick in he hand and soon have caught the pig. Uncle Billy say, "Jimmy! Do for God sake don't let that pig got way out that bag. Carry him to Maussa for me, Jim!"

(Mother to son)

"Don't throw clods of dirt! Might get some in Uncle Mike's milk!"

Mike: "Missus, done drink this milk now! No dirt get in 'em.)

"Uncle Jimmy pick up the bag, and KNOWN the pig wuz in the bag cause he bring 'em out the pen. Uncle Billy call behind 'em as he move off, 'dont let that pig git way!' Jimmy answer, 'Know he in the bag and know I catch Maussa home cause it dinner time!'"

So he leave to carry pig to Maussa. After he gone a good ways down the road, Uncle Jimmy has to pass the shop. While he going by, a man wuz in the door. Ask Uncle Jim where he gwine. Uncle Jim told him—(skeeter bite me here till I whale up!)—where wuz I at? Yes SUH! Uncle Jim told him,

"I going far as Maussa house!"

He ask him—he say,

"Jim what that you got in that bag?" Jim say,

"Its a pig. Shop man say,

"Why don't you rest yousef awhile wid you pig?" Invite him in and after Jimmy GOT in he say,

"Uncle Jimmy, does you drink?" Jim say,

"Oh, yes SUH!" The old body need warming up this cold morning!"

So the shop man get he glass and bottle and pour out a drink for Uncle Jimmy. Uncle Jimmy jump up and smack he tongue and knock he feet rejoicing for that drink. But the trouble wuz outer door! Somebody been meddle Uncle Jimmy bag!

"So time come to retire and Uncle Jimmy give 'em gladly thanks. He come on out the shop. Gone where he leave he bag under the old barren-mulberry.

The bag wuz tie up jess (just) as when he went in. Gone on down to his Maussa house. Call up the serbant and ask for his Maussa. And after Maussa appear he say, 'Maussa! I come to bring Uncle Billy bacon!'"

And Maussa smile and take he pipe out he mouth and say, walk wid 'em to the pen for delibber up the pig. And when Uncle Jim leap over the pen and loose up the bag to turn out the pig, Maussa been standing looking in the pen, and when Uncle Jimmy shake out the pig—it wuz a PUPPY! Uncle Jim squreal out, "Oh, God! I done Maussa! I never been in such trouble before! Put a pig in the bag in the pen to Uncle Billy place and now he is a puppy!"

Poor old man too upsot. He grab he sack and hasted out back to Uncle Billy pen wid diss here puppy. When he got to shop where he stop, man halt 'em agin! Say, (nother drink, Sonny!)

"Where you going old man?" He tell the shop man,

"Great God, Cap'n, something happen to me never happen yet!"

Shop man say," How come dat?" Uncle Jimmy told him,

"I put a pig in the bag to Uncle Billy pen for Maussa, and when I pass you here the pig tie up in the bag. And when I get to Maussa pen and shuck out the pig—it wuz a puppy!"

"The man invite him back in. He have some peculiar (mischie'vous) boys exchange the pig for the puppy again—(for that what they had done in the fuss place!) Yes! While Uncle Jimmy gone in to get a drink, these boy take the bag and carry 'em round the shop, empty out the puppy and put the pig back in the bag! And they set the sack the same place—the same place Uncle Jimmy leave 'em when he gone in to get the drink—right there under that BAD LUCK MULBERRY TREE.

"When Uncle Jimmy come out that drink still have 'em happy. The shop man tell 'em,'Jimmy don't go back to Uncle Billy! Go back to Maussa. Tell 'em you sho got the pig in the bag this time!'"

And he take up the bag for the last and gone stagger down to Maussa hog crawl one last time! And this time Maussa didn't go again wid 'em to the pen. He sent a witness back to prove is it the pig this time! The serbant wuz all surprise to see how quick exchange wuz made. Serbant went and tell Maussa, 'You sho got the pig DIS time!'

Poor old Uncle Jimmy bumfumbling! Tell Billy? Lord, NO. Missus, it wouldn't never do tall, tall for Maussa neither Billy to know bout that drink. And you know that old Uncle Jimmy been worry till his call come bout that accident. Sometimes he blame it on them bad-luck mul-berry and say that pig (must have) musser been worked on wid some sorter conjur or ritchcraft—but he ain't never know. But they been one thing he has learn—when he going errant he never take no more drink to that shop man store."

Jim Moody

In the early thirties the Kimball family bought Wachesaw plantation from the Willcox family. Since the Kimballs were interested in the land as a hunting preserve, they kept Thomas Chandler on as caretaker. Thus the Chandler family continued to live on the land as it had before the sale. Jim Moody worked for Chandler as an assistant and general farm laborer. He was an almost constant presence in and around the Chandler household in those days.

In 1934 Chandler began building a log cabin intended for the Kimballs' hunting trips. In laying the foundation, he and his crew found what appeared to be a Native American grave site. The skeletons of thirteen young women were buried in a circle, the apparent victims of a deadly epidemic. The skulls were filled with beads, which led archeologists to surmise the women's bones had been picked clean prior to burial. Apparently they had been exposed to the elements for some time, then dressed with ornaments, and interred. After the crew discovered them, the skeletons were once again removed from the earth and laid out for examination.

At some point during the excavation, Moody took teeth from one of the skeletons as a charm—a souvenir he came to regret. Moody's confession is the subject of the one interview presented here.

As an unfortunate footnote, it was around the time of these events that Chandler's daughter, Genevieve (a coeditor of this volume), became ill with diphtheria. Doctors surmised it was contracted by exposure to the excavation. Chandler's daughter survived, but in the process of fumigating with sulfur candles, the Chandler's house at Wachesaw caught fire and burned to the ground.

When the Kimballs decided to move permanently to Wachesaw, the Chandlers moved to Murrells Inlet. Moody, however, stayed on at Wachesaw, working for Kimball much as he had for Chandler.

Wachesaw, the Place of the Great Weeking.[1]

"Man, dat critter carocoss!"

"No, man!"

"Cap'n,[2] what you tink he is?"

"Don't-know. Dig on."[3]

"Cap'n, boss! Dish her human! Looker he skull!"

And sure enough there was a skull, one skull, two skull, three skull, four skull, five skull! Skull on each side! Skull to der foot! And bones! Man, der bone! Dig man, dig.

"Dem skull full er thing! Wha dat?"

The skull were full o'tings. The white foreman's eyes fairly protruded as he knelt and scraped up handfuls of treasure spilling from broken skulls-beads, beads, beads! There were transparent glass beads that had imprisoned the blue Italian skies; long white ivory-like pendants that appeared to be carved from sea shells, big dull black beads that glowed like fire opals having gathered color from the soild, while hidden from the sun these two hundred years or more.

Beads that looked like mosaic, red and black and blue stripes running horizontally along their sides; little red glass beads exactly like holly berries, black spot and all; cupfuls of tiny white beads like seed pearls, dull opaque blue beads that seemed like turquoises, ruby red beads! It was a matter of a few hours, such a fascination has buried treasures, before the news spread and cars and people literally stramed to the isolated plantation, Wachesaw, by the smoothly flowing Waccamaw to see and handle with their hands. No trepass signs availed nothing. Every man, woman and child was a souvenir hunter.

They must have what they had come for. Though the skeletons, much broken by careless, untrained hands, do rest in the museum at Charleston, many of the beads, bits of skull and teeth walked off in the pockets of visitors. The banker's lady knelt and for bones sifted sand as patiently as had the day laborer in worn overalls, searching for more beads.

Among those much interested in the excavating by amateurs was Black Bob.[4] All of Bob was black save the whites of his eyes, his ivories and his

1. "Weeking" is a corruption of "weeping." Local folklore holds that the Native American word *Wachesaw* translates as "place of the great weeping."

2. Tom Chandler.

3. This digging was done in preparation for the foundation work and construction of Ed Kimball's home at Wachesaw.

4. A pseudonym, albeit an unfortunate one, chosen by Genevieve Chandler to protect Jim Moody's identity.

comspicious blue gums that were visible every time he spoke or smiled. Nobody dreamed Bob was a souvenior fiend. When the white overseer salvaged the copper anklet that still encircled the moldy, green ankle-bones, thrown last from the grave and the interesting trified or hare's-foot spoon-Bob said nothing, but one could see whites of his eyes.

Later, when these proved identical with those excavated in Rhode Island and Massachusetts said to have been buried in the early seventeenth century, Bob looked on occasionally—wielding a spade but doing no talking. The whites of his eyes grew whiter but he said nothing. No one saw when he stooped and rising, slipped a closed black fist in his pants pocket.

At sunrise the next day—Sunday,—remembering that the colored people were to have a "Baptising" at the foot of the Indian Mound in the waters of the Waccamaw, the caretaker thought best to put the bones out of sight. These, therefore, were carefully gathered into a tub and put out of sight in a near-by mill-house. As the white folk engaged in his gruesome task hurried to finish the hob before the white robed minister and his candidates arrived, they were startled from their absorption by hearing a voice say:-

"Cap'n, Boss, I'se brung back dem teef. Ef I hadn't been too feared, I'd a brung 'em in der night. I ain't got no res. I'se bin trouble all night."

"Why, Bob, what's the matter? You sick?"

"Oh, no sir. Not to say sick. I wuz trouble wid de speits. De Injun sperit. De ghost. Dey come to me en de say". " Bring back us teef! Bring back us teef! En I git feared. Dey wuz a big missy en er lil missy. Dey all two bofe had on long white robe and er hair hang down en he face been red same lak de brick in de chimbley. Jes when I too tired and ready for ter sleep dey walks right in troo de do en hit barred: En de wails out same lak leetle screech owl.

Bring back us teef! Bring back us teef! Bring back us teef! Dey scare me too bad. En when I gits meh speech I say: 'Jes you wait tell day come, missy, and I sho takes 'em back."

So here dey is, Cap'n Boss, en please trow 'em back in de grabe. I don rob no grabe no more. I don bother no more wid ded peoples. Dem two missis look so sad like and cry so pitiful, 'Bring back us teef! Bring back us teef! Bring back us teef!'

And with this Bob sowed his handful of teeth in the grave and joined the procession winding down the live-oaks grove down to the river's edge for baptising.

(Submitted: May 30, 1936)

William Oliver

William Oliver was born into slavery (in approximately 1858) on the Oliver place in Horry County. His recollections of slavery appear to be particularly lucid. He recalls means by which slaves like his father could make a marginal profit hiring themselves out as stevedores and reimbursing their owners for less than the total wage they were paid. Other memories include the kinds of food that were most common, clandestine educational practices, and the severe reputation Texas held regarding slave punishment.

Oliver was the son of Caesar Oliver and Janie Oliver. Both parents were originally from the Jewitt family plantation near Little River. Oliver's father, Casear, was a the plantation driver.

Oliver was one of sixteen siblings (four boys and twelve girls), including Trizvan, Sarah, Martha, William, Mary, Lizzie, Emma, Alice, Joanna, Havilla, Ella, Redonia, Caesar, Zachariah, and Eddie. At the time of his marriage, Oliver indicates, his own occupation was "working turpentine." In other words, he worked in the woods tapping and draining sap from the longleaf pines. The sap was used in the naval stores industry to make turpentine and paint thinner. U.S. Census data from 1920 describes Oliver's work as general farm labor. At that time he was married to Martha. They were then raising a two-year-old niece, also named Martha, and living in the Knoxville community. By the time of his interview with Chandler however, Oliver—then approximately seventy-five years old—was a widower.

(Recollections of Uncle William Oliver)

"Underground Railway? They give it that name being they had this way to transfer the slaves. T. O. Jones was one of the officers. Growed up in Illinois.

"I was born in Horry—eight miles this side of Conway. The old Oliver place. Father Caesar Oliver; Mother Janie. Mother born near Little River[1]–Jewitt place. Joe Jewitt raise my father. Had four brother; twelve sister;

1. Little River, South Carolina, which is north of Myrtle Beach, South Carolina.

One - Trizvan
Two - Sarah
Three - Martha
Four - William
Five - Mary, the fifth
Six - Lizzie, the sixth
Seven - Emma, the seven
Eight - Alice, the eighth
Nine - Joanna
Ten - Havilla
Eleven - Ella
Twelve - Redonia
Thirteen - Caesar
Fourteen - Zackie
Fifteen - Eddie
Sixteen - (He could not remember)

"Three boys so scattered about you can't tell anything about them. All chimney, clay. All chimneys that day, clay. Moved right away soon as Freedom came. Women done cooking and washing same as now. Shuck mattress. My mother was a weaver. Old timey loom. Cotton and wool. Sheckel (Shuttle?)

"I remember one song my mother sang:

> 'Do Lord, remember me!
> Remember me when the year go round!
> Do, Lord, remember me!
> Why can't you die
> Like Jesus died?
> He laid in His grave!
> He crippled some.
> Some He saved.'

"I can't get it all.

"My father head man on the plantation. Indigo? Cut the bush down. Put it in sacks. Let it drip out. Call that indigo mud. Raise cattle and hogs loose over the County. No cash money was give to slave. Had to get a ticket. Hire they self out as stevedore—anywhere they could—and pay Massa so much for the time. Smart slave do that. Oh, yes, my father do that. If they keep themselves alive after freedom, they doing well.

"Schooling? Only by night. And that couldn't be known. When he could get any body to teach him 'A-B-C' but wasn't allowed to go to any school.

"We'd eat peas, rice, cornbread, rye bread, sweetbread. Most molasses. Game was all over the woods. Everybody could hunt everybody land those days. Hunting was free. When I come along had to work too hard to hunt. Could get pike out the lakes. Go fishing Sabbath. That was day off. Sunday free day. Wild turkey. Possum. Don't bother with no coon much. Possum and squirrel all we could get. Had our garden. Different bean and collard. Turnip.

"Clothes? Regular wool and cotton. Maple dye and indigo. Red, blue, gray. Lot of gray. Big slave owners had a shoemaker. Plenty of hides. Cow hides, deer hides.

"When I married, was working turpentine. Rent timber and cut boxes.

"The cruelest treatment I know of in the United States and all the other states was done in the Southwestern states. Take New Orleans. Galveston? Was fixing to get to Texas. Texas beat the country for cruelty. They tell me when your Master and Missus in this country want to make you do your task, they threaten to sell you to Texas. Had a regular 'Vanger Range' in New Orleans. Place they keep the slaves and auction them off. Man by the name of Perry Ann Marshall. He was sold out there. He told my father he'd be out in the field in the morning—hoe in hand. Had to get out there fore it was light, hoe in hand. Boss man there with whip. When light enough to hoe, give order, 'Heads up!' Then lots of women fell dead over the hoe. Give order, 'Heads up!' you chop! Breakfast bring to you in the field. Set right there by you hoe and eat till he say, 'Heads up!' When women fell dead, lie right there till night where the body drop—till you knock off. That's Texas! I call Texas 'Hell.' Even today black man can't get no first class ticket Texas!

"When you come right down to the truth, we always got up fore day most of time. You could go visiting other plantation, but must have you a ticket. Patrol catch you they whip you."

Given by Uncle William Oliver
A boy in slavery time
Murrells Inlet, S. C.
May 20th, 1937.

Minnie Knox: (Referring to dog) "Sport think he people. Must a got German police and shepherd mix. He the sensibilest dog I know. Sport think he mix with people. He come and knock at the door like somebody. And he sit up to the fire and hold he paw up to the fire. We get up and pull off to go to bed, Sport pull off too! We go to bed. Sport gone in the bed, too. The other night I miss Sport. Gone in my room and there Sport his head up on my pillow sleep—he fore paw all stretched like chillun hand."

Uncle William Oliver: "You know, one time I had a little dog named Terry was the sensibilest thing to be sho. Just like a child in the home. Daughter and I there and wife. Terry find three babies. One die. Raise two. Then I say,

"Wont keep all these dog."

Market man buy beef from me say he want one. Man name gone all out of my mind now. All right. Man say,

'I'll give you two hen for puppy.'

Man never didn't give me hen—Man mother was right agree-able. She got sick. Sick some ciderable time. That little dog wouldn't leave that woman bedside. Stay right there. When they take her out the house to bury her, (she dead you know)—little dog follow right long hind the box to cimitery. Folks of the family didn't give dog a thought. Look around when they get home for the little dog. Say,

"Somebody take Ma little dog!"

Next Sunday they gone to cimitery. Little dog was all hurdled up curdled up on top of the grave. Been there a week and was so poor and thin and weak she could hardly walk. Had to prize her from that spot. She brace herself! Take her home. Wouldn't eat. Just mince. Gone back to that cimitery and hurdled down in that hole and stay there. He stay right there till she dead right there. The old people say dog been the first animal people tame. Man best friend—dog.

Minnie Knox age 25
William Knox[2]*—age 78*
Murrells Inlet, S. C.
October 1937.

2. Apparently Genevieve Chandler or a typist has made a mistake here since the William interviewed is identified in the text as William Oliver.

Maude Esther Lee Pickett

PICKETT WAS IN HER LATE TEENS when Genevieve Chandler interviewed her. She was the daughter of Olie and Julia Knox Pickett and thus the granddaughter of Gabe and Addie Knox. According to 1930 U.S. Census records, the Picketts had five other children (Ceaphus, Willie, Middie, Billie, and Alice). Maude Esther Lee Pickett's interviews with Chandler reveal her to be a quite humorous—if acerbic—social critic. Pickett shares two trickster tales about the wily slave John (referred to in one as "Jack"). Also her insights about "Uncle Sam"—including his resemblance to "Sandy Claw," or Santa Claus—provide some rare commentary on the dubious relationship between the southern black population and their white governors.

Maud Esther Lee Pickett:

"When I was little I thought Sandy Claw and Uncle Sam the two BEST thing in the world. I thought Sandy Claw was giving you all them thing you mama have to pay for. And I thought UNCLE SAM was a good man too. I thought he was sittin' up there in his office in Con-o-way and I thought when you paid your tax Uncle Sam just saved it all for you. And when you needin' money I just thought you could go right there to Uncle Sam and get your money. I thought they was two ugly people too. Uncle Sam picture so ugly. I don't think Uncle Sam so good now. Make you buy the land and keep on paying the tax. I calls that NO business.

"Now the meanest thing in the world? I thought that was the 'forebliceman. I see him catch us own people and RUSH'EM off to jail. I seen'em run down a man to 'forerest him. 'foreBliceman run him down—cut 'forecross front of him in he motor cycle, And hold he gun on him. The Sheriff and the 'foreblicemans can sho talk rough to you."

SOURCE: *Maude Esther Lee Pickett*
Age 15
July 1938
Murrells Inlet, S. C.

Strong Man Jack

"They was Jack, Once upon a time they was Jack was a very wise nigger. Cap'n brag on Jack. Cap'n say:

"'Jack can beat all swimmin' !'

"Then he come tell Jack:

"'Jack, tomorrow a man coming here to swim with you. Want you to swim two three miles. Want you to beat him. I bet money on you. You must beat him so's we can get all that money.'

"Now Jack can't swim nary lick. He go get him a stove, grits, meal, meat, and lard and ALL and put 'em on his back. Man come to swim with Jack he say:

"'What you got them bundle for and goin' swimmin'?'

"Jack tell him:

"'You think I goin' swim three four miles 'forethout any sumptin t'eat? You must think I a big fool!'

"And the man what come think if Jack goin' swim so far he have to stop and cook rations long the way he better down.

"Jack Cap'n got all THAT money! "

SOURCE: *Maud Esther Lee Pickett. Age 18 ? Burgess, S. C. (Horry County)*

The One 'bout Jack

"(Miss Jin, Capers[1] he know all the JACK story
'bout Strong man Jack. I don't know Jack so
good. I'm telling 'bout JOHN!)"
6-JOHN

"Well, one time slavery time Maussa tell he wife:

"'You know I'm goin' kill John! That nigger too wise. He learn too much. He might kill me!'

"So now one day the Maussa take him to the river and put him in a sack and set him down on a little stool close the river bank. Then he say:

"'I won't kill you now. I'll go home fust and get my dinner. Kill 'em after dinner.' And Maussa gone to he dinner.

"Here John in the sack start to sing!

"'Anyhow! Anyhow, my Lord! Anyhow!
At the Holy Ghost we may bide!

1. Capers Pickett.

Lord, I goin' up to Heaven anyhow!'

"Old woman pass goin' to the store to the Ark.[2] Say:

"'Aints that John?'

"And John talk out the sack:

"'Yes, this John! I goin' up to Heaven today!' The
old woman say:

"'John, I'd sho' like to go up to Heaven. But I got to go to the store and get some grits and coffee and sugar and cream.'

"'Well you hurry and get 'em and come back. I can go up any old day. I'll let you go in my place.'

"She come back. She had hurry and she come back. And John say:

"'Loose the sack and let me out. Now you get in.'

"And he tie the sack mouth back.

"Maussa come back take the sack and throw it in the river! Didn't say 'A' ner 'M' ner nothin'. Didn't call John ner nothin'.
And here the old lady in the river. And her coffee and sugar and all gone in the river!

"Johnhe stay gone two three days. Come back by the pastor.
(Maussa don't know nothin' 'bout the cows. He don't keep up with the cows) Here he come back drivin' a big bunch o' Maussa cows.

"His wife look 'forecross to the seacoast:

"'Ain'ts that JOHN?'

"And Maussa say:

"'NO! I done kill that —— nigger!'

"John come walkin' up.

"'Mornin' John! Mornin' John!'

"And John say:

"'Mornin' Maussa!'

"'John,I thought I kill you!'

"'Yes, Cap'n, you kill me! I been all to Heaven and come 'round by Hell. The Devil have these cow. Say he ain't want 'em. You want 'em?'
"'Drive 'em in the stable John. John, you know where my money?'

"'I know where your money 'fore I leave.'

"'Well you go get that money and spend it for anything you want.'

"So John come to be a rich colored man."

SOURCE: *Told by Maude Esther Lee Pickett. Age 24 (?)*
Burgess, S. C.

2. Ark plantation.

Reverend Aaron Pinnacle

Aaron Pinnacle was a highly respected United Methodist minister, operating within the United Methodist Conference. In the Waccamaw Neck region, Pinnacle preached at Brown Chapel as well as Heaven's Gate. Pinnacle was most likely in his midforties when Chandler interviewed him. He was a close friend of the Knox family, referred to simply as "the Rev" by Zackie Knox. He is fondly remembered by Mary Small as, "Singin' Pinnacle! E could sing." Pinnacle's parents came from the Charleston area. His father, Hazel, was born into slavery. In 1910 the U.S. Census reports the Pinnacle family was living in Berkeley County. At that time Aaron Pinnacle was living with his father and mother (Hazel and Hariet) and his four brothers (John, George, Alonso, and Abraham). The 1920 and 1930 census records find Pinnacle still living in Berkeley County, in his own home, with his wife, Ida Pinnacle. In 1930 they had seven children (Mary, Nathaniel, Myrtle, George, Rosa, Naomi, and Ruth).

The present volume features two interviews with Reverend Pinnacle. In one, Pinnacle describes his father and grandfather. In another, he retells a trickster tale about two elderly slaves that was passed on to him by his father. Pinnacle adapts the story to the local community by employing the names of two local residents, Hardtimes and Pleasant Sparkman. Traveling folklorist John A. Lomax referenced the reverend in *Adventures of a Ballad Hunter* in his retelling of Ben Small's funeral.[1] Chandler also made a transcript of these proceedings. We have placed it here because much of the text is reportage of Reverend Pinnacle's sermon, prayers, and remarks.

1. "Ben's pastor, the Reverend Aaron Pinnacle, in the midst of his sermon, the core of which was the warning question, shouted again and again, 'Who will go next?' 'One day,' he added, 'Death is coming to our chamber. What are you doing to get ready to meet him? You can get around to paying the store kind of debt. You can say you haven't got the money. But when Death comes, you got to pay the debt principally! You can get used to anything except Death. Whenever he comes, you ain't acquainted with him. He is always new.' The solidly built black minister kept his heavy voice at such a high pitch that it became more and more difficult to follow his words.

Being Remarks Made and Extracts from Prayer at Brother Ben's Funeral.

Mom Hagar: "She'll never get over it! Lyin' there speechless ever since he shoot! Ben's death gwine kill he Ma!"

(Extracts from Sermon.)
St. Peters Church in the Free Woods.

"Paul said I know that when this earthly tabernacle dissolve, it shall drop off this mortal flesh and have a new house. And Saul looked at man as man fight in war. Man got to meet death by hisself. So we find Brother Ben Small.[2] Find him at St. Peters. Find him service the Lord. Brother Ben ain't live no Christian life. That good mother! Tell him he ought to live to inherit eternal life. Tell him how he ought to live.

On last Friday he went out from home and have a weakness and things of the world overcome him. When Brother Ben went out on Friday night, Satan went and surround him. But by some means he come to Sister Hannah house. And he brudder and sister went over there. Hear that gun shoot. Stamp a stamp! They take Ben to the hospital. Way of Satan. Come on time! I want you to stand up right!"

(Congregation in a frenzy. Mad orgy of emotionalism.)

"I see darkness! Sin in my path. Ben will not come here to worship no more! St. Peters will meet him no more! 'Tell my Mudder and Fadder I am comin' home! Tell my Mudder and Fadder I am comin' too!'"

(A girl (niece) is overcome. Stiffens like a board. Arms waving in time to singing. Three men held her up before altar. Each member of congregation keeping time. Some standing, dance. Smiles. Perfect unison. Perfect rhythm.)

"Oh I say to gentle Jesus 'I'm comin' too." Lord will must be done. Lord will must be done! All got to take it. All got to die. Friends, just a statement.

As a climax he spoke in a trembling falsetto: 'No more will we see Brother Ben in Sunday school; no more will Brother Ben lead the prayer on Wednesday night; no more will we hear Brother Ben's voice in the choir. Brother Ben will meet us, way somewhere in the noncomitant of an uncloudy day.'

'Thank you, Lord,' shouted the audience, while many feet tapped the floor in an ever faster crescendo of grief. This tapping rose and died away in unison with the inarticulate moaning that swept the room, just as the moaning grew in volume and sharpness with the jumbled shouts of the preacher." John A. Lomax, *Adventures of a Ballad Hunter* (New York: Macmillan, 1947), 211.

2. Mary Brown Small's husband. Hagar Brown's son-in-law.

Iowes you. Here together we'll be until the hour of our departure come. I will say it will be a good chance. When we read Bible text, when we recites that beautiful prayer! One line, 'Let Thy will be done on earth as angels does it in Heaven.' God goin' to do his will. Can get used to many things but, when death come, we never come acquainted with death. New every time he come. Say the life of the man while he give up the Ghost. (Say it not in his behalf. He finish his work.) Say over his remainder he have finish his course. He finish his race. Finish. Race won. Yesterday morning 'bout six o'clock! We got to pay that debt! You can get 'round payin' the store account but that debt you 'foregree yo pay. You can go up and say, 'I haven't got the money!' But death one debt must pay.

"We been tryin' many years to die death. Who is death? His name? But I say this mornin' he name is JOSH!" (Josh was the man who shot Brother Ben) When we get it in our hearts the understanding, man born of woman have but few days to live full of misery. Grown up in the morning, cut down in the day and wilter in the grass. He flee like a shadow. Man got the understanding. Meet that just man. He is comin' into our chamber. Are we prepared to meet him?" (Sad chant like death march. Heads bobbing in unison. All sing or hum and keep time.)

Prayer.

"Almighty Everlasting One! Everlasting Thou Art God! Before whose sight Thou have decree I come, Thank You! We thank you for the care and keepin' the heart. Kept us from out early risin'. Even from out infancy Thou hast brought us. Thank Thee. Thank Thee for the breeze. Thank Thee for health. More especially thank Thee for the knowledge we shall die for Thy Son Jesus give us deep repentance. For our sin. Thou art God. Beside the omnipotence, omniscience, and omnipresence, we ask, "Come in our midst! Shine one of Your Jehovah smile. Come in our midst but come not in death. Come not in judgement. Come not in anger. But come in mercy. Mercy have a case this morning! Time come to stand before the judgement seat. and give 'forecount. of deeds done in the body. Side of the river is dark. Battle done been fought! Call soul in from the battle-field to stop at the feet of Jesus. Study war no more. Battle fought. Meet us somewhere! Some where out yonder!"

(Revents Pinnacle leads 'Steal Away')
"By the lightning!
"By the thunder!
The lightning flashes!
Steal away, christian!
Steal away,sinner!.

Steal away to Jesus!"
(Preacher exhorting)

"NEED to steal away to Jesus! Near the end of the journey! Sho to ax our self the question, 'Lord, will I be next?' Death is old; death is new. Twice or three times a week it new. But consider, Lord's will must be done. Lord's will must be done."

(Song)

Lord, I'm Out On The Ocean Sailing.

1.

Lord I'm out on the ocean sailing!
Lord I'm out on the ocean sailing!
Lord I'm out on the ocean sailing!
Who! Who! Who!

2.

I'm goin' sail till I meet my Mother!
I'm goin' sail'till I meet my mother!
I'm going sail 'foretill I meet my mother!
Who! Who! Who!

3.

I'm goin' sail my way to Heaven!
I'm goin' sail my way to Heaven!
I'm goin' sail my way to Heaven!
Who! Who! Who!

4.

I'm goin' sail Till I meet King Jesus!
I'm goin' sail 'foretill I meet King Jesus!
I'm goin' sail 'foretill I meet King Jesus!
Who! Who! Who!

5.

I'm goin' tell him how Satan do me!
I'm goin' tell him how Satan do me!
I'm goin' tell him how Satan do me!
Who! Who! Who!

6.

Satan roll me over and over!
Satan roll me over and over!
Satan roll me over and over!
Who! Who! Who!

7.

I'm goin' sail till I get to Heaven!
I'm goin' sail 'foretill I get to Heaven!
I'm goin' sail 'foretill I get to Heaven!
Who! Who! Who!

8.

I'm goin' tell Him what a trouble I had!
I'm goin' tell Him what a trouble I had!
I'm goin' tell Him what a trouble I had!
Who! Who! Who!

9.

I'm goin' sail 'round the thrones of Glory!
I'm goin' sail 'round the thrones of Glory!
I'm goin' sail 'round the thrones of Glory!
Who! Who! Who!

10.

I'm goin' to meet my mother when I get there!
I'm goin' to meet my mother when I get there!
I'm goin' to meet my mother when I get there!
Who! Who! Who!

11.

Lord I know by her livin' here!
Lord, I know by her livin' here!
Lord, I know by her livin' here!
Who! Who! Who!

12.

I'm goin' try on my long white robe!
I'm goin' try on my long white robe!
I'm goin' try on my long white robe!
Who! Who! Who!

13.

I'm goin' try on my slipper shoe!
I'm goin' try on my slipper shoe!
I'm goin' try on my slipper shoe!
Who! Who! Who!

14.

I'm goin' try on my wings and fly!
I'm goin' try on my wings and fly!
I'm goin' try on my wings and fly!
Who! Who! Who!

15.

I'm goin' tell my God how you treat me!
I'm goin' tell my God how you treat me!
I'm goin' tell my God how you treat me!
Who! Who! Who!

16.

I'm goin' tell Jesus 'bout my trouble!
I'm goin' tell Jesus 'bout my trouble!
I'm goin' tell Jesus 'bout my trouble!
Who! Who! Who!

17.

Oh, tell me where you find your religion!
Oh, tell me where you find your religion!
Oh, tell me where you find your religion!
Oh, Who! Who! Who!

18.

I find'em in some lonesome valley!
I find'em in some lonesome valley!
I find'em in some lonesome valley!
Oh, Who! Who! Who!

19.

Why don't you shout like you got good religion!
Why don't you shout like you got good religion!
Why don't you shout like you got good religion!
Oh Who! Who! Who!

20.

I'm sailing to make the harbor!
I'm sailing to make the harbor!
I'm sailing to make the harbor!
Oh, who! Who! Who!

Questioner: "How you Auntie?"
Auntie:[3] "I ain't do wuth (worth). Headed to Ben funeral. Grave done dig."
Taken down at funeral

Summer 1936
SOURCE: *St. Peters Colored Church*
(Horry County) Free Woods.
Burgess, S. C.

3. Hagar Brown.

My Grandfather

"My Grand-father put his shoe on his shoulder—mostly to save his shoe. In sight of the church stop and put on his shoe. He would cut two and a half cords of wood on potatoes and meat. (With nothing for food except potatoes and meat) My Grand-father lived at Midway—near Bamberg.[4] My Mother's father was named Mallit. Mostly followed up street work. My Father was educated by his father. He went home and taught Grand-father. Grand-father didn't know 'A' if it were big as the house. Father was the leading choir. He'd go to Ladsden[5] and all round Summerville[6] and Charleston to Camp Meeting and took me. His church 'The Wesley M. E. Ladsden.' He inspired a lot. Born 1853."

(When asked his idea of how the spirituals were born he said, in effect, that they were inspired. This was the way he answered:

"One day a writer sat with his pencil in his hand and a little bird flewed in the window and he couldn't understand. He looked up to find the cause and there were a hawk. The hawk were chasing the bird. The writer turned and wrote 'Rocks of Ages.' That were inspire. That is the way the spirituals were. They were inspire."

(Hawk was prounced 'hock.')

(This is not verbatim but 'flewed' and other unusual words are as given.)

Reverend Pinnacle said that his father could play on the violin, cornet and later learned to play the organ. In fact as he expressed it, he could make music on any instrument.)

Told by Rev. Aaron Pinnacle
(Negro)
Pastor Heaven's Gate M. E.
Church—Age 45.
Murrells Inlet, S. C.

(Story Given by Rev. Aaron Pinnacle That His Father Gave Him.)

Uncle Hardtimes and Mom Pleasant.[7]

"Uncle Hardtimes and his wife been out o' money. They wonder how they going to do. So they talked and planned it out one day. Uncle Hardtimes say,

4. Bamberg, South Carolina.

5. Ladson, South Carolina.

6. Summerville, South Carolina.

7. Hardtimes and Pleasant Sparkman. Hardtimes was the plantation carpenter at Richmond Hill.

"'I going to my boss man[8] and ax for money to bury you!"

Then he gone on down the road. When he come to the boss' house, the Cap'n been setting on the porch cooling his foots.

"'Boss,' he say, 'I in trouble.'

"'What the trouble, Hardtimes?'

"'I lose Mom Pleasant last night!'

"'What?'

"'Please, Cap'n Boss, loan me twenty-five dollars to put Pleasant away right.'

"'That enough, Hardtimes?'

"'Twenty-five dollars been enough, Cap'n.'

The money was deliver. Hardtimes gone on. Show the twenty-five dollars to Mom Pleasant and tell 'em,

"'Pleasant, old gal, I got the money. Now you seen the Cap'n coming, you better been dead. I tell the Cap'n you dead!"

"'Next morning Mom Pleasant going down the road and she meet up with her white Missus.[9] She pass the time of day but when she think how she got to be dead, she look sad. So Missus say,

"'Mom Pleasant anything wrong? You say you good as common but you ain't look too happy?'

And Mom Pleasant say,

"'Well Missus, now you ax, sumpting got me worry up! Don't feel none too good. Going to miss my old man too much!"

"Where Uncle Hardtimes?"

"'He dead.'

"'Dead? Hardtimes dead?'

'Yes Missus, and I needs twenty-five dollars to put him away right!"

"Twenty-five dollars?"

'Yes Missus. That been enough. That'll beat the spense. Twenty-five dollars will put my old man away nice!'

So Mom Pleasant Times gone on home and Uncle Hardtimes hear what she tell the Missus. Uncle Hardtimes perceive from his loss twenty-five and here Mom Pleasant say:

"Tell my Missus YOU been dead so here I got my money too!"

Ain't that pitiful! Ain't that pitiful! And that night the boss and Missus meet. Boss say,

"'So Mom Pleasant dead?'

And Missus say:

8. Dr. John D. Magill was the owner of Richmond Hill plantation.

9. Mary Vereen Magill, the wife of John D. Magill.

"'No! Uncle Hardtimes the one what dead! I know cause I loan Mom Pleasant money to put him away right!'

"You must be wrong," say the Cap'n boss. "I loan Hardtimes twenty-five dollars to bury Mom Pleasant.'

"And they say,

"'We best ride over there and find out who it is been dead!'

"And so the two bosses get in the buggy and gone on.

"Well the two old colored people been finish up the best supper they relish in a long time and they just setting cooling on the joggling board[10]—just a-sotting out in the porch slapping mosquitoes. They hear hoofs coming and they know it been the Cap'n horse. And Hardtimes say,

"Sho as today Satdy, that the Cap'n!"

And Pleasant say,

"And I hear the Missus!"

"And they ain't have but one thing TO do. All two both fall dead—Stretch out! Lay same like two old fat possum! And it ain't been too long fore the boss man and the Missus hit the step and they see they two old friends stretch out! So the Cap'n say:

"'I'd give twenty-five dollars to know which one dead first.'

And Hardtimes jump up and say:

"Me dead fuss!"

And the old woman jump up and cry:

"Me dead fuss!"

So both dead fuss!"

Story told by
Revents Aaron Pinnacle
Murrells Inlet, S.C.
(Told Rev. Pinnacle by his father who was born in slavery—near Charleston.)

10. Once a common style of porch seat, the joggling board is a long flexible plank suspended between two supports. The flexibility allows for bouncing, or joggling.

Fred Poinsette

MOST OF THE INFORMATION AVAILABLE about Fred Poinsette comes from the U.S. Census material and is therefore of uncertain reliability. According to the 1900 U.S. Census, Fred Poinsette was born in June 1874. Poinsette's parents were Friday and Christina. The 1880 U.S. Census suggests he had seven siblings (Bonaparte, Paul, Abraham, Noah, Sheadon, Sarah, and Catherine). Poinsette was married twice. First, he was married to a woman variously referred to as Bella (1900 census) and Isabella (1910 census). Isabella Poinsette was reportedly born in May 1877. They had at least three children (Lucille, Lucinda, and Annie Bell). Later Poinsette married Emma. The 1920 U.S. Census finds Annie Bell, now seventeen, still living in the house. It also reports a fourth daughter (Chatritha, age nine).

Poinsette worked as both a turpentine hand (1900 census) and a farm laborer (1910 census). Although he was not formally educated, he was listed as literate in the 1930 census. This census also suggests that he lived in close proximity to the Singleton, Keith, and Bryant families. The one interview Chandler recorded with Poinsette presents him as a sage old man, meticulously planting a grapevine.

(Verbatim Conversation)

"You ax Lottie[1] the text? She ain't know? Don't remember none the song. Some people don't bring a thing home. I go to church to get something to feed on.—something to take home for the soul to feed on next week.

"To-morrow night we going to have a flat-form service. Tached (taxed) each member fifteen cent pay to leader and leader turn into the Treasurer. Raise money to go to 'Ladies Age' (Ladies Aid'). Going to summer convention. Got to make a report.

"Gripe! Gripe the stummick! Last dose I take it faint me. Knox say, 'What the matter?'

I say, 'Hand me the cold water.'

1. Lottie Pickett.

He say, 'You take that black dross (draught)[2] last night? Tear you up like double team in new ground.'

"Thing faint me. Take none since."

Questioner: "Lottie, you go to Gordon Chapel last night?
Lottie: "Yas'm. I been there.
Questioner: "What was the text?
Lottie: "I'm plumb forgot. I'm easy forgetful."

Auto-giro passes—***Lillie:*** "Missus, look at that air-ship with a wind mill on top of it!"

Uncle Fred Poinsette brought the grape-vine and guaranteed it would live—a scuppernong. Carefully he digged the hole; carefully he arranged the roots then, turning to his cart, he rummaged around and got a bushel bucket. It contained dirt—black dirt.

"What's that, Uncle Fred?" I asked.

"Dirt. Home dirt. So it'll feel homey. So it'll feel at home.

Fred Poinsette—age 75
Murrells Inlet, S. C.
April 26th, 1937.

2. Black draught was a purgative taken for constipation.

Carrie Pyatt

Very little biographical information exists for Carrie Pyatt. The possible reasons for this are numerous, but her absence from U.S. Census data can most probably be explained as a consequence of her residence on Sandy Island. The remoteness of this community seems to have discouraged many census takers. Alternatively it is possible that "Carrie" is a basket name, by which she was known among familiars but which would not have been given to a government official.

The one interview featuring Carrie Pyatt amounts to a record of her gossiping with Lillie Knox about recent events in the local marital scene, including new marriages, remarriages, divorces, and abandonments.

Bella
(Verbatim)

Lillie: "Bella workin' to Miss Smith.[1] You know that pretty little bluish thin dress your cousin Lucile buy? Bella pass on the color and say her chillun have a dress make off that piece. I buy it and you know what color it been? Navy! And now see it white! I say if she make her chillun little panties and waisses out that piece and bile it long with her white things ——————————:

"How Bella chillun gettin' on she left?"

Visitor:[2] "Fine! Fine!"

Lillie: "She left four—Three girls; one boy. Jimmy have on dress when Bella die."

Visitor: "Her husband find 'forenother wife, ain't he?"

Lillie: "Yes."

Visitor: "Chillun by he last wife?"

Lillie : "Yes."

Visitor: "You know that last wife?"

Lillie: "Yes, gal. I been know Josephine too long!"

Visitor: "I hear she marry that man 'forecause he have too much o' cattle."

1. Mrs. Gilmore Smith, one-time mistress of Sunnyside.
2. Carrie Pyatt.

Lillie: "That so."
Visitor: "I hear they have a dispute 'bout that cattle. That so?"
Lillie: "I'm tellin' you!"
Visitor: "Didn't have to go to LAW 'bout it, did they?"
Lillie: "No. All sell. She have but the two yoke of ox leave."
Visitor: "Ox cost nuttin' to keep. Wampee, peas vine, fodder grass. Some feeds off with rice straw. Never been any mule but one on Sandy Islant. One man had one. He died. (Man dead not the mule.) Wife sell the mule off the islant."
Lillie: "Hear Wash little girl—jest a child—marry here Sunday gone."
Visitor: "They does marry sixteen, seventeen. Can marry fifteen. I one marry fourteen. He died 'bout three months ago. Died to New York. We wuzn't livin' together when he died. His Mother got a telegram. She ain't but fifty sumpin'. She knows when my Mama and Papa wuz chillun. Turkey? No turkey—but Lord the duck!

"That man gone off and leave me after them two twins come. Sent back money for his Ma to take the chillun to New York to see him. He didn't sick them. He didn't have sense to come back live. Say he was comin' and the same month and very day he say he wuz comin', they bring his body. Bring his dead body. No. I didn't 'foretend the funeral."

SOURCE: *Carrie Pyatt, Sandy Island, S. C., and Lillie Knox, Murrells Inlet, S. C. September 1937.*

Hackless Riley

ACCORDING TO GENEVIEVE CHANDLER, Hackless Riley was born Hekerlez Riley, named after the Greek hero Hercules. Peter Wood in his 1974 book *Black Majority* notes of the name, "One reason that the name *Hercules*—often pronounced and spelled *Hekles*—was applied to strong slaves may well be the fact that *heke* in Sierra Leone, was the Mende noun meaning 'a large wild animal.'"[1] Whether Hackless Riley's name found its origin in the ancient legends of Western culture or in the lexicon of the West African coast, he seems to have had an awesome physical presence. Riley presents himself as an authority on alligators: championing them as a delicacy, offering anecdotes about human encounters with them, and opining about the best way to fight them.

Chandler probably made Riley's acquaintance while he was working as a ditcher for the WPA. Apparently he lived south of Murrells Inlet, near Pawleys Island. He was married to Julia, and the couple had eight children (James, Levi, David, Andrew, Sarah, Aron, Anna, and Hackless Jr.). Riley had at least two grandchildren (David and Margaret Riley). The 1910 census records Riley's age as thirty-five, making him approximately sixty-one in 1936.

Halligator (By Hack)

"Halligator eat good.[2] Yas'm When yinnah say halligator in dese kennel (canal) yuh mek a man puah hongry fer dem bittle. Ef I hab dem steak now, I could puah feas. En dem ration gib yuh strong mussel en strength fer dig dese ditch. Dem halligator bin quare critter.

Born centuries ago in ancient Greece he would have been Hercules. On Waccamaw in the South Carolina low-country, his dark-skinned mother affectionately christened him Herkerlez. That was over half a century ago. Names,

1. Peter H. Wood, *Black Majority: Negroes in Colonial South Carolina from 1670 through the Stono Rebellion* (New York: Knopf, 1974), 183.

2. "Eat good" is a common Gullah inversion meaning "is good to eat."

like much worn garments, change shape. They adopt themselves to the form and character of the wearer. Like this Hekerlez has work down. Been cut short. Fits. To-day to his friends, this strong, black man is Hack.

Were you to meet Hack on a lonesome path your impulse would be to run. Unprepossessing. A big, black ogre. One glance and you are in African jungles. But when you stop and search, you read nothing mean in his countenance. Ignorant, Superstitious. Faithful. Grateful for kindness. And work! Hack eats it up. A ditch-digger. Watch that spade!

Down-full-up-toss!

Down-full-up-toss!

Wound up! Only stopping this regular, rythmical, motion when a stump says "stop" or a live-oak root makes a natural bridge, that must be tackled with an ax. And loves his job. Ambitious. Ambition? To make his ditch as good a ditch as may be ditched. Putting out. The juice flowing. No man in the gang can out-ditch Hack.

He waves a wet bandanna over a sleek brown shoulder from which perspiration flows in rivulets. I am glad the ditch is running in the shade to-day, with the mercury reading 104 out-of the-sun!

And an alligator has been seen in this canal! If possible Hack is working even more zealously since learning this. May be he can dig out that alligator! Fresh steak would make his arrival at home an event. How they could feast! He and the old woman and the children.

"Yas'm. Dem bin quare! Dey fer tek a long ress. Dat critter 'foree fer hab er long sleep. Dem hab warm hole fer house. Dey place wha dey go een bin onder de water lebbel en peoples ain fer rech 'em. Dey ain fer git 'um. En when dey gits een dere, dey hab room mek wid long, flat, mud, shelf bove de ribber lebbel en dere dey ress high en dry. Dey lies dere same ez lawg en sleeps all de cold wedder tru.

"Missus, dem halligator cooter sleep too. En dey fer crawl een dat halligator den en dey climbs on 'foree shelf en dey gits on 'foree back en dar dey stays 'foretwell hot wedder bin git here. En dey tink dey fer hab 'foreer snug bunk.

"Dey wuz man ober we way call Cooter Diber Austun. Dat man could find dem halligator den. En een be cole season 'foree would dive een dat do en tak sack wid 'em tie ter 'foree wais. 'foreE would pick cooter off dat halligator back same lak yuh bin pick dem big black fig off'en dat figs tree. When Cooter Diber poke 'foree hed out dat halligator hole 'foree hab his sack weight down wid puah halligator Cooter. Dem sho mek good soup. Mak nourishment fer chilluns en good bittle fer de ole wha ain hab tooth.

"Dem halligator slow growin. De mammy she lay a bushel ob aig. Dem look same lak fowl aig but dey bin long lak lizzard en snake aig. Hab on'em de hard shell. Not soft lak de turkle aig. En de mammy gator mek ness ob dem rotten lebe in leetle scranch en mud. 'foreE mek ness on de ribber bank er nigh de pond. En 'foree lay aig en kibber dem wid leaf en scranch (little branches) en mud. En 'foree lay mo aig. En 'foree fer kibber dem. En mo aig. En kibber. Dey keep on 'foretwell dey fer lay sixty aig. En some hab lay 200 aig—fix een layer lak dem cake de missus bake fer Chrismus. Aig, mud, scranch. Lak cake icin, nut-clean ter de top 'foretwell all de aig fer lay. Hot sun fer hatch 'em—same lak Missus bator[3] wha hatch de fowl aig. En dem young halligator when dey fust hatch bin bout eight inch long. En de mammy halligator ack same lak duck. 'foreE led 'em ter de water en say, "Dere's yer home." Dem slow growinest ting yuh ebber seen. Tak 'em fifteen year fer mek two, tree foot. Mah ole Pa bin wuk de rice-fiel in 'foree fer kno halligator. 'foreE rassel wid 'em when 'foree fer mend dem bank. En meh pa bin tell me when halligator reech sixteen foot he bin heah long time. 'foreE hab wan hundred (100) year of age when he reech sixteen foot.

Ef yuh goin try fer kill halligator, don git ter 'fore e side. Dem big critter kin trash en trash en trash 'foree tail worser dan flail een de rice-barn een er strong man gras.' Yas'm. Halligator strong critter. En 'foree mek strong meat. 'foreE ain too hard fer kotch. Jess doan let 'em turn side-er way fer yuh. Knock yuh ter pieces. Uh-huh! Fac 'em! Knock 'um! Gin 'em lick on dat knot on 'foree hed. Ax de bes weppin. Lick 'em on de hed. Doan let 'um git chance ter flail yuh wid 'foree tail. Uh-huh!

"You bin heah bout Marcus Nickleson, enty? (ain't you) Dat wan brabe man. 'foreE all de time fer say Plat Eye ner hag ner hant ner ghos' ain fer harm 'em. 'foreE ain fear de dark nohow. En peoples say ,'Mark, yuh trabble dem lonesome road too much. Why ain yuh fer tote flash-lite?" But dat man ain eben ez much ez tote lantun. 'foreE doan bodder wid lightard torch ner nuttin. 'foreE trabble blin'. 'foreE truss gawd. Ain 'foree preacher? Enty?

"Mark wife good sense gal. She walk behin'. She follow de ole man. She ain fer kno dem snake habit. She ain fer kno de ole man safe. She ain fer kno de fuss mans rous'em en de nex fer feel 'foree pang. En when de paat bin dark, she fer beg Marcus,

"Look good, Marcus! Dey bin say pilots en cotton-mouf en rattle-snake tick in dese heah woods. En dey ain no black chicken[4] here fer tie on ter dreen out de pizen ef dem rattler pop yuh on yuh laig.

"En wan nite Mark en Mary start home late from de ribber landing. Ain no one come on de ole Comanche boat but dem two. De moon bin set but dey is light nuff fer Mark ter see 'foree road bin block. En 'foree tink him black dawg. En 'foree say, 'Go on bout yuh bizness.' En when dat critter ain

3. Incubator.

mube, Marcus rais 'foree foot fer kick 'um en 'foree stick 'foree laig een big halligator mouf! Jess lak sayin,

'Halligator, yuh hongry? Hep yuhsef!'

En een less time dan I kin tell'um, dat beas hab 'foree holt en Preacher Marcus wuz down. En ef I hab wife lak Marcus' Mary, I'd fer wash she foots fer er yeah. You hear wha dat oman fer do? Aw rite! Aw rite! Mark bin down on 'foree side en she feel in 'foree pocket en de pocket dat wuz up, hab 'foree knife een 'um. En dat gal fotch 'um out! She blood up. She fightin sperrit rous. She step cross dat halligator. She hab dat open knife een she han. En she hab dat critter onder 'foree fore leg. She jab! She jab! Aw rite! Aw rite! En no hep een hearin distant. En Mary bin desprit. She hab realize de condishun. En she ain fer see good so she feel, en dat gal brabe! She pray fer strenth. En Gawd hep'em. En she rech down. She fix 'um. She wan! Wid wan leetle knife. She fer cut dat halligator troat! 'foreE loose 'foree grass! 'foreE mouf drap! Marcus loose! 'foreE releas!

"Mundy mornin come fust lite, Mary en she Pa come. Dey wan fer see jist how long dat halligator bin. Marcus bin down. 'foreE most fer lose 'foree laig. Dey hab fer fotch de doctor frum Jargetown. So Mary come. She en she Pa. En when dey fin' 'em dat halligator bin ober ten foot long. Gawd troot. Aw rite! Uh-huh!

"Hit bin er dry drout dem time en dat critter bin lebe 'foree dry pond en sarch fer water. 'foreE bin hed fer de Wakmaw ribber.

"Yas'm. Dem critter eat good. Haligator tail eat fine. Fuss I tas 'em I ain fer kno dat halligator 'foretwell I fer finish meh potion. Yuh ain fer lick (can't be overcome) ef yuh rais on dem ration. Good bittle. Yas'm. Marcus' halligator bin good en hongry. Dry Drout.

"When dat critter close 'foree jaw on Marcus Nickleson laig 'foree smile tuh 'foreesef en fer tink 'foree hab good fat caf fer dinner. Dat halligator bellow en Marcus holler. All two bofe bin fer holler. En dat halligator tink him hab good steak But, Missus, Marcus bin de wan fer feas on steak dat day! Um-huh! Yas'm! Stidder halligator feas on Marcus, Marcus feas on halligator! Um-huh! Yas'm!

And as Hack brought his narrative to its happy conclusion his guffaw was repeated by his fellow workmen up and down the ditch. He looked more than ever like a great black ogre. Ghoulish. Unattractive. Not quite human.

A chuckle. A final 'foreAw rite! Aw rite!' A humorous roll of his eyes and the spade was back in harness.

Down- Full- Up- Toss
Down- Full- Up- Toss.

The strong. muscles fed on halligator steak resumed their rythmic routine. Hack revels in his job. Halligator steak. Herculean muscles. Dig ditch. Hack and Hack's spade. Making a scar on the face of Mother Earth. Was the first Hercules happier supporting the heavens?

(Submitted: August 3, 1936)

Sabe Rutledge

Sabe Rutledge was born into slavery at John Tillman's Ark plantation around 1861. His mother was Martha Rutledge. His father, James "Jas" Rutledge, was the driver at the Ark, a position he assumed following in the footsteps of his own father, Roderick Rutledge. Sabe Rutledge had at least three siblings (David, Francis, and Jane). He was married twice, first to a woman named Elizabeth from Pawleys Island and then to Nancy Holmes, Monday Sampson Holmes's sister. Rutledge raised numerous children (Eddie, James, Belle, Peter, Joseph, Mary, Thadeus, Lagrande, Lillie, Mary, Daniel, John, Morris, and Alene).

Rutledge lived and worked at the Ark. As an entrepreneur, landowner, and farmer, Rutledge was a well-respected leader in the African American community. Rutledge's largest enterprise was the fishery he operated at the Ark beach, also know as Floral Beach Fishery. In the fall months he could be found watching the ocean from a small tower, looking for schools of mullet, which appeared as large dark clouds among the waves. When the roe mullet were particularly abundant, the fishery often had an attendant air of festivity. Fish were piled in great heaps on the beach, and people came from up and down the Waccamaw Neck to eat mullet and to get a portion to salt down for winter.

Rutledge owned his own home and farm with some twenty-five acres under cultivation. A piece of land called "the Ridge" that he owned was the highest point between the ocean and the Waccamaw. It was also known locally as the "Sand Ridge." Along with the usual agricultural staples, Rutledge grew upland rice.

Rutledge was a fantastic storyteller; his favorite tales were those of Budder Rabbit. His granddaughter Sadie Bellamy reminisced: "Used to come prop up his feet by the fire. Wanted to finish dinner so we could hear Buh Rabb!" Budder Rabbit stories, told after dinner, were a long-standing family tradition. According to Sabe himself, "How come I know all these Buh Rabbit story, Mudder spin you know. Have the great oak log, iron fire dog. Have we chillun to sit by the fire-place put the light-wood under—blaze up. We four chillun have to pick seed out the cotton. Work till ten o'clock at night and

Sabe Rutledge at his farm, Oak Ridge, with his mule Bessie. *Photograph by Bayard Wootten. North Carolina Collection, University of North Carolina Library at Chapel Hill*

rise early! Mudder and Father tell you story to keep you eye open! Pick out cotton seed be we job every night in winter time—cept Sunday! When we grow bigger, Mudder make one card. One would spin and then Mudder go to knitting. Night time picking these cotton seed out; day time in winter getting wood!"

Rutledge was also literate. His granddaughter Sadie Bellamy remembered his love of reading. He kept a cedar chest filled with his prized possessions: newspaper articles, letters, and other documents. Unfortunately these were either lost or discarded after his death.

Uncle Sabe

"I know the old Doctor[1] and I know he brudder.[2] He brudder Charlie one fine man I tellin' you! My sister DOWN and I take her to Brudder Isaac house there to Brookgreen gate and Doctor Charlie had come home 'forecause his sister sick. He doctor my sister three long weeks. Then she WELL and he figure the bill 'round $70 dollars and he say: 'Sabe, you give me $5 and call it settle.' Yes suh! Doctor brudder Charlie sho a fine man.

1. Ward Flagg.
2. Charles Ebenezer Belin Flagg.

"Fire? You talk Miss Yewton[3] fire? That the time Miss Yewton get loss and they put fire out. Put fire in the woods and it make a clean sweep way down to the Belin's Bay.[4] Some calls it the 'Big Bay.' I'm 77 (Seventy-seven) and never in my recollection and not in my father's[5] time had that Big Bay burn. That the first in memory of man. Here we surround that bay. Tryin' to keep the fire hem up in there. We string fire all 'round the bay and here come the deer! Come outer there SMOKIN'! Big buck they come first. Doe and fawn follow buck. Stop still, doe and fawn stop behind him. Smellin'. He smellin'. Don't NEVER go by what they SEE. It what they SMELL. Depends on they nose altogether. And rabbit! More rabbit come out. And we see Possum and coon have they eye BURN CLEAN OUT. Blind and scorchify crawlin' 'round in the woods.

"I study all kinder study". (When he heard of the woman.)[6] "I couldn't realize it. This same mornin' her Grandson wanter go place they call 'Beaver Dam.' She say 'NO.' And he went and hitch up the two little steers and drove off anyhow. And she miss him. She got oneasy. Look. Didn't find boy. See the cart track. Outcry was make. Nobody could give no recollection. I help search. I know these woods. Twenty years later here they find the carcass. They subscribe it as her. Her tooth. Her buckle. Her button.

"Time come for the two old man[7] to die people nurse them too good. Think they goin' to learn something! First old man have a stroke. Gone. Don't talk. CAN'T talk. Next man go. He don't talk. Disappoint all the people. SOMEBODY had to know something 'bout it. I did know the woods. I know buzzard. Buzzard would give way a thing like that. Was put way mighty conceal. When they DID found it, it right on top of the ground.

"I 'foremember him too good. Come out the woods ridin' a flea-bitten horse. Hail me:

"'Oh, Uncle Sabe! You see the dog and the deer?'

"'I HEAR the dog and SEE the deer!'

"'Look like he hit?'

"'Didn't TOUCH him Cap'n!'

"'He was broad-side to me. I don't see why I didn't!'

"I have to laugh at the Cap'n that day. Morest of the deer run out THAT bay, if they misses them they takes the sea! Deers a SWIMMIN' animil. Gone right on out there two miles and float till he get sea-sick. He can stay out there

3. This woman went missing in the Freewoods. As Sabe Rutledge reports, her remains were found twenty years later.

4. A bay in the Freewoods area.

5. Sabe Rutledge's father was James "Jas" Rutledge.

6. When asked about Miss Yewton's disappearance.

7. Two men were originally suspected of foul play in the disappearance.

three or four hours. Dogs and man got the strand. No hope for the buck. Doe will go out but not stay long like a big old buck. Men see they track in the sand. See they track. No hope for them."

"Did I give you the tale 'bout the turtle and the crow? I had a tale 'bout that you know. Now the turtle he wanter go travelin'. Crow come long one day say they can carry him over to the other pond. Say they can FIX 'FORE-RANGEMENT for carry him. Carry him if he do like they say do.

"Crow come back now brought a stick. Say: 'One of we take one end of the stick; one the other end. You take a holt in the middle and we'll rise. You take the middle but mind, don't open you mouth to say a word.'

"They rise. Come in view of the other pond. The turtle say:

"'MY, that a big pond over yonder!'

"Down he come! Crow tell him: 'You ain't do like we say do! You walk now. We carry you no more.'

"You know the one 'bout Budder Deer and Budder Cooter run the race? Budder Deer and Budder Cooter make a bargain.one time to run a race. Budder deer say he'll beat him three miles. So they make and put up a mile post EVERY MILE. Post put up every mile.

"Old Budder Deer the first one lead out. Budder deer he lead out.

"Old Budder Cooter put one he chillun to every mile post and he old lady to the last one. When Budder Deer come to the first mile post he hail!

"'Hey, Budder Cooter! Whey you is?'

"'Here I is!'

"Next mile post:

"'Hey, Budder Cooter!'

"'Here I is!"

"Keep on like a dat till he reach the last mile post. he hail:

"'Where you is Budder Cooter?' And Budder Cooter wife come crawlin' out:

"'Here I is Budder Deer! Been here till I turn 'round!"

"Missis, you take that ocean there. A mystery to the world. Never still. It make you THINK. When you sittin' on the lookout studyin'. I have time on the 'Lookout' to study. MAN couldn't do THAT. Must be some great place to contain that water till it explore again. It go some where low tide. It don't station and it revolve but we can't preserve it.

"You ought to been there Monday. Catch a sea monkey. You couldn't argue it from a monkey. Curl he little tail up. Move he little head quick like just like a monkey. Brown. Have on little old fuzz just like a goslin'-down on him.

Like a real monekey. He like a monkey I'm tellin' you. Little nubs for feet. Work he little nub. Work it backwards and fowards. Work'em just like they feet. Every thing on earth out there in that sea.—and MORE. Bound to be. 'foreCause there more water than there LAND."

SOURCE: *Uncle Sabe Rutledge*
THE ARK FISHERY
Burgess Post Office, S. C.
Horry County.

Folklore
Uncle Sabe Rutledge

(Testimony given by old man born 1861, The Ark Plantation, Horry County—owned by Mr. John Tillman)

"Fust thing I realize to remember, I nuster cry to go to the old boss—old Massa—for sugar. Massa say:

"'Martha,[8] what Newman (he call me that) crying for?'

Ma say, 'Wanter come to you for sugar!'

"'Bring the boy here, Martha!'

"He gie me sugar.

"Boil salt? Pump! Pump! Pump it! Had a tank. Run from hill to sea. Had a platform similar to wharf. And pump on platform. Fetch good high. Go out there on platform. Force pump. My Grandmother boil salt way after Freedom. We tote water. Tote in pidgin and keeler[9]—make out of cedar and cypress. No 'foreting to crove 'em (groove 'em) compass. Dog-wood and oak rim. Give it a lap. (This was his description, with pantomine, of way pidgin and keelers were made by plantation carpenters)

"My Grandmother had two pots going. Boil all day and all night. Biling. Boil till he ticken (thicken) Cedar paddles stir with. Chillun eat with wooden spoons. Clay pot? Just broken piece. Indian had big camping ground on beach near the Ark. After big blow you can find big piece of pot there. I see Indian. Didn't see wild one; see tame one.

"Indigo? Old man Lashie Tillman nuster plant indigo. Seed lak a flax. Put myrtle seed in with indigo to boil. Gather and boil for the traffic. All the big

8. The Rutledges' owner, John Tillman, refers to Sabe Rutledge's mother as Martha though her true name was Ellen according to Charles Joyner in *Down by the Riverside: A South Carolina Slave Community* (Urbana: University of Illinois Press, 1984), 217. Likewise, Sabe is called Newman. It may be that Ellen and Sabe are basket names. On the other hand, Tillman may have blindly insisted on giving his own names to the slaves he kept.

9. A keeler was a shallow tub used for household purposes.

folkses plant that fore the rice. Rice come in circulation, do way with indigo. Nuster (used to) farm indigo just like we work our corn. Dind't have nothing but ox. And the colored folks—they came next to the ox—Hill keep advancing out. Reckon you wouldn't blieve it, but I ken cummember (Uncle Sabe stutters a bit) when all that beach been cultivate field. Must be nature for sand hill to move. Time most got too fast now for the people to live.

"Storm? Oh my Lord! Flagg Storm? Sea naturally climb right over that hill like it wasn't nothing. Water come to King Road. Reckon it would come further if the wind didn't shift.

"Calls this 'The Ridge.' Why? I first man settle here. Oak Ridge. (It is the highest land between Waccamaw river and the ocean.) Just name it so.

"Member the shipwreck. Two men and lady come to the Ark. Stormy time. Massa take them to town. Old anchor there now. Come a blow you kin see it. Water rise over it high tide.

"Ma tell me bout they had the to-do. Blockade at Inlet. Had 'em out to drill (The Yankees came to shore to drill.) Old man John Tillman lose all he China-a-way! (chinaware.) Every bit of his china and paints (panes of glass) out the window. Yankee gun boat sojer (soldier) to Magnolia to drill. They tack 'em (attacked 'em) to cut 'em off. When Rebs tack 'em, small boats gone back. She had to brace 'em. Shoot dem shell to brace. (Gun boat fired to frighten Rebs who were cutting Yankees off from escape) I hear old man Frank Norris—lived right beyond Vettrill Deas—I hear him (nuster come home to the Ark and trap)—I hear him say lot of 'em bog. (Ella, Agnes and Johnnie Johnson fadder been there) Bomb shell hit the hill and bury them in the sand. Cap "H" had to dig out.

"Old man John Tillman my boss. Sho treat his people good. Don't see why his folks (slaves) went to blockade (tried to escape and join Yankee gunboats). Sho treat his colored folks good. My Grandfather, Rodrick Rutledge, driver from a boy. Time he big nuff to handle it till Freedom.

"Couldn't marry widout consent of boss." (Remark from Uncle Sabe's sister, Mom Jane, who is quite acid. All her information inherited—she Freedom child)

Mom Jane: "Been to devil and come back now!"

(Comparing slavery to the lower regions)

Uncle Sabe—continuing:

"Have sick house; have chillun house." (All in this section tell great tales of the 'chillun house.' Sounds a lot like the nurse houses in Russia to-day. All the babies were in this day nursery in care of the older women, too old for field work.) Corn. Meat—pig, beef, fish—plenty milk." (Some cow 'coffee cow'—that is give just enough milk for the coffee.)

"Any rice?"

Aunt Jane: (interrupting) "Pick you teet (teeth) to find the rice! Great God! Now I can buy my rice!"
Uncle Sabe: "Could plant up-land rice to Ark. (This on coast away from fresh water)

"Ash cake? Meal, salt, water. Not a grease! Not a grease! See Mudder cook it many a hundred day!"
Mom Jane: "Put it in the stove today,—nothing!

Rather have it any day!"
Sabe : "Wrap it in brown paper, mostly. Cows free in woods. Alligator tail good. Snail built up just like a conch (whelk). They eat good. Worms like a conch. Bile conch. Git it out shell. Grind it sausage grinder. Little onion. Black pepper. Rather eat conch than any kind of nourishment out of salt water."
Mom Jane: "Conjur? Wouldn't turn a hucks bread for 'em. (Give a crust.)
Sabe: "What God got lot out for a man he'll get it."

"Flat boat full up (with slaves trying to escape) gone down Waccamaw. Uncle Andrew Aunt the one got he eye shoot out (by patrollers) took 'em to camp on North Island.[10] Never see so much a button and pin in my life! Small-pox in camp. Cap "H" had to leave 'em.
"Captain Ben and Captain Tom fadder—look how he die! Looker the blood!! Looker the people! Looker the blood! His boat call 'The Bull River.' Up and down Pee Dee river. Meet flat! Bore hole in flat and women and chillun go down! Take men off. He COME TO THIS COUNTRY. (Came down from North before Civil War) Them darnish Yankee very percruel. (Peculiar?)

"My Great-grandmother Veenia, pirate captured and took all they money in English war. (Revolution) Dem day Ladies wear bodkin fastened to long gold chain on shoulder—needle in 'em and thimble and ting. Coming down from New York to get away from English. My great grandmother little chillun. Pirate come to her Missus. Take all they money—come cut bodkin off her shoulder. Grandmother ma gone on the boat and twiss herself in Missus' skirt. Pirate put 'em off to Wilmington. Come on down settle to Pitch Landing near Socastee. Keep on till they get to Ark.

"My Great-Grandma Veenia didn't have a teet in her head—one hundred ten years old and could eat hard a bread as any we."

Uncle Sabe Rutledge
Burgess, S. C.—P.O
Horry County
Age 76 (Born 1861)
Ark Plantation.

10. North Island lies south of Debordieu and forms the south bank of North Inlet.

Folklore
Uncle Sabe Rutledge
(Ex-slave Story)

"They call him Rogerick Rutledge for shortness. My Grandpa REAL name Jim. First time I big enough to realect (recollect) him he have on no pants but something built kinder like overall and have a apron. Apron button up here where my overall buckle and can be let down. All been dye with indigo. Have weave shirt—dye with blue indigo boil with myrtle seed. Myrtle seed must-a-did put the color in. Old brogan shoe on he foot. Old beaver hat on he head. Top of crown wear out and I member he have paste-board cover over with cloth and sew in he hat crown. My Grand-mother wear these here gingham cloth call gingham twill.

"Now the chillun! I member I was a big boy grown when I get my first pants. All boy chillun wear a shirt—long down to knee and lower. Have belt round the middle—just like you belt to hold 'em. Chillun have not a shoe! Not a shoe for chillun on us plantation to the Old Ark. First shoe I have, Pa get a cow hide and tan it. And a man name Stalvey make my first pair of shoes. I was way near bout grown. Make the sole out the thickness of the cow hide. Short quarter. No eye—just make the hole. Last! Yes man! Yes man! Yes man! Keep 'em grease! Them shoe never wear out!

"We raise all we get to eat. Hominy, cornbread, peas, potatoes, rice. Morest we plant this here yellow corn. I cry many a day bout that yellow corn! We say, 'Pa, this here yellow corn make hominy look like he got egg cook in 'em; red corn look like hominy cook in red molasses!

"But yellow corn stronger feed! Stronger feed! And Pa know 'em.

"Sunday come go to church in that same blue shirt! Little old pole church—(gone now)—call ' Dick Green Bay Church.' (Named for a local character.) When we go to church before freedom, Mudder and them have to have the ticket.

"Old man John Tilghman at the Ark Plantation have no overseer—have 'Driver". Most folks on Waccamaw have overseer and 'Driver". My Pa been the Ark 'Driver'.

"Old man Zachariah Duncan been the preacher. That the same man build the first 'Heaven Gate' church after freedom. He got drift lumber on the river and on the beach. Flat 'em—make a raft and float 'em over to the hill and the men haul 'em to 'Heaven Gate' with ox. Yes. 'Heaven Gate' built outer pick up lumber.

"Before freedom Parson Glennie—he was piscopal—he would come give us a service once a month on the plantation—so mother said.

"Patches of indigo all through the woods. You know cow eat indigo. Us have too much ox! Have to haul rail all the time keep up the old fence. Woods full up with cow. Cattle loose—free. When you want beef have to hunt for 'em like we hunts deer now. I member some ox I helped broke. Pete, Bill, Jim, David. Faby was a brown. David kinder mouse color. We always have the old ox in the lead going to haul rail. Hitch the young steer on behind. Sometimes they 'give up' and the old ox pull 'em by the neck! Break ox all the time. Fun for us boys—breaking ox. So much of rail to haul!

("You can't tell me bout this pension? Look like to me somebody trying to smother something. Letters come. Cards come. My name on outside alright. Tell me to put my name on cards and hand 'em out to my friends. Say send twenty-five cents. Next time say 'Send thirty-five cents.' He cool off then and another man—Mr. Pope come in. Got two letter from him and he tell me be still till I hear from him again. J. E. Pope. Last blank I got from Mr. Pope he say not to look for more than thiry or thrity-two dollars a month. Say there ain't going to be no two hundred a month.)

"How come I know all these Buh Rabbit story, Mudder spin you know. Have the great oak log, iron fire dog. Have we chillun to sit by the fire-place put the light-wood under—blaze up. We four chillun have to pick seed out the cotton. Work till ten o'clock at night and rise early! Mudder and Father tell you story to keep you eye open! Pick out cotton seed be we job[11] every night in winter time—cept Sunday! When we grow bigger, Mudder make one card. One would spin and then Mudder go to knitting. Night time picking these cotton seed out; day time in winter getting wood!

"Fall—harvest peanut, peas, 'foretater!

"I member all then Buh Rabbit story! Mudder tell 'em and we laugh and wake up! They was one bout Buh Rabbit and Buh Patridge. You know Buh Patridge the onliest one get the best of Buh Rabbit!

"Buh Rabbit bet Buh Patridge (Buh Rabbit think he so sharp you know!) He bet Buh Patridge if he fly off down the road a piece and lit Buh Rabbit can find 'em.—Buh Patridge bet him he can't! So Buh Patridge take off and fly down the road a piece and lit—like a Patridge will do—lit and turn up on he back and rake the leaves over him and kiver (cover) his body all cept he two foots sticking up like stick!

"Now Buh Rabbit come! He hunt and he hunt and he hunt! Couldn't find 'em and he get so hot he take off he coat and hang it on Buh Patridge foots!

"He go on hunting and after while he call out,

11. Before the invention of the cotton gin, seeds had to be removed from harvested cotton by hand.

"' Well I can't find Buh Patridge! Can't find Buh Patridge!'

"And Buh Patridge sing out,

"' Well, Buh Rabbit, here I is! You hang you coat on my feet!

"Buh Rabbit have to pay the bet! (I don't member what the bet was). So Buh Patridge was the onliest one I ever hear bout could get the best of Buh Rabbit!

"When Father and Mudder tell them story we chillun noddin'! Some cackle out and all jump up and go back to picking out cotton seed!

"There is another one bout Buh Bear. They goes out my head. I'll think them Buh Rabbit up fore you come back Missus!'

And Uncle Sabe, who was sitting on the 'LOOK OUT' at the Floral Beach Fishery, continued to let his eyes play all over the sea like searchlights, ready to wave the black flag and march down toward the fishery holding it aloft keeping himself in a line with the fish if fish were sighted. Since way before what he called 'the big war' he and his people have eaten mullet and rice for the three fall months. His home was visited before Uncle Sabe was located and children and grand-children, wife, sister and neighbors were found seated and standing all over the kitchen floor and piazza floor and steps—each one with a generous tin plate of rice and fresh, brown, hot 'spot'—a fish not so valuable in summer but choice in fall and winter. Two hounds and a large cat worked around among the feasters for their well chewed bones.

SOURCE: *Uncle Sabe Rutledge, The Ridge, Burgess, S. C., (Horry County) Born first year of the Civil War.*

(He owns his house and land,—some twenty-five acres under cultivation. This is located on what appears to be a 'height of land' lying between the Waccamaw and the Atlantic. Locally it is known as 'The Sand Ridge.')

John Simmons

Most of the available biographical information concerning John Simmons comes from U.S. Census data. His wife was named Affie, and together they had nine children (Joseph, Larry, Richard, John, Marie, Benjamin, William, Allie, and Mac B). In 1920 he is listed as owning his own home, but in 1930 he appears to be a renter. He is listed as a farm laborer and as a public works laborer. Chandler most likely encountered him in the latter of these two professions, probably working on a WPA ditching crew near her residence.

Murder Reported Poaching

"You know we had a man died Saturday gone! You know? You hear bout that man get kill Emerson place?[1] Then one my cousin died after they delibber the baby. From Monday yesterday till to-day. Missus, I tell you the fact I had on the saddest feeling I ever had from Monday since Satday. Throw reflection on me. From Monday till to-day. I don't know no more bout it than I hear. I didn't know anything bout how accident happen. Maybe kill by rattlesnake? I ain't know. No snake bite. You jest as well come in he own yard and shoot him. Near Emerson line. In he hog crawl.

Simmons kin give you the straightness of it."[2]

Simmons: "He been in the swamp. Hunting the squirrel. And he went a little below the line. The game ward man[3] been out there thirty minutes waiting for 'em. When Albert got up near to 'em, he halt 'em. And he tell to tro (throw) his rifle down. And he laid it down to side of 'em. Tell to consider heself be arrest. Tell 'em go before him in his car. 'Less I kill you!' Albert slow moving, and he shot him—in left side. Albert fell on his right. Call his wife. Second his boy. He (game Ward man) bent rifle twice to tree. He went off. My brother heard the call. Went to Albert house. Ax he wife where is Albert.

1. Arcadia plantation.
2. Lillie Knox is probably the speaker throughout the opening of this interview.
3. Game warden.

Say he went out in back. Say, 'I heard someone call very mournful and a gun shot. Out deah. He went out there and deah he found 'em. Found him lying down on his side. Went back and tell his wife. Albert wuz shot. Brother come up in meantime—in car. He told 'em. Both went in there. Brought him out and take him to town. Take him Doctor. Few minutes after he wuz git there, he wuz die.

John Simmons—about 50
Waverly Mills, S. C.
August 15, 1937.

Reverend Cato Singleton

Born into slavery (ca. 1859) on the Singleton plantation along the banks of the Pee Dee River, Cato Singleton answered to the name "Black Cat." He served as the driver at Richmond Hill plantation from roughly 1880 through 1890, overseeing rice production in its last days on the Waccamaw. He and his wife, Catherine Gary Singleton, had at least nine children (Queen, Abraham, Andrew, Claude, Susan, Cato, Samuel, George, and Viola); they lived at Richmond Hill until roughly 1912. Singleton was a master carpenter. He led the construction of several of the lasting structures on the Waccamaw Neck, employing both traditional mortise-and-tenon construction and, when nails became more readily available, balloon-frame construction. Structures of particular note included Vaux Hall and the Beaty home in Murrells Inlet as well as Gordon Chapel, which was later demolished. His crew also cut shingles from bald cypress in the swamps, which he would load onto boats at Wachesaw landing for sale in Georgetown. Singleton's sons followed their father into carpentry and worked as a family crew. His grandson George Kato Singleton remembered that as they worked they would "roll their hammer and carry a tune with it."

De Flagg Storm
(Rev. Cato speaks).

"Reckon dey calls it dat cause it done wipe out mos ob de Flagg family, Yas'm, Dere's wha dey wuz. Right. Right dere on Magnolia. Magnolia Beach bin turn to islands at high tide. All de mans en omans en lil gal wuz dere too. One lil gal. No'um, Not more dan eight year old. Old Colonel wuz de magistrate en he call a court fer try man who had argumint wib he wife. She git cut up. My ole ooman[1] en me wuz call fer witnesses. Yas'm. Us start bout sundown.

"De court bin ober. Ole ooman en me wuz gwine home. Hab ter ford de end of de salt crick in dem time. Want no shell cause-er-way lak Mr. Huntington done mek. Hab ter do-what-you-do when de tide gone out. no-um, not walkin. Us wuz in ox-cart. De tide ain't run out dat day. Not eben fer

1. Catherine Gary Singleton.

Reverend Cato Singleton. *Photograph by Bayard Wootten. North Carolina Collection, University of North Carolina Library at Chapel Hill*

show de ister rock, ner neither san bar. She is go low nuff fer de mash[2] ter sho he head. When us come ter de ford, she she <u>rushin</u> in. Behin' us cross de san beach, de sea bin lite up.

Miss Jin, he bin lite same lak lantern lite de house. He look same lak fire. Us wuz anxious fer git cross dat ford. Dat sea mek us tink—ob jedgement en hell. He look lak he on fire. En us hit de crick. En de crick bin lite up. Sea and crick bin shine. En us urge us ox. En de tide, she roll in fas. En you know dat bawg place. Us sho taut us hab fer lebe de critter den en ris de shark en wabe. But she pull out. De ole ooman she bin dribe. Yas'm, I prize en push. En us two bofe bin pray. Us call on de Lord en he carry us tru. I kin hear de ole ooman jist lak it wuz yisterday. Us reach de hill en she bin shout,

'Gin Him de praise! Saf at las! Us bin sabe fer dis time! Tank Gawd!'

"Yas'm, it sho wuz bad on de hill,[3] too. De moss wuz flyin frum de trees same lak bird. De win talk en moan same lak human. De Plat Eye bin frequent. Yas'm, en ebery which-er-way de tree snap. De rotton lim he fall all roun. Us bin try fer reach de open groun. Dat big corn-field ub de wilderness plantation min us ob a haben of res. En after too much trabail, us come in soun ob de"Will Go" Dey wan't no church dere den en fer prayer us ud gether at the "Will-go-Lodge.[4]

"De Gospel Train dat wus mostly fer de young fry. But de ole mens en omans hold ter de "Will-Go." De soun ob de prayers bin reach we, when us near nuff ter lose soun ob Gawd's win en wabe. Dey wuz all prayin. Good en bad wuz unite. De woorser de sinner, de stronger dey pray. En bout dat time ole man Nisbit come cross Collinses Crick. He us oldest citizen. He us leader in Saint's Res Church.[5] En, too, he de big boss ob de "Lodge." When he call—us turn out. Ole en young. Yas'm, he hab powerful voice fer man goin on a hundred. En he bin call, "Erf-quake![6] Dis ain't jedgement! Dis erf-quake! People, go down in prayer! Tak wid de good Gawd! Ax him fer speak ter de win en wabe. Ax him fer cam de elements! Beg him say"Peace! Be still!"

Miss Jin, de prayer-meetin bin nite en day while he las. Yas'm, dey doan wait fer call. Dey hants dat "Will-Go Lodge." En de prayin bin done. En de young men inspire. Dey preach, dey testify, dey pleads wid Gawd. Dey gal, dey shouts. Dey bin shout "twill de flo gib way. Dey doan cook. Dey doan eat.

2. Marsh.

3. Richmond Hill plantation.

4. The meeting place for the Will-Go Society, located on the Old River Road (see pp. 34–35, n. 72).

5. An antebellum church. The name is probably incorrect and/or of Genevieve Chandler's manufacturing.

6. The earthquake of 1886.

Dey doan drink. Dey doan crabe no bittle. De sperrit hole em up. De sinner, he fall in trance. Dey lie same lak dead human. Dey has to be tote off after de element bin calm down. Dat rebribal bin las, too. It las long time. Dey ain no drinkin ner neither hawg steal fer nigh on six months. Ober to de iland? How dey fares? Lord, Missus, de house done bin wash out ter sea. Fust de wabe lick in an he tak out ole Miss, en de Cap'n,[7] he cry,

"Miss Georgie[8] gone! I gone, too." En he turn loose he holt! He leggo de bed post what anker him down. En de big wabe roll out de deep. En de lik out de cap'n. En de doctor.[9] Him bin young den. He see him mudder float right en he pa follow. De storm lick em out. An when de wabe wash him close de beach cedar, he grab he holt. Dem beach cedars bin sent from Gawd ter sabe de doctor. Him bin sabe fer tender us cullud people all dese year. Dere he hol. Der wabes try to loose em, but he truss Gawd en grip en grip he holt en tighten he grass. He look up en Mom Adeline[10] bin floatin by, en de doctor grab he holt en he raise he voice bove de element,

'Hold on, Mom Adeline! Hold on! En mom Adeline hol on, and Gawd speak! He call de waters! He talk wid de win! He call em back! He wheel em! Yas'm, de doctor bin testify ef Gawd didn't speak, ef Gawd had er let her run—he race, de ocean an ribber would er meet. She bin shake hand wid de Waccamaw.[11] But dat ain't He plan. He call em back. De wabe obey. De swell rollout. De water go back ter de deep. En de doctor hear him moan en complain. Doctor say him talk lak man. He resis. But Gawd hab He way. En ez he trun back he hear Him say,

' I done mah wuk!
I done mah wuk!
I done mah wuk!
I done mah wuk!'

He groan en he resis. But Gawd tell em,

'Go back!' En he go.

Der peoples on de hill? Dey tuk de woods en de make a run fer higher groun. O, Yas'm. Much corpse hin lie in de dead mash de dead. Cow bin res in de libe oak. De carcass bin hang high. De buzzard bin feas. En de good

7. Arthur Belin Flagg.

8. Georgianna Flagg, wife of Arthur Belin Flagg and mother of Ward Flagg.

9. Dr. Ward Flagg.

10. Mom Adeline was a former Flagg slave whom Ward Flagg saved during the hurricane.

11. The Flagg storm flooded the Waccamaw Neck. As a result, the river and the ocean met.

doctor, en he uncle[12] who bin sabe in de Hermitage spen all dey time en sabings fer hep de distress. De white folk ter town, de fear de plague. Dey wusn't no Red Cross dem time. No'um. En de Rev. Ca'lina[13] he volunteer. He say: 'I hear de call! I go to my distress brethren!' En de white folks, dey bear de spence. He bury dem what drownded. He impress. He see how Gawd turn de sea loose. He inspire. He lif up. When he preach, you two years wide open! You hang on he ebery word. Gawd put de word in he mouf. He exhort same lak Isiah. He splains Gawd's jedgement on Jerusalem. He preach de prophet Daniel.

'Serve not other Gawds ner worship dat golden image. Neither eat ner drink ter offen. Let dem git us pulse ter eat en water fer drink.' He talk jedgement. He warn de sinner. He bin mak use ob de reberlation. He tell embout Mount Seir. He say, 'Son ob man! Set your face 'foregainst Seir en prophecy 'foregainst it! Thus saith the Lord, Gawd. Behold, Oh, Mount Seir. I am against thee! and I shill stretch out my hand 'foregainst thee, en I shill mek thee mos desolate. I will lay thy city waste, thou shalt be desolate. En thou shill know that I am de Lord, Gawd. En his mountain shill be fill wid slain mens. In thy hills en all thy ribbers, shill be slain human. De sea shill swallow dem up, en thou shill know I am de Lawd. When de whole earth do rejoice thou shill be desolate. Oh, Mount Seir! En thou shalt know I am de Lord!

He preach Reberlation and judgment. He trabbeled from Genesis ter Reberlation. He go de whole course. He tell 'em.

He hair on he head bin white lak wool en white ez snow. En he eye bin a flame of fire. En he feet lak dey burned in furnace. En he voice lak de soun ob many waters. En he open de six seal.[14] En lo! dere wuz great erf-quake. De sun wuz black. En de moon wuz blood. En de sea bin lit up. En mountain en iland en sea done move out'en dey place. I will give ebery man cording ter he wuk. I see yer wuk. You is not hot, neither cold. You is luke-warm. I shill spue dem out'em my mouf in de sea, en de sea his-sef shill know I am de Lord Gawd Jehovah!'

En all de people tak notis. En Rev. Ca'line bin wuk day en nite. En he wuz belled. He sho wuz. On ebery tongue. He done rite de song en teach us fer sing'em.

And once seen and heard one could never lose this picture from his mental gallery.

12. Allard Belin Flagg Sr.
13. Albert Carolina.
14. References to the book of Revelation.

The quite sooty black man, the wrinkled old preacher, grey hair, celluloid collar and all, bent over his milkin-stick,[15] both hands caressing it—sittin there on his coolin bench[16] seeing himself painting what he saw for me.

'Kin I sing'em? I mos fergit'em.

And the plaintive, wailing quaver was one with the soughing of the pines:-

'De win so high
He blow so hard
We just doan know what fer do.
Den we recognize in it de wonderful power o' Gawd.
Two hundred body
Come floatin by.
We ain't know jes what fer do.
Den we recognize in it de wonderful power o' Gawd.
Two hundred body
Come floatin by.
We ain't know
Jes what fer do.
Den we recognize in it,
De wonderful power o'Gawd.[17]

15. Cato Singleton's cane, also used to drive the cow for milking.

16. Usually the cooling bench was used for laying out the dead.

17. A spiritual Genevieve Chandler believed to have been written about the Flagg storm. More likely, it originated in Beaufort, South Carolina, where far more people were killed by an earlier hurricane.

Claude Singleton

Claude Singleton was one of Rev. Cato Singleton and Catherine Gary Singleton's sons. He was born at Richmond Hill in 1893. Claude Singleton had at least eight siblings (Queen, Abraham, Andrew, Susan, Cato, Samuel, George, and Viola). He was a literate carpenter, working in the lumber mills at the time of the 1930 census. To hear him tell it, Claude Singleton had his share of tough luck. A heavy drinker by his own confession, disfigured in a fight, and deceived by his wife, Florence, Mr. Singleton was struggling at the time Genevieve Chandler interviewed him. Nonetheless his tone was hopeful, and he seemed to think, despite his physical scars, that past misfortune could be overcome if not completely forgotten.

(Verbatim Conversation)

Claude Singleton: (Not quite sober.)

"I say, 'Somebody knock me!' "

It was a white man. He raise me fifteen years. I take 'em in the creek. I learn 'em how to fish and oyster. October fifteenth he call me. 'Please, Claude help me push my car.' I was drinking in the day of that time. I have a quarter. Boy have a quarter. All we have. I say, 'Only thing to do is mortgage us necktie!' Then I say, 'I already mortgage my knife.' And when I say I already mortgage my knife he say, 'I going fight' I say, 'I got to tief!' And the white man say, 'Give Claude a pint of liquor. Give Claude a pint!'

We gone on to Rooster[1] house. That man lay hand on my shirt. I say,

'Do, Cap'n must not to tear my shirt!'

When I know myself, that white man standing there and say,

'Claude don't know me!' And he take a brick and knock me in my face. Ruin me like this for life. Have to let my jaw go.

"Twenty-one or eighteen days of July I marry my wife. Want to do the best I can. I skin little bit of cash. Went to a white man. Bought a acre of land. My Daddy[2] give me two acres.

1. Basket name for Ben Horry.
2. Rev. Cato Singleton.

"Time come I find out my wife think a whole lot of J——. She think more of him than she do of me. I works. Makes $10. a week. Picks swimps[3] and thing and earns three in tip. Found my wife in way she could not be own self.[4] She say.

'Oh, Claudie, I faid you gun!'

I go to the Revents. He say, 'Now Claude, you sold you gun it be all right!'

Time gone. I caught her doing a night ride with J——. She say,

'Claude, don't kill me!'

I going marry soon. Another woman. Want her to let me alone. That woman fool me. You read 20th. and 18th. St. Luke, 'Somebody in world make a great mistake!.'

Yes. Find her and J—— in automobile. Holding hands. Girl raise on Pee Dee—by the white doctor. Wouldn't thought he'd a treat me like that! Tell 'em 'You want J—— and J—— want you, take 'em!

Probated Judge told me to Marion I got a right to get another wife! Andrew and Fred Poinsett, Secretary and Leader in us church, gone to her and she say she don't want me no more.

Doctor say he got to give me shot. Wasn't able to raise money to make 'em. I miss three shot now. Doctor tell me not to well 'em too quick." (Referring to broken jaw.)

"That frizzle?[5] When a frizzle cry out at the back door DON'T COME OUT! They was root people and a ting call hippertize. Man give you a bottle and you drink 'em—Can't keep you husband!

SOURCE: *Claude Singleton—About 40. August 1937. Murrell's Inlet, S.C.*

3. Shrimp.

4. Claude Singleton is suggesting that his wife became pregnant with another man's child.

5. A frizzle chicken has ruffled feathers and is purported to bring good luck. Their condition is explained as resulting from having come out of the egg backwards. A frizzle chicken is featured prominently in the Genevieve Chandler's story "O, Precious."

George Kato Singleton

George Kato Singleton was the son of George Parker Singleton and Sarah Sanders Singleton. His father was the youngest of the Reverend Cato Singleton's sons. George Kato Singleton is a unique subject within this body of work for several reasons. He is the youngest of Chandler's subjects contained in this work—aged nine and ten at the time of the interviews—and his knack for storytelling is remarkable for one so young. Due to his longevity, Singleton was able to participate in this work again some fifty-five years later when the editors of the present volume began their initial fieldwork.

Singleton left the Waccamaw Neck only a few years after being interviewed by Chandler, and he returned only occasionally to visit family. In the 1990s, after a distinguished career in the military, Singleton moved back to Murrells Inlet. His memory of late 1930s Murrells Inlet and its inhabitants was as vivid as anyone's in 1993. Unlike other informants who had spent their entire life in the area and had seen the changes come and go through the years, Singleton remembered the Murrells Inlet of his youth as though it were frozen in time. His memories of the area and of the "old livers" strongly influenced this volume's sense of the place and its people.

Tar-baby
(A version of JOEL CHANDLER HARRIS' famous tar-baby)

"They wuz a rabbit and a Billy goat. Dey dry land now." (time of great drought). All the animal ain't have no water. Didn't know how to git water. So the Billy goat ask the rabbit, 'Buh Rabbit! Whey you gettin all you water frum? We can't get no water!'

Buh Rabbit tell 'em: 'Oh, man I wake up soon in duh mornin' and git my jew![1]'

Duh Billy goat tell 'em: 'No, man! We try dat! We don't git no water!'

Buh Rabbit tell 'em: 'You ain't quick nouf!' (Yinnah won't be quick nouf!') (Buh Rabbit have a well dig. Didn't want none to know! Billy goat watch 'em that night an Buh Rabbit gone down to he well just a whistl-ering. Billy goat

1. Dew.

gone tell all the animal. And they set a tar-baby. Make a PRETTY tar-baby! Set 'em close to Buh Rabbit well. Buh Rabbit gone down that mornin' and see the tar-baby.)

"Hey, oh deah, Pretty Gal!

Tar baby ain't say nuttin.

"You better talk wid me! Oh, if I slap you one time wid my right hand, I broke you jaw!

Tar-baby ain't say nuttin and he right hand stick!

"If I slap you wid my left hand one time I slap you face one sided! I slap a gal wid my left hand one time and I have to pay twenty-five dollars fuh 'em."

Tar-baby ain't say nuttin' and he left hand stick!

'If I kick you wid this foot, I buss you belly open!'

After he done kick 'em wid he foot, dat right foot stick!

"Oh, I wouldn't want to kick you wid my left foot! I don't know what wouldn't become of you! If I kick you wid my left foot—Oh, Gal, I ain't know what he done for you!'

And all two both he foots stick!

"'Well, I know one thing! I got a belly! I ain't wanter butt you wid my bell tall—tall ' I got a belly here. I butt you my belly I buss you open!'

He butt 'em wid he belly. Dat stick!

'Well I got a head here and a teet!

'Oh, I got a head! If I butt you wid dis head and bite you wid dis teet, you don't do nuttin' but die!'

He knock 'em wid he head and he bite 'em wid he teet and all dat stick!

He stop. Can't do nuttin' now.

Billy goat come. All duh animal come. Tell Buh Rabbit,

'Oh! Have we got you now! How come you tellin' we you gittin' water off duh jew and now you to you well?'

And the Billy goat and all the animal take Buh Rabbit frum the tar-baby and carry him home and tell 'em: 'We carry you home now and we don't know what we do wid you!'

And dat all I know—."

Cato Singleton[2]
Age—9 (Fourth grade)
Murrells Inlet, S. C.

Buh Rabbit and Buh Guinea

"They once was a rabbit and a guinea. They love to work together,—Buh Rabbit and Buh Guinea. One day they meet a cow. So they tief the cow and

2. Kato Singleton spells his name with a *K* rather than a *C*.

kill her and left her there. Have all the entrail done clean. Then Buh Rabbit say,

"'Oh, Buh Guinea! See that red fire yonder? Go get a piece of that fire and we'll cook a piece this cow and eat her!' And Buh Rabbit show Buh Guinea the red sun.

"Buh Guinea fly and fly. Buh Guinea fly a day and a night 'fore he can get to the sun and then he couldn't get there. So he turn back. When he get back didn't seen the cow. But he seen Buh Rabbit. Buh Rabbit say,

"' I went off in the bush just now and wink my eye and I come back all the cow done sink in the ground. Ain't nuttin' but the tail out! Now you and me can pull the tail and get the cow! (Buh Rabbit had carry all the meat and give it to his kin animal—all the animal kin to him.)

"So they pull and they pull. Buh Rabbit he pull and Buh Guinea he pull and the tail pop off! Then Buh Rabbit say,

"' Less us dig! '

"And they dig and they dig and they dig and they dig till they come to water! And they didn't find the cow! So Buh Guinea he say,

"'I hongry! Better roast this tail and eat cause I hongry!'

"So Buh Guinea roast the tail and eat a piece and fall back and say he dead—

"Then Buh Rabbit think that meat must a-been pizen. And he ain't want all his kin animal to pizen so Buh Rabbit run round and fetch all the meat back where he was.

"When Buh Rabbit bring all the meat back where he was Buh Guinea pitch up and say,

"' Buh Rabbit, you fool Buh Patridge, but you not fool me! We gwine share this meat even! '

"And Buh Guinea jump up and share it out even and started home. And Buh Rabbit pick up the share and start home.

"The man what own the cow see 'em. Start to shoot them. Drop they meat in the bushes and run! Man gone. They come back, get they meat—gone on home.

"So Buh Guinea catch up with Buh Rabbit.

"Step on the tin

"Tinny wouldn't bend

"That the way

"My story end!"

"Where you get that story Cato?"

Erline:[3] "Bubba[4] just study them up 'forecause he got nothin' to do!"

"What you do, Erline?"

Erline: "I mind the baby. Bubba pump the water. Daddy get the wood. Mama just does the work in the house."

SOURCE: *Cato Singleton—Age 11, Erline Singleton—Age 10*
Murrells Inlet, S. C.

3. Erline Singleton.
4. Brother, meaning Kato Singleton Jr.

Boss Skinner

Little is known about Boss Skinner's origin or his relatives. Chandler reports that he lived in Conway and was at least eighty, meaning he was a former slave.

Uncle Boss Meets the Bank Robbers.
By Uncle Boss Skinner

"I was comin' down to my home, you know, over Yauhannah Bridge.[1] The tow-road turns off and I was comin' to the bridge to Mr. Bowman where he was fishin'. Understand me now? He have a daughter work for Mr. Don Richardson I jump out the road! Car comin' down that tow-road toward me careerin'! The driver took the pine sapling thicket. I said to myself: 'Well I 'foreblive I'll go!' Then I see a one seat car comin' the same direction. I say: 'That a whiskey car. I goin' tell Sheriff!'

"When I hit the bridge there Bowman daughter talkin' to her father. I not wantin' to cut 'forecross while white people talkin'. She tellin' her Papa 'bout a Bank Robbery. She sayin' they had the blue Dodge number. I say:

"'You got the blue Dodge number but you ain't got the one seat number. Mr. Bowman, I can tell you where your blue Dodge but I can't tell you where your single car. Three head in'em, Missis. Broke top down like a buggy top. The blue Dodge is settin' off in a pine sapling thicket. It's just as considerable (confortable?) as a chicken in a egg shell! Three hundred steps from the road. I been think that a whiskey car. I protect it were the Sheriff in that back car, Had on a vest. Didn't had on no coat. Broke car top down. I didn't know 'bout the robbin'. I caught the licent Norse Calina and caught the other Souse Calina. That blue Dodge been a run! That blue Dodge in that road like rabbit. Had to go on through my settlement. They said it had make a roll of dust

1. A bridge over the Pee Dee River near Plantersville, South Carolina—between Conway, South Carolina, and Georgetown, South Carolina.

high as that shed! It could hunt the road! I didn't have no expission[2] it were the car broke in Boss Bank! Lemme make you good understandin'. I steps over here and he just see me and he whip this-a-way. I stood there and watch five minutes. I say 'Howdy do, Cap'n.' They gone RIGHT ON TOWARD CHERAW![3]

"They ain't but two nations of Skinner in Georgetown County. Bright Skinner is head of the white nation and DICK Skinner the head of the colored nation."

SOURCE: *Uncle Skinner*
Over 80
Conway, S. C.

About Eagles and Hags

"They be come if they see you up that tree. Lays two eggs; stays in nest two months. I tell you that stone something extry. Have it REDRESS. Loses strength. I've never had one I see a man had it. I see him went in Bank. They couldn't keep him in jail! Once I been on a job with a man name Tom Collins. Spend all his maney but 80cts. Had that lodestone. Come out all his money in his pocket.

"You gone to that nest here the eagle comin' like car beenc comin'. They pick you eyes out. Fight you.

"Hag? Not Jimmy John. They take a gourd. Cut out like a neck. and if they like you they goes at night and sucks you blood and puts it in the gourd. And let it get cold and cut it up like jelly and eat it on bread.

"I know a man have two daughter. All was settin' up to the fire. Have company. Old Pa was noddin'. Company man was a hag. That hag jump on that gal right there. Pa get he ax and was goin' to kill'em.

"I tell you how to get rid of'em. Take a bottle that long and full it half full of chamber lye and take a English stopper new bran cambric needle and when the hag come and you partner holler out SHOVE IT IN and call you partner. He's a gone gobbler. (The hag!) Next mornin' early somebody come to borry a match or a seasonin' of salt or a seasonin' of sugar. The FIRST PERSON come next mornin' may have a SACK of salt at home. They comin' for a PINT. (point) The one tryin' to catch the hag sleep on the front of the bed and let this somebody (The one worried by hags) sleep on the back.

2. Suspicion.

3. Cheraw, South Carolina; named for the Native Americans who formerly occupied the district.

"If you don't turn'em way they'll swell yp big as a barrel. Sho as buck is to a bay, dat's DEM. Willin' to bet you my throat. If they ever taken to like you they'll drindle way or they'll swell up big like a barrell and BUST.

"Take a broom and turn it 'forecross you front door., (To turn hag away) or a handful of pot salt. You can do now turn horse heel up—one over every window and door."

SOURCE: *Boss Skinner (colored)*
Age 80 plus.
Conway S. C.
July 1938

Ella Small

Ella Small was born at Wachesaw plantation in one of the old slave cabins along what was known as Wachesaw Street. She was one of eight children. The two siblings Ella Small mentions by name are her sister Diana and her brother Frank Wallace. Small's maternal grandparents were Prince and Caline Drayton. Ella married Footie Small in her mother's home. According to the 1910 U.S. Census, they had seven children, five of whom survived (Rosa, Perry, Primus, Richard, and George). In the data from 1920, a second daughter (Rachel) is listed. She may have been a later addition to the household rather than a "blood relation."[1] Small worked as what the 1910 census terms a "washerwoman." In 1920 she was employed as a farm laborer. Genevieve Chandler guessed Ella Small's age to be about seventy at the time of their conversation. According to the 1900 census, which places Ella Small's birth in 1873, Small was closer to sixty-four. Small's one interview with Genevieve Chandler is a testament to her sense of loss after bearing and raising many children throughout her youth, losing some in their infancy to illness and losing others to migration and the responsibilities of adulthood.

Mom Ella Small:(Entering kitchen)

"Good morning coz![2] How you feeling darling?"

Mom Ella: "Have to come see Missus! Been a long time since my eye ress (rest) on 'em. Didn't get to Dave[3] funeral. Couldn't get good sense bout the funeral."

Lillie: "I meet Uncle Quinvy. He saw lots 'foreo trouble. Deth come. That trouble. I say, 'Yes. Got to look for deth.' And he say, 'You must not understand. I lost Dave.' And I say, 'You lost your onliest one then! All the other son-in-law jess (just) a name! Dave smart! Smart boy!' John have to left every

1. For more on kinship models among former slaves and their descendants, see pages xxxvi–xxxvii.

2. Ella Small.

3. Dave Knox.

morning six o'clock — for his job. Beulah (Dave's widow)[4] live good ways from Harriett. She in the house with those seven head and don't know when she going down. Going to come back with her Pa at night. Lessie been with Dave when he dead. Say he left good testimony. He had a large funeral—most as much out the door as in the church."

Mom Ella: (On being asked her age)

"Tell you truth, Missus, can't tell you! They stroyed my age."

Lillie: (To Mom Ella's daughter who has been deserted by a city man who stayed in community just long enough to marry, then passed on)

"When you hear from James?"

Carrie:[5] "Don't hear from James. Don't care tho, Miss Lillie!"

Mom Ella: (On being asked how her youngest daughter's baby was—girl not married—too young to marry)

"Baby dead. Dead with rheumonia. Dead. Didn't want in there but atter he there—! Dead in leven months."

Lillie: "Lost mine too, Mom Ella! My little Silas Warren Harding[6] too pretty to stay here. Gone to the kingdom. Good Master say fore the Devil out do him. 'He take the baby from the mother breast.' He kingdom must full."

"Mom Ella, how many boys you have?"

Mom Ella: "George—tuh Baltimore; Primus—dey up tuh Reginnia; Perry—tuh Mullins."[7]

Lillie: "Uncle boy come home from North. Ben to Heaven Gate Sunday. Uncle didn't know he own boy! Oldest boy by his fuss (first) wife. Bet Levi and Miller come popping up here some 'foreo these days! Uncle Say, 'Lillie, who this boy here?' Uncle marry four times."

Mom Ella: "Those boys lost. Ride by coz Andrew house. Ax way to you Uncle George. Then Andrew correct him (direct him). Say, 'Take this same River road on to the old store. Then turn and keep the straight road on till you have to turn again!' Say they get letter from Lutella. Lutella say she marry—marry tuh New York. Say she going come home. Can't come home after you marry! Can't move as you choose. Smart! Clean! All of us has a weakness you know! Ain't but one perfect man—that God! Lutella? Her girls sho grow! So far from school. Rain so much. Way back in that swamp didnt get too much 'foreo schooling last year. Aint right for no child to let young-uns stay in her parents house till they big nuff to pick up a turn 'foreo wood

4. Beulah Knox.
5. Ella Small's daughter.
6. Silas Warren Harding Knox, Lillie Knox's son.
7. George Small, Primus Small, and Perry Small—all sons of Emma Small.

and then take 'em out. Don't see how she can do Uncle that way. Them chillun jess (just) big nuff to pick cotton![8]

"Can't believe all you hear! All object—(opposite)—other way. Course they in good hand. Miss Patient good to 'em all right—but they Grandaddy have all the trouble wid dem."

"Paul wife staying home. Help Aunt Wisa wid Uncle. Carrie there too but she got too much chillun to do much. Uncle up now; got he pants on."

Aunt Ella: (Answering question as to her age when married)

"They tell me when I marry Footie[9] I wuz fifteen—but I don't blive it! I blive I been older than that! Born to Wachesaw street. My ma have the eight head—Diana been one; Frank Wallace and me brudder and sister. Don't know all they name.

"Run way? Wouldn't run way with man no-how! Marry in my Maw house! Salem preacher! Baptist—Alex Wilson—Eleanor Grand-pa. When Footie dead my boy George in he three months.

"My Grand-Ma been Caline Drayton. Caline and Prince Drayton live right there to Hermitage. Took Diana.

"When that cunjur been throw at the obersheer (overseer) and hit my brudder Frank, I run two three times a day from Watsaw here to Doctor Flagg. Time git way, Missus! Great ting to have friend come to you refuge in sickness—great ting!

"We had started to the crick and when I hear the car I wheel back. I yeddy dem say, 'I spect to find you home Carrie!' Say the man got a Drug (Drug Store) in town."

"Your boys help you, Mom Ella?"

Mom Ella: "Duh trut! (truth) Wouldn't story on dem! Boys hep (help me)! Marry ones help and them aint marry help!

"Man say, 'Mom Ella, aint got nothing but fifteen cent. Get you bacco!'

"He leave wid seven head. Say, 'Work till I dead.' Wife gone. Nother woman come in there. Look'm hard at his chillun! Aint marry! Bella come there! (Eddie oldest son marry Richard Miles daughter!) He aint marry yet! He say, 'Yes. Hard to find a settle mind now! Can't make no good settle wife now! Big picture show to-night! She wanter go! Got to have a party dress and new slipper.' I say, 'Change will come!'"

Lillie: "Change gwine come!"

8. Emma Small is decrying Lutella's desire to reclaim the children she left to be raised by her parents. It is Emma Small's contention that those who raise children should benefit from the children's labor once they reach laboring age.

9. Footie Small.

Mom Ella: "Oh, yes! Change will come! Good wife fuss (first) time. Faid (afraid) won't get good one next time!"
Lillie: "That the truth!"
Mom Ella: "Yes he is! Yes he is!
Lillie: "Saw Aunt Jane to funeral. Say she got nothing to worry her now cept study bout get in His kingdom."
Mom Ella: "You boy big now?"
Lillie: "Leven. Twelve come sixteenth September."
Mom Ella: "Yes? Yes? Child favor he Paw. Sho is! Coz, I gone! Yeddy?"

Conversation in kitchen between: Mom Ella Small
(Age got stroyed—nearing 70
Murrells Inlet, S. C.
Lillie Knox—age 35
Murrells Inlet, S.C.
July 6th, 1937

Lewis Small

Lewis Small gave Genevieve Chandler one trickster tale. He was approximately thirty years old at the time of the interview, and he lived in the Freewoods community of Burgess. U.S. Census data suggests Small was the youngest son of Toby Small of Richmond Hill plantation and Annie Glover Small of the Burgess area. By 1910 Lewis Small's mother, Annie (then aged forty-five), had had fifteen children, thirteen of whom were still living. Lewis's siblings Julia, Jane, Rosa, Henry, Patrick, Benjamin, Walter, and Louis were still living at their parents' home at the time. The entire Small family was listed as literate. Lewis attended school and in 1930 was a farm laborer.

Buh Rabbit and Buh Wolfe

Visitor: "Lewis, you know any stories bout animals or beasts?"
Lewis: "I member one bout Buh Rabbit and Buh Wolfe and the 'butter tree.' They had a 'butter tree' together. Buh Rabbit say, (You see they been down there hoeing rice). Buh Rabbit getting hongry (hungry) and he look up and say,

'Buh Wolfe, I'm going to the house now! My wife called.

Buh Wolfe say, 'all right, Buh Rabbit. Buh Rabbit gone on, slipped to the 'butter tree' and eat butter! Full up on butter he come slipping back through the bushes. Grab he hoe. Gone to hoeing and tell Buh Wolfe,

'My wife got a young 'foreun at home and she want me to give it name!'

Buh Wolfe say, 'what you name it, Buh Rabbit?' Buh Rabbit tell 'em, 'JEST (just) START!'

They hoe on the rice till Buh Rabbit get ready to eat again. He raise his head and say,

'My wife call! I got some more chillun home to name!' He gone slipping back to that 'Butter tree' and full up! Come back Buh Wolfe say,

'Buh Rabbit, what name you give that young 'foreun?' Buh Rabbit say, 'MOST HALF!' And gone to hoeing rice. He hoe and he hoe till just thinking bout that 'butter tree' have him pure hongry. So he stretch up, drop he hoe and say,

'Buh Wolfe, my wife call. Must want me to name another chillun!' Gone slipping through the gallberry[1] bushes and get full up at the 'butter tree' and come back. Buh Wolfe ask 'em,

'What you name it now Buh Rabbit?'

'MOST GONE!' And Buh Rabbit gone to hoeing like he wanter make up for lost time. Just fore noon Buh Rabbit feel too hongry! So he lean on he hoe like he listening and then he throw down the hoe and say,

'Buh Wolfe, got to go name that last chillun!' He gone so fast he come back he most lost wind. Buh Wolfe ax,

'What you name the last one in the litter, Buh Rabbit?'

'ALL GONE!' Buh Rabbit tell 'em and gone to hoeing and hoe till Buh Wolfe call,

'NOON! Time to go eat us butter, Buh Rabbit!' Buh Rabbit make him answer,

'Yes suh! Let's go get us some butter!'

When they come to the 'butter tree' all the butter gone! Buh Rabbit look at Buh Wolfe and say like he been mad, 'Buh Wolfe, you eat all the butter!' (Buh Rabbit sharp all right!)

Buh Wolfe tell 'em, 'NO, Buh Rabbit! This the first I seen us 'butter tree' since yesterday!' So then Buh Rabbit say,

'Tell you what less do! (let's) Less lay down in the sun and the one who eat the butter, when the sun shine hot and melt it, it'll run out he mouth!' Buh Wolfe aint have nothing to say but, 'All right!'

Sun warm. Get hot. Buh Wolfe so tired. Gone to sleep. Buh Rabbit take he pay and take butter off HE OWN mouth and wipe it on Buh Wolfe mouth! Then, when Buh Wolfe wake up he call out, 'Buh Wolfe, you know you eat the butter cause it on you mouth!'

Given by Lewis Small—age about 30
Free Woods, Burgess, S. C.
(Horry County)
(When this was read to Zackie Knox he said, "Yes. That's one. I heard that story all my life but that ain't the way I hear it! The way I hear it had such a disgracful ending that I didn't tell you that one. But Lewis fix it up all right!")

1. The gallberry is a bitter, wild berry that looks like a huckleberry.

Liza Brown Small

According to the 1900 U.S. Census, Liza Small was born in approximately 1867. She claimed, however, to have been "born the very day freedom was declared," which most like refers to Robert E. Lee's surrender to Ulysses S. Grant on April 9, 1865, but which could also conceivably be taken to refer to the Emancipation Proclamation, issued January 1, 1863. She was born on Sandy Island but raised on the mainland at Turkey Hill plantation, also the home of Welcome Bees. At fifteen, as Small describes it, she "marry out the Brown to the Small." Her husband was Samuel Small, a farmer, to whom she had been married forty-nine years at the time of the 1930 U.S. Census. The couple had three children (John, Samuel Jr., and Eliza Jane). This interview features an example of Genevieve Chandler using the name of her brother, Dr. Dick Willcox, as a guarantee of her own trustworthiness. Like so many of Chandler's informants, Small is interested in supernatural phenomena, although she initially seems a bit reluctant to admit it. Ultimately she reveals her nightly struggle with hags and her belief that a hag may have caused the death of one of her grandsons during infancy.

Visit with Aunt Liza Small
(Went to see the 'old bush')

The path led through an abandoned field overgrown with nut-grass to Aunt Liza's door. The cabin was more pretentious[1] than the usual one found there to-day; strongly built, two rooms across the front, kitchen across the back with the usual front and back piazzas found in the South. Aunt Liza watched my approach, and even after I had spoken entered the porch, and seated myself in the swinging seat, she kept an "on guard" position at the door, braced against the jamb. Her attitude was not hostile but a bit chilly until, inadvertently, in the attempt to start conversation, she mentioned her 'high

1. Liza Small's cabin was an antebellum slave cabin. By "pretentious," Genevieve Chandler intends to suggest the cabin is more attractive and well built than most cabins built during Reconstruction.

blood'[2] and her doctor, and she learned he was my relative.[3] No longer was Aunt Liza chilly or luke-warm; she was my friend. I could be trusted. She had been to my house; she had seen my parents; we were old friends.

"Aunt Liza, did the old captain leave any Grans?"

Liza: "I know he raise chillun for he wife. Now great gran, I ain't know. This he two wife."

"Aunt Liza, who were you before you married Uncle Sam?"

Liza: "I marry out the Brown to the Small."

"Where were you born?"

Liza: "Yeddy den! 'You hear me then!) I ain't born nowhere. Not Turkey Hill Plantation. I raise Turkey Hill. Born Sandy Islant (Island). When that been in civilization, truth to tell, I was (she said 'wuz!') too young! The old man been here he could straighten you. He was born to Oaks; he was Oaks labor." (Meaning he was a slave on Governor Allston's Plantation, The Oaks.)

"When I know myself, I started to Turkey (Turkey Hill Plantation). If you want to get that straight, see the old bush. (Meaning her husband—the old man). Some big white house been to the water front. To the Nanny Gully? Oatland church? Oatland and Turkey (Turkey) Hill jine on plantation." (Oatland and Turkey Hill adjoined).

"Aunt Liza, when they moved the old Oatland church, the pillars were full of bees and honey."

Liza: "Bee ever did stay in that church."

"Uncle Welcome[4] helped build Oatland church for the missionary, old Parson Belin[5], and Uncle Welcome is one hundred and four years old."

Liza: "Old man Welcome have a good memorandum, old as he is. These big church that flourish lak-a-now, didn't been. Turkey Hill, holding meeting in the Class room."

"Where were you married?"

Liza: "Class Room. That been in. White veil over you face; wreath round you head. Cease you racket! (Last three words addressed to the cur who had begun to bark louder than his size and condition led you to expect he could). Just good for bark round the house. Ain't so much good. Sick so."

Her high cheek bones and ginger-bread complexion and taciturn manner led me to ask,

"Aunt Liza, haven't you some Indian blood?"

2. High blood pressure.
3. Dr. Dick Willcox, Genevieve Chandler's brother.
4. Welcome Bees.
5. Rev. James L. Belin.

Thinking of how she was suffering from the high blood, her reply was, "Missus, what kind of sick that been?"

"Aunt Liza, I see you have all the doors and windows painted sky blue. Why?"

Liza: "Board tak 'em."[6]

"Why blue?"

Liza: "Old man buy 'em."

"I always heard blue would keep the hag out."

Liza: (Roused—excited) "That ain't so! That ain't so! I prove that. Sometimes they ride me till I can't keep up next day!"

Her grandson arriving in the rain from school, I asked:

"How many grans?"

Liza: "That boy name Harry. Girl behind him Annie, girl, Lucy. She stop breed."

"You used to have such pretty corn on this hill."

Liza: "Ain't have nothing to pay hire hand. Charge you same price they charge white man."

"When will I find Uncle Sam home?"

Liza: "If he ain't got arrant, he here every day in week."

"See you have peanuts coming up. When is the best time to plant peanuts?"

Liza: "On the full man or dark night any one. Miss the moon, ketch the wind." (If you fail to plant on the full moon, wait, for a time when the wind is not 'East.')

Liza: "Peanuts? Plant full—on the full man or dark night—anyone."

"Aunt Liza, wasn't the old man Bees[7] married twice?"

Liza: "Emma Brown he second. Took sick suddenly. Didn't last too long."

Liza: "Young head say old one have no sense. I say they keep everything together till the young head come! I'm a poorly person to remember.

6. Here Liza Small seems to be evading the question. She may be uncomfortable discussing superstition. Painting door and window frames sky blue is said by some to repel supernatural forces.

7. Welcome Bees.

"I ain't been in the world in the shaking[8] but I had a sister born bout that time. Born in Brookgreen street, Charlotte Reese baby born. Aunt Babbit born fore Freedom. Her baby born in the shake.

"My daughter (Aunt Liza said 'Datter') have the two boy. Lose one. I low (allow) hag (must have) musser lock he jaw. Couldn't suck."

"Aunt Liza, if the old man can't work and you are sick too, how do you manage?"

Liza: "Just how this chile mother feed this chile, we eat through."

Suddenly the grand-child who had just come in from school, called, "Grand-ma! Grand-ma!"

We ran behind the house. The cur dog was eating a little biddy while the mother hen was leading the surviving ones to safety.

Liza: "Name of God! Gimme a rope! Beat him over dem. (Meaning 'Beat the dog over the dead chicken.') Fowl been sick! Eat up sick one; start on well one! Going to put a taste on him this evening (Aunt Liza said, 'Diss seben-ing') he didn't have! Fetch a rope! Dat what I feed you for? You ketch the good one and eat 'em? Get a taste? I'll give 'em a taste he ain't have!"

Aunt Liza Small—age 70 to 72
Parkersville, S. C.—P. O.
Waverly Mills, S. C.
(Born the very day Freedom was declared.)

8. The earthquake of 1886. There is an apparent inconsistency in Liza Small's claim to have been born after the earthquake and in Genevieve Chandler's claim, at the end of the interview, that Liza Small was born "the very day Freedom was declared."

Rebecca Washington

No U.S. Census data is available for Rebecca Washington. The only record we have of her personal struggles comes in the following recollection of her "to-do-ment," which was probably narrated to Chandler by Lillie Knox. As Chandler indicates at the end of this interview, Washington lived in the Burgess area of Horry County. She had a daughter named Anna, and at the time of the interviews, Washington's husband Jake had recently moved to Conway to work in a lumber mill. He had stolen her life savings just before his departure. She doubted she would ever see Jake or her money again.

Jake and Becca "To-do-ment"[1]

"Becca 'foresplode on me this mornin.[2] Pour all her trouble out on me, there to the road! Becca say:

"'I work for fifty cent a day. Save a quarter. Work in the field. Hoe work. Work to the wash pot. Long time ago meat and thing cheaper than they is now. You could get a big piece o' meat for ten cents. I have just me one and the girl[3] to fee—till I marry with Jake! And I save little by little till I have over a hundred dollar hide away when I marry with Jake. Had it hide away in the top of the loft in a glass fruit jar—so the rat couldn't make way with it. Marry with Jake when his wife gone back to her people—and I ain't stop work ain't stop savin'. Puttin' money in another fruit jar.

Here a month ago Jake come in and say:

"I have a job to the Big Mill, Con-o-way. You going with me?"

I say:

"Yeah!" Nothin' else to say. "I'll go anywhere you can get a job".

1. "To-do-ment" is a way of referring to Jake and Becca's "story," probably a corruption of "predicament."

2. Lillie Knox is probably speaking.

3. Rebecca Washington's daughter, Anna.

"'Here Gabe come with he car. Jake pile all he thing in, and tell me he'd send when he get a house and get settle. Great God! Don't want to lay my eye on that boy no more. Wouldn't surprise me Jake got three or four wife.

"'The fortune teller tell Jake where the money was. He went to the Fortune Teller to the fair and give her his last dollar! Told Jake I have it in the loft. Way up in the dark loft corner hide back under some old rags in a glass jar! Had to go through a little hole in the house top to get to it. Was some strip nail up side the wall so's you could climb up there—most good as a ladder. When Jake come in the house the first he axed 'bout that and I tell him that was to climb up on case o' fire.

"'Last fall all that downpour come and it rain three week. Jake was needin' boot. Here he had to wade to get out the yard. —so flat in them Savannah—and he keep on sayin', if he had just had a boot what all he could do. So one day when he had waded off in his old shoe I climbed up in the loft and open one them money jar and sent to Conway by the MAIL MAN and when Jake come home that night there was the boot. Then all that rainy time nobody couldn't get out to do no work—and here I was feedin' all three—that girl and me and Jake. And he knowed I wasn't feedin' the whole bunch on promise. He knowed I wasn't askin' no man for credrick. So he was askin' me "Where you get money for new boot? Where all these rations come from? How you buy boots and pants and thing for the house?" I tell him "For rainy day you have to have a little lay by! Here rain! Rain! Rain! Can't do no work—no kind!" Then he ax to borry $1. Ain't know I have money! You can't let people know you have money! They'll kill you for it! And here now! All what hurt me he CARRY MY MONEY and leave me FLAT! If I was took down now no money—Why I even put Jake in the INSURANCE! Ever two weeks thirty cent—so if he die he can be put away right."

Becca Washington Burgess, S. C.

Lill: "Miss Rina come by. I say:

"'Grand mama, come in and wait on me a minute. I'll go long to church with you.'

"She say. 'Lill, child, how you tell me you just have to comb your hair? How big you going to grow no how?' She gone on to talk and tell me 'bout Jake and Becca 'To-Do-Ment.'

"Miss Rina say when Jake come home he'd just make up something and blame it on her. He say he going off to work. Becca ain't mind. She too tired of so much news and quarrelment. And she know she have money hide away if push come to shove. She say Becca tell her 'Miss Rina, I can't say nuttin'. Can't tell no-body nuttin. They go back and tell Jake. And tell him more'n what I say! I got a chance to married Jake. I already have one girl—Anna. I marry. Think if I marry I'll shut these mouth up. And it HOT TAR WATER for me! I have Anna twelve years 'fore I marry Jake! I tell Becca:

"'Anna your CROSS! That your CROSS!'[4] Becca say:

"'Wait, let me talk! Times was I couldn't say my prayers. There Cousin Quinn. That old man act so pious like. Big leader in the church.

"I tell her. Oh but Becca, you mustn't 'foreblive nothin' you hear and half you see.' She say,

"'If Jake just hadn't carry off all my money with him I wouldn't hate it so. All these years 'fore I see Jake I work these two hand—"

Becca Washington—Burgess, S. C.

4. The stigma of being born out of wedlock, carried by Anna, is also a constant impediment to her mother, Rebecca Washington.

Lula White

Lula White was forty years old when she was interviewed by Genevieve Chandler. She was from Florence, South Carolina. U.S. Census data for Florence County suggests that she was the daughter of Sharpee and Susan Pervis. She had two sons (Cleveland and Edward). In 1920 she lived with her husband, Sam White, despite having previously appeared in the 1910 census as a widow, living with her parents. It is unclear what this incongruity in the record signifies. White may have come to Murrells Inlet as a domestic employee in the summer of 1938. Chandler's notation at the end of White's first interview, "Care of Mrs. Walter Harper," is probably a reference to White's employer. The content of all three interviews featuring Lula White refers in some way to religion, and she displays a religious enthusiasm that is rarely foregrounded by Chandler's informants.

Love Feast Meetin' to Town

Lula: "Oh, that church to town the most beautifulest niggerish church I been in yet! The biggest sounding post I have sawn YET. 'bout sixteen choirs in they costume. Most beautiful thing. Here they coomin' marchin' singin' and keepin' time. And that church full! Full! Our church had 'FORENUSTER been full up like that but since that piccolo come out and that NUMBER—that gamblin' number! I tell dem that I hits a number every Saturday. That MY pay day. I hits a number.

"After the choirs come a little girl gone up in the pulpit and repeat the ten commandment.

"And then a woman read 'bout a 'Messigish for God!"

Lillie: "Lula, you something like myself. You can go to church and come back and tell somebody something. Some don't so much as carry the text home."

Lula: "This woman say, 'Mary was a messigish! Mary was a messigish for God!'"

Lillie: "You learn any new song?"

Lula: "Yes, gal! I hear a song sing! They say it just come in! The preacher preach and a woman prayer. She make a prayer. She thank God the blood still runnin' warm in her vein. She thank him the sun rise; she thank him for the settin' sun. And then a slim little woman TOO light on her feet was comin' down the aisle way. She sing as she come and little white fan in her hand and here she keepin' time. Keepin' time! That was a song. And I catch it ALL. I goin' ring that Song nex Sunday in love feast to Mount Zion if THAT BUS RUN and take me home!

1. Oh, is JOY in that city (Oh YES!)
   Oh, is Joy in that city (Oh YES!)
   Oh John, just seal up the book!
   Fold up the paper, John!
   John don't you write no more!

2. There's HOPE in that city (Oh, YES!)
   There's hope in that city, (Oh yes!)
   Oh John, just seal up the book!
   Fold up the paper John!
   John don't you write no more!

3. There's love in that city (Oh, yes!)
   There's love in that city, (Oh yes)
   Oh John, just seal up the book!
   Fold up the paper John!
   John don't you write no more!

4. I'm goin' walk down in that city (Oh yes!)
   I'm goin' walk down in that city, (Oh yes!)
   ('Here she come walkin' down the aisle way headin' to the pulpit!)
   Little white fan keepin' time!
   Oh John, just seal up the book!
   Fold up the paper John!
   John don't you write no more.
5. Oh, I'm goin' shout in that city etc.

6. Preacher, you goin' preach in that city (Oh yes)
(Here she singin' to the preacher. Actin' accordin' to the wordiments)."

SOURCE: *Lula White (colored)*
Age 40 years.
August 20th., 1938
Florence, S. C.
Care Mrs. Walter Harper

Satan, I'll Tear Your Kingdom Down!

Lula: "There's a Leader in our church name King Field. He does love that song and ever time they pitch it it carry me back to old Lady Patty Wine settin' up."

"It were 'bout a couple of years ago. A lady had died by the name of old lady Patty Wine. You know how these things is done. She live by herself. House fallin' down.

Lillie: "Yeah!"

Lula: "Old house shacky!"

Lillie: "Yeah!"

Lula: "And they was all there singin'. House full up singin'. Had the house pure rockin'!

"Satan, I'll tear your kingdom down!
Satan, I'll tear your kingdom down!
Well I heard a voice from Heaven say
Old Satan your kingdom must come down!

And just as they work up and singin' 'Your kingdom must come down' here the floor give way and the end fall and the roof start to comin' down on'em and here they gone! Right out the window! Out the door puntop (upon top) one another. And one man sing out: 'It comin' down! Satan kingdom comin' down!"

SOURCE: *Lula White—age 40—August 22nd., 1958.*
Florence, S. C.

Vision

Lula: "I 'foremember my Ma never touch 'forenothin' to eat on FRIDAY. Not even to so much as DRINK till noon gone! Steal away to fence cornder and pray. Gone to her seekin' ground! Never eat a meal Friday. When her time come she say: 'I feel death but it nothin' but a cool breeze.' She tellin' another old lady she sawn a vision.

"One time I sawn a vision. I been too sick. Everybody give me up. The doctor medicine mis the pain and I worse stead o' better. And a white lady with a white fan in her hand come walkin' in my room. A white face. Wave that fan slow like over me and sing:

"Go run Mary and Martha, go tell my Lord!
Go, run Mary and Martha, go tell my Lord!
Go, run Mary and Martha, go tell my Lord!
True believer find a home at last!

"I ax'em ALL can't they see that white lady and I tell Ma that song I say: 'Can't you hear that lady singin''? 'And then my Ma pitch it and they ring that song! And I feel too good! I get up and WALK! Ma say that a old time song."

SOURCE: *Lula White—Age 40*
August 22., 1938
Florence, S. C.

Willis Williams

Willis Williams was born in Rock Creek, North Carolina. As a young boy and presumably as an adolescent, Williams worked as a house servant or "house boy," as he put it, for a white family with the Williams surname. During the Civil War a party of Federal soldiers raided the Williams plantation for livestock and supplies. They also took young Willis Williams with them. He followed his northern liberators to Fayetteville, North Carolina: "Kept me with 'em till Johnson surrendered in Raleigh,—then they kept me in Goldsboro and took me on to Petersburg." While with the Union army, Williams worked as a cattle herder. After the war he was put on a train back to Fayetteville. Upon his return Williams labored as a turpentine hand. He also worked in a lumber mill. According to Williams's own report, he was married at least five times. Jinny Lind, Mary Dickson, and Caressa Pyatt are the only three wives, however, whom Williams mentions by name in the interviews. The 1920 census reports Williams (age seventy) married to Caressa (age sixty-five) with one adopted son, Henry Allen (age one). Williams was then working in a sawmill. At the time of his interview with Genevieve Chandler, Williams lived in Conway, South Carolina, thirty miles north of Murrells Inlet. Chandler estimated Williams's age to be between eighty-nine and ninety, and the 1920 census agrees with this estimate.

Ex-slave Story
Uncle Willis Williams

"When wuz I born? Born in August. When I wuz born been August. I wuz a man grown pulling boxes, (turpentine boxes) when the shake wuz.[1] I know the very night the shake come—on a Wednesday night. I wuz on door step loosing my shoe string. There wuz more religion then than they is now . Praying and prayer meeting for a month. Everybody tend meeting.

"I been with the Yankee. I kin tell you bout the Yankee. They come home there to Rock Creek when the war wuz breaking up and carried me to Fayetteville. (N.C.) Kept me with 'em till Johnson surrendered in Raleigh,—then

1. The earthquake of 1886.

they kept me in Goldsboro and took me on to Petersburg.[2] After everything over they give me free transportation back home. Free on train back to Fayeteville. They had put all the Yankee clothes on me,—all the blue shirt, blue coat and bumps on the shoulder,—and when they start me home took all the Yankee clothes way from me. Put gray clothes on me and sent me back. I member they took me up in a way-up-yonder building—to Richmond. Couldn't tell you the depth of it. Man on the ground looked like boy.

"The man I belonged to been Mass John A. Williams. (Born on the Cape Fear.) I goes by Mass John name—Williams. His sons been John, James, Charlie, Wallis, William, James. James come home from army sick. Had the mumps; thirty days furlough.

"Member when the Yankees come. Been Sunday morning. Ride up to the gate on horses. Old Boss happened to come out and walk to the lot. I happened to be at gate. They took his watch out his pocket, his pistol—had it girded to him—and took all he whiskey and catch chickens and guinea and take them all. Then they gone in the lot and took two breeding mares and hitch them in wagon and loaded wagon full o' corn. Then they took the two carriage horses and hitched to carriage, and gone to smoke-house, and fill that carriage full of all Mass John sides of meat and ham and shoulders. I been following and watching to see what all they going to take, and a soldier looked at me and say,

"'Come on little Nigger! Wanter go?'

"And I done like another fool! I rode off behind the two brood mares, on the corn, and where they rested that night, I rested right there.

"It was mighty cold up there. I suffered a heap in the cold fore I got back home. They give me a horse,—saddled and bridled,—and a little bayonet gun. Put me on that horse to drive cattle. Tell me to take all I see. Didn't except nobody cattle.[3] Night come put 'em in pasture put 'em in anybody field—on the oats, rye, wheat.

"Sometimes rain sho fall.—Had to tend that bunch of cattle rain or no rain. Didn't kill one beef and stop! (Kill) FOUR beeves a day. Go out git the hog and kill 'em. Skin 'em. Didn't scald 'em and clean 'em like we do.[4] Just eat the ham. Rest throw way. Gone to Wilmington, Fayetteville, Rockfish and Beaver Creek.

2. Petersburg, Virginia.

3. Here a double negative is intended to indicate a positive. The Union soldiers told Willis Williams to take cattle and to exercise no discretion in doing so.

4. Willis Williams was troubled by the recklessness with which the Union troops plundered livestock: hurriedly slaughtering them, taking only the choicest cuts, and abandoning the rest.

"General Sherman? Has I hear bout him? I SEEN him! He had a big name but he warn't such a big man; he was a little spare made man. I member now when I seed him the last time. He had two matched horses going down to Petersburg. Six guards riding by the side of his turnout. Oh my God, what clothes he had on! He was dressed down in finest uniform.

"When I leave the Yankee they give me $35.00 in money. I been so fool had never seen no green back. Throwed it away eating crackers and peanuts. And I bought some brogan shoes. If I'd a helt on to that, I'd a been some body today.

"I members it was Sunday morning that General Johnson throwed up his hand at Raleigh. Done with the war!

"Before Freedom I have a good enough time. Just lay round the house and wait on my boss. When Freedom come and I did have to get out and work it most kill me!

"After Freedom my mother wash for family to Beaver Creek. And after Freedom my father went to working on shares. Old Mass John called 'em up and tell 'em,

"' You free, Asa. You free, Lewis. You free, Handy. You free, Wash. You can do as you please. You have to fadge for yourself now.'

"Mass John Williams had four hundred slaves. He was a man had the colored people. He didn't work all on his own plantation. He'd hire out his people to work turpentine.—Put 'em out for so much a year. He'd give 'em blanket, suit, coat, pants. First of the year come, Boss would collect wages for all he hire out.

"That there my second wife. You know how a man is. How many wife I had? Two or three. Lemme see! (Looking at present wife) You is one! You the last one! Fust one been Jinny Lind. Next one been Mary Dickson. And Caressa Pyatt been one! And there been another one! I forgot that woman name! Got it in my mouth and can't call it! I'll call the name of them others I take up with in a little while! One was Caline; one was Tissue; (Tisha?) I take them a little while and if they didn't do to suit me, I put 'em out! Some I didn't stay with long nuff to find out they name! Jinny Lind sister was Tissue. Jinny Lind gone, try her sister. Just a 'make out.' If they didn't do to suit me, I'd give 'em the devil and put 'em out

"Don't know bout beating woman. Some say that bout,

'Woman, dog, cypress knee
More you beat'em the better they be!'

"But some woman, the more you beat 'em the worse the devil gets in 'em. Get so they won't 'GEE' nor 'HAW.'

"When I was house boy for old Mass John, waiting on white people, that was the best and easiest time I ever had. Ever Satdy drive Mass John to Fayetteville. Ever Satdy they'd think that store belong to me! I'd eat lumps of brown sugar out the barrel, candy, crackers. Did as I please then; NOW do as I kin!

"'Ways of woman and ways of snake deeper than the sea!' I take that to mean—mighty few can tell by the trail of a snake whether its coming or going—

"I hear story bout the rabbit and the fox—all them old things—Some times my mind franzy. Been break up too much! Break two ribs to the lumber mill. Jump out a cart one day and run a ten penny nail through my foot. That lay me up two months. Some mean people ketch me up by that tree yonder with a car and that lay me up sixty-five days. They pick me up for dead that time. All that make my mind get franzy sometimes. Come and go—Come and go."

SOURCE: *Uncle Willis Williams. Age, 89 to 90 years old. Conway, S. C. (Horry County).*

Martha Wright

ACCORDING TO THE 1910 CENSUS, Martha Wright was born in 1880. This information is also corroborated by another interview (not contained in this volume). Therein she reveals that her mother died when she, Martha, was "just a little thing." According to this same interview, Wright's mother was still alive during the earthquake of 1886. Martha Wright had at least two children, one of whom predeceased her. The 1910 census reports her as living with Andrew Wright; her relationship to him is listed as "second cousin," and both are listed as widowed. Ten years later the census reports that Martha is Andrew's wife and that they have a son Rufus (age nine). They are also living in close proximity to the Willcoxes, including an unwed Genevieve Chandler, age twenty-eight and a schoolteacher. By 1930 Martha Wright is again listed as widowed. At that time her occupation is recorded as "hoe hand."

Aunt Martha's Hant!

"Man, yes man! Hant was there in Tom Pryor house all right! Wouldn't give me no rest tall, tall! Turrible. Come in there and have more noise on that stove than enough. The noise sound peculious. He always come in the KITCHEN part. He stays in the kitchen part to the stove and cut up all he craziness in there. Don't come to the BIG half of the house and talk. Have more rattle up on that stove! Sound like he goin' BREAK UP the stove! Francis Gadsden and Georgie sit up with me more night than one for company me.

"They tell me when Tom Pryor die they been a time in that house. He die a wicked death. Something terrible. They tell me thay have to take and tie him on the bed! I could-a been there when he die. Everybody ELSE been there. But I didn't choose to been there. If I'd a -seen how he die, I'd not a stay in that house.

"One night sumptin' talk to me in my room there from 'forehind my room door. I got mad and I say: 'I want you to talk again so's I can hear you!' Didn't NO MORE! Not THAT night. I been 'foretween sleep and wake. And he talk kinder funny TWO time. And I say: 'I want you to talk ONE MORE TIME so I can catch the voice!' Never had such a thing happen to me in my life before since

I born from my Ma! Everbody tell me: 'Martha, you got a MIND to stay THERE!'

"I gone two time to Parkersville[1] and tell the root doctor GOOD how that hant done me and he say: 'Auntie, tell you, you wuk (work) diss here! Wuk you KNEE!' (He mean say my 'pray.')

"And I gone home and done some prayin'. If I didn't a -have the Lord in me, he would -a kill me! No rest. Catch a little nap by DAYlight! Set by fire and nod so! Catch a little nap. Go in my bed can't sleep.

"Missis, can you take me a picture like you take for Cun Annie? I want my guerrotype[2] take 'fore I go off again.

"Shoe? Have to cut it. Man didn't give me no number seven. He give me a number EIGHT and I have to cut that shoe. Have a BURNER[3] on my foot."

SOURCE: *Aunt Martha Wright*
Murrells Inlet, S. C. 1938.
Age 70 plus.

1. Parkersville, South Carolina.
2. Daguerreotype.
3. Bunion.

Appendix A
Memo from Mabel Montgomery

October 1, 1937

Negro Dialect

Memorandum

TO: Workers Who Prepare Ex-Slave Stories
FROM: Miss Mabel Montgomery
SUBJECT: Ex-Slave Stories

I have recently spent several days reading a large number of ex-slave stories before the copy goes to our Washington office. I found in them a wonderful amount of human interest, ranging all the way from stark tragedy to carefree humor, including considerable hemelt wisdom. I only wish that each of you could have read, as I did, these stories coming from many sections of the State, and revel, as I also did, in the information give. I enjoyed them so much that I wish to congratulate the workers on the excellent material which most of them have contributed and to urge attention to several details in preparing further stories.

You of course realize that the aim of the ex-slave narratives is to preserve a picture of life at that period. Unless secured now, the sources of material—the old Negroes themselves—will not be available much longer, after these ancient men and women have passed away. It is encouraging to remember that through the ex-slave interviews, we are aiding in the preservation of history for future generations. The contemplated volume will probably contain many verbatim stories; others will be summarized and the main facts given.

Please follow carefully the instructions, originating in Washington, which have been sent you from time to time, particularly those relating to modified dialect. Some of you have transgressed in this regard. Consult the list of tabooed words and do not use them. Our desire is for easy reading and a complicated dialect does not produce that result. We who live in the south are so accustomed to Negro speech that we forget how difficult it is to be understood by people from other sections.

Please further follow the Washington suggestion that Negroes be visited several times in order to establish a friendly relation, some material being secured at each visit, and the whole woven into a consecutive story.

With assurance of my warm personal interest, even though I do not find time to tell you of it very often, I am

Cordially,
(Miss) Mabel Montgomery
State Director Writers' Project

Negro Dialect Suggestions

DO NOT WRITE

Ah for I
Baid for bed
Bawn for born
Capper for caper
Coase for Cose
Com' for come
Cose for 'cause
Cot for caught
Daid for dead
Do for dough
Ebry ev'ry for every
Fiuh for fiah for fiah
Fuh for for
Gi' for give
Gwainter for gwinter (going to)
Hawd for hard
Hit for it
Ifn for iffen (iff)
J'in for jine
Kin' for kind
Mah for my
Moster for marster or massa
Muh for my
Ole, ol' for old
Oman for woman
Othuh for other
Ovah for over
Poar for poor or po'
Poe for po'
Ouh for our
Ret, right for right
Snaik for snake
Sowd for sword
Stow for store
Teh for tell
Tho't for thought
Tuh for to
Twon't for thought
Undah for under
Useter, useta for used to
Utha for other
Uz or uv or o' for of
Waggin for wagon
Wha for whar (where)
Whi for white
Wuz for was
Yo' for you
Yondah for yonder

Approved Dialect Expressions.

ain't
and
arranged
after
against
bout'
b'long
behin'
befo'

'cause
chillun
Carryin'
'cept
'cused
'cussing
countin'
'cided
'clare

didn't
de
daddy
dese
dis
dere
dat

done
'dopt
diggin'
eat
ever
fightin'
for
fust
gotta
git

gwine
goin'
gonna
gimme
gal
hoss
have to
hold

if
I's
just

knowed
kinda
killed

lak
livin'
lightenin'
'liminated
Master
Mistress
more
Mammy
'member
'nough
'nother
Nigh

onliest
of
petitions

rather
strength

settin'
'spects
sumpin'
'sponsibility
'scuse
sho'
see

seein'
set
stickin'
took
them
'tween
then
truth
told
to
they
tryin'
themselves
toted
'tachment
vittels
wasn't
we'd
wid
what
workin'

yonder
yes'm
zackly

Appendix B
Memo from Folklore Department

Folklore

Field workers must learn to survey their towns and districts with fresh eyes. Very often they fail to recognize that lore and customs known to them al, their lives are novel and interesting to people from other parts of the country. The Sales Mondays of South Carolina county seats are as strange to the eastern Pennsylvanians as are the costumes of the Pennsylvania Mennonites to South Carolinians.

INSTRUCTIONS FOR FIELD WORKERS

1. Workers will record carefully exact sources of information, giving names of persons interviewed, their ages and addresses, and the dates of such interviews. Source bibliographies, if any have been used, must also be recorded. Obviously, leading citizens of towns are not always the best sources for lore. Rather an old cook, washerwoman, gardener or other retainer of some long-established family should be contacted. Oldest residents, close to the soil, who, because circumstances have cut them off from education and progressive enlightenment, are repositories for local lore, legend and superstition, would be ideal sources for the field worker. Of course, cultured citizens in various localities may be interested in the lore and customs of their regions and may have done local research for their own amusement or purposes. These, if ascertained and properly approached by the field worker, would cooperate and be valuable consultants.

2. For accuracy, it is always well to get more than one account from different sources of the same legend.

3. Workers must write down on the spot the information exactly as given by consultant or narrator. They must not attempt to correct, embroider or interpret according to their own conclusion. Under no circumstances must homely phrasing, idiom or pronunciation be altered. Wherever possible the precise language of the narrator should be used.

4. If more than one version of the legend, lore or custom exists, each version should be recorded. If there is a factual basis for the legend or custom, it, and the source of information, should be noted. When the origin of a custom is known, it must be given. Eg: The dress of the Pennsylvania Amish. The Amish first began shaving their mistaches, retaining their luxuriant beards, using hooks instead of buttons on their clothes when they were opposing civil authority in Switzerland where buttons and mustaches were then being taxed. These customs yet prevail.

5. Field workers will also record unusual dialect, slang, pronunciations, place names, local expressions.

Eg. 'culch,' 'finnicky,' 'kerhoot,' 'mosey,' 'faze,' 'caint,' 'axes,' (for asked); Tombstone (Arizona), 'The Road to Ruin (name of a Texas saloon), doggie (motherless calf), etc.

6. Peculiar epitaphs in old cemeteries should be recorded. Note with these name of person memorialized, dates, name of cemetery and place.

Appendix C
Memo from Henry Alsberg

Memorandum

June 9, 1937

TO: STATE DIRECTORS OF THE FEDERAL WRITERS' PROJECT
FROM: Henry G. Alsberg, Director

In connection with the stories of ex-slaves, please send in to this office copies of State, county, or city laws affecting the conduct of slaves, free Negroes, overseers, patrollers, or any person or custom affecting the institution of slavery. It will, of course, not be necessary to send more than one copy of the laws that were common throughout the state, although any special law passed by a particular city would constitute worthwhile material.

In addition, we should like to have you collect and send in copies of any laws or accounts of any established customs relating to the admission to your State of bodies of slaves from Africa or other sections, the escape of slaves, etc. Also, we should like to see copies of advertisements of sales of slaves, published offers of rewards for fugitive slaves, copies of transfers of slaves by will or otherwise, records of freeing of slaves, etc. Public records of very particular interest regarding any transaction involving slaves should be photostated and copies furnished to the Washington office.

Furthermore, contemporary accounts of any noteworthy occurrences among the Negroes during slavery days or the Reconstruction period should be copied, if taken from contemporary newspapers. If such records have been published in books, a reference to the source would be sufficient. We have been receiving a large number of extremely interesting stories of ex-slaves. The historic background of the institution of slavery, which should be disclosed with the information we are now requesting, will be very helpful in the execution of the plans we have in mind.

Copies sent to:

Alabama	Georgia	Maryland	North Carolina	Tennessee
Arkansas	Kentucky	Mississippi	Oklahoma	Texas
Florida	Louisiana	Missouri	South Carolina	Virginia
				West Virginia
				Ohio
				Kansas

Appendix D
Second Memo from Henry Alsberg

Memorandum

July 30, 1937

TO: STATE DIRECTORS OF THE FEDERAL WRITERS' PROJECT
FROM: Henry G. Alsberg, Director

The following general suggestions are being sent to all the States where there are ex-slaves still living. They will not apply *in toto* to your State as they represent general conclusions reached after reading the mass of ex-slave material already submitted. However, they will, I hope, prove helpful as an indication, along broad lines, of what we want.

General Suggestions:

1. Instead of attempting to interview a large number of ex-slaves the workers should now concentrate on one or two of the more interesting and intelligent people, revisiting them, establishing friendly relations, and drawing tem out over a period of time.

2. The specific questions suggested to be asked of the slaves should be only a basis, a beginning. The talk should run to all subjects, and the interviewer should take care to seize upon the information already given, and stories already told, and from them derive other questions.

3. The interviewer should take the greatest care not to influence the point of view of the informant, and not to let his own opinion on the subject of slavery become obvious. Shuld the ex-slave, however, give only one side of the picture, the interviewer should suggest that there were other circumstances, and ask questions about them.

4. We suggest that each state choose one or two of their most successful ex-slave interviewers and have them take down some stories *word* for *word.* Some Negor informants are marvelous in their ability to participate in this type of interview. *All stories should be as nearly word-for-word as is possible.*

5. More emphasis should be laid on questions concerning the lives of the individual's since they were freed.

Suggestions to Interviewers:

The interviewer should attempt to weave the following questions naturally into the conversation, in simple language. Many of the interviews show that the workers have simply sprung routine questions out of context, and received routine answers.

1. What did the ex-slaves expect from freedom? Forty acres and a mule? A distribution of the land of their masters' plantation?
2. What did the slaves get after freedom? Were any of the plantations actually divided up? Did their masters give them any money? Were they under any compulsion after the war to remain as servants?
3. What did the slaves do after the war? What did they receive generally? What do they think about the reconstruction period?
4. Did secret organizations such as the Ku Klux Klan exert or attempt to exert any influence over the lives of ex-slaves?
5. Did the ex-slaves ever vote? If so, under what circumstances? Did any of their friends ever hold political office? What do the ex-slaves think of the present restricted suffrage?
6. What have the ex-slaves been doing in the interim between 1864 and 1937? What jobs have they held (in detail)? How are they supported nowadays?
7. What do the ex-slaves think of the younger generation of Negroes and of present conditions?
8. Were there any of the ex-slaves in your community living in Virginia at the time of the Nat Turner rebellion? Do they remember anything about it?
9. What songs were there of the period?

The above sent to: Alabama, Arkansas, Florida, Ga., Kentucky, La., Md., Mississippi, Mo., N. Car., Okla., S. Car., Tenn., Texas, Virginia, W. Va., Ohio, Kansas, Indiana

Stories from Ex-slaves

The main purpose of these detailed and homely questions is to get the Negro interested in talking about the days of slavery. If he will talk freely, he should be encouraged to say what he pleases without reference to the questions. It should be remembered that the Federal Writers' Project is not interested in taking sides on any question. The workers should not censor any material collected, regardless of its nature.

It will not be necessary, indeed it will probably be a mistake, to ask every person all of the questions. Any incidents or facts he can recall should be written down as nearly as possible just as he says them, but do not use dialect spelling so complicated that it may confuse the reader.

A second visit, a few days after the first one, is important, so that the worker may gather all the worthwhile recollections that the first talk aroused.

Questions:

1. Where and when were you born?

2. Give the name of your father and mother. Where did they come from? Give names of your brothers and sisters. Tell about your life with them and describe your home and the "quarters." Describe the beds and where you slept. Do you remember anything about your grandparents or any stories told you about them?

3. What work did you do in slavery days? Did you ever earn any money? How ? What did you buy with this money?

4. What did you eat and how was it cooked? Any possums? Rabbits? Fish? What food did you like best? Did the slaves have their own gardens?

5. What clothing did you wear in hot weather? Cold weather? On Sundays? Any shoes? Describe your wedding clothes.

6. Tell about your master, mistress, their children, the house they lived in, the overseer or driver, poor white neighbors.

7. How many acres in the plantation? How many slaves on it? How and at what time did the overseer wake up the slaves? Did they work hard and late at night? How and for what causes were the slaves punished? Tell what you saw. Tell some of the stories you heard.

8. Was there a jail for slaves? Did you ever see any slaves sold or auctioned off? How did groups of slaves travel? Did you ever see slaves in chains?

9. Did the white folks help you to learn to read and write?

10. Did the slaves have a church on your plantation? Did they read the Bible? Who was your favorite preacher? Your favorite spirituals? Tell about the baptizing; baptizing songs. Funerals and funeral songs.

11. Did the slaves ever run away to the North? Why? What did you hear about patrollers? How did slaves carry news from one plantation to another? Did you hear of trouble between the blacks and whites?

12. What did the slaves do when they went to their quarters after the day's work was done on the plantation? Did they work on Saturday afternoons? What did they do Saturday nights? Sundays? Christmas morning? New Year's Day? Any other holidays? Cornshucking? Cotton Picking? Dances? When some of the white master's family married or died? A wedding or death among the slaves?

13. What games did you play as a child? Can you give the words or sing any of the play songs or ring games of the children? Riddles? Charms? Stories about "Raw Head and Bloody Bones" or other "hants" or ghosts? Stories about animals? What do you think of voodoo? Can you give the words or sing

any lullabies? Work songs? Plantation hollers? Can you tell a funny story you have heard or something funny that happened to you? Tell about the ghosts you have seen.

14. When slaves became sick who looked after them? What medicines did the doctors give them? What medicine (herbs, leaves, or roots) did the slaves use for sickness? What charms did they wear and to keep of what diseases?

15. What do you remember about the war that brought your freedom? What happened on the day news came that you were free? What did your master say and do? When the Yankees came what did they do and say?

16. Tell what work you did and how you lived the first year after the war and what you saw or heard about the Ku Klux Klan and the Nightriders. Any school then for Negroes? Any land?

17. Whom did you marry? Describe the wedding. How many children and grandchildren have you and what are they doing?

18. What do you think of Abraham Lincoln? Jefferson Davis? Booker Washington? Any other prominent white man or Negro you have known or heard of?

19. Now that slavery is ended what do you think of it? Tell why you joined a church and why you think all people should be religious.

20. Was the overseer "poor white trash"? What were some of his rules?

The details of the interview should be reported as accurately as possible in the language of the original statements. An example of material collected through one of the interviews with ex-slaves is attached herewith. Although this material was collected before the standard questionnaire had been prepared, it represents an excellent method of reporting an interview. More information might have been obtained however, if a comprehensive questionnaire had been used.

Notes by an editor on dialect usage in accounts by interviews with ex-slaves. (To be used in conjunction with Supplementary Instructions 9E.)

Simplicity in recording the dialect is to be desired in order to hold the interest and attention of the readers. It seems to me that readers are repelled by pages sprinkled with misspellings, commas and apostrophes. The value of exact phonetic transcription is, of course, a great one. But few artists attempt this completely. Thomas Nelson Page was meticulous in his dialect; Joel Chandler Harris less meticulous but in my opinion even more accurate. But the values they sought are different from the values that I believe this book of slave narratives should have. Present day readers are less ready for the over-stress of phonetic spelling than in the days of local color. Authors realize this: Julia Peterkin uses a modified Gullah instead of Gonzales' carefully spelled out Gullah. Howard Odum has questioned the use of goin' for going since the g is seldom pronounced even by the educated.

Truth to idiom is more important, I believe, than truth to pronunciation. Erskine Caldwell in his stories of Georgia, Ruth Suckow in stories of Iowa, and Zora Neale Hurston in stories of Florida Negroes get a truth to the manner of speaking without excessive misspellings. In order to make this volume of slave narrative more appealing and less difficult for the average reader, I recommend that truth to idiom be paramount, and exact truth to pronunciation secondary.

I appreciate the fact that many of the writers have recorded sensitively. The writer who wrote "ret" for right is probably as accurate as the one who spelled it "right." But in a single publication, not devoted to a study of local speech, the reader may conceivably be puzzled by different spellings of the same word. The words "whafolks," "whufolks," "whi'folks," etc., can all be heard in the South. But "white folks" is easier for the reader, and the word itself is suggestive of the setting and the attitude.

Words that definitely have a notably different pronunciation from the usual should be recorded as heard. More important is the recording of words with a different local meaning. Most important, however, are the turns of phrase that have flavor and vividness. Examples occurring in the copy I read are:

durin' of de war
outman my daddy (good, but unnecessarily put in quotes
piddled in de fields
skit of woods
kinder chillish

There are, of course, questionable words, for which it may be hard to set up a single standard. Such words are:

paddyrollers, padrollers, pattyrollers	for patrollers
missis, mistess	for mistress
marsa, massa, maussa, mastuh	for master
ter, tuh, teh	for to

I believe that there should be, for this book, a uniform word for each of these.

The following list is composed of words which I think should not be used. These are merely samples of certain faults:

1. ah	for	I
2. bawn	for	born
3. capper	for	caper
4. com'	for	come

5. do	for	dough
6. ebry, ev'ry	for	every
7. hawd	for	hard
8. muh	for	my
9. naked	for	naked
10. ole, ol'	for	old
11. ret, right	for	right
12. snaik	for	snake
13. sowd	for	sword
14. sto'	for	store
15. teh	for	tell
16. twon't	for	twan't
17. useter, useta	for	used to
18. uv	for	of
19. waggin	for	wagon
20. whi'	for	white
21. wuz	for	was

I should like to recommend that the stories be told in the language of the ex-slave, without excessive editorializing and "artistic" introductions on the part of the interviewer. The contrast between the directness of the ex-slave speech and the roundabout and at times pompous comments of the interviewer is frequently glaring. Care should be taken lest expressions such as the following creep in: "inflicting wounds from which he never fully recovered" (supposed to be spoken by an ex-slave).

Finally, I should like to recommend that the words darky and nigger and such expressions as "a comical little old black woman" be omitted from the editorial writing. Where the ex-slave himself uses these, they should be retained.

This material sent June 20 to states of : Ala., Ark., Fla., Ga., Ky., La., Md., Miss., Mo., N.C., Ohio, Okla., Tenn., Texas, Va., and S.Car.

Negro Dialect Suggestions
(Stories of Ex-Slaves)

Do not write:

Ah for I	*Gwainter* for gwineter (going to)
Poe for po' (poor)	*Oman* for woman
Hit for it	*Ifn* for iffen (if)
Tuh for to	*Fiuh* or *fiah* for fire
Wuz for was	*Uz* or *uv* or *o'* for of
Baid for bed	*Poar* for poor or po'

Daid for dead
Ouh for our
Mah for my
Ovah for over
Othuh for other
Wha for whar (where)
Undah for under
Fuh for for
Yondah for yonder
Moster for marster or massa
J'in for jine
Coase for cose
Utha for other
Yo' for you
Gi' for give
Cot for caught
Kin' for kind
Cose for 'cause
Tho't for thought

Index